WHY
DISSENT
MATTERS

WHY DISSENT MATTERS

**Because Some People
See Things
the Rest of Us Miss**

WILLIAM KAPLAN

McGill-Queen's University Press
Montreal & Kingston • London • Chicago

© McGill-Queen's University Press 2017

ISBN 978-0-7735-5070-4 (cloth)
ISBN 978-0-7735-5084-1 (ePDF)
ISBN 978-0-7735-5085-8 (ePUB)

Legal deposit second quarter 2017
Bibliothèque nationale du Québec

Printed in Canada on acid-free paper that is 100% ancient forest
free (100% post-consumer recycled), processed chlorine free

McGill-Queen's University Press acknowledges the support of the
Canada Council for the Arts for our publishing program. We also
acknowledge the financial support of the Government of Canada
through the Canada Book Fund for our publishing activities.

Library and Archives Canada Cataloguing in Publication

Kaplan, William, 1957–, author
Why dissent matters : because some people see things the rest of
us miss / William Kaplan.

Includes bibliographical references and index.
Issued in print and electronic formats.
ISBN 978-0-7735-5070-4 (cloth).
ISBN 978-0-7735-5084-1 (ePDF).
ISBN 978-0-7735-5085-8 (ePUB)

1. Dissenters – Canada. 2. Dissenters – United States. 3. Social
change – Canada. 4. Social change – United States. I. Title.

JC328.3.K37 2017   303.6'1   C2017-901279-7
                                       C2017-901280-0

For J.L. Granatstein

Contents

Preface

We all know one important thing about life. Some of our most fiercely held beliefs will turn out to be completely wrong.

Consider South Africa and Northern Ireland. There was no possible solution to the continuing crisis in either country: just unrelenting irreconcilable hatred and mutual loathing between the oppressor and the oppressed. No one thought it would or could ever end. But after decades of violence, with thousands of people murdered, terrorized, tortured, imprisoned, and maimed, suddenly there was peace. Real peace. Lasting peace. It came about thanks to the dissenters who had challenged the status quo along with everything that had once been believed to be true.

In another example, it looked as though the Cold War would last forever. And then it was over.

What happened? The Berlin Wall came tumbling down. It had been built to keep people in the east end of the city from going west, thereby turning all of East Germany into a huge prison state. It was guarded by murderous, bloodthirsty soldiers with orders to shoot on sight. But on 9 November 1989 East German border guards lowered their machine guns. The next day, deliriously happy East and West Germans began to reduce the wall to rubble, and the entire Soviet Empire completely disintegrated, almost overnight. Because of the wisdom and restraint of a true and brave dissenter – Mikhail Gorbachev – the Eastern Bloc collapsed not with a bang but a whimper. "Recent years," activist Naomi Klein has written, "have been filled with moments when societies suddenly decide they have had enough."[1]

If you need more proof about how quickly things can change, look no further than the rapid acceptance of a group of citizens once considered criminal: the lesbian/gay/bisexual/transgender (LGBT) community.

In 1965 a Northwest Territories mechanic named Everett George Klippert was jailed for "gross indecency" after admitting to engaging in sex with other men. A court-appointed psychiatrist determined he was "incurably homosexual," which was undoubtedly correct. Two years later, the Supreme Court of Canada confirmed that he could be held in prison indefinitely as a dangerous sexual offender for having consensual sex with other adults. That was 1967, the year that amendments were introduced to Canada's Criminal Code. Justice Minister Pierre Elliott Trudeau told Canadians that "there's no place for the state in the bedrooms of the nation," but it was too late for the jailed Klippert. The struggle for equality was about to begin. Strikingly, it began to gather steam in the wake of the AIDS epidemic – and also in response to it.

In the 1980s, as the AIDS plague ravaged gay communities, tens of thousands, and then hundreds of thousands, of gay men were dying. Nobody seemed to care and some actually approved, seeing God's plan at work. The rage that erupted from this public and political indifference soon mobilized LGB communities. The AIDS Coalition to Unleash Power (ACT UP), founded in 1987, was one of the groups that fought back. Its motto was: "Silence = Death." There was nothing silent about the organization, which began by demanding greater access to experimental AIDS drugs. ACT UP played a huge role in mobilizing LGB communities across North America, giving birth to the modern LGB equal-rights movement. Many became advocates for equal marriage (the first Canadian court challenge to recognize same-sex marriage was in 1974). For most Canadians – and this was only a few years ago – the idea was incomprehensible: men marrying men, women marrying women? The dissenters were fighting an uphill battle, but they soldiered on with persistence and courage, often in the face of unbelievable hostility.

Attitudes did begin to change. LGBT people became increasingly visible, more people came out to their families and friends, where most commonly they were welcomed, and this change in attitude was reflected in society at large, especially in popular culture. On television, *Oprah* interviewed gay couples, *Ellen* broadcast the famous coming-out episode in 1997 (along with a parental advisory), and *Friends* had its own gay wedding.

Canadian public-opinion polls began to show increasing acceptance for marriage equality. In 2002 the *New York Times* announced that it would begin publishing reports of same-sex commitment ceremonies in its *Sunday Styles* section, with executive editor Howell Raines stating that "public celebrations of commitment by gay and lesbian couples ... [are] important to many of our readers, their families and their friends."[2] On 10 June 2003 the Ontario Court of Appeal approved equal marriage, followed later that day by the first marriage of a same-sex couple at Toronto's City Hall.

One of the authors of the court judgment was none other than Chief Justice Roy McMurtry, who, in an earlier incarnation as Ontario's attorney general, had allowed the prosecution to proceed of men arrested during the infamous bathhouse raids – the Canadian consciousness-raising equivalent of the 1969 Stonewall Riots. During "Operation Soap," as the Toronto police called it, more than 300 men were taken into custody in the 5 February 1981 sweep – the largest apprehension in Canada since the 1970 October Crisis. The first Pride parades were protest marches against this very raid. But things quickly changed. Today, the Pride March is a community celebration, and McMurtry, once burned in effigy, became the gay community's patron saint.

In June 2016 the Toronto police chief issued an official apology for the raids. And Klippert? He was kept in jail until 21 July 1971, and he died in 1996. In 2016 Prime Minister Justin Trudeau announced his government's plan to recommend a posthumous pardon. By then, equal marriage was a widely accepted fact of life, and not just in Canada. In 2015 the Supreme Court of the United States ruled that it was unconstitutional to limit marriage to one man and one woman. It was a close call, five to four. One of the dissenting judges was the chief justice, John G. Roberts. While he opposed the majority result, he could not help but acknowledge the moment: "Many people will rejoice at this decision," he wrote, "and I begrudge none their celebration."[3] That night the White House was lit up in rainbow colours, and President Barack Obama called it a "victory for America." The unthinkable had become the new normal.

Dissenters are everywhere.

Some people dissent because they are assigned that role – the devil's advocate, for example. Others dissent because it is an expected part of their job – appellate court judges. And a few dissent because they have to: their conscience leaves them no choice but to speak up. In addition to these lone wolves who have left the pack, there are mass protest movements where dissenters against one thing or another come together in a common cause and clamour for public attention. We meet all these different dissenters in the pages that follow. What unites them all is that they challenge received wisdom and the status quo.

Dissenters are important. They force us, sometimes uncomfortably, to look at the other side. Without them, we could easily go down the wrong path. With them, we may still go down the wrong path, but there's a better chance that we will change our minds and get it right. Dissent is noisy, messy, inconvenient, costly, often misplaced, sometimes laughable, usually badly timed, and almost always time-consuming. Many dissenters are self-interested and misanthropic. Some of them are just crazy. Others are principled and prescient. We often pay lip service to dissent, just another box to be checked off. But the price of not listening to dissenters is far higher than its costs, even when the dissenters are all wrong. Some dissenters have truly important things to say.

One such dissenter was a quiet Canadian, doctor, and scientist, Frances Kelsey, who stood up to a huge pharmaceutical company, prevented an American tragedy, and became a true hero. The nature writer and scientist Rachel Carson connected all the dots before anyone knew they even existed and then pulled the fire alarm, warning the world of an unfolding environmental disaster that quite possibly threatened all life on the planet. A dissenting jury can change the law. It happened in Canada when jury after jury refused to convict Dr Henry Morgentaler of performing an illegal abortion when on the facts he had done just that, thousands of times.

Judicial dissent is another matter. It is "an appeal to the brooding spirit of the law, to the intelligence of a future day, when a later decision may possibly correct the error into which the dissenting judge believes the court to have been betrayed."[4] We will read in this book about judges who had the courage to stand up, all alone, and say no to injustice. Sometimes they save lives, or at least try to. Often, it is all about the evidence. And destroying the evidence is exactly what happened in Canada over the course of a dark decade when the Conservative government of Stephen Harper did everything it could to ensure that voices that might have informed public policy were silenced.

Occupy Wall Street was a truly international protest. There were more than one thousand occupations in 2011 in eighty-two countries. Who were the occupiers, what did they want, and what influence did they have?

Another growing international movement is BDS: Boycott, Divest, Sanction. It is directed at Israel. It is a cliché, but history may be repeating itself. In October 1973 Israel faced military defeat because its leaders could not even see the enemy armies amassing around it. The credulous, the brave, the righteous, the wicked, the principled, and the frauds all find a home under the BDS umbrella. Still, dissenters in Israel and around the world are screaming their heads off, and Jewish voices are among the loudest.

Our world has been saved by authentic dissenters: people who have been attacked, bullied, ostracized, jailed, and sometimes, when all is over, celebrated. We need to know what they know. They don't dissent because they have been told to. They dissent because they have to. Suppressing dissent is bad – for the dissenter – but worse for the rest of us. Listen – and decide – before you shut them out.

WHY
DISSENT
MATTERS

Chapter 1

The Tenth Man

In the years before the Holocaust, no one foresaw the Final Solution to the Jewish Problem. Arresting Jews, stealing their property, making them work in camps were all conceivable; a pogrom here, and a killing there, but not mass murder. Some Jews, far too few, could see the writing on the wall and left Germany and other countries, or tried to. But most others, patriotic citizens through and through, could not imagine the unimaginable, and there were only a handful of dissenting voices pointing to the impending disaster. Through the extermination of millions of people, the world learned that outlandish scenarios deserve careful attention. The canary is in the coal mine for a reason: threats we cannot see are the most dangerous. Israelis know this better than anyone – at least, they should.

Israelis have reason to live in constant fear of attack, and the Israeli government must never underestimate threats to national security. Any danger, no matter how small or insignificant it may seem, demands careful attention and clinically dispassionate consideration. The October 1973 Yom Kippur War – known in the Arab world as the Ramadan War – is proof. It is the classic intelligence failure in Israeli history.

The Concept of Arab Intentions

The Directorate of Military Intelligence Branch, known as AMAN, is the most important section in Israel's intelligence establishment. It not only prepares the national intelligence estimate but is required to investigate and assess all threats to national security. As a cornerstone of Israel's national security doctrine, the Israeli Defense Forces (IDF) must never be taken by surprise. The IDF relies on AMAN. AMAN needs to know not just what the enemy is capable of doing but what it intends to do. In 1973 it promised to provide at least forty-eight hours' notice of any Arab attack. An early-warning system would allow for the rapid mobilization of well-trained reserves backed by a superior air force.

Eliyahu Zeira. One of the principal architects of the Concept, Zeira simply could not see the gathering storm. (Credit: Israel Defense Forces)

In October 1973 AMAN's director of intelligence was the smart and self-assured Major-General Eliyahu Zeira. Promoted to the position the previous year, Zeira firmly believed that the Arabs would not attack, telling the prime minister in December 1972 that "the chance that Egypt would initiate war is not high ... the probability that they will try to cross the [Suez] canal is close to zero."[1] Like much of the Israeli defence establishment, he was of the view that, in the aftermath of the Six Day War, 5–10 June, 1967, the surrounding Arab countries would not start a war unless they were convinced they would win. Egypt had lost that war disastrously: Israeli forces had seized the Sinai up to the Suez Canal (depriving Egypt of oil revenues and Canal fees), much of the Golan Heights from Syria, and the West Bank from Jordan. In the 1969–70 War of Attrition that followed, Egypt suffered more than 10,000 casualties.

President Anwar Sadat took power in October 1970 and had a different approach. "We want peace," he said over and over again, peace that would include the return of seized territories and justice for Palestinians.[2] He called upon the United Nations – and the world – for help. Israel said no, leaving Egypt with no choice but to prepare for another war. But no one took Sadat seriously. When he declared 1971 "the year of decision," he was ridiculed when the year came and went with nothing being decided, unless the decision he was referring to was to do nothing.

The extraordinary 1967 victory ironically laid the basis for future instability. Most Israelis, and much of the world, concluded that Israel was militarily superior to its neighbours and closed their eyes to the increasing professionalism of the Egyptian high command, bolstered by virtually non-stop Soviet rearmament. The prevailing received wisdom was that Syria would not fight unless Egypt did, and while Jordan and Lebanon might eventually be persuaded to join the party, they would never, ever act alone. These events and assumptions form the context for "the conception of Arab intentions," or the Concept, which dominated Israel's government and intelligence services in the months leading up to the Yom Kippur War. It was also widely believed that Egypt would not begin a war until it had advanced weaponry – planes, missiles, and tanks – to attack Israel and to defend Egypt effectively from the inevitable response.

There are always threats to Israel and Israelis, but in the early 1970s all the danger seemed to come from terrorists. In May 1972 the Japanese Red Army killed twenty-six and wounded more than seventy, mostly Christians on a pilgrimage to the Holy Land, at an attack at Tel Aviv's Lod Airport. That summer, eleven Israeli athletes were massacred at the Munich Olympics by the Black September squad of the Palestine Liberation Organization (PLO). Israeli intelligence concluded that the Arabs had resorted to terrorism because they could not win a conventional military campaign.

Israeli officials dismissed Sadat as "intellectually low-level, narrow-minded ... a mediocre statesman,"[3] an "untalented fool," a "hypocrite and opportunist," while other reports declared he was "incapable of leading and making tough decisions."[4] AMAN even sent a sample of Sadat's handwriting to a graphologist and took the results seriously. Born in a poor Nile Delta village, Sadat was the grandson of a freed Sudanese slave (his enemies, referring to his skin colour and ancestry, called him "the dark donkey"). His heroes included Mahatma Gandhi, Kemal Ataturk, and Adolf Hitler – a mixed bag, certainly, but all nation builders. The Israeli assessments were outrageous and completely untrue: Sadat was imaginative, curious, intelligent, brave, and strategic, capable of dramatic, impulsive, and independent action. He was also extremely determined.

In mid-January 1973 credible intelligence came in from Cairo. Israel had several spies close to Sadat. One of them was Ashraf Marwan, the son-in-law of former Egyptian president Gamal Abdel Nasser. Marwan

Ashraf Marwan (with his bride, Mona, and father-in-law,
Egyptian president Gamal Abdel Nasser). A Mossad agent –
or was he playing both sides of the street? He repeatedly
warned Israel of the coming attack.

was actually a Mossad agent, a "walk-in" recruited in 1970. Marwan –
who committed treason for a number of reasons, but mostly because he
liked the money, reported (as he had the previous November) that Egypt
would attack Israel. The report was assessed, checked against the Concept, and rejected. The rumblings and rumours nevertheless increased.[5]
In March, intelligence reports indicated that Egypt was planning a major
military offensive, perhaps as early as April or May. Sadat made no secret about his plans once the diplomatic door was shut in his face: "The
resumption of hostilities is the only way out," he told *Newsweek*. The
headline to the article – *The Battle Is Now Inevitable* – said it all, but just
in case, even that was spelled out: "Everything in this country is now
being mobilized in earnest for the resumption of the battle."[6]

It certainly seemed that way. "Seldom has a leader of a country bent
on war enunciated so clearly his intentions to the world," Israel's president, Chaim Herzog, wrote later.[7] There was objective evidence supporting these reports: Egyptian troops were on the move, while airplanes
and expeditionary forces from Algeria, Iraq, Libya, and other countries
began making their way to Egyptian lines. The extremely well-paid Marwan for the second time that year told his controller there would be war.

In the spring of 1973, Lieutenant-General David Elazar, a career military man who had been the IDF chief of staff since December 1971, believed Marwan's report and ordered, at great financial cost, the Blue and
White Alert. Two reserve tank brigades were mobilized and war prepa-

David Elazar. Better late than never, the IDF chief of staff finally summoned the reserves just hours before the war began. (Credit: Bettmann/Getty Images)

rations initiated. It was all for nothing. The Year of Decision (1971) had come and gone. Warnings in late 1972 and the spring of 1973 turned out to be false alarms. Would the Cry Wolf Syndrome now take root?

To be sure, by this point, Zeira, one of the principal architects of the Concept, had become its main cheerleader and he had just been vindicated by a pointless call-up that he had opposed. When he was asked how Israel would know if the Egyptians were about to attack, he answered, "By the preparations: the preparation cannot be hidden."[8] Elazar knew that the barometer was rising in direct relation to Egyptian frustration about the stalemated peace talks, but it seemed that many Israelis cared more about the cost of the unnecessary mobilization – around $35 million – knowing nothing about what was actually taking place in their own backyard. There was even public pressure to reduce military spending.[9] By the beginning of August, the IDF had returned to its normal state of readiness. Military officials, at the highest level of command, were now convinced that they had overreacted, a conclusion bolstered by another internal AMAN intelligence estimate prognosticating that Sadat intended to focus on some of Egypt's serious domestic problems; he had obviously put war with Israel on the backburner.[10]

Israel was "so strong" that "the problem of security has ceased to be its main problem," Ariel Sharon, the future prime minister, bragged, adding, "We have one of the strongest armies in the world."[11] No one considered the possibility that the mobilization of the reserves in May 1973 had made the Egyptians reconsider, or that they were deliberately shaking the tree, or, perhaps, that they really did intend to attack – just later. For his part, Sadat wrote in his memoirs that he had no intention of starting a war in the spring of 1973; the bellicose statements and troop movements were "part of my strategic deception plan."[12] Moshe Dayan, the minister of defence, told *Time* magazine in July 1973 that he expected the borders to be frozen for the next ten years.[13] He even mused out loud about reducing the period of compulsory service for the regular forces and the reserves, a sure crowd-pleaser in the run-up to the fall general election.

Dayan could have been sent from Central Casting, except he was the real deal. Israeli-born, the second child delivered on the first kibbutz, he joined the Haganah at the age of fourteen and fought bravely in the War of Independence. His black eye patch was his trademark, but it was his success, especially in the Six Day War (and also the bedroom), that made him famous – a bona fide international celebrity occupying one of the most important and prestigious posts in Israeli public life. In his view, not only were the Israelis virtually invincible, but the Arabs were stupid and weak: "It is a weakness that derives from factors that I don't believe will change quickly; the low level of their soldiers in education, technology and integrity."[14] On another occasion he explained, "There is a large gap between us and the Arabs ... a qualitative gap."[15]

Indeed, an official Israeli study of Egyptian soldiers captured during the Six Day War found they were of "significantly lower intelligence" than their Israeli counterparts. Egyptian officers had "shallow and inadequate personalities and were psychologically weak, emotionally immature," and "lacked a sense of responsibility toward their soldiers."[16] This "thorough study" was accepted by Israeli intelligence "as well-based and reliable."[17] Certainly, it reflected popular prejudices. In the eyes of most Israelis, the Arabs were incompetent and disorganized, would rather run than fight, and their sabre rattling was but routine red meat for the streets.

This notion of Israeli superiority, together with its suggestions of Arab racial inferiority, permeated Israeli society. It left military planners, intoxicated by their historical success, holding fast to a general strategic approach that refought the last war instead of anticipating the next one. Many Israelis believed that their Army and Air Force were invincible. This exaggerated and swaggering sense of self-confidence reflected the Concept – now the national consensus. There would be no Arab attack, the military and intelligence establishment argued, ignoring the fact that the magnitude of the Israeli victory in June 1967 had seriously injured Arab pride, honour, and self-respect, all of which would eventually have to be avenged. That meant war, although Sadat continued to promote peace.

In September 1973 Henry Kissinger, the US national-security adviser, was appointed secretary of state. Kissinger was no stranger to the Middle East peace process. In late February 1973 Sadat had sent his own national-security adviser, Hafiz Ismail, to the United States to meet secretly with Kissinger and other American officials. Ismail presented a comprehensive peace plan – not just between Israel and Egypt but between Israel, all of its neighbours, and the Palestinians. Kissinger's response then, and several months later, was not encouraging. He told Ismail to tell Sadat to be realistic: "We live in a real world and cannot build anything on fancies and wishful thinking. Now in terms of reality you are the defeated side."[18] Yitzhak Rabin, the Israeli ambassador to the United States (and future prime minister), admitted that the Sadat proposal had some "interesting expressions." However, the Israelis treated the Egyptian initiative, offering real peace and normalization of relations and international guarantees in exchange for Israel's return to its 1967 borders, as a nuisance. It was a squandered opportunity, not the first or the last.

The prime minister, Golda Meir – "We just will not go along with this!"[19] – was the culprit, Kissinger the handmaiden.[20] Kissinger was, in his defence, overextended, directing his resources elsewhere: détente with the Soviet Union, resolving the war in Vietnam, and engagement with China. There was no appreciation that the summary rejection of a legitimate, realistic, fair-minded peace plan posed a huge future threat.[21] Even though various discussions continued, they were pointless. More importantly, the situation on the ground was becoming ever more untenable. Sadat was under intense domestic political and military pressure to achieve results, leaving Egypt with little choice but to launch a war – not a total war, but enough to spark a crisis and attract superpower (meaning US) intervention.[22] As it turned out, the Arabs were not so stupid after all.[23]

The Arabs Prepare for War

Sadat began by lowering the rhetorical temperature. He instructed his ministers to express Egypt's peaceful intentions in discussions with their Western counterparts. He knew his peace initiative would fail, but his objective was diplomatic deception: to create the impression that a peaceful resolution was being sought.[24]

Stories were planted in the Arab press, which the Israelis monitored, about the neglect and deterioration of Soviet radar and missile-guidance equipment that had been left behind after some 15,000 Russians were expelled in July 1972. It was almost certainly all for show. The "freeze" in Egyptian-Russian relations did not last long; as the flow of weapons accelerated, the advisers began to trickle back, and the lease on the Soviet naval base was quietly renewed.[25] It became widely "known" that Egyptian personnel had no idea how to operate much of the Soviet kit, and they were understood to be running out of spare parts. In another rumour, Egypt and Syria were said to be on the outs. In fact, there were many top-level war-planning meetings. From Jerusalem's perspective, however, it was business as usual, situation normal: Egyptians would not be going to war even if they were so inclined, and it was obvious they were not – or so the Israelis thought.[26]

Golda Meir, the Kiev-born, American-raised Zionist and prime minister, was a force to be reckoned with. Founding Israeli prime minister David Ben Gurion called the seventy-five-year-old grandmother "the best man in government" – and he meant it as a compliment. Empathy was not her strong suit, however. "Put yourself in Egypt's shoes," someone once suggested to her. "Not a chance," came the response.[27] A rigid, hawkish nationalist, Meir once famously declared, "There are no Palestinians" (she later claimed to have been misquoted).

Over the spring, summer, and fall of 1973, American sources shared their intelligence with Israel. The United States also believed that the situation was stable. "Our difficulty," State Department Intelligence Chief Ray Cline recollected later, "was partly that we were brainwashed by the Israelis, who brainwashed themselves."[28] Nevertheless, as a precautionary move, the United States and the USSR (which knew that war was

David Ben Gurion and Golda Meir. (Credit: David Rubinger/Getty Images)

likely) pre-emptively launched satellites. They were now ready for battlefield surveillance.[29]

In September, King Hussein bin Talal of Jordan secretly flew by helicopter to a Mossad safe house outside Tel Aviv and told Meir that an attack was imminent. Hussein, said to be a direct descendant of the Prophet Muhammad, was a moderate; he had an unusually close relationship with Meir and had met with her and other Israel leaders three times previously. Jordan had lost the West Bank to Israel in the Six Day War, but Israel quietly helped Hussein withstand Palestinian and Syrian attacks during September 1970 (Black September), and the king had no desire to become embroiled in further conflict. On two earlier occasions, he passed on reports about impending hostilities. There was the usual small talk before Hussein turned to the real purpose of his visit. Speaking in English, he told Meir that Sadat was completely frustrated and desperate because of the stalled peace talks:

HUSSEIN: All the Syrian units are now in attack positions … all this was done under the cover of training exercises, but the information says that these are pre-jump positions. The meaning of this is not known. I have doubts, but nothing is certain.
MEIR: Could it be that Syria will do something without Egypt?
HUSSEIN: I don't think so. I think they would cooperate.[30]

Jordan and Israel were still technically at war, but at this top-secret meeting the king told the prime minister with typical Middle Eastern elliptical nuance that Israel would be attacked and that Egypt and Syria were cooperating. It was a bombshell and should have blown the Concept to smithereens. At the very least, the king had reported advanced Syrian military preparations. Even if it was still true that Syria would not go to war without Egypt, was it now possible that Egypt and Syria were about to launch a joint attack? "No war, no peace," was untenable from Sadat's point of view and, ultimately, would be existentially destabilizing to his leadership. King Hussein had made a special trip to Israel. He obviously thought it was important. But the Israelis were not listening. When war did break out, Hussein released some Palestinian prisoners and committed two armoured brigades to Syrian service. But he also made a side deal with Israel: the Jordanian troops would not fight, and the Israelis would not attack them.[31]

Sadat had to break the deadlock and do something to bring Israel to the negotiating table. He needed help and turned to Syrian President Hafez al-Assad, an Air Force commander and future mass murderer of his own people who had seized power in 1970. Assad needed no convincing; he was unrelentingly hostile toward Israel and could not even contemplate its continued existence. He was more than happy to participate, especially since Sadat did not make his real and limited intentions of a bridgehead war known: the Egyptian president shared some fake war plans that would purportedly tie up Israeli forces in the Sinai, making it easier for the Syrian Army to liberate the Golan Heights.[32] Egyptian and Syrian military leaders accelerated their joint preparations.[33]

On 29 September a Syrian-backed terrorist group in Austria, the "Eagles of the Palestinian Revolution," held up a train carrying Soviet Jews from Moscow to Vienna. They would not agree to free the hostages until Austria's cowardly chancellor, Bruno Kreisky, agreed to close Schönau Castle, a transit centre used to forward "refuseniks" to Israel. Then Kreisky set the terrorists free. Israeli society was absorbed by these events in Europe, diverted, as quite possibly intended, from what was actually taking place on their own borders.

In fact, a full disinformation campaign was underway. Egyptian military officers were ordered to follow their usual routine, cadets were told to report to courses in early October 1973, many men were given leave to travel to Mecca on the *umrah*, a minor pilgrimage, and the

Egyptian press reported that 20,000 reservists had been demobilized (not mentioning how many remained on duty). Sadat was even rumoured to be sick and considering treatment in Europe. At the Canal, special troops were deployed and instructed to move about as visibly as possible without helmets and to swim, fish, and eat oranges as if they did not have a care in the world.[34] An attack seemed unimaginable to just about everyone: in late September, Muslims were observing Ramadan, Jews were celebrating Rosh Hashanah, and Yom Kippur was coming up. With an Israeli election just weeks away, all the politicians were preoccupied with campaigning.

On 1 October an Israeli intelligence officer, Lieutenant Benjamin Simon-Tov, drew attention to an Egyptian military build-up along the Canal. Since the Six Day War, Israelis had occupied the Sinai: they were on the east side of the Canal, and the Egyptians on the west. Every fall the Egyptian Army organized practice manoeuvres, and once again the training had been publicly announced. Simon-Tov's first report, *Movement in the Egyptian Army – the Possibility of Resumption of Hostilities*, pointed to a growing mobilization of Egyptian forces. His follow-up report two days later analyzed the data and concluded that the Egyptian activities were for real. "Why," he asked among other questions, "have the Egyptians prepared some forty descents for boats on the banks of the canal?"[35] None of this activity had ever been previously observed. These were the biggest training exercises ever, and they indicated advanced war preparations. In 1968 Soviet forces had used a large military exercise as cover for its invasion of Czechoslovakia. Had the Egyptians taken their cue from the Russian playbook?

There was really nothing secret going on: the stockpiling of supplies was openly visible, along with five Egyptian divisions with 100,000 soldiers ready to go. Israeli soldiers guarding the Canal could hear the roar of armoured columns arriving day and night and watch bulldozers levelling the approaches for tank ramps and future bridges and pontoons.[36] At the water's edge, the appearance of transport boats left little doubt about the plan: first, vessels to carry artillery battery, then ferries to deploy troops, and finally pontoon bridges to transport tanks and trucks. Nevertheless, the senior intelligence officer in the Southern Command, Lieutenant-Colonel David Gedaliah, remained true to the Concept and promptly buried Simon-Tov's findings. "They stood in contradiction to Headquarters' evaluation that an exercise was taking place in Egypt,"

even though it was "unprecedented in its scale and direction."[37] Gedaliah's assessment did not change even after aerial reconnaissance produced
photographs several days later providing irrefutable evidence of the
Egyptian military build-up.

Back in Cairo, there was still no sign that the Israelis knew anything.
"This seemed incredible to us," Mohamed Hassanein Heikal, the Sadat
confidant and well-connected editor-in-chief of the influential and widely
circulated Egyptian newspaper *Al-Ahram*, later recalled.[38]

Wednesday, 3 October, the day of Simon-Tov's second report, was
also the day that Meir returned from Europe. She had attended a pre-
scheduled meeting in Strasbourg at the Council of Europe but made an
unscheduled stop in Vienna on the way home. She got nowhere with
Kreisky. "He didn't even offer me a glass of water," she complained.
Back in Israel, Meir assembled her most trusted advisers at her home –
the kitchen cabinet – including Dayan; Yigal Allon, a cabinet minister
and military hero from the 1948 War of Independence; Israel Galili, the
Haganah chief of staff from the War of Independence and perhaps Meir's
closest adviser; and Benny Peled, the commander of the Israeli Air Force.
Elazar and Zeira's deputy, Brigadier Aryeh Shalev (the IDF's director of
research, Intelligence Branch), were also in attendance (Zeira was sick).

After two hours, they reached their conclusion – nothing had changed:
there would be no war. No one questioned the intelligence estimates or
expressed concern. "Nobody at the meeting," Meir later explained,
"thought that it was necessary to call up the reserves, and nobody thought
that war was imminent."[39] If there was an attack, the regular Army could
hold off the enemy until the reserves were mobilized. AMAN, after all,
had promised forty-eight hours' notice, if not more.

The cabinet met later that day, but the hot topic was events in Europe,
not the Egyptian and Syrian military build-ups. A regular cabinet meeting was scheduled for the day after Yom Kippur, Sunday, 7 October.

On Thursday, 4 October, Israeli reconnaissance reported that Syrian
tanks were positioned "hull down." Dug-in tanks are defensive, designed
to resist an attack, not launch one, as any soldier looking at pictures
would have concluded. About one month earlier, the Israeli Air Force
had shot down thirteen MIG-21 Syrian warplanes, establishing Israeli
dominance over Syrian airspace and demonstrating once again the superiority of Israeli forces. In these circumstances, a Syrian attack of any
kind was considered most unlikely. Israeli intelligence believed that any

military build-up – the observable movement of artillery and tanks toward the front, for example – was a response to the earlier clash or in preparation for the expected reprisal for the recent Syrian-backed terrorist activities in Europe. Dayan expressed uncertainty: the artillery placement seemed off, "not a normal defensive move." Elazar dismissed this concern: an attack was highly improbable.[40] Radio Damascus reported that Assad was about to begin a nine-day tour of the eastern provinces, making a war in the west unlikely.

Around this time, it was learned, in another unmistakable signal that war was imminent, that families of the remaining Soviet advisers, and many of the advisers themselves, had begun to leave both Egypt and Syria on a succession of Aeroflot passenger planes. The arrival of giant Antonov 22 cargo planes packed to the brim with war materiel was just around the corner. Dayan continued to believe there was little probability of war – and the top military brass reached the same conclusion when they met in Jerusalem. It was a central tenet of the Concept that Syria would not act without Egypt. However, the joint evacuation provided proof that the two countries were working together.

The next day, Friday, 5 October, was the day before Yom Kippur. AMAN's Egyptian expert, Lieutenant-Colonel Yonah Bandman, prepared a report detailing what was clearly an offensive large-scale Egyptian military build-up at the Canal. Zeira inordinately relied on Bandman, but gray was not part of Bandman's palette – he saw things entirely in black and white and believed that the Concept governed. Aerial photographs taken the day before showed tens of thousands of Egyptian troops and their crossing equipment massed along the west side of the Canal. "From the numbers alone you could have a heart attack," Dayan observed.[41]

Even though the report catalogued a long list of advanced Egyptian military preparations, Bandman knew what he knew: "Although the deployment showed apparent signs of offensive intent, no change had taken place in the Egyptian view of the balance of power between them and the IDF, and consequently the likelihood that they intended to renew the war was low."[42] Indeed, Bandman, despite what he could see in the photographs, and what Israeli soldiers could see on the ground, described the Egyptian military activity as "routine."[43] This conclusion did not change even after credible information arrived that Egyptian soldiers had been ordered to break the Ramadan fast.[44] In Washington, Central Intelligence Agency (CIA) officials briefed the president: "The military preparations that have occurred do not indicate that any party intends to initiate hostilities."[45]

In Cairo, Sadat was obsessed with learning what the Israelis knew. Saad El Shazly, the dashing and distinguished Egyptian chief of staff who had served with the United Nations in the Congo, received Ranger training in the United States, and taken a course in the USSR, reassured him.[46] We are a jump ahead, he told Sadat.[47] El Shazly was the kind of soldier and leader who spent time in the field with his men, not in the officers' mess.[48] In truth, he was astonished by the lack of Israeli response (after the war was over El Shazly served in the diplomatic corps, was dismissed when he criticized the government, went into exile in Algeria, and on his return to Egypt was put into prison).[49] The Egyptian war plan took as a given that Israel would know Egypt's intentions possibly fifteen days before the attack, and certainly no less than three days beforehand (almost mirroring the official Israeli assessment).[50] Zeira had promised Meir that if the Egyptians were preparing an attack at the Canal, he would be able to provide both a tactical and an operational warning "a number of days in advance."[51] El Shazly could not believe his good luck.[52]

Egypt's preparations escalated. The head of civil aviation cancelled all commercial flights and closed the Cairo airport in yet another signal that hostilities were about to begin (though the order was quickly countermanded when El Shazly found out). The Egyptian press announced a general call for blood donors. Russian naval ships could be seen leaving Egyptian ports. AMAN knew, and had known for at least six months, that Egypt had the men, the bridging equipment, and the boats to cross the Canal, as well as fighter-bombers and hundreds of new and advanced Soviet tanks and artillery, including state-of-the-art missiles to attack Israeli planes, tanks, even cities. In fact, the objective evidence from aerial reconnaissance was "irrefutable."[53] In both the Canal Zone and in Syria, the military movements were massive, methodical, and visible to the naked eye.

Reports also began to trickle in that Syria had cancelled all leaves and was calling up its reserves. The head of the IDF's Syrian desk insisted that Syria was about to attack, but he was silenced and scheduled for disciplinary action.[54] The Concept held that Syria would not attack without Egypt, and Egypt was not going to attack, so no authority in Israel assessed these "curious" developments as a real threat. A self-satisfied Elazar did, however, send some modest reinforcements to the Golan

Heights. "We'll have one hundred tanks against their eight hundred," he observed; "that ought to be enough" (additional tanks were sent later). In this single sentence Elazar summed up the long-held Israeli belief that regular forces could hold off any attack until the reserves arrived.[55] Not that there was going to be a war. Nothing, he said, could "be more idiotic."[56] The Syrian tanks soon redeployed into offensive formation, and even more heavy artillery and additional Syrian tanks began moving to the front lines.

When Meir was informed, she convened a meeting on Friday morning, 5 October. Elazar and Zeira were both there. Elazar had by now received conclusive evidence that the Egyptian army was in attack formation, "the magnitude of which we have never seen before."[57] He issued a dire warning: "I cannot say that they are not going to attack."[58] Zeira seemed confused in his assessment. "Technically," he said, "the Egyptians and the Syrians are ready, prepared and able to start a war at any time."[59] Yet, clearly disassociated from reality, he continued, "I don't see either the Egyptians or the Syrians attacking."[60] Even though every single piece of information screamed out that a war was about to begin, he could not bring himself to abandon the Concept. If there was a war, "it would be Sadat's mistake, not his," he said.[61] Zeira was not alone. "I did not hear anyone say that war was about to break out," Dayan later recalled.[62]

Although most cabinet ministers had left for the Jewish holiday, Meir summoned those who were available for an emergency briefing at her Tel Aviv office just before noon. They reviewed a document that outlined in detail numerous "alarming indicators," but they too were told that war was unlikely. Zeira conceded that there were "things for which we have no explanation," such as, for instance, the coordinated Russian evacuations in Cairo and Damascus, but when one of the ministers pushed back, Zeira let him have it: there was little probability of war, but if one started "the least probable move is the crossing of the Canal. And the highest is raids and perhaps shooting here or there."[63] Elazar backed Zeira up: "We do not face a war," he told the assembled ministers.[64]

Meir was uncomfortable and worried. "It is difficult to believe," she told the group, "that with all their force [on the border], they will suddenly shell one settlement or another for five or ten minutes."[65] She was also extremely disturbed about the evacuation of the Soviets from both Egypt and Syria. "It reminded me of what happened prior to the Six Day

War and I didn't like it at all." But no one else seemed alarmed. When Meir was reassured that there would be adequate warning,[66] she decided to trust her generals, though the rump cabinet delegated her the authority to direct a full mobilization of the reserves if need be. She also contacted Henry Kissinger through his deputy, Brent Scowcroft. Tell the Arabs that if they attack, Meir said, "Israel will react militarily, with firmness and great strength."[67]

An AMAN estimate made available early in the afternoon of 5 October gave succour to both Elazar and Zeira. Its first thirty-seven paragraphs outlined in great detail the massive Syrian and Egyptian military build-ups and the Soviet evacuation. But it concluded that "the probability that the Egyptians intend to renew fighting is low ... The probability of a Syrian independent action (without Egypt) remains low."[68] Before leaving for the holiday, Zeira addressed a meeting of senior staff, including Elazar. He stayed on script: the likelihood of a coordinated attack, he advised was "even lower than low."[69]

Elazar accepted the advice (although he quietly, and behind-the-scenes, deployed additional troops to both the Golan and the Sinai, declaring a "C" alert, the highest, for regular forces and previously mobilized reserves). On his way home that night, Elazar asked himself "whether we weren't overdoing it?"[70] That evening, however, there should have been no denying the information that began to flood in that Egypt and Syria were hours away from war. Very early the next morning – Saturday, 6 October – at a hastily arranged meeting with the head of the Mossad in London, Marwan confirmed the report he had forwarded his Mossad controller two days earlier – "something is going to happen"[71] – obviously meaning that there would be a war, adding now that it would start at 6 p.m. that day Israel time.

Predicting war was exactly what Marwan had done the previous March and earlier, and it had not happened on either occasion. But this time it was true, and Marwan even handed over the updated Egyptian battle plan (after an epic snafu, it was eventually put to good use by the IDF).[72] Moreover, Marwan's credibility had, weeks earlier, been given a big boost when he spilled the beans about a terrorist plot to shoot down an El Al plane in Rome, leading to the would-be perpetrators being quickly rounded up. (As a side note, Marwan may actually have been a double agent. Much of his behaviour, including numerous false reports of impending war, suggests as much. In June 2007 he was thrown to his death from the fifth-floor window of his posh London flat just off Trafalgar Square by men of "Mediterranean appearance."[73] His body came to rest in a small rose garden.)

The red phone beside Dayan's bed rang at 4:00 Saturday morning, and the military men met just before 6.00 a.m. Dayan held to the Concept – there was "not going to be a war"[74] – and he actually resisted a full-scale call-up. Elazar, though understandably reluctant to be dismissed once again as an alarmist who wasted public money on unnecessary mobilizations, nevertheless now demanded that the reserves – all 200,000 of them – be immediately activated. He also argued in favour of pre-emptive strikes. "The Chief of Staff wants to mobilize troops for a counterattack in a war that hasn't even begun?" Dayan taunted. He also outright rejected any pre-emptive strike: it was not worth risking the loss of American support.

Around 8:00 a.m., the prime minister was briefed. Zeira now conceded that the Soviets were evacuating because they believed that Syria and Egypt were about to start a war. But, he insisted, war was far from certain. Zeira had earlier admitted that he could not reconcile his estimate with the evidence. However, referring to Sadat, he suggested to Meir, "Perhaps at the last moment he will draw back."[75] Meir ignored him. Zeira was clearly insane. Meir did reject a pre-emptive attack – she too was concerned about American reaction – but even though Dayan told her it was "superfluous,"[76] she finally began to listen to her instincts and ordered a partial but significant mobilization of 120,000 soldiers.

"The organic structure of our army," Dayan wrote in his memoirs, was based on the "orderly mobilization" of the reserves. The transition, he added, from "desk, tractor, and lathe to the battlefield is not at all easy."[77] Even so, and even in the face of the mounting evidence, Zeira and others continued to defend the indefensible, and Dayan even taunted Elazar, "What will you do with all these reservists if war doesn't break out?"[78] Pessimistic, indecisive, wavering, unfocused, and blinded by about just everything that was going on around him, including the extremely unbalanced ratio in forces on the two front lines, Dayan could not see the forest or the trees. The prime minister, however, was a different story. Immediately after the meeting, Meir met with the American ambassador. "We may be in trouble," she told him.[79]

The Yom Kippur War

At noon the Israeli cabinet assembled in Tel Aviv: "On the basis of information we have now," Dayan reported, an attack "is impossible."[80] Indeed, Bandman had just sent in another report estimating the possibility of war as low. Elazar again made his case for a full mobilization and first strike. Meir, chain-smoking unfiltered Chesterfields, knew that Dayan and Zeira were wrong, but she also understood that a pre-emptive strike was a complete non-starter. Kissinger had made it clear that Israel could not expect any American assistance if it started another war in the Middle East. It was no use appealing to the president: Richard Nixon was frequently intoxicated, depressed, and distracted by Watergate and its aftermath, particularly the "Saturday Night Massacre" of his attorney general, deputy attorney general, and special Watergate prosecutor, and the imminent resignation of his crooked vice-president, Spiro Agnew. Impeachment was some months away, but the impossible was becoming increasingly inevitable.

As Dayan was explaining, again, that there would be no war, the air-raid sirens sounded. Just before 2:00 p.m. local time the Egyptian-Syrian coalition launched a "surprise attack." The Concept was so ingrained that "the mere fact that we start an attack at all will be the most important element of surprise," General Abdul Munim Riad, the Egyptian soldier who commanded Jordanian forces in the Six Day War, had predicted.[81] Though most wars begin with deception and surprise, this one was not well concealed. Even so, the Israelis had not seen it coming. The surprise lay not just in the fact that the attack had happened but that its military objectives were so limited and its political goals so specific.

In the south, Operation Badr was underway.[82] Dayan had described the Suez Canal as one of the best anti-tank ditches in the world. Water crossings are always confounding for invading armies, but the Suez Canal posed special challenges to building bridges and getting troops, artillery, and tanks across. It had very steep banks reinforced with concrete, while the tide changes and rapid current made construction of pontoon bridges problematic. Israel, at enormous cost, had built the Bar Lev Line in case the tanks that could never cross it actually did get across. Completed in 1970, and extending approximately 145 kilometres along the eastern side of the entire Canal, but not at Great Bitter Lake, where the width of the lake was wrongly thought to make a Canal crossing unlikely, the Bar Lev

Line was an approximately eighteen-metres-high sand and concrete wall. Inclined at a 60-degree angle, it was designed to prevent armoured and amphibious vehicles from reaching the desert, assuming they succeeded in crossing the Canal.

Behind the wall were twenty-two forts incorporating thirty-five strong points – all of which cost a staggering sum, equal to half the total for the Aswan Dam. In addition, there were soldiers, trenches, minefields, barbed wire, mortars, anti-aircraft weapons, artillery guns, fortified bunkers (with air conditioning), and Israeli battle tanks backed up by the Israeli Air Force. The Israelis even designed an underwater pipe system to pump flammable crude into the Canal to create a sheet of fire. A test run threw off flames and dense clouds of black smoke that attracted the attention of watching Egyptians. Israeli military planners believed that their defences were invincible.

It was not to be. In the first minute of the war came a massive artillery bombardment from 2,000 guns – more than 10,000 shells were launched – and then the Egyptians began to lay their pontoon bridges and operate their ferries from the crossings they had earlier and openly built. They quickly overran the Bar Lev Line. The supposedly impregnable wall – guarded by about 450 soldiers (a hodgepodge of reservists putting in their annual month of service, some professional soldiers, disgruntled Orthodox Jews angry about missing Yom Kippur, and new immigrants with only the briefest of basic training) – was demolished in less than two hours.[83]

Working from small boats, Egyptian forces used high-powered British- and German-made water cannons attached to dredging pumps in the Canal to attack and disintegrate the sand wall, creating more than eighty breaches in the line. Israeli intelligence had earlier considered whether water cannons might pose a threat but had dismissed the idea as "unfeasible."[84] Egypt had 250 planes or more (Soviet MIG-21s, 19s, and 17s), five infantry divisions, two armoured divisions, and three mechanized divisions (100,000 soldiers) boasting at least 1,500 tanks. There were no sheets of fire stopping them or even slowing them down, since frogmen had blocked the underwater pipe openings with concrete. Within three hours, more than 30,000 Egyptian soldiers were well east of the Canal, followed by tens of thousands more the next day, and Egyptian flags were flying again on Egyptian soil. About half the Israeli soldiers guarding the Bar Lev Line were killed, and almost all the others taken prisoner.

At the same time as Egypt was routing the Israelis in the south, Syrian forces under Assad's leadership – three infantry divisions with 35,000 soldiers – were, along with hundreds of tanks and artillery pieces, on the move and ready for battle in the north. Here, too, the odds were stacked against Israel as this overwhelming force faced off against Israel's vastly outnumbered soldiers. For a brief time, it seemed that Israel's northern settlements – Tiberias, Safed, Haifa, and Netanya – would soon be under Syrian control. Dozens of Israeli warplanes were shot out of the sky.

The Yom Kippur War was, without question, the most traumatic event in the country's history, and most Israelis still regard the decision not to mobilize the reserves fully in the days preceding it as the worst and most tragic decision ever made.[85] Even in as small a country as Israel, ample advance warning to assemble the reserves was critical and the opportunity had been lost. In one fell swoop, Egypt and Syria demolished two of the three pillars of Israeli national security: that Israel's military superiority would deter its enemies, but that in case it didn't, Israel would have sufficient advance warning of an attack to respond immediately. Only the third remained: the military ability to win a decisive victory no matter what.

It was also a brilliant tactic for Egypt and Syria to begin the war on Yom Kippur. Israel mobilized its reserves by broadcasting codes on radio, but on that holy Jewish holiday Israeli Radio shut down. Yom Kippur also fell squarely within Ramadan, when Muslims do not eat or drink during daylight hours. Who would possibly begin a war then? The Israelis had alternative means of mobilizing the reserves, but the timing of this war made summoning the reserves unnecessarily difficult, enabling early Arab success and dealing Israel and Israelis a huge psychological blow, one that worsened as the casualties mounted.

On the second day of the war, an increasingly alarmist Dayan told the prime minister and many others, "This is the end of the Third Temple" – the demise of the Jewish state.[86] At one point he burst into tears, telling a subordinate that "everything is lost."[87] Dayan could not believe how well the Egyptian and Syrian armies fought. "As for the fighting standard of the Arab soldiers, I can sum it up in one sentence: they did not run away."[88] Old prejudices die hard, but this one hit like a ton of bricks.

Dayan was almost certainly clinically depressed: on a tour of the southern front, he lurched around, walking slowly and apathetically, "as if he was not there."[89] Meir was completely rattled: "If everything Dayan forecasts will take place ... I will commit suicide," she warned. She knew she should have paid attention to her "feelings and fear," not to Dayan and the generals.[90] She finally stopped listening to her minister of defence as his mood – apocalyptic – and his judgments and advice became increasingly suspect: "Dayan wants to talk about the terms of surrender."[91] Not on Meir's watch.

The Arab armies fought valiantly and, initially, were successful. Israel was on the verge of defeat and placed its Jericho missiles on alert, giving a clear signal that it was arming its nuclear arsenal.[92] This was done for show: opening the kimono for just long enough for Russian and American satellites to photograph the missiles (although to many, it truly seemed that Israel's fate hung in the balance).[93]

By the third day, Israel had lost 500 tanks, 400 on the Egyptian front alone, and 50 aircraft. How was that possible, Kissinger asked? The Israeli Armed Forces attaché to Washington confided that many of these tanks had been lost on their way to battle because they were run too fast and had been inadequately maintained. Israel's ambassador, Simcha Dinitz, conceded that something "obviously went wrong." So much for Israel's vaunted military superiority and technical prowess.[94] Meir begged President Nixon for help. Kissinger advised the president that an Israeli loss would be a geopolitical disaster.

American politicians, under great pressure from the Jewish community, made their wishes known, and, after a while, the United States responded by initiating a massive airlift of conventional arms that soon saw American aircraft landing in Tel Aviv every fifteen minutes. The Soviets beat them to it, and even urged Arab states sitting on the sidelines to join the battle. What was a regional conflict now had the potential to become an international one.

In short order, Israel regrouped and retook the Golan Heights and, within the week, beat the Syrians back and was actually shelling the outskirts of Damascus. The fight in the Sinai was more complicated, but soon enough the Egyptians were on the run, with Israeli forces, under the leadership of General Ariel Sharon, yet another future prime minister, now on the west side of the Canal, encircling and ready to destroy Egypt's beleaguered Third Army, and just 100 kilometres from Cairo. The nuclear alert was lifted.[95] The American strategy was to let Israel come out ahead, but only after it had bled a bit and agreed to engage in

With Egyptian President Sadat.
August 25, 1975.

Henry Kissinger and Anwar Sadat. Brave and visionary, Sadat would later share the Nobel Peace Prize with Israeli prime minister Menachem Begin. (Credit: United States Library of Congress)

peace negotiations.[96] "We've got to squeeze the Israelis when this is over," Nixon instructed Kissinger, "we've got to squeeze them goddamn hard."[97] Kissinger made it clear to Sadat that America understood Egyptian interests: "The US side will make a major effort as soon as hostilities are terminated to assist in bringing a just and lasting peace to the Middle East."[98]

On 24 October, three weeks after it started, the war was more or less over. Two days later, Israelis and Egyptians had their first direct talks in twenty-five years. An uneasy quiet returned to the region. The Yom Kippur War not only restored Arab honour but set the stage for a more vulnerable and realistic Israel to reach arrangements with Egypt and Syria in 1974 and 1975, and several years later a real peace with Egypt, kick-started by Sadat's dramatic and unforgettable 1977 visit to Jerusalem. (Incidentally, Kissinger proved to be a much better judge of character than the Israelis were of others and of themselves: "He [Sadat] is really very farsighted, he is one of the greatest political leaders I have ever met." The Israelis, on the other hand, have "a low ability to analyze complex situations and to conduct long term policy."[99])

Egypt's military defeat actually led to its political victory, just as Sadat had planned. Syria would never make peace, because the Golan Heights remained under Israeli control, but everything was, and has remained, relatively quiet on the northern front. (The Israelis and the Syrians have exchanged blows, directly and indirectly, in Lebanon, but Syria has much bigger fish to fry now in dealing with ISIS within its own borders. The two countries may actually be cooperating against this common enemy.)

Even before the war was over, the fallout started to spread. Soon enough, America and its allies settled in for a tougher winter, courtesy of the retaliatory Arab oil embargo that initially saw crude prices quickly increase by 70 per cent. The embargo – production cuts and price increases – inevitably cascaded, contributing to a global recession that caused real damage to the international economy, including an inflationary spiral that lasted for about a decade. Although the embargo was lifted the following March when Israel was persuaded to pull back from the Sinai Peninsula and part of the Golan Heights, the economic damage took much longer to repair. In the meantime, Israel was reeling.

Israel lost almost 3,000 soldiers – more than twice as many as were killed in the Six Day War and, by any measure, devastating to a country of just 3.3 million.[100] Many thousands more were wounded, and those taken prisoner – about 300 in number – were reportedly subjected to unspeakable atrocities. The country was in mourning.

On 6 October, Meir had addressed the nation: "For a number of days our intelligence services have known that the armies of Egypt and Syria were deployed for a coordinated attack on Israel … Our forces were deployed according to plan to meet the impending danger."[101] But no one believed a single word of it because it was demonstrably untrue (and she said nothing about her summary rejection of Sadat's repeated efforts to begin peace talks).

"How could we have been so unready?" Meir was asked as she toured the front lines after the ceasefire. Meir replied that she was not an expert and had relied on Dayan and Elazar. "Because you don't understand these things I lost fifty-eight men?" a tank battalion commander shouted at her.[102] The prime minister was not just out of her depth but was weak, as she later confessed: "I couldn't handle a confrontation with the head of Military Intelligence or the Chief of Staff."[103] It was curious to say the least that this formidable person – imperious, intransigent, decisive,

Golda Meir and Moshe Dayan. Their explanations for "the blunder" enraged
Israeli society. (Credit: Stringer/Reuters Images)

no-nonsense – had been so easily intimidated and had so readily deferred
to military advice.

Dayan also came in for his share of public abuse. The hero of the Six
Day War was taunted wherever he went with calls of "murderer."[104] The
impact of this war would be felt years later as some Israelis pivoted right,
for example, to Gush Emunim (Block of Faithful), committed to settling
occupied lands, or left to Peace Now, willing to trade land for peace.[105]

At the first meeting of the Knesset – Israel's parliament – after the
ceasefire, future prime minister Menachem Begin, then leader of the Likud
opposition party, asked the question on everyone's mind: "Why ... did
you not call up the reserve forces and mobilize the weaponry? What prevented you from doing this simple and fundamental thing? Who prevented you from doing it?"[106] There were immediate demands for an
independent investigation into what became commonly known as *ha'Me-
hdal*, The Blunder. By the end of November, Prime Minister Meir had
announced the appointment of an inquiry known as the Agranat Commission. Heads would roll.

Shimon Agranat. His commission of inquiry led directly to the establishment of the Tenth Man. (Credit: Government Press Office/Israel National Photo Collection)

The Agranat Commission

A graduate of the University of Chicago law school, Shimon Agranat was born in the United States in 1906 and was only forty-two when he was appointed to the Israeli Supreme Court. By 1973 he was chief justice, and, just weeks after the war, he and four colleagues (including two former IDF chiefs of staff) were asked to investigate what had gone wrong. One of the key questions concerned intelligence and preparedness: "The intelligence available from before the war on the intentions of Syria and Egypt; the analysis of the intelligence by the authorized civilian and military units; the general preparedness of the IDF to fight, especially on the date of October 5, 1973, the day prior to the outbreak of the war."[107] The Agranat Commission held hearings, listened to witnesses, and, on 1 April 1974, published the first of its three reports. Even in its redacted form, the report caused a sensation.

Moshe Dayan and Golda Meir both got a pass, as politicians often do. The commission concluded that they had not been negligent. Dayan was absolved of all responsibility because his conduct was beyond the inquiry's scope and he had, in any event, acted as a "reasonable minister of defence." Instead of standing with his officers, Dayan developed a separate legal strategy and, when he testified before the commission, he blamed them for what had happened. He portrayed himself as an innocent cabinet minister misled by his military team.

This absolution was breathtaking. Dayan had been appointed minister of defence because he was a military expert and a war hero, yet he was judged not by the usual parliamentary system of ministerial responsibility but by an imaginary standard of reasonable behaviour that ignored his military qualifications. Agranat's biographer, Pnina Lahav, concluded that applying this standard to Dayan "smacked of excessive legalism, a manipulation of semantic techniques designed to set Dayan free."[108] The conclusion seemed to be that, so long as Dayan accepted the opinion of his advisers, he could not be held responsible. Dayan's cynical self-preservation, and the commission's apparent complicity, enraged Israelis. Dayan resigned in due course, though he made a comeback in 1977 when Menachem Begin appointed him foreign minister, and he partly rehabilitated his reputation during the Camp David talks that led to the Egypt-Israel peace agreement.

Israel is a small country with a self-protecting elite that extends across party lines – and the prime minister benefited from this protection as well. The commission found that Meir had acted "wisely, with common sense ... performing a most important service for the defence of the state,"[109] even though she admitted she had failed to act on the vital question, "Why didn't I say anyway: 'Gentlemen, let's call up the reserves?'"[110] But what is the purpose of political leadership? As former foreign minister Abba Eban concluded, "It is certainly not to accept, willy nilly, the conclusions of others, particularly where she knew better."[111]

Assessing political responsibility was properly beyond the scope of the commission – the voters would do that – but surely Israeli intransigence under Meir's leadership, most notably her refusal to engage in mediated peace discussions, had something to do with Egypt going to war. More importantly, no matter how you look at it, both Meir and Dayan should have listened to Elazar when he, admittedly belatedly, insisted on all of the reserves being summoned for duty. "In Israel," however, "responsibility always stops one level below the politicians."[112]

Sadat was actually a tactical genius. By waging war, he achieved more than what he had been willing to settle for in the abortive peace negotiations that predated the attack. "What no one understood at first," Kissinger wrote in his memoir of the crisis, "was that Sadat was aiming not for conquest but to change the equilibrium in negotiations he intended to start. The shock of war, he reasoned, would enable *both* sides, Israel as well as Egypt, to show a flexibility that was impossible while Israel considered itself militarily supreme and Egypt was paralyzed by national humiliation."[113] It came at a terrible cost: "Israel's tragedy was that it had to pay such a high price – in human and material losses – in order to comprehend the limits of military power and … to realize that the only means by which it could attain peace and security was through the return of all Egyptian territory occupied in 1967. It was … fortunate that in 1977 Menachem Begin finally understood what Golda Meir refused to accept in early 1973."[114] Israeli triumphalism also played a major part in informing public attitudes and impairing judgment across all levels of Israeli society.

Even though she was "commended" by the commissioners, Meir could not survive politically. Almost every Jewish family in the country had lost someone, and thousands of angry demonstrators took to the streets. Just nine days after the first report was published, Meir was out of office. "Cover-up" and "fundamentally defective" were just two of the more polite press responses to the report, and the criticisms and condemnations became more vitriolic over time. Most of the report was censored, so Israelis did not know even half the story. Most galling of all was the double standard: absolution for the politicians, and condemnation for the military, deserved though much of it was.

Agranat and his colleagues recognized the danger inherent in evaluating historical events with the benefit of hindsight, but they had no difficulty in pointing their finger at the soldiers and holding them accountable. Their critical finding was direct and to the point: because of the Concept, the IDF was not ready. Even if correct at one time, the Concept had not been adequately reconsidered in light of changing circumstances, particularly the overwhelming evidence of two enemy armies poised for war on Israel's borders.

The commission identified the theoretical framework underlying the Concept, which encouraged Israeli decision makers to believe that there would be no attack – the self-confidence, mixed with stereotypes, about the military superiority of the Israelis and the inferiority of the Arabs, who were considered incapable of coordination and sophistication. Sadat had talked of war before but nothing had happened. In addition, there were structural factors and numerous very bad decisions.

Belief in the Concept had mesmerized Israeli officials and led them to ignore countless signals and irrefutable evidence from both Egypt and Syria that they were about to wage war: "These efforts were part of an imaginative, intensive, and well-orchestrated strategy of deception which brought rich rewards. Particularly effective was the exploitation of Israeli weakness by deliberately acting in such a way as to confirm the Israeli leaders' known belief that the Arabs were not ready and not willing to go to war."[115] Within AMAN, the entire IDF and senior Israeli political leadership, the dominant group, marginalized and silenced any colleague who dared to suggest an alternate approach or perspective.

It would, however, be simplistic to say that the entire blame for the surprise attack rested with the Concept. To be fair, the Concept had been vindicated on several previous occasions. But that did not mean it was still true. "We didn't believe Sadat was capable of surprising us," Lieutenant-General David Elazar admitted to the commission.[116] Indeed, he testified that between 1 and 6 October, everything was "most normal … I did not observe anything extraordinary."[117] The report called him to account: "The chief of staff bears direct responsibility for what happened on the eve of war, both with regard to the assessment of the situation and the preparedness of the IDF."[118] On the morning of 6 October, Elazar had urged full mobilization of the reserves as well as a pre-emptive attack, but it was too late and he was, in any event, overruled. Once the report was released, Elazar resigned. He had a lot to answer for, of course, but some of the responsibility should have been appropriately shared with his political masters.

The commission also recommended that Zeira be dismissed. Not only had he got it all wrong but he had withheld information and misled both Dayan and Elazar. Israel had eavesdropping devices planted on strategic communication lines in Cairo – "the special means" – which were supposed to be turned on in the case of a true emergency. When asked if they had been activated, Zeira replied: "Everything is quiet." That was partially correct: they had not been activated.[119]

Zeira was no traitor – like every officer and soldier he loved Israel – but he was captivated by the Concept. Obviously he had to go. In the words of the report, "in view of his grave failure … [he] cannot continue in his post as Chief of Military Intelligence."[120] Zeira later claimed that if he had been shown some of the other information – AMAN received some 400 messages indicating that war was imminent in the immediate run-up to the attack – he would have made different decisions. Maybe. But why did he intimate to Dayan and Elazar that the surveillance was operational and producing nothing when it had not even been turned on?[121] Referring to Zeira and his deputy, Shalev, the report could not have been more damning: "These two," the commission concluded, displayed "doctrinaire adherence" to the Concept and "failed to provide the IDF with adequate warning."[122] Lieutenant-Colonel David Gedaliah suppressed information that contradicted the Concept, while Lieutenant-Colonel Yonah Bandman fiddled with evidence to make the border look quiet when it was not. The commission recommended that they also be dismissed. In the end, blame for the disaster was attributed to five men: Elazar, Zeira, Shalev, Gedaliah, and Bandman.

A second interim report was published in July 1974 and the final 1,500-page document was published at the end of January 1975. Much was redacted, marked "top secret." The "complete" report was released in seven volumes in 1995, with large portions still blacked out. Even today, four decades after the Yom Kippur War, the full story of the intelligence failure, at least from the Israeli point of view, is not completely known. Just about everyone involved in the war, Arab and Israeli, wrote memoirs absolving themselves of responsibility for any wrongdoing and identifying others as culpable. (Moshe Dayan's were particularly self-serving and deceitful, no high bar in that group, all of whom were very busy pointing fingers at each other.)[123]

What we do know is that military intelligence completely failed. AMAN had all of the information it needed well before the attack, but ignored it. In the days before the war began, the evidence was overwhelming, but because of blind adherence to the Concept, it was not correctly assessed. The likelihood of war was deemed "smaller than small."[124] In the run-up to the Yom Kippur War, two subordinate officers dared to speak up. One was sidelined, and the other faced disciplinary action for telling the truth.[125]

Key information that demanded the immediate reassessment of the received wisdom was simply discounted, for example, King Hussein's visit to Tel Aviv. As Shalev later admitted in his rather sad, self-justifying account, "the information provided by Hussein should have been taken more seriously and regarded as a warning."[126] Add to that the racist and ridiculous, not to mention superficial and ill-founded, Israeli assessment of Sadat and his soldiers, the massive visible troop build-up (and the known acquisition of the very weapons said to be a precondition for Egyptian resumption of hostilities, a key pillar of the Concept), the coordinated Russian evacuations from Egypt and Syria, Marwan's tip from London ... the list just goes on and on.

Although it was easy to identify and blame the Concept, fixing the problem was more difficult. Abba Eban testified before the commission-·ers that freedom of opinion in assessing intelligence was indispensable, as was "pluralism of assessments."[127] Meir agreed, saying that there must be "a proper counterbalance of assessment ... It has become absolutely clear to me that we must not be in a situation where only one person is making the assessments."[128] The Agranat Commission reached the same conclusion. Exclusive dependence on AMAN's intelligence assessment was one of the explanations for the fiasco. A counterweight was required. That meant a cultural change, one where contrary opinions could be safely expressed. The commission made all sorts of recommendations that led to various organizational reforms, but the one that really struck a chord was the Tenth Man.

The Solution

The Tenth Man is a devil's advocate. If there are ten people in a room and nine agree, the role of the tenth is to disagree and point out flaws in whatever decision the group has reached.

Killing the messenger is self-defeating. AMAN had to change the way it did business, and in the aftermath of the Agranat Commission it created two new tools: the position of the Tenth Man, also referred to as the Revision Department, and the option of writing "different opinion" memos. "The task was to generate intelligence estimates that ran contrary to Research Department assessments ... This approach was important because it allowed for the consideration of a number of possible intentions of the enemy, including those deemed less probable than others."[129] After all, the opposite might be true. If this system had been in place in October 1973, AMAN would have produced two assessments: the first indicating on the basis of the overwhelming evidence that the Concept was defunct and that war would begin, and the second that the Concept continued. Faced with these alternative assessments, Israel's political leadership would have almost certainly called up the reserves even if it decided, for political reasons, to let Egypt and Syria launch their attacks.

The Tenth Man's job is to challenge conventional and received wisdom. The aim is to look at things creatively, independently, and from a fresh perspective, to engage actively with and to reconsider the status quo. Tenth Man "analysts search for information and arguments that contradict theses constructed by the intelligence community's various production and analysis departments. One anomaly is sufficient to refute a thesis, or at least to warrant a reexamination."[130] The Tenth Man also looks at subjects that have not, but perhaps should, receive attention, and it provides a sounding board for lower-level analysts who wish to raise issues that might not otherwise be considered at senior levels in the chain of command.

The task of the Tenth Man is to explore alternative assumptions and worst-case scenarios, and they can do so without fear of damage to their careers.[131] Can the same data used to support one conclusion also be used to support another? Applying that simple test to the evaluation of the intelligence accumulated in September and October 1973 would immediately have led to competing intelligence assessments.[132] The Tenth Man has high status within AMAN: it is free to obtain any intelligence data it needs and to criticize existing views. Its reports cannot be ignored; they must be considered. Tenth Man reports go directly to the director of military intelligence – the position Zeira held – as well as to all the major decision makers, including the prime minister and the minister of defence.

The idea of the Tenth Man is not a panacea. Many seasoned intelligence professionals think it is ridiculous; more importantly, it is seen as unproductive because it doesn't work. That's what the eminent historian Walter Laqueur concluded. The Tenth Man was without "conspicuous success."[133] In the intelligence world, the detractors criticize it as pseudo-intelligence, beginning with a preordained conclusion that the contrary of something is correct, instead of following the evidence no matter where it goes. There is also some reason to believe that "the routine use of this mechanism ritualizes it and results in it being ignored."[134] Benny Gantz, the IDF chief of staff, observed: "We need an organizational structure that encourages all ranks to be critical, to cast doubt, to reexamine basic assumptions, to get outside the framework."[135] There are those who claim that these contrary opinions "have never changed the intelligence assessment," while proponents insist that such opinions are an "extremely important educational tool."[136] Persuading professionals to assume the role of permanent critic also presents certain practical difficulties in recruitment and retention as team players advance and unhappy campers are isolated and ostracized.

Pluralism in decision making is no guarantee against getting it wrong, but it's the right approach and it transcends any particular time and place. Israel is not alone in facing threats to its national security: the challenges are international. The enemy will launch a ground war, an air war, a nuclear war; it will use chemical weapons; it will engage in a single act of terrorism or multiple acts; it will hit at home or hit abroad. We actually cannot rule anything out, at least not without evidence of capability and an understanding of intentions.

Meir did not stand up to the military when she instinctively knew better and understood she should do so. AMAN was an arm of the military. A case can be made that, in a country like Israel, intelligence gathering and assessment are opposite sides of the same coin. But, in general, the military, where hierarchy, discipline, and obedience govern, is probably not the best institution to assess intelligence. Soldiers see threats and want to destroy them. Fair enough – that is their job. But public-policy decisions are more complicated and nuanced, and need to consider all possible angles. In October 1973 the information was good, but it was poorly evaluated. Chaim Bar Lev – the person after whom the line was named – summed up the situation in these words: "The mistake lay in the evaluation of the intelligence data and not in the absence of accurate and reliable information."[137]

Obviously, hindsight is perfect. And it would be beyond naive to believe that there will always be time to consider carefully every option in the midst of a true crisis. In general, people really do try hard to get their decisions right, and they deserve some understanding when they get them wrong. Still, what could be worse than getting them very badly wrong by not even considering actual available evidence?

Ultimately, the Israelis deceived themselves: their adherence to the Concept, their belief in their military superiority, their inability to consider a limited military campaign with a political objective, their racism, and many other factors led them down the path to disaster and the very real possibility of national collapse. They did not put themselves in the shoes of their enemies when they should have examined everything from the perspective of the other guy.

"The 'Concept' was not," Moshe Dayan later recalled, "the invention of a mad-genius ... but it emerged from very critical information which we thought was the best one could have acquired."[138] That may have been true once, but the Concept should have never been chiselled in granite.

Forty years after The Blunder, Zeira was asked what went wrong. He had a number of explanations, some self-serving, others not, and two that would have been wise if they had not been so predictable: "The first mistake was that we did not understand that the Egyptians' main problem was shame ... If I had understood this point, I would have understood that they desperately wanted a victory, even a small one." His second mistake was related to the first: "We did not have a mechanism for probing the soul of the Egyptian people."[139] But just like the amassing enemy forces, both explanations were sitting in plain sight.

Israel's founding prime minister, David Ben Gurion, had identified the real threat to Israel's security years earlier. Referring to Sadat's predecessor, Gamal Abdel Nasser, and the Arab defeat in 1948, Ben Gurion said: "Nasser is suffering from a psychological injury; he is humiliated, and he will not make peace before he has healed his injury, in other words before scoring a victory over Israel."[140] A Tenth Man could have pointed this out.

The day before the Egyptians and Syrians attacked, Zeira advised the prime minister not to worry about the evacuation of Russian personnel from Egypt and Syria. If the Soviets were leaving because they feared war, "they do not know the Arabs very well," he told Meir.[141] In fact, it was Zeira who knew nothing. The Israelis suffered a mental blackout that completely impaired their intelligence assessments and decision making. Not only did they not see what they were seeing, their governing assumptions about their enemies were just wrong, whether based on racism, myth, fantasy, or plain wishful thinking.

When Israel rejected Egypt's realistic peace initiatives, when Egypt acquired advanced jet fighters, Scuds, and Surface-to-air-missiles, when Sadat out-thought his enemies and came up with a good plan, he caught Israel and its military and political leadership by surprise even though every action he took was in plain view in broad daylight. It even turned out, though the information was suppressed for many years, that the IDF had actually obtained the battle plans for the Syrian offensive in April 1973 (with an update courtesy of the CIA at the end of September) but did not believe them.[142] The intelligence was completely accurate, in terms of manpower, materiel, location, approach, and strategy.[143]

This type of self-inflicted blindness was not unique to Israel and its leaders (battle-hardened rugged individualists). "Wooden-headedness, the source of self-deception," celebrated historian Barbara Tuchman wrote, "is a factor that plays a remarkably large role in government. It consists in assessing a situation in terms of preconceived or fixed notions while ignoring or rejecting any contrary signs. It is acting according to wish while not allowing oneself to be deflected by the facts."[144] For the Israelis, their warped world view aggravated the problem: "You cannot suspect a stupid enemy of deceiving you[,] who are smarter, because the mere fact that that he can deceive you makes him smarter than you."[145] In October 1973 Israel knew that Egypt had the capacity to start a war but ignored Sadat's intentions. Why? Because, "we had nothing but contempt for him."[146]

The Elusive Pursuit of Good Decision Making

Three years after the Yom Kippur War, on 27 June, 1976, an Air France flight from Tel Aviv to Paris via Athens was hijacked by members of the Front for the Liberation of Palestine joined by a couple of comrades from Germany – members of the Revolutionary Cells, an extremely dangerous leftist group. After a stopover in Benghazi, Libya, the plane was flown to Entebbe Airport in Uganda where the terrorists were warmly welcomed by His Excellency President for Life, Field Marshal Alhaji Dr Idi Amin Dada, VC, DSO, MC, CBE. Amin was actually a psychotic cannibal. (Yasser Arafat served as best man at one of his many weddings: to a nineteen-year-old go-go dancer.) Realizing that the Ugandan leader was in cahoots with the terrorists, the Israelis decided to come up with their own rescue plan as it became increasingly obvious that there would be no diplomatic solution.

The logistical problems in orchestrating a rescue thousands of kilometres from home seemed insurmountable and suggestion after suggestion was rejected as the clock ticked closer to the terrorist deadline. Defence Minister Shimon Peres, another future prime minister, however, instructed the IDF "to continue raising new ideas and checking them out, no matter how weird and crazy they sounded."[147] This is exactly what they did until they finally came up with a plan that could work. On 4 July 1976 an elite team of Israeli commandos executed a daring raid. Only one IDF soldier lost his life in the rescue mission – the commander, Yonatan Netanyahu – and his death is widely credited with inspiring his younger brother, Benjamin, Israel's current prime minister, to enter politics.

In some cases, like Operation Thunderbolt, the name given to the Entebbe rescue mission, the process of leaving no stone unturned, considering every option, and welcoming the expression of all suggestions has a relatively happy ending; in others, the opposite occurs, the Iraq War being a case in point. In the run-up to the American-led invasion, the head of AMAN instructed the Tenth Man to prepare a contrary analysis to the claim that Iraq had weapons of mass destruction (WMD). The Tenth Man concluded that Iraq possessed chemical and biological WMD but no nuclear weapons. "Although there was doubt among AMAN analysts concerning Iraq's capabilities, the doubts did not supersede fears that Saddam nevertheless had a remnant ... of such weapons, as well as a small number of missiles."[148]

Just like the Americans and the British, Israel's Tenth Man got it completely wrong. The truth was that Iraqi programs to develop and produce chemical, biological, and nuclear weapons had been long dismantled. Perhaps fear trumped other considerations, or politics won, or none of the AMAN intelligence officers objected to any pretext for war against Iraq: Saddam was, after all, a loathsome, war-mongering tyrant, a mass murderer, a terrorist sponsor, and a dictator unrelentingly hostile to Israel and his neighbours (including Iran and Kuwait). It certainly looked like he had something to hide. Yet how could the Tenth Man conclude, on the basis of no evidence, that there were WMD when clearly there were not? The point in institutionalizing dissent with the Tenth Man was to hard-wire autonomy, independence, and space for contrary points of view in the decision-making process. The purpose was to provide intelligence estimates based on fact. There is no shame in admitting that there is insufficient information and that no conclusions can be reached. Better that than getting it wrong. Yet there was no stopping the American and British march to war. The Tenth Man failed.

It may make sense to exaggerate threats and prepare for them rather than underplay them, which is exactly the opposite of what happened in the run-up to the Yom Kippur War. But overestimation of threats clearly has costs too. Intelligence to please, if that is what it was, is not intelligence. Politicized intelligence is not intelligence. In the years since the 2003 invasion of Iraq, at least 500,000 people have died – some say the number is closer to 1 million or even more – and those totals, dreadful though they are, are on top of continuing violence, human suffering, and material damage of hideous and still escalating proportions. The world is now far less safe. We live in challenging times. Nothing is certain. Peace, collective security, even the future of the planet are hanging in the balance. We have to get it right and that means really seeing the threats to our world. Israel should know this better than anyone. Instead, it is, once again, facing disaster.

Chapter 2

There Really Is Nothing New under the Sun

The list of intelligence failures is long. The Americans might have avoided Pearl Harbor if they had picked up on the signals.[1] There was no way that the Russians were going to avoid Operation Barbarossa, but they should have seen it coming. In 1941 there was ample information that the Japanese in the Pacific, and the Germans on the Eastern Front, were poised for war, just as the Egyptians and Syrians were in October 1973, but neither the US military nor Soviet dictator Joseph Stalin wanted to believe it. Like the Israelis, the Americans and the Russians were caught off guard. In similar fashion, South Korea ignored North Korea's expansionist and imperialist intentions in 1950, and the British were surprised when Argentina attacked the Falklands in 1982.

The lessons from all these intelligence failures are clear: good decision making requires freedom of thought and diversity in views.[2] Good decisions depend on dissenters.

Cuba Two Ways

The Bay of Pigs invasion of communist Cuba was a fiasco. In its aftermath, the inexperienced new president, John F. Kennedy, who had been in office for only three months, realized that not only had he failed to see what was coming but had convinced himself, against all the evidence, that the plan would work. He had received poor advice from some of his generals – who promised a "fair chance" of success – and outright lies from the CIA. As soon as the exiles landed, director Allen Dulles told him, there would be a popular uprising, and the dictator, Fidel Castro, would be overthrown.[3]

But why would the Cuban people rally behind the invaders? Castro had displaced dictator Fulgencio Batista (an American puppet and Mafia stooge) and was popular at the time for his social and economic reforms, which resonated in the impoverished but proud island nation. The notion that a handful of hastily trained irregulars could defeat Cuba's huge professional army was simply far-fetched. Moreover, the Cubans knew they were coming.

In January 1961 a front-page *New York Times* story disclosed that the United States was training Cuban patriots at a secret base in Guatemala, and, inevitably, the Cuban exile community in Miami spread the news. Four days before the attack, Radio Moscow's English-language service predicted the invasion: it was a plot hatched by the CIA using "criminals," it reported. "More and more details about the Cuban operation are appearing in the papers," presidential aide Arthur M. Schlesinger, Jr, noted in his diary.[4] American political and military leaders nevertheless convinced themselves and each other that the invasion would succeed and that the world would believe that the United States had nothing to do with it.

On 17 April 1961 approximately 1,400 underequipped Cuban volunteers (unfortunately including Batista-era criminals and a handful of truly discreditable ex-Cuban army types) attempted their invasion on a beach in the Bay of Pigs, and most were killed or captured by 20,000 readily assembled soldiers. One ship carried the bulk of the ammunition reserve, and it was immediately sunk. "Many fine men have been killed or lost," Schlesinger wrote, and, regretfully, "one cannot resist the belief that it was an ill-considered and mistaken expedition."[5]

There were no mass uprisings of popular support; rather, most of the Cuban people supported the revolution (although 200,000 of them were apprehended by Cuban authorities and herded into theatres and auditoriums as a precautionary measure). The United States paid more than $50 million in ransom in food and drugs to secure the freedom of the captured members of invading Brigade 2506. Not long after, Che Guevara approached an American official at a cocktail party in Punta de Este, Uruguay, and expressed Cuba's thanks for the invasion: it had been a "great political victory for them," he said, and "enabled them to consolidate."[6]

Kennedy was beside himself: "How could I have been so stupid?" he asked his advisers. It was not just Dulles who had misled the president: so had the Joint Chiefs of Staff and the secretary of defense. "They all spoke with the sacerdotal prerogative of men vested with a unique understanding of arcane matters."[7] Yet the plan was poorly conceived from the beginning. Kennedy was even told that if the rebels encountered any problems, they could "melt away" to the Escambray Mountains – but those mountains were 130 kilometres away, separated from the rebels by swamps and jungle. An unofficial post-mortem catalogued a completely misconceived undertaking, politically, militarily, and technically, one informed by wildly inaccurate assumptions and intelligence, fuelled by bravado and bluster.

There were a great many meetings in the run-up to the invasion, planning for which began during the Eisenhower administration (it was actually Vice-President Richard M. Nixon's idea). Kennedy's advisers were eager to please – it was no secret that the president was committed to Castro's overthrow – and there had already been several American-backed attempts to assassinate the Cuban leader.

No one in the inner circle really spoke up, at least not in a way that mattered and registered. As Schlesinger recalled, "our meetings took place in a curious atmosphere of assumed consensus,"[8] a candid admission from the court historian. The only real pushback came from the talented Senator J. William Fulbright: Cuba, he told the president, was a thorn in the flesh, not a dagger to the heart. But by then it was too late; when everyone else on the team participated in a straw vote on the eve of the invasion, they were all on side. "Had one senior adviser opposed the adventure," Schlesinger wrote, "Kennedy would have cancelled it."[9] Well, maybe.

Kennedy later confided to *Washington Post* editor Ben Bradlee that, "the first advice I'm going to give my successor is to watch the generals and avoid the feeling that because they were military men their opinions on military matters were worth a damn."[10] He resolved never again to rely entirely on insiders and to expand the range of those to turn to for advice. His brother Robert insisted, in the future, that "there be a devil's advocate to give an opposite opinion if none was pressed."[11] The Bay of Pigs was an abject failure, but it set the stage for the next tangle with Cuba – the Missile Crisis.

As might have been expected, American aggression pushed Castro right into the arms of the Soviet Union. In October 1962 the CIA reported there were thousands of Russian soldiers on the island, just 145 kilometres off the US coast (there were actually more than 40,000). Even worse, U-2 surveillance flights revealed Russian medium-range nuclear missiles pointed at Washington and other cities along the eastern seaboard. "It was a staggering project – staggering in its recklessness, staggering in its misconception of the American response, staggering in its rejection of the ground rules for coexistence among the superpowers."[12]

American officials – even the hardened Kremlinologists – had not anticipated any of it, despite the escalating Cold War. The previous month the national intelligence estimate concluded that placing longer-range ballistic missiles in Cuba or establishing a base for missile-launching Soviet submarines "would be incompatible with Soviet practice to date and with Soviet policy as we presently estimate it."[13] It also ignored credible reports of giant tubes being unloaded at Cuban ports, yet their only purpose could be as silos to fire nuclear missiles.[14] A post-mortem attributed this major intelligence failure to misconceptions about the Soviet Union. This time round, however, a seasoned, more experienced President Kennedy was at the helm, with lessons learned from the Bay of Pigs debacle.

Kennedy gathered the Executive Committee of the National Security Council, but gave ExComm, as it became known, new and improved marching orders. He stayed away from most meetings and directed that the usual rules of hierarchy and rank be ignored. Members should not represent their departments or institutions; rather, as they considered the problem and its possible solutions, they should "put themselves in [Chairman Nikita] Khrushchev's shoes."[15]

Khrushchev, a true believer in the Soviet system, made no secret of his long-term goal: "We will bury you," he told Western diplomats in Moscow. With his earned reputation for ruthlessness and barbarity, this threat could not be dismissed. Not surprisingly, American military leaders began to prepare for a surprise attack followed by invasion and strongly urged that outcome on the political leadership, where it initially found considerable favour.

But President Kennedy adopted a more reflective approach. He instructed ExComm, instead of reaching a consensus and agreeing on a single recommended course, to present alternatives. "In effect, the members walked around the problem … first from this angle, then from that … thinking aloud, hearing new arguments, entertaining new considerations."[16] Lower-level officials were periodically invited to join the deliberations, mixing things up and adding fresh information and perspectives. In marked contrast, however, Khrushchev could not see beyond his initial assessment of the president. He had bullied the younger Kennedy at the June 1961 Vienna summit. The Soviet premier returned to Moscow convinced that, if pushed, the American president would fold.

ExComm members – Secretary of State Dean Rusk, Secretary of Defense Robert McNamara, Vice-President Lyndon B. Johnson, the new director of the CIA, John McCone, the US ambassador to the United Nations, Adlai Stevenson, and nine other first-rate men – were divided into smaller groups to consider the options and were asked to bring them back to the larger group for discussion. "As a result," Robert Kennedy recalled in *Thirteen Days*, his best-selling memoir of the crisis, "the conversations were completely uninhibited and unrestricted. Everyone had an equal opportunity to express himself and to be heard directly."[17] ExComm settled on two possible alternatives: military intervention or blockade.

Acquiescence was inconceivable. The missiles were capable of killing 80 million Americans, and that fact alone ruled out doing nothing. With mid-term elections around the corner, there were also secondary political considerations. The Republicans had already identified Cuba as a hot-button issue in light of the massive Soviet armament of the island. A blockade, or quarantine as they called it, coupled with a demand that Soviet missiles be removed, would show that the Americans meant business and allow for a peaceful resolution, all the while preserving the military option if necessary.

The genius of the blockade was that it would buy time – stopping ships, boarding ships, seizing ships, all opportunities for reflection and reconsideration – but keep the door open for negotiations. It was a political tool meant to avoid resort to a military one. At the same time, the assembly of 200,000 American troops in Florida, the arrival of hundreds of tactical fighters within easy striking distance of Cuba, and the deployment of the US Navy to the region signalled resolve and readiness to pursue the military option.

Irving Janis, the research psychologist from Yale University who became famous for his theory of "groupthink," credited this problem-solving approach for breaking up premature consensus that may well have led to a nuclear war. Avoiding a nuclear catastrophe remained Kennedy's priority throughout.[18] In using ExComm in this way, "a basic choice had yielded to a richer, more sophisticated menu of choices, enabling the president to calibrate US actions more carefully, find the precise spot where he felt the greatest confidence, and give more clear operational guidance to his subordinates."[19] (Dean Acheson, the grand old man of the Truman administration, however, had a different take; he favoured targeted air strikes and objected to the "freewheeling academic seminar" instead of a "presidential council of war."[20])

American officials *did* learn something from their mistakes: "The cast of characters in both dramas [was] mostly the same; the team that bungled the Bay of Pigs was the team that performed brilliantly during the Cuban missile crisis."[21] The president had recently read Barbara Tuchman's book *The Guns of August*, and he understood how easy it was to stumble into war. Determined to understand the adversary, he knew exactly when and how hard to push and when to pull back.

In October 1962 Kennedy was at the top of his game and, fortunately, in Khrushchev he had a willing if occasionally erratic partner. Thirteen days after the crisis began, a negotiated agreement was reached between the superpowers – the war-mongering maniacs in both countries were benched, and the world breathed a sigh of relief. A full-scale nuclear war was averted, in part because Kennedy insisted on considering all options – including dissenting points of view. Good instincts and intuition and pure blind dumb luck also played a part.

The received version of events asserts that it was Khrushchev who blinked, having completely misjudged Kennedy's mettle. There is, however, an alternative narrative: Khrushchev achieved his goals: an American promise not to invade Cuba and a secret agreement to have US nuclear warheads pointed at the Soviet Union removed from Turkey. Kennedy won the propaganda war – just before the mid-term elections – but Khrushchev came out ahead.

Iraq

Since 20 March 2003, myriad post-mortems have been conducted of Operation Iraqi Freedom, the invasion of Iraq by Coalition forces – some forty countries led by the United States but not including Canada. President George W. Bush explained that the justification for the war was as simple as it was straightforward: "to disarm Iraq of weapons of mass destruction, to end Saddam Hussein's support for terrorism, and to free the Iraqi people."[22] The reasons that motivated President Bush and UK Prime Minister Tony Blair to go to war against Iraq are complicated, but they had nothing to do with weapons of mass destruction: in truth, there weren't any.

The various assessments of the Iraq disaster agree on a few things: there was a rush to judgment and little, if any, consideration of alternative explanations of the evidence supposedly demonstrating that Saddam was still developing WMD. For example, Iraq was subject to all sorts of United Nations (UN) sanctions, and it used front companies and intermediaries to sidestep the international embargo. Bush and Blair realized, however, that they could make no compelling case for regime change in Iraq unless WMD were involved – these terrifying weapons were the linchpin. So, if evidence about their existence did not exist, they would have to fabricate it. Bush easily convinced an adulatory Blair to go along: "I will be with you, whatever," he wrote to the US president.[23]

Prime Minister Blair's 2003 "dodgy dossier," widely circulated to enlist public support for war, claimed that the assessed intelligence established "beyond doubt" that Saddam was producing WMD, even though it was filled with plagiarized and dated material. The misinformed US secretary of state, Colin Powell, not only gave it his approval but praised it.[24] "Such bad food," Woody Allen once said in an entirely different context, "and small portions too."[25] Bush even claimed in his 2003 State of the Union Address that "the British government has learned that Saddam Hussein recently sought significant quantities of uranium from Africa."

There was no truth to any of it – the documents were easily detectable forgeries. True, at one time Iraq was developing WMD, but, when UN sanctions were imposed in 1991, the program was terminated and stockpiles were destroyed (although some equipment and expertise were retained to restart production after the sanctions were lifted). Saddam could have laid all the concerns to rest had he cooperated with the UN's Special Commission on Disarmament, but he sealed his and Iraq's fate when he expelled the international inspectors. A last-minute turnaround came too late.

Meanwhile, the WMD claims were not challenged by the American client states that joined the Coalition and that collectively failed to consider sufficiently any option other than going to war. Preparation for the war and contingency planning were completely inadequate, and the ill-planned occupation resulted in devastating and continuing consequences for Iraq, its people, and the world. That was one of the findings of the twelve-volume *Report of the Iraqi Inquiry Committee* (2016), better known as the Chilcot Inquiry. Sir John Chilcot also concluded that it should not be possible "to engage in a military or indeed a diplomatic endeavour on such a scale and of such gravity without really careful challenge analysis." There was no absence of external dissent: people protested all over the world, but they were ignored.

Chilcot's report blasted Blair and his Labour government for its decision to invade Iraq, pointing out that the underlying intelligence added up to nothing: it was torn from context, ambiguous, embellished, concocted, or completely unverifiable, coming as it did from suspect sources. In fact, the British government knew that Saddam was not developing WMD months before the prime minister lied to the British people and sent his country to war. On 23 July 2002 the "Downing Street Memo" had reported that American authorities were tailoring the facts to support their policy of removing Saddam.[26] Political leadership had no intention of allowing actual evidence to interfere with decision making, even if it meant making stuff up to justify the unjustifiable.

Public trust took a hit as people in the United States, United Kingdom, and all over the world learned that the American and British governments could not be relied on to tell the truth. A study by the Center for Public Integrity found that President Bush and his top officials had, in the two years after 9/11, made almost 1,000 false statements to the American people.[27] This is not a new phenomenon. Far from it. Another important lesson was that "all aspects of any intervention need to be calculated, debated and challenged with the utmost rigour."[28] In short, dissenting voices need to be heard.

Cognitive Barriers to Good Decision Making

"Why do people so often fail to look into the available alternatives when vital consequences are at stake?"[29] Janis asked in the aftermath of the botched Cuban invasion. It was an obvious question and his important 1972 book, *Victims of Groupthink*, began by taking a long hard look at "A Perfect Failure: The Bay of Pigs."

Janis found this episode perplexing: "Like the President, all the main advisers were shrewd thinkers, capable of objective, rational analysis, and accustomed to speaking their minds," he wrote. "But collectively they failed to detect the serious flaws in the invasion plan."[30] How did these smart guys get it so wrong? The answer: groupthink.

"According to the groupthink hypothesis, members of any small cohesive group tend to maintain esprit de corps by unconsciously developing a number of shared illusions and related norms that interfere with critical thinking and reality testing."[31] Groupthink is a psychological phenomenon that leads people in some groups to make bad decisions, but not all groups get it wrong. ExComm got it right because it was subject to clear rules for disciplined decision making. President Kennedy got it wrong in the spring of 1961, as did the Israelis in October 1973. In both instances it was classic groupthink, although not all of its many variables were present in each case. In general, though, there was an overwhelming desire to achieve consensus. With blinkers on, the Americans marched down a path to their desired result, one that was littered with obviously dangerous potholes, while the Israelis held true to a concept that had been disproven by overwhelming evidence to the contrary. In neither case did anyone call for pause to reconsider or re-evaluate.

What happens with groupthink is that a small group of people actively suppresses dissent, creativity, and independent thinking because they are determined to reach a consensus decision, often a preferred outcome that is known in advance. Group loyalty requires all members to go along as they discount information that runs contrary to the group's collective beliefs in favour of internally generated information, even if that means rejecting expert advice. Without all the evidence, there is little opportunity for critical appraisal or informed debate of assumptions, potential risks, or alternatives. If considered at all, they are rationalized, downplayed, or dismissed. Group members who raise an objection are silenced or forced to conform. At best, lip service is paid to contingency planning and risk assessment because the group is satisfied it has made the correct decision. An overwhelming belief in its moral superiority blinds the group to the ethical and moral consequences of its decisions. The end result, as Janis described it, is a predictable and likely cognitive deterioration in mental efficiency, reality testing, and moral judgment, all the result of group pressure.

Groupthink can be countered and decision making improved, as happened in the Cuban Missile Crisis. The key is getting the evidence – as much of it as possible – and creating a space for people to feel free to disagree vigorously. Debate is about encouraging the active consideration of risks, alternatives, and contingencies, about promoting informed dissent from people with different backgrounds and perspectives, no matter what place they occupy in the pecking order. And it is about trying to understand the other guys. What motivates them? What are their interests and objectives? Real leaders foster the conditions for good decision making by establishing a truly diverse group – not only demographic diversity but also diversity in race, gender, background, experience, ideas, and perspective. And they create an environment where group members can honestly say what they think and reveal their fears: they also welcome the introduction of new information from non-traditional sources.

Janis made a number of specific suggestions about how to improve the decision-making process. The leaders should stay away. The group should be split and, although all assigned the same task, the subgroups left free to do their job independently and only then to report back to the larger group. All alternatives should be examined and outsiders consulted, both by individuals on their own and by the group. Janis also recommended that every group member be assigned the role of "critical evaluator," to help counteract spontaneous pressures that give rise to premature consensus, and that at least one member be asked to serve as devil's advocate. Before a final decision is reached, a "second-chance" meeting should be held where participants have the opportunity to express residual doubts. In a nutshell, that is what President Kennedy did during the Cuban Missile Crisis.

Under the right circumstances, groups are very smart, especially diverse groups. Collective judgment can be excellent. Yet adopting Janis's prescriptive approach, or any other similar ways of improving group decision making that have emerged over the years since, is not without risk: "By institutionalizing dissent and opening up group deliberation to a wide array of outside forces, the decision making process may break down under political factionalism and bureaucratic in-fighting."[32]

However, deliberation without dissent serves little purpose: it is nothing more than an echo chamber. In any circumstance in which like-minded people discuss issues without being exposed to competing views, they tend to move toward even more extreme positions in a process called group polarization.[33] "When people are hearing echoes of their own voices, the consequence may be far more than support and reinforcement: "group members, move and coalesce, not toward the middle ... but toward a more extreme position."[34] People want to be favourably perceived by others, and they adjust their positions in the direction of the dominant view.

Life is filled with examples: organized religion is one of them. Religious groups amplify religious conviction, especially if external influences are minimized or even prohibited. The antidote is obvious: mix the group up and make sure that competing views can be heard. "What is necessary is not to allow every view to be heard, but to ensure that no single view is so widely heard, and reinforced, that people are unable to engage in critical evaluation of the reasonable competitors."[35]

Groupthink, or elements of it, are part of many bad group decisions. "I am obliged to confess I should sooner live in a society governed by the first two thousand names in the Boston telephone directory than in a society governed by the two thousand faculty members of Harvard University," William F. Buckley once said, and his point was a good one. Eggheads are great, but others also have important things to say. Lack of diversity is but one element: confirmation bias is another. "The trouble with the world," Mark Twain observed, "is not that people know too little, but that they know so many things that ain't so."

People seek information that confirms beliefs, and they ignore or discount information that contradicts it. Thucydides understood this human trait, as did Dante, Francis Bacon, and Leo Tolstoy. The latter wrote: "The most difficult subjects can be explained to the most slow-witted man if he has not formed any idea of them already; but the simplest things cannot be made clear to the most intelligent man if he is firmly persuaded that he knows already, without a shadow of doubt, what is laid before him."[36]

The beliefs and views we hold have extraordinary persistence, even in the face of contradictory, irrefutable evidence that should lead to a change of mind. The Semmelweis Reflex is another example of this. Ignaz Semmelweis was the Hungarian obstetrician who figured out, years before the confirmation of germ theory, that dirty hands were responsible for spreading infection and causing death. He insisted that doctors begin to wash their hands and for doing so faced fierce resistance: "Doctors are gentlemen, and gentlemen's hands are clean."[37] Dr Semmelweis was correct however, and the reflex named after him describes the human tendency to reject innovation whenever it contradicts received wisdom, prevailing attitudes, or established paradigms.

There is no doubt about it: "Our way of looking at and thinking about the world is tough to change and our biases are remarkably sticky."[38] People fit new information into existing theories and established views: they assimilate it to what they already know and believe. Most of the time that makes sense: information has to be organized or it becomes unmanageable and overwhelming. And yet simple psychological experiments demonstrate that with the right nudge people can be convinced to see something that isn't there – the Asch conformity experiments prove that – and sometimes they can't accurately interpret what is plainly there.

Cognitive dissonance, counterfactual thinking, blind spots, "recency" bias, wishful thinking, tunnel vision – the list of psychological barriers to good decision making goes on and on. How we frame and anchor questions directs answers. If we assume that knowledge of these barriers is sufficient to mitigate against them, we are the victims of optimism bias. Whether we are opening a business or starting a relationship, we are often overly optimistic, unrealistic in the assessment of our prospects. On a personal level, it would be hard to approach life any other way. But we should factor it into our decision making. Unfortunately, knowledge does not liberate us: "Just knowing about our biases does not make us less susceptible to them. Indeed, knowledge can easily have the opposite effect, encouraging people to think that they are immune to bias precisely because they know so much about it."[39]

That is one of the reasons why Janis recommended using the devil's advocate to institutionalize dissent. The idea has been around for hundreds of years, along with the red team, independent directors, and the Westminster parliamentary system, which balances the government in power against the loyal opposition. They are all supposed to serve the same purpose as the Tenth Man: to make sure that dissenting voices are heard. The question, however, remains: Does institutionalizing dissent work?

The Devil's Advocate

God has had his advocate, the *Advocatus Dei*, and so too has the Devil, the *Advocatus Diaboli*, since 1587. That's when the Roman Catholic Church established the Devil's Advocate Office to argue against the beatification or canonization of a candidate for elevation and veneration. At the time, the Vatican was a saint factory, or at least it appeared so. The

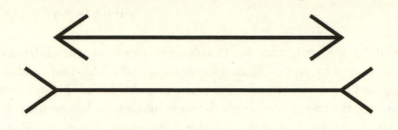

Müller-Lyer illusion. Each horizontal line is the exact same length. (Credit: Adapted from Wikipedia user Fibonacci)

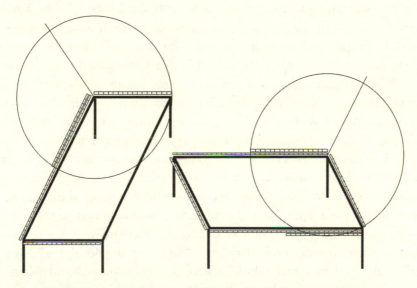

Shepard's Tables illusion. The shape and size of the two tabletops are identical, as the small bars and circles help illustrate. (Credit: Aaron Sloman, https://www.cs.bham. ac.uk/research/projects/cogaff/misc/rotated-table-illusion.html)

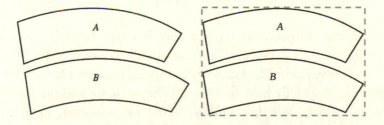

Jastrow's illusion. The shapes and sizes of A and B are identical, as can be seen when they are centred within the rectangle for reference. (Credit: Adapted from Wikipedia user Fibonacci)

job of the devil's advocate was to argue against raising a candidate to the rank of saint by proposing alternative explanations for that candidate's supposed miracles – miracles being the essential proof of sainthood. In that way, the theory went, only the worthiest would be anointed. If the deeds of a prospective saint were truly miraculous, they should stand up to the most searching scrutiny.

As the years went by, it became evident that the function had serious limitations. The devil's advocate role was an artificial one: he argued against something because that was his job, not his belief. The Vatican tried to imbue the task with status and importance: it gave the job to "a well-respected, well-trained, high-ranking official."[40] But the problem remained. In 1983 Pope John Paul II basically abolished the position.

When someone playing a role is an actor putting on a performance, everyone knows it and treats the advice accordingly: "Role-playing techniques may be less effective than authentic minority views in stimulating divergent thought because the role-player creates ambiguity regarding whether his arguments come from conviction and the reality that he cannot change his mind because his role is scripted."[41] Devil's advocates can become the proverbial broken record, saying the same thing over and over again. President Lyndon Johnson, for instance, assigned his aide Bill Moyers the devil's advocate role during the Vietnam War. Soon enough the president began to refer to him as "Mr. Stop the Bombing." Moyers was relegated to a pigeonhole, where he was ridiculed and where he remained, except when he was let out to repeat his ignored mantra.[42] At best, the devil's advocate "facilitates a more sophisticated inquiry into the problem at hand."[43] At worst, contrived dissent is a complete fiction providing little more than convenient cover.

Red Teams

Red teams are independent organizations that explore alternatives, usually in the case of a planned military or intelligence operation. They are ExComm on steroids. The US Army's *Applied Critical Thinking Handbook* explains exactly how they do it. They assume nothing and challenge everything, whether military, political, cultural, or personal assumptions. When that's done, they look for hidden assumptions. They take a proposed plan of action and deconstruct it to the granular level, then put it back together and do it all over again, a second and a third time, always with a completely different perspective and approach. They identify and put into place measures to counteract cognitive barriers, and they assemble all the facts, keeping an eye out for anomalies.

They take Donald Rumsfeld seriously: "Reports that say something hasn't happened are always interesting to me, because as we know, there are known knowns; there are things we know we know. We also know that there are known unknowns; that is to say we know there are some things we do not know. But there are also unknown unknowns – the ones we don't know we don't know."[44] A special military university has been established to teach the techniques: the University of Foreign Military and Cultural Studies located at in Fort Leavenworth, Kansas.

In this process, huge amounts of time and resources are spent to ensure that every single risk is identified, every blind spot illuminated, and every worst-case contingency anticipated, and that a plan, or two or three, is proposed to deal with it. Only supermen and superwomen are recruited: "The ideal critical thinker is habitually inquisitive, well-informed, trustful of reason, open-minded, flexible, fair-minded in evaluation, honest in facing personal biases, prudent in making judgments, willing to reconsider, clear about issues, orderly in complex matters, diligent in seeking relevant information, reasonable in the selection of criteria, focused in inquiry, and persistent in seeking results which are as precise as the subject and circumstances of inquiry permit."[45] Loners, mavericks, oddballs, contrarians, and skeptics are encouraged to apply, especially if they are fearless and can imagine themselves in someone else's shoes. Careerists and toadies are definitely unwelcome.

Red teaming is used not only in military conflicts but for terrorist threats too: the CIA formed its Red Cell the day after 9/11. There are also important commercial applications. Knowing what your competitor is doing, or might do, can provide a competitive advantage. Knowing what your competitor knows about you is hugely valuable information. A red team works only if it is supported at the very top and used sparingly. Not every decision needs dissection, and it would be devastating to morale if everyone was always second-guessed. But sometimes the effort is worthwhile, and when that decision is made, the bad news needs to be welcomed just like good news, or the whole operation is a waste of time.

It is definitely comforting to believe that there are people out there who can really figure stuff out, who can uncover what mere mortals cannot see. And maybe it's true. The problem is that we will never know for sure because the work takes place in secret – and stays that way.

Independent Directors

Independent directors, sometimes referred to as outside directors, are selected by shareholders at annual meetings to supervise management. They can have no material relationship with the company other than pocketing their director fees. Under some regulatory regimes, they cannot even be shareholders. In carrying out their responsibilities, they have a legal obligation to exercise independent judgment. In general, a majority of board members of publicly traded companies must be independent.

Part of their task is to ensure statutory compliance – and to do so with care, diligence, skill, integrity, and experience. They oversee strategy, performance, key appointments, decisions, and direction and approve mission, values, and vision. Independent directors are definitely not elected to represent the public interest, marginalized groups, special interests, or the environment, nor are they chosen to advocate for employees, social responsibility, or consumer protection. In Canada their foremost obligation is to act "in the best interests of the corporation" – and that means the shareholders.

The 2008 financial meltdown put big business and the financial industry under the spotlight. Unsound financial decisions, fraud, and government deregulation led to the crisis, but, whether fair or not, the watchman – the independent directors – were accused of falling asleep on the job. Even before the fiscal crisis, board composition had become a concern, particularly the homogeneity of white men in suits. Diversity is the touchstone of our times, and most people believe that important institutions should reflect contemporary society.

Not everyone agrees: in the run-up to its initial public offering, Facebook announced that its board members were all men. "We have a very small board," founder Mark Zuckerberg told the *New Yorker*. "I'm going to find people who are helpful, and I don't particularly care what gender they are."[46] A furor followed: "It doesn't make sense for a company that claims to be so forward looking to not have any women directors," Susan Stautberg of Women Corporate Directors told *Bloomberg*

Technology. With this stand, Facebook is exceptional: societal imperatives and social pressures have placed enormous pressure on corporations and boards to diversify their composition in terms of gender and ethnicity supposedly because doing so is both good for the bottom line and ensures better governance. But are these claims true?

In their comprehensive 2014 review of the literature, Stanford Law School professors Deborah Rhode and Amanda Packel found that, "although empirical research has drawn much-needed attention to the underrepresentation of women and minorities on corporate boards, it has not convincingly established that board diversity leads to improved financial performance."[47] Other researchers agree: "There is no solid evidence that independent directors improve corporate performance."[48] But does a diverse board improve governance and decision making?

In 2009 the question was often asked, "Would Lehman Brothers have gone bankrupt if Lehman Brothers had been Lehman Sisters?" When the issue came up at the World Economic Forum in Davos, the general consensus was "probably not."[49] Iceland presents an interesting case study. Several businesswomen there had warned the government that the country was on the verge of economic collapse, but they were ignored. Shortly after, the banking system failed. In 2008 the three largest banks went bankrupt. The *krona* declined in value, interest rates jumped to 15 per cent, inflation soared, unemployment skyrocketed, and the stock market took a 90 percent nosedive. It was a national disaster brought about by completely reckless behaviour.

To turn things around, the government did many things, but unique to the rest of the world it began by calling the wrongdoers to account. The Office of the Special Prosecutor was established, and many people (some of them highly placed) went to jail. The new prime minister, Johanna Sigurdardottir, promised to exercise "prudence and responsibility" as she righted the listing ship. Her spokesperson was blunt: "Men, especially young men, made a mess of things."[50] But women did not just take political charge; they also moved into the corporate boardroom and the executive suite – and recovery followed. Iceland has been ranked first in the world when gender equality is measured. In 2010 the Icelandic parliament passed a new law, effective 1 September 2013, requiring that women account for at least 40 per cent of directors on the boards of all publicly traded corporations and some private ones.[51] Sixteen countries in the world have enacted similar requirements.

In terms of gender equality on corporate boards, North America lags: in 2015 the United States was ranked twenty-eighth in the world, and Canada thirtieth, well behind countries such as Burundi and Moldova. In December 2014, however, the Ontario Securities Commission introduced a new regime requiring listed companies to disclose the number of women on their boards and in executive positions.[52]

In 2015 women held just under 17 per cent of the board seats on Fortune 500 companies, but more than three-quarters of these companies had at least one minority director. The representation of Asian Americans and Latinos on boards has significantly increased, but the same cannot be said of African Americans. The most powerful positions – chair of the audit, compensation, and nominating committees – continue to be overwhelmingly held by men.

According to a major research study by the market research firm MSCI – it looked at 6,500 corporate boards around the world – companies with gender-diversity guidelines that exceeded regulatory minimums had fewer instances of governance-related scandals.[53] There were a number of interesting and related findings: companies with more than average numbers of female directors scored higher on the metrics for management of environmental and social risks as well as governance ones. Women are not inherently more moral than men, but gender diversity usually means cognitive diversity, and that leads to better problem solving and results. Law professors Rhode and Packel agree: "Diversity may lessen the tendency for boards to engage in groupthink."[54] But that can happen only if the directors are brave enough to speak out.

Therein lies the rub. Independent directors do not prevent major governance failures: Enron and WorldCom are just the two most notorious cases on point. The US Senate Committee report, *The Role of the Board of Directors in Enron's Collapse* (2002), revealed that the directors had been persuaded by their $400,000 annual compensation not to ask any hard questions.[55] In the years leading up to the company's collapse, every board decision was unanimous.

If gender equality and minority representation are achieved on major corporate boards, the presence of diverse independent directors may make a difference. But perhaps not. "Women and minority directors tend to have educational, socioeconomic, and occupational backgrounds similar to other directors." The potential benefits of board diversity, Rhode and Packel conclude, "should not be overstated,"[56] though others disagree.[57]

Space-Shuttle Stories

Most of us are not asked to serve as the devil's advocate. We don't know anyone who is part of a red team, and we are unlikely to be invited to join a corporate board. But what if, in our professional or our personal lives, we feel we should speak up? Most of us don't.

Think of NASA's space shuttle. It was amazing: proof of American technological innovation and excellence. The rocket assembly was fifty-six metres long, the shuttle the size of a DC-9, and each of the two rocket boosters produced 3 million pounds of thrust. One minute after takeoff, it would be flying with its seven astronauts at 5,500 kilometres per hour and still accelerating.[58]

On 28 January 1986 the *Challenger* blew up over the Atlantic Ocean after just seventy-three seconds in the air. This tragedy was entirely foreseeable and avoidable. Engineers at Morton Thiokol Inc. were concerned about the O-rings in the boosters and had been for years. In October 1985 one of them, Bob Ebeling, wrote an e-mail with the subject line "Help" asking that more resources be allocated to the rocket-seal task force. The e-mail signed off: "This is a red flag." The O-ring was meant to keep the pressurized gas inside the boosters, where it belonged. Ebeling and some of the other engineers wanted the Challenger launch to be delayed when it became clear that the temperature would be colder on launch day than in any previous testing conditions.

Their request was widely discussed at the operational level and a consensus reached, initially supported by senior management, that the launch had to be postponed. But the night before the scheduled takeoff, Morton Thiokol managers reversed themselves, "without one shred of supporting data," probably because of "intense customer intimidation" from NASA.[59] Other shuttles had been launched in similar circumstances, the argument went, the *Challenger* had already been delayed, the launch window was closing fast, and NASA was getting antsy. If Morton Thiokol could not prove that the O-ring was unsafe, then the launch would proceed.

It was minus-one degree Celsius on launch day, and the *Challenger* had not been certified, never mind designed, for takeoff in such low temperatures. As it happened, an O-ring seal on the right solid-rocket booster failed: the cold made it so stiff that hot combustion gases leaked from the booster and burnt through to the fuel tank. Hundreds of tons of propellant immediately ignited, causing the space ship to explode. Everyone on board was killed, including the first schoolteacher sent into space, Christa McAuliffe. There were also erosion and other problems that had been known long before the *Challenger* launch. But the real cause of the tragedy was twofold: pressure to launch, demonstrating that space travel was safe and could be reliably scheduled; and NASA culture, including "can do" and "go fever" – a culture marked by overconfidence and a need to complete a project at any cost and despite any risk.

The investigation commission led by former attorney general William P. Rogers described "a flawed decision-making process."[60] Although the red flag had been raised, it was not waved high enough. In response to criticisms in the Rogers Commission report, released on 9 June 1986, NASA created the Office of Safety, Reliability, Maintainability and Quality Assurance. But, although NASA tinkered with a few details, the management structure and workplace culture remained much the same. The Morton Thiokol mechanical engineers who urged management not to bend to NASA's will were all shunned back at the plant, referred to as the "five lepers."

"One of the assumptions behind the modern disaster ritual," Malcolm Gladwell wrote, "is that when a risk can be identified and eliminated, a system can be made safer."[61] Experience indicates this is not true. When the space shuttle *Columbia* launched on 16 January 2003, seventeen years after the *Challenger* blew up on takeoff, the crew, much like the one on *Star Trek*, was an almost perfect cross-section of humanity: two women (including an Indian) and five men, one of whom was an African American and another an Israeli. It was the 113th flight of the space-shuttle program: eighty-seven missions – each costing $500 million – had gone off without a hitch since the *Challenger*.

Eighty-two seconds after the launch, a piece of foam disengaged from the *Columbia*'s left external fuel tank. About the size of a briefcase, it travelled at more than 800 kilometres an hour and struck the orbiter's left wing. Foam shedding was a common occurrence, and because nothing had happened on previous flights, NASA management assumed that all would be well this time too. Instead, *Columbia* disintegrated sixty kilometres above Texas as it re-entered earth's atmosphere on 1 February. All seven members of the crew perished. Perhaps the piece of foam was larger this time or it hit the orbiter in a vulnerable place, damaging one of the heat shields that protected the ship as it returned home. That

Linda Ham. The chair of the Mission Management Team, Ham could not see that the flight crew was in real danger. (Credit: NASA)

such a thing could happen should have been recognized. Making matters worse, there was time to consider remedies.

However, senior management repeatedly demonstrated a complete unwillingness to discuss anything other than their optimistic view that the space shuttle would safely return as usual. Low-resolution video from an Air Force tracking station had captured the hit, "producing a spectacular shower of particles. It was unclear from the images whether the debris cloud contained foam, ice, or bits of Columbia's heat tiles."[62] Certainly, it was something to look into, but in a message to the *Columbia* crew, Flight Director Steve Stich wrote: "Some debris ... came loose and subsequently impacted the orbiter left wing ... Experts have reviewed the high speed photography and there is no concern for ... tile damage. We have seen this same phenomenon on several other flights and there is absolutely no concern for entry."[63] Yet some people were worried: the tiles protected the ship and its crew from intense heat on re-entry.

Concerns were expressed by key contractors and NASA engineers. "Any more activity today on the tile damage, or are people just relegated to crossing their fingers and hoping for the best?" landing-gear specialist Robert H. Daugherty asked NASA engineers on 28 January.[64] Up to three dozen engineers and analysts were running models, considering contingencies, and trying to figure out what to do. A consensus quickly developed that NASA needed to know more about the extent of the damage. It was time to bring the chair of the Mission Management Team, Linda Ham, into the loop.

Decisive, no-nonsense, and sure of herself, Ham was brusque, arrogant, and insular: "I really don't think there is much we can do," she said. "So it's not really a factor during the flight because there is not much we can do about it."[65] Later Ham told one engineer pressing for action, "We don't have a tile repair kit ... there isn't anything you can do about it. You just have to hope it holds."[66] Some engineers were still concerned – knowing there was ample opportunity to consider the problem and its possible solutions. "Relevant information that could have altered the course of events was available but not presented."[67] Some managers and contractors spoke up, too softly as it turned out, while others had concerns but kept quiet.

Requests were made three times from two different NASA departments for in-orbit high-resolution photographs of the left wing. But they came from middle managers, and at NASA hierarchy ruled and status determined who was listened to and who was ignored: "Some engineers would later say they felt an unspoken pressure to validate management's belief that the foam strike wasn't a flight safety issue."[68] Everyone apparently assumed someone else would step forward, but no one did. There were plenty of opportunities – meetings filled with senior NASA officials, scientists, and important contractors. Still, "no one spoke up."[69] Instead, more information was sent Ham's way confirming her initial assessment: "no safety of flight issue."[70] Ham herself was more focused on preplanned maintenance when *Columbia* returned – the shuttle program had to be kept on schedule – than on what turned out to be a life-threatening danger to the ship's crew.

Ham's team was both isolated and isolating – a highly cohesive in-group that discouraged dissenting opinions, refused to seek expert opinion, and, suffering from optimism bias, failed to consider properly a wide range of alternatives. Ham, who was married to an astronaut and cared about the safety of the crew, simply could not see that the *Columbia* was in real danger. She made some terrible decisions, especially when she failed to accept advice to obtain the in-orbit imagery that would have answered the question whether the *Columbia* was at risk.

In the aftermath of the disaster, she became Public Enemy No. 1, regularly and uniformly vilified by an increasingly misogynistic press.[71] Posters were plastered all over NASA: "If it is not safe, say so." But years of budget cuts, and an eroding and corrosive safety culture with its increasing acceptance of technical deviance – nothing had been learned since the *Challenger* – played their part in the catastrophe. The independent safety board was more lapdog than watchdog.

In its 26 August 2003 report, the Columbia Accident Investigation Board (CAIB), appointed by the president to investigate the disaster, identified eight missed opportunities to determine the extent of the damage. Photographic images from powerful military telescopes and satellites could have been requested. A simple spacewalk would have answered the question immediately. However, NASA's culture was toxic: it humiliated people found to be wrong, actively discouraging even the mildest expression of dissent.

Instead of following sound engineering practices, NASA relied on past success as a harbinger of future safety and stifled professional differences of opinion. "Given the obvious potential for a catastrophe, one might expect that someone would have gone directly to Linda Ham ... to make the argument in person for a spacewalk or high resolution photos, to do something, anything. However, such were the constraints within the Johnson Space Center that no one dared. They later said that, had they made a fuss about the shuttle, they might have been singled out for ridicule. They feared for their standing, and their careers."[72]

The *Columbia*'s crew knew that something had happened on launch, but they were not told any details. Admiral Harold W. Gehman, Jr, who led the official investigation, concluded that the system for engineers and others to express safety concerns was broken, making it almost impossible for anyone to say anything unless it was fully supported by data, which in this instance was impossible because no one was willing to press hard for the data to make the case. Just like the *Challenger*, the *Columbia* disaster suffered from "increased acceptance of risk; concerns of engineers that were ignored or never heard."[73]

In earlier years NASA had a protocol in place – the "Tiger Team" – a group of experts assigned to solve a technical problem. They were experienced, specialized, uninhibited, innovative, fearless, and smart, with the imagination to track down relentlessly every possible source of failure, consider all possibilities, and develop and propose solutions.

Gene Kranz. "Failure is not an option." (Credit: NASA)

That is exactly what happened in April 1970 when, fifty-six hours into its mission to the moon, and 330,000 kilometres from earth, an oxygen tank exploded on *Apollo 13*. The crew's report, "Houston, we have a problem," was how NASA learned about the disaster. Immediately, Gene Kranz, NASA's flight director, went to the front of Mission Control and began speaking: "This crew is coming home. You've got to believe, your people have got to believe." Failure was not an option. The three-man *Apollo 13* crew scrambled to the lunar lander as the Tiger Team on the ground figured out how to return them to earth safely.

"What I want from every one of you is simple," Kranz told the team, "options, and plenty of them."[74] Ron Howard's award-winning movie, *Apollo 13*, starring Tom Hanks and Kevin Bacon, accurately depicts the dedication and resolve that can be deployed to respond successfully to a true space emergency. As Kranz recalled in his memoir of the rescue mission, "with a team working in this fashion, not concerned with voicing their opinions freely and without worrying about hurting anyone's feelings … everyone became a part of the solution."[75]

However, no Tiger Team was assembled when the *Columbia* was damaged on takeoff. There was no gathering of all of the evidence, no consulting widely, and no considering options. Senior management characterized the flight as routine, and many went away for the Dr Martin Luther King long weekend.

After the fact, the CAIB determined that there were actually two possible rescue scenarios: one, a challenging but potentially feasible mission deploying the space shuttle *Atlantis*; the other, a high-risk spacewalk to repair the breach, with no way of knowing whether an improvised patch would have worked. But NASA chose to do nothing.[76] The parallels between the *Challenger* and the *Columbia* disasters were stark. The CAIB concluded that both spacecraft were lost "because of the failure of NASA's organizational system."[77] Space travel is risky, but NASA had learned nothing from the *Challenger* disaster. The same "flawed decision-making process" that led to the loss of the *Challenger* was responsible for the destruction of the *Columbia* almost two decades later: "NASA has shown very little understanding of the inner workings of its own organization."[78]

Authentic Dissent

What makes some people dissent while others slink away? The problem is that most people do not want to stand out. They do not want to express unpopular views or be wrong. There is strength in numbers, and responsibility is easier to bear, and avoid, when it is shared. Dissenters are generally disliked, especially if their objections affect co-workers' lives. Studies show that "people are ... aware of the likely dislike and rejection that ensues from ... persistent dissent."[79] Most simply fall into line. Criminal acquiescence is an entirely different matter – for example, the Ford Motor Company's management team that decided to continue manufacturing the deadly firetrap Pinto because it would cost more to retool – $137 million – than pay out on future accidents (a projected 180 burn deaths a year, not to mention serious injuries).

A Tenth Man or devil's advocate might have prevented the *Challenger* and *Columbia* disasters, but probably not. Still, one solution suggested after the *Challenger* blew up on liftoff was "to rely more on outsiders who, uncoopted by membership in the system, can introduce contradictory signals that challenge entrenched worldviews."[80] However, a devil's advocate, the Tenth Man in other words, is an artificial technique: someone is role playing, and everyone recognizes it as such. What really matters is authentic dissent. Corporate directors should be able to provide it, but because they generally come from similar professional backgrounds, they more often than not see things the same way.

"Only authentic dissent shows the consistency, confidence and commitment that makes the minority influential. Only authentic dissent has taken the risks and, by implication, argued from a position of belief."[81] As a result, authentic dissent leads to an informed discussion, to the identification of more and creative alternatives.[82] Role playing, by its very nature, is less compelling. Recent social-science research indicates that "an authentic dissenter generates more divergent thinking than does a role-player."[83] Dissent is important because we are so often prone to being wrong. We often cannot see what is in plain view.

Authentic dissent makes a difference because it requires us to engage more fully with others and to reassess what we think in light of what the dissenter says. "The most creative spaces are those which hurl us together. It is the human friction that makes the spark."[84] Devil's advocates and the like may even be counter-productive: "Armed with the belief that they have considered alternatives by virtue of exposure to the Devil's Advocate, people may become even more convinced of the truth of their initial position and possibly more rigid and resistant to reconsideration."[85]

As observed in the Book of Ecclesiastes, there really is nothing new under the sun. We know all about the impairments to good decision making, and have for a very long time. In 1859 John Stuart Mill wrote *On Liberty*. He also understood that only authentic dissent was credible. Balance was important. Mill knew that too. But the only arguments that really matter, the only opinions that truly persuade, Mill observed, come from people "who actually believe them."[86]

Chapter 3

A Woman of Fortitude and Determination: Frances Oldham Kelsey

Frances Oldham was born on 24 July 1914 in Cobble Hill – a village just north of Victoria on Vancouver Island. Her English father, Colonel Frank Trevor Oldham, a retired British Army officer, had married a young Scotswoman, Frances Katherine Stuart. Their daughter was one smart tomboy, graduating from high school when she was only fifteen. "I always knew I'd be some kind of scientist," she recalled.[1] One aunt was a lawyer, another a doctor, and no one was surprised when Frankie, as she was called, was accepted at McGill University in Montreal. At twenty she received her bachelor of science degree and, the following year, a master's degree in pharmacology – the branch of medicine and biology that studies the interactions between living organisms and pharmaceuticals.

Kelsey graduated in 1935, the middle of the Great Depression. "There were absolutely no jobs," she remembered, "and the few openings that there were were almost invariably filled by men." It was either graduate studies or the breadlines, and she "decided that graduate work would be more interesting."[2] The University of Chicago was the place to go. Dr Eugene Maximilian Karl Geiling from Johns Hopkins University had been hired to set up a new pharmacology department, and he and Kelsey were both interested in focusing their research on the posterior pituitary gland.

At the time the anterior pituitary gland was considered the master gland – "the conductor of the endocrine orchestra" – and the posterior lobe, Kelsey's particular concern, was seen as a "rather drab affair." For Kelsey, the shared interest was a lucky break. Why don't you write him and ask if he needs a research assistant? Kelsey's supervisor suggested – and she did. The response was off-kilter but encouraging. "Dear Mr. Oldham," Geiling's letter began, offering the applicant admission to the doctorate program and a research assistantship. It was her big break, and Geiling never admitted whether he would have offered her the opportunity had he realized she was a woman.

Elixir Sulfanilamide

In the fall of 1937, one year after Kelsey began her studies in Chicago, "Elixir Sulfanilamide" began killing people. Sulfanilamide was a German wonder drug that for several years had proved extremely effective in fighting bacterial infections. It had been safely used in tablet and powder form but needed to be taken in large doses. Not surprisingly, a demand developed for it to be available as a liquid. But there was a problem: the ingredients were not soluble in alcohol or water.

One manufacturer, Massengill Company of Bristol, Tennessee, directed its chemist, Harold C. Watkins – a dubious individual who had previously been caught selling fraudulent nostrums – to figure out how to make the drug pleasant and tasty, especially for children. Watkins dissolved it in antifreeze – diethylene glycol – and mixed in pink colouring and raspberry flavouring.[3] It was tested for taste and appearance but not toxicity. The 1906 Pure Food and Drugs Act did not require that safety studies be performed on new drugs. Essentially, it focused on food safety while banning the sale of some narcotics.

Soon after Massengill released the new drug, more than 100 people were dead, many of them children being treated for sore throats and other minor infections. First came one to three weeks of nausea, vomiting, stupor, and convulsions, accompanied by intense and unrelenting pain, and then an agonizing death. The Food and Drug Administration (FDA) turned to Dr Geiling and asked for his help. He immediately directed all his graduate students to test the drug – on dogs, monkeys, rabbits, and rats. In short order the laboratory confirmed that the antifreeze was the culprit. Making matters worse, a few simple tests before the elixir was sold would have established that it was deadly.

In the aftermath of that tragedy, the 1938 Food, Drug and Cosmetic Act was passed by Congress and signed into law by President Franklin D. Roosevelt.[4] Under the new regime, drug manufacturers were required to provide proof that new products were safe. In theory, outright poisons like Elixir Sulfanilamide would be caught before they left the laboratory, but there was still no obligation to prove that they were effective. Moreover, one huge loophole remained: there was no restriction on the use of drugs in clinical trials. A company could test unapproved drugs on thousands of people with no oversight whatsoever. In the meantime, Massengill paid a small fine under the 1906 act for labelling a preparation as an elixir when it contained no alcohol, and Watkins was rumoured to have committed suicide.

Elixir Sulfanilamide, however, was just a precursor of what was soon to come.

The Right Training for the Job Ahead

Kelsey received her PhD in 1938 after presenting her dissertation. The job market had not improved, so she stayed in Geiling's laboratory. Everything changed for her once the United States entered the Second World War in December 1941. After the fall of the Dutch East Indies in March 1942, almost all the world's supply of quinine disappeared – just as American troops fighting the Japanese were being bombarded by malaria-carrying mosquitoes. The mosquitos had to be killed, and a pesticide named DDT was deployed for that purpose (we will return to that wonder chemical shortly).

Meanwhile, the disease itself had to be treated. Dr Geiling and other scientists were asked to find new anti-malaria drugs, and some 14,000 drugs were screened as potential anti-malarials. The most promising prospects were tested on inmates at the Statesville Prison in Joliet, Illinois (including the infamous Nathan Leopold, one of the murderers of Bobby Franks in the "crime of the century"). In one set of animal experiments, Kelsey observed that adult rabbits could metabolize quinine quickly, but pregnant rabbits were less able to do so and embryonic rabbits not at all. She concluded that the drug, retained within the fetus for a longer period, could be toxic to it but not to the mother. Kelsey found this work interesting, important, and exciting, and she continued on at the laboratory. In due course she married one of her colleagues, F. Ellis Kelsey, another scientist with a doctorate who was working with Geiling.

At war's end, Kelsey began medical school at the University of Chicago and, before she graduated in 1950, the couple had two daughters. She accepted a position with the *Journal of the American Medical Association* and, together with Geiling and her husband, published *Essentials of Pharmacology*, a widely used introductory textbook. In 1952, when Ellis became head of the Pharmacology Department at the University of South Dakota Medical School in Vermillion, a small town on the banks of the Missouri River, Kelsey taught at the medical school and worked as a country doctor in the nearby small communities. Then, in 1960, a job offer arrived from the FDA's director of the Bureau of Medicine, Dr Ralph Smith, who, like Kelsey, was from Canada and a pharmacologist.

Geiling had recommended his "brilliant" former student for the position. Kelsey, who had become an American citizen in 1955, began work on 1 August 1960 in Washington in a ratty uncarpeted cubicle in a dingy temporary office building on the National Mall. She was appointed one of a handful of medical reviewers of new drug applications (NDAs). Kelsey didn't know it at the time, but her predecessor, Dr Barbara Moulton, had quit the FDA in disgust because her superiors regularly overruled her. It was nevertheless noteworthy that the FDA hired women professionals (as did the United States Bureau of Fisheries, which hired a young scientist named Rachel Carson. She comes up next).

The FDA Approval Process

When a pharmaceutical company believed it had a drug ready for market, it submitted an NDA to the Food and Drug Administration. The company provided a list of the drug's ingredients and a full description of its chemistry. In addition, it catalogued the animal studies and clinical trials that had been conducted to establish that the drug was safe for human use. However, the law did not explicitly require proof of efficacy. The FDA had about a dozen medical officers in all, some of whom worked halftime. As Kelsey would quickly discover, the pressure from pharmaceutical companies for early approvals was unrelenting.

One month after Kelsey was hired, the NDA for a drug called Kevadon, or thalidomide as it is better known, arrived at the FDA offices. Kelsey was given the file – her second assignment. "They gave it to me because they thought it would be an easy one to start on," she said. "As it turned out, it wasn't all that easy."[5] The applicant was William S. Merrell Inc. of Cincinnati, an American pharmaceutical company with plans to manufacture thalidomide under licence from Chemie Grünenthal, a family-owned West German company. As it turned out, Grünenthal had a record of rushing bad and inadequately tested drugs to market.[6]

Grünenthal's brain trust was led by Dr Heinrich Mückter, a chemist who had joined the company at the end of the Second World War. He was a bad man in bad company, working alongside an astonishing array of Nazi party members, sympathizers, and war criminals who made their way onto the company payroll.[7] During the war he had conducted research

Frances Kelsey. Examining new drug applications. (Credit: US Food and Drug Administration)

for the German Army, using Polish prisoners as guinea pigs for various experimental vaccines. Merrell was not Grünenthal's first choice for an American partner – the first choice did some testing and then said no thanks – but this company, anxious to break into the big league, was game.

Thalidomide and Merrell were made for each other. A subsidiary of the Vick Chemical Company – makers of Vicks VapoRub – Merrell knew little about medicine, employed no senior scientists, and had no laboratory dedicated to research. It had next to no capacity to conduct its own

testing on products it wished to bring to market, but it owned large production plants and a national promotion and distribution network.[8] It
was the perfect partner for a company like Grünenthal with something
to hide.

The NDA for thalidomide was contained in three or four blue- and
black-bound folders, each about the size of a city telephone book (most
NDAs today occupy hundreds of volumes). Synthesized in 1954, thalidomide was developed as an anti-convulsant drug. In fact, it did nothing
to prevent seizures but was a powerful hypnotic and directly induced
sleep. The company catalogued some of the identified side effects as unre-
markable when they clearly were not, while others, such as reducing the
desire in teenage boys to masturbate, were saved for use later. Grünenthal had to include some animal-testing results in many national-approval
applications, so it tried the drug on a few small laboratory animals in
some truly laughable experiments later determined to have zero scientific value. Instead of conducting thorough and cautious investigative
human trials, Grünenthal provided the medicine to a group of West German doctors who were paid to try it out on their patients. After the company gathered these clinical results at a "symposium," it issued a report
pronouncing the drug safe and effective.

Grünenthal then submitted the results to West German and other
authorities. In West Germany, the regulatory approval process was, to
put it mildly, primitive and pro forma. It followed something called the
"principle of self-monitoring"; pharmaceutical companies got to decide
how to test new drugs, and there was no requirement to consider possible impacts on the unborn.

Thalidomide was first sold over the counter in West Germany in October 1957 and soon travelled to fifty countries. Local authorities were
happy to ape the "decision" of the West German regulators.[9] Grünenthal also gave out free samples to its own employees: thalidomide's first
documented victim, born on 25 December 1956, was the daughter of a
staff member. Soon enough, five more Grünenthal families would have
children injured by the drug.

Thalidomide, an inexpensive drug, was an immediate success. Marketed under the trade name Contergan in West Germany, Distaval in
Britain, and Talimol in Canada, it may have been the best sleeping pill
ever invented: it actually cured insomnia and provided prompt, deep, and
natural sleep. It also relieved pain, headaches, coughs, and colds. It was

especially effective for pregnant women suffering from morning sickness. The manufacturer insisted there were no side effects.

In August 1958, even though it had conducted no studies on thalidomide's safety in pregnancy or its effects in animal reproduction, Grünenthal wrote to West German doctors declaring that thalidomide was the best choice for pregnant and nursing mothers. Marketing material in the United Kingdom likewise claimed that the drug was perfectly safe for pregnant women and their children.

By 1961, after a massive advertising campaign, thalidomide was the best-selling sedative in West Germany and, overall, represented 50 per cent of Grünenthal's total income. Employee ranks tripled.[10] Senior executives saw their bonuses, directly tied to thalidomide sales, expand exponentially. Men like Mückter became extremely rich. America would produce vast profits. And there were other markets to exploit. A liquid form was developed: Contergan Saft (Contergan Juice); the drug was referred to as "the babysitter," and many European parents used it to sedate their children.

In the 1950s millions of people all over the world were looking for something to make them feel better. The demand for barbiturates, sleeping pills, and amphetamines was huge – and growing. Publication of Jacqueline Susann's *Valley of the Dolls* was imminent. It became one of the best-selling novels of all time (and, arguably, one of the inanest books ever written). The "dolls" were the different pills available on the market. Most of the sedatives were barbiturates, which made people feel relaxed and euphoric, but the death toll from overdoses, deliberate and accidental, was rising. Thalidomide promised to change all that: the company claimed it was impossible to overdose on the drug. As it turned out, even this claim was untrue: taken in syrup form, thalidomide killed laboratory animals, but Merrell kept quiet about these results. There was another bonus: thalidomide was not addictive, or so they said.

The NDA rules required a decision from the FDA within sixty days. Merrell was so confident of speedy approval that it planned a massive marketing campaign for the beginning of March 1961 and began to stockpile supplies. The long-term plan was for the drug to be made available over the counter, but first the FDA had to say yes.

Under the leadership of FDA Commissioner George P. Larrick, the relationship between the regulator and the pharmaceutical industry was closer than it should have been. There was the usual wining and dining

at the top, and from time to time the coziness decayed into outright crim-
inality. One senior official was exposed in 1960 after he accepted more
than $250,000 from the antibiotics industry. When the Merrell NDA
arrived, three FDA employees were assigned to the file: Kelsey, the medical officer; a chemist named Lee Geismar; and a pharmacologist, Oyam
Jiro. Soon after they began their investigations, Geismar and Jiro had
some concerns, and Kelsey had a lot of questions.

First, the animal studies seemed incomplete. People given thalidomide
lapsed into almost immediate sleep, but rats did not. There were a number of possible explanations. Perhaps the rats were not absorbing the
medicine. It's not uncommon for substances to have different effects on
people and animals, but in this case Kelsey rejected the argument that
the drug would not have toxic effects on humans simply because it had
shown no harmful effects on rats.

Second, although the regulatory framework did not require randomized, double-blind, multi-site, placebo control studies – the gold standard
– Kelsey felt that those submitted with the application were incomplete
to the point of being meaningless. The claims drawn from them were
simply "not supported by the ... studies."[11] Several of the clinical reports
were written by hacks with established reputations for selling their services to the highest bidder; others were casually summarized notes from
doctors who had participated in the study by distributing free samples
to their patients. "Works wonders" was a common refrain. Kelsey found
encomiums unpersuasive.

Third, the supporting materials were a mess, with many obvious mistakes in translated texts. The overall sloppiness raised alarms for Kelsey:
clearly, Merrell thought its application would be a "pushover," and that
was "one of the possible reasons why it was so poor."[12] Thalidomide
had been given the nod in most other countries, so Merrell assumed that
US approval would be a mere formality.

The way the approval system worked at the FDA, if staff identified
issues within the sixty days, a notice could be sent requesting further
information. The company would have to submit a new NDA, and the
sixty-day clock would begin to run all over again. Two days before the
deadline, on 10 November 1960, after which approval would be auto-
matic if she did nothing, Kelsey mailed a notice declaring the application
incomplete; in her words, "the chronic toxicity data are incomplete and,

therefore, no evaluation can be made of the safety of the drug when used for a prolonged period of time."[13] She also asked for more information on the animal studies, and many other items. As one analyst has written, "Kelsey's doubts were piqued early on by the vagueness of the application and the grandiosity of the claims."[14]

Kelsey was particularly concerned about the clinical trials and wanted more detail on those underway in the United States. "My job," she said at the time, "is to pick these new-drug applications to pieces."[15] American law allowed the experimental use of drugs while the approval process was ongoing. Drug companies routinely sent free samples to doctors – to begin laying the foundation for future sales. As for the patients, no informed consent was required by law.

When Kelsey asked for more information, Merrell pushed back – hard. Because of concerns that the FDA was captive to the industry, Commissioner Larrick had recently promised Congress that pharmaceutical companies would not be allowed to contact examiners during the approval process. That did not stop Merrell: on more than fifty occasions, aggressive industry representatives visited the FDA and hounded Kelsey and the other medical reviewers.[16] Sometimes they sent a good cop, offering assistance, and other times a threatening bad cop. Some representatives were accompanied by respected clinical investigators – window dressing really – to bolster their case.

Company executives insisted that Kelsey was depriving the American people of an amazing drug. They complained to Kelsey's superiors that she was fussy, nitpicking, stubborn, unreasonable, and obstructionist, a completely gendered critique that almost certainly would never have been applied to a man. "Most of the things they called me, you couldn't print," she said.[17] It was clear to Kelsey that Merrell considered her "an unreasonable female."[18] Many pharmaceutical companies applied pressure to obtain FDA approval, but "in no instances was it as severe as with this application."[19] But still she would not budge.

Kelsey's thorough approach seems to have "put her at odds" with older members of her organization. Internal disagreements have been described as a "civil war."[20] But Kelsey had the support of her boss – Ralph Smith – and she was not being obstinate without reason: she followed the best scientific practices. She conducted a thorough literature review, consulted colleagues and other researchers, carefully studied the underlying research design of Merrell's supporting studies, scrutinized thalidomide's chemical composition and stability, and did her best to verify Merrell's various claims.

In mid-January 1961 Merrell resubmitted the Kevadon NDA. All the questions about the drug's metabolism, excretion, absorption levels, and toxicity remained unanswered. Kelsey was not prepared to rush: it was a sleeping pill, after all, and plenty of safe brands were already available. Then, in late January or early February, she read a short letter in the *British Medical Journal* from a Dr A. Leslie Florence. Titled "Is Thalidomide to Blame?" Dr Florence reported that some patients taking thalidomide were experiencing peripheral neuritis – a painful tingling in the arms and legs.

Although a pharmacologist and a physician, Kelsey could make no sense of this report from any scientific or medical perspective. "Peripheral neuritis did not seem the sort of side effect that should come from a simple sleeping pill," she reasoned.[21] Kelsey got some reassurance at home. Her husband was a respected scientist in his own right. He looked at the revised NDA and described it as a "collection of meaningless, pseudoscientific jargon, apparently intended to impress chemically unsophisticated readers." It was worse than bad: "I cannot believe this to be honest incompetence," he concluded.[22] Relieved to have her suspicions confirmed, Kelsey deemed the second application incomplete. Again she wrote Merrell asking for additional information and more proof about safety.

Kelsey soon learned that the side effects mentioned in the doctor's letter were already documented in Europe, though they had never been mentioned in the NDA. When Grünenthal's American representative was asked about them, he replied, like Sergeant Schultz in *Hogan's Heroes*, that he knew nothing. "I had the feeling," Kelsey wrote after one meeting with company representatives, "that they were at no time being wholly frank with me."[23]

Merrell then made matters worse by claiming, after an investigation, including a trip to England and West Germany, that the reports about neuritis proved not to be serious, and that the symptons were, Grünenthal advised, reversible; moreover, they were possibly connected to vitamin deficiencies and poor diet, not to thalidomide. The truth was that the side effects were severe, widespread, and directly related to the drug.

Grünenthal had known since October 1959 that there was a connection between thalidomide use and peripheral neuritis.[24] In one telling incident, patients at a Hamburg psychiatric hospital were given massive doses of thalidomide to sedate them. When one of Grünenthal's marketing representatives visited the site in April 1961 to book another order, he was surprised to learn that none of them were experiencing this side effect he had heard so much about. "Maybe," he concluded in a report to headquarters, "the idiots are happy when there's tingling!"[25]

Although Kelsey had no way of knowing, by the time Dr Florence's letter was published, Grünenthal had received hundreds of reports of severe peripheral neuritis attributable to thalidomide, and 1,500 reports of other side effects, all of which the company summarily dismissed.[26] Privately, however, the company was worried, and with good reason. It took a baby step and ended over-the-counter sales but it was too little and too late. Documents uncovered as part of a class-action lawsuit in Australia started by a thalidomide victim named Lynette Rowe revealed that Grünenthal's lawyers were, at the time, repeatedly warning it of a legal "avalanche coming at us."[27]

As if on cue, the West German medical press was soon filled with articles about the dangers of thalidomide. It was now revealed that doctors, including those paid by Grünenthal to test the drug, had complained from the start about its safety. In response to these complaints, Grünenthal always played dumb: "We feel obliged to say that this is the first time such effects have been reported to us"[28] was a standard and completely untrue response. Based on Dr Florence's letter alone, however, Kelsey had demanded all the background clinical reports and research. When Merrell failed to follow through on its promise to provide the documentation, Kelsey became convinced that thalidomide really was too good to be true.

In April 1961 Merrell changed tack with its application for approval. Thalidomide might have problems, company representatives advised Kelsey, but it was better than most barbiturates that were commonly used to induce sleep. It now admitted that its own studies had shown that rats could be killed by the drug. Kelsey asked the company point blank how it could submit a NDA without disclosing the evidence of neurological toxicity. In her opinion, it was impossible to approve this application: the animal and clinical studies were unpersuasive and incomplete, there was no proof the drug was safe, and information indicating other problems had been withheld.

But Merrell did not see it that way. "They thought I was nuts," Kelsey recalled. When Kelsey wrote Merrell observing that "evidence with respect to the occurrence of peripheral neuritis in England was known to you but not forthrightly disclosed in the application," the company appealed to her boss and grumbled about "libel" and the "meddlesome fool" who was standing in their way.[29] Still Kelsey would not give in – and upped the ante.

Just at this time the FDA was becoming interested in the effect of drugs on fetuses and had begun to develop guidelines. Kelsey knew from her time at Chicago that drugs affected adult rabbits and rabbit fetuses differently. She also knew that drugs could and did pass through the placental barrier. Some drugs caused malformations, or teratogen, in fetuses. When steroid hormones were prescribed in threatened miscarriages, for instance, some babies were born with heightened masculine qualities.

This was not rocket science, but established science. There were hundreds of published papers, references in leading texts, and international medical conferences devoted to the phenomenon. Kelsey now asked Merrell about thalidomide in pregnancy. "Here was a drug that, given for three or four months, could cause severe neuropathy. With thalidomide, a growing infant might, perhaps, be exposed to it for five or six or up to nine months,"[30] she remarked, and so she wanted to know whether it might have an adverse effect on a child. Merrell had no answer. Apart from one study conducted during late pregnancy, the company had not even considered the question. It later turned out that thalidomide, even a single pill, caused deformities if taken between the twenty-seventh and fortieth day after conception.

Testing for birth defects should have been normative. Merrell had conducted reproductive testing on several of its drugs, but not this one, having relied on Grünenthal's assurances. While Grünenthal would endlessly repeat that it followed best practices, this was not so. Major pharmaceutical manufacturers including Burroughs Wellcome, Hoffman-La Roche, ICI, Lederle, Merck, Parke-Davis, and Smith Kline and French throughout the 1950s tested the teratogenic potential of their new drugs. It would have taken about one month, and cost about $100, to run a thalidomide test on pregnant mice – a test that would have immediately revealed its numerous damaging effects.[31]

The one thing Grünenthal did say that was correct was that there was, at the time, no legal obligation to conduct these tests. Maybe that is why Merrell rejected Kelsey's invitation to conduct a study, offering instead,

in return for FDA approval, to put a warning on the label that thalidomide should not be taken during pregnancy and that peripheral neuritis
was one possible side effect. When this offer was rejected, Merrell
"ordered" Kelsey to approve the drug within one week or else, and provided some of what would soon to turn out to be completely fabricated
studies attesting to thalidomide's safety. Again, she stood firm: if the drug
could save lives, that would have been one thing, but it was just a sedative in a market saturated with them. "The field of usefulness of the drug
is such that untoward reactions would be highly inexcusable," Kelsey
replied coolly.[32]

Injured Babies the World Over

By now a year had passed since Merrell first submitted the NDA for
thalidomide in September 1960. Formal approval had been prevented by
a slim, well-mannered, and shy woman who turned out to be an obstreper-
ous and obdurate bureaucrat – at least in the manufacturer's eyes. Sales
of sedatives and hypnotics traditionally spike around the end-of-year holiday period, and with the second one approaching since it first applied,
Merrell increased the pressure. "We want to get this drug on the market
before Christmas," it wrote to Kelsey.[33] When that tactic did not work,
it resorted to bullying, again to no avail.

"Then, quite suddenly, the news came in from Europe about horrible deformities."[34] In November 1961 a German pediatrician, Widukind
Lenz, head of the children's clinic at Hamburg University, determined
that a growing number of mothers with deformed children had taken
thalidomide during their first trimester – the period scientists call organo-
genesis, when limbs and organs are formed.

Dr Lenz called Grünenthal and spoke to the chemist, Heinrich Mückter, who was disturbingly nonchalant. Lenz thereupon put his concerns
in writing to Grünenthal, outlining the epidemic of a "certain type of
deformity" that could be traced back to 1957. The one common denominator was thalidomide. Lenz presented his findings at a pediatricians'
meeting in Dusseldorf, and then to local governmental authorities. He
demanded that the drug be immediately withdrawn from sale. Grünenthal initially refused to withdraw the drug, threatening lawsuits and publicly vilifying Lenz as a "half- wit" intent on "murdering thalidomide by

spreading rumor."[35] Even though the company now knew better, or should have, Grünenthal insisted that thalidomide was safe but offered to affix a warning that the drug should not be taken by pregnant women.

At almost this exact moment, information came in from Australia that left no doubt that thalidomide was causing serious side effects (as did private reports from the British manufacturer). The German press got hold of the story, which became big news throughout the fall of 1962. *Welt am Sonntag* (World on Sunday) reported that a popular sleeping drug was injuring babies. It did not have to name thalidomide – everyone knew. And so it was that Grünenthal finally agreed to withdraw the drug. Reports of massive numbers of birth defects, spontaneous abortions, and stillbirths began to flood in from all over the globe.

Astonishingly, Grünenthal continued international marketing until the end of January 1963. Some countries like Canada dithered and dallied: there were thirty more victims before regulatory authorities finally woke up in March 1962 (including some truly remarkable Canadians like Fiona Sampson, the tireless human-rights advocate who received the Order of Canada in 2015). Japan was the worst: for more than a year, Grünenthal did not withdraw the drug from Japan, where mothers could buy it as an over-the-counter medication. Several hundred additional thalidomide babies were hurt, completely unnecessarily.[36]

In the United States, Merrell continued to protest, claiming that "it was a false association."[37] Whatever was going on, Merrell claimed, thalidomide was not the cause. It even went so far as to suggest with a straight face that thalidomide was a good thing: "Thalidomide did not damage the fetus, but on the contrary somehow allowed otherwise badly damaged fetuses to survive until birth rather than being spontaneously aborted."[38] For almost the next fifty years it claimed that thalidomide had no teratogenic effects. But the jig was up.

The effects of thalidomide were extreme, a situation made even worse because it was all entirely avoidable. It was not just missing or shortened limbs but toes sprouting directly from the hips, flipper-like arms, missing eyes and ears, and malformations in the genitals, heart, kidneys, and digestive tract. Brain damage was common, though many victims were within the normal range of intelligence. The data was shocking, demonstrating a massive increase in affected children.[39]

Before thalidomide, most doctors would go their entire career without encountering a single case of phocomelia – the condition in which the limbs are attached close to the trunk or are grossly underdeveloped or missing. Beginning in the mid- to late 1950s, that condition was no longer rare – but without a national registry, doctors took a while to put the pieces together. It was a different day. Doctors communicated by telephone and mail; sometimes they met at conferences. Specialists could be unaware of events occurring around the corner and across the street and understandably had no idea about the epidemic unfolding right in front of them. That took one intrepid doctor, Widukind Lenz. In the end, West Germany, where the drug had been available over the counter for years, was hit the hardest.

On 30 November 1961 Merrell informed the FDA that it was discontinuing clinical trials. Kelsey was the first to hear the news in a telephone call from one of her chief Merrell tormentors. Finally, in March 1962 an application to withdraw the NDA was submitted. Grünenthal now conducted some real scientific experiments. The first one immediately established that thalidomide easily crossed the placental wall. Others demonstrated that some animals given thalidomide during their first trimester gave birth to offspring with the same deformities found in humans. The only upside to this part of the tragedy was that the techniques developed to test thalidomide were of general application and could be used to screen new drugs for possible teratogenic effects.

Kelsey continued to collect information. She soon learned that Merrell's effort to notify American doctors conducting clinical trials were dilatory at best. An FDA investigation revealed that 1,267 doctors had been given 2.5 million tablets and that they distributed them to 20,000 patients. Kelsey was flabbergasted – the applications had said nothing about these clinical trials and the FDA had assumed, quite wrongly, that only a small number of clinical investigators had been given the drug. In fact, these were clinical trials in name only, run by the company's marketing team, not its medical department.

The participating doctors were told they had no need to report results "if they did not want to."[40] Merrell sales representatives had been directed to tell doctors that the "drug was virtually ready to be approved."[41] The salesmen were instructed to pander: "Appeal to the doctor's ego – we think he is important enough to be selected as one of the first to use Kevadon."[42] The doctors were advised that, in addition to treating morning sickness, the drug was good for treating bedwetting, nightmares, poor school work, marital discord, and premature ejaculation. Merrell even ghostwrote articles for medical journals extolling thalidomide's safety and efficacy.

One doctor, Ray Nulsen, submitted his "clinical results" to the *American Journal of Obstetrics and Gynecology*. His study concluded that there was no danger, even if thalidomide "passes the placental barrier." Dr Nulsen had no idea whether it did or not. He had studied nothing, of course, but he agreed to put his name on the cover page because he wanted money and would do as he was told to get some. Clearly, these were the furthest thing from normal clinical trials, nothing more than a poorly disguised first step in a planned national sales campaign.

Despite the mounting evidence, FDA Commissioner Larrick was slow to react – bumbler or industry sop, it was hard to tell, but he was ultimately fired – as Kelsey kept working behind the scenes to galvanize the agency. In the end, although no accurate count is possible, about seventeen proven thalidomide babies were born in the United States (seven from thalidomide acquired abroad), but the real number of victims was probably much higher. For nineteen months, Kelsey had held Merrell at bay, and she continued on the case until every pill she could muster was withdrawn. Still, vast quantities remained at large. Merrell's recall efforts were abysmal: two tons of the drug were never accounted for. According to conservative estimates, had the drug been approved in the normal process, it would have claimed at least 10,000 US victims.

Honours for the Heroine

On 15 July 1962 the headline on the front-page story in the *Washington Post* said it all: "'Heroine' of FDA Keeps Bad Drug off of Market." It was a classic tale of good guys versus bad guys:

> This is the story of how the skepticism and stubbornness of a government physician prevented what could have been an appalling American tragedy, the birth of hundreds or indeed thousands of armless legless children.
>
> The story of Dr Frances Oldham Kelsey, a Food and Drug Administration medical officer, is not one of inspired prophecies nor of dramatic research breakthroughs.
>
> She saw her duty in sternly simple terms, and she carried it out, living the while with insinuations that she was a bureaucratic nitpicker, unreasonable – even, she said, stupid ...

What she did was refuse to be hurried into approving an application for marketing a new drug. She regarded its safety as unproved, despite considerable data arguing that it was ultra safe.

President John F. Kennedy went on national television and asked Americans to check their medicine cabinets. Suddenly, everyone was talking about the government doctor who prevented untold tragedy. She was featured in the *New York Times*, *Saturday Review*, *Life Magazine* – "a woman of fortitude and determination."

Two weeks later, Senator Hubert Humphrey held an oversight hearing on the FDA. At the very same time that Merrell was pushing thalidomide, it was also touting a cholesterol-lowering drug with the brand name Triparanol, which had been approved over the objections of a pharmacologist but with the consent of one of Kelsey's medical-officer colleagues. Unfortunately, Triparanol caused blindness, cataracts, and other severe side effects, as routine tests quickly established. Then it was learned that Merrell had faked test results for the drug and submitted a completely fraudulent approval application. In the end, three senior scientists pleaded "no contest" to criminal charges in an obviously cooked deal and received six months' probation. Merrell paid a small fine and an estimated $200 million to 500 Americans who had been seriously hurt by the drug.[43]

The near miss with thalidomide gave ammunition to politicians who had been fighting for years for a more muscular regulatory regime – one where public policy and public health were based on science. Senator Estes Kefauver of Tennessee, a populist Democrat and long-time proponent of increased pharmaceutical regulation, demanded proof of safety and effectiveness. When the Kefauver-Harris Amendments were signed into law by President Kennedy on 10 October 1962, Kelsey was there in the Oval Office.

The new law, which modified the 1938 Food, Drug and Cosmetic Act, completely changed the process for seeking and obtaining regulatory approval. It was now recognized that a drug had to be proven safe and effective before it could be marketed. Proper clinical trials conducted by qualified experts became mandatory.

Merrell immediately went into damage control. "We followed the normal course of all responsible American pharmaceutical manufacturers," it claimed. "In our trials, the drug appeared both safe and effective." Sure, company executives explained, we had differences of opinion with the FDA, but that is normal. They asked us lots of questions, and

Frances Kelsey. With JFK receiving the President's Distinguished Federal
Civilian Service Award. (Credit: US Food and Drug Administration)

we answered them. That was the reason for the many contacts between
us and Kelsey. It was just business as usual. When we heard the news
from West Germany in November 1961, we took immediate steps to
ensure that the drug was not given to pregnant women. Even so, the
information was "incomplete," a Merrell spokesman told *Life Maga-*
zine in August 1962: "We have not minimized the possibility that thalidomide may be connected with congenital malformation in some way not
now understood."[44]

It was complete nonsense, of course, and it was subsequently established that Grünenthal did everything it could from the earliest opportunity to suppress scientific concerns about the effect of thalidomide,
including smearing the name of any doctor, not just Lenz, who raised the
alarm. Throughout, Merrell was a willing accomplice. Astonishingly, no
one from Grünenthal or Merrell was ever imprisoned. In the United
States, the Justice Department determined that, while "questionable,"
Merrell's promotional practices were not strictly proscribed.[45]

The President's Award for Distinguished Federal Civilian Service was presented to Kelsey in August 1962. Although she was not originally on the list, it would have been unthinkable not to include her among the recipients, especially after she had been lionized by the *Washington Post*. The ceremony was held at the White House on the South Lawn. Kelsey was there along with her husband, her daughters, her brothers, several colleagues from the FDA, Dr E.M.K. Geiling from Chicago, and Dr Barbara Moulton, her predecessor at the FDA.

President Kennedy praised Kelsey for her exceptional judgment and thanked her for preventing a major tragedy. "Doctor," he said, "I know you know how much the country appreciates what you have done."[46] "It was a team effort," she recalled years later, and I accepted the medal "on behalf of a lot of different federal workers."[47] The picture of a demure but competent, cerebral and circumspect Kelsey accepting the award from the smiling president became the iconic image of the FDA at a time when people still believed government could be a force for good.[48]

Senator Kefauver, however, said it best: "Dr. Kelsey's contribution flows from a rare combination of factors: a knowledge of medicine, a knowledge of pharmacology, a keen intellect and inquiring mind, the imagination to connect apparently isolated bits of information, and the strength of character to resist strong pressures."[49] In December 1962 Gallup announced that Kelsey was on the list of the ten "Most Admired Women in the World."

The Bureau of Medicine within the FDA was also reorganized. Kelsey was put in charge of a new branch that handled the investigational new drug (IND) applications – the notices seeking approval for exemptions for new drugs before the beginning of clinical trials. Other assignments followed as the FDA's work exploded. Kelsey helped establish best practices for institutional review boards – responsible for monitoring biomedical and behavioural research – which were created after questionable drug-testing trials were exposed in nursing homes, mental institutions, and prisons. She retired in 2005, when she was ninety, after forty-five years at the FDA. After that she played bridge, watched birds – together with Rachel Carson (our protagonist in the next chapter), she was a member of the Chevy Chase chapter of the Audubon Society – and, every day, she enjoyed a glass of sherry at 11:00 a.m. and a real cocktail at 5:00 p.m.[50]

Repercussions of the Tragedy

Around the world, in contrast to the United States, the thalidomide story was just starting. It is hard to know for sure, but perhaps as many as 10,000 people were affected in about fifty countries, not counting the thousands of spontaneous abortions and stillbirths. Many infants did not survive their first birthday. Whole families were destroyed by the guilt, shame, rage, and terror.[51] The financial burdens were overwhelming.

In Canada the situation was made much worse than it should have been. Thalidomide was not ordered off the shelves until March 1962, and it could still be found in some pharmacies as late as mid-May, three months after West Germany, England, and dozens of other countries had banned its sale. In April 1962, notwithstanding the weight of the evidence, the head of Canada's Food and Drug Directorate mused that thalidomide approval might be reinstated.[52] Fortunately, saner heads prevailed. Today, estimates indicate that there are about 3,000 survivors worldwide, with just less than 100 in Canada. While formally approved for sale in April 1961, free samples of thalidomide had been given to doctors as early as 1959. Senseless tragedy could have easily been avoided if Canadian regulators had exercised proper vigilance.

There were lawsuits, and demands for justice. It was not easy anywhere; it was a pitched fight everywhere. In Britain, survivors now receive an annual pension of around $88,000 a year. In West Germany, it's about $110,000 a year. In Canada, the then minister of health, Jay Waldo Monteith, promised in 1963 to care for the victims in "the best possible manner," which apparently meant doing nothing.[53] Canada provided a one-time payment in 1991 – a pittance – and the process was a farce. Desperate people in financial need will often compromise their legitimate claims.

Many survivors were in terrible shape. By and large, they could no longer rely on their parents – some abandoned them immediately, others struggled and did their best, but almost all are now deceased. Many of the victims were too disabled ever to work – the average annual income was only $14,000 – and most of them endured decades of grinding poverty and social isolation, fear, and shame. All of them experienced a lifetime of chronic pain and physical ailments.

That changed in May 2015 when the Conservative government of Stephen Harper, bowing to public and media pressure, and in one of the few compassionate actions in its entire ten-year term, and thanks in large part to Health Minister Rona Ambrose, announced a generous funding package. It did not go as far as the victims and their advocates had requested, but it was a long overdue step in the right direction.

Because of thalidomide, the bar in most countries for drug approval was raised, beginning with the institution of basic standards for clinical studies including obtaining informed consent. The FDA was given the power to withdraw the approval of any drug if satisfied that there was an imminent hazard to public health. Though smart and necessary, the new rules led, in turn, to a host of other complicated, vexing, and overlapping problems. As a practical matter, FDA approval is the difference between commercial success and failure.

It can take years and billions of dollars to prove that new drugs are safe and effective before the FDA application is even made. And then there is no guarantee that the drug will be approved. Meanwhile, people are dying. It's the classic "damned if you do and damned if you don't" situation: difficult to estimate the numbers who would have been saved had the drug been approved, and easy to count those who got hurt or died because a drug was approved instead of rejected. Mistakes have consequences – to individuals and to the FDA itself – and it's no surprise that some drugs have been approved for sale despite serious and foreseeable risk, while others that could have saved people languish in a regulatory maw. It's a challenging no-win situation all round.

On 20 December 2000 the *Los Angeles Times* published a prize-winning report by David Willman which tracked seven drugs, all approved by the FDA, that had to be withdrawn as suspected deaths mounted – exceeding 1,000 in all. None of the drugs was essential to save lives – one a diet pill, another for heartburn. The manufacturers pocketed $5 billion before the dangerous drugs were withdrawn. "Never before," Willman wrote, "has the FDA overseen the withdrawals of so many drugs in such a short time."[54]

Dr Janet Woodcock of the FDA explained the context for the debacle. "There are economic pressures to get drugs to the market as soon as possible," she said, "and these are highly valid." In a follow-up interview, she alluded to the difficulty in turning down a proposed drug that had cost a drug company millions of dollars to develop.[55] Woodcock was not alone: "If you raise concern about a drug, it triggers a whole internal process that is difficult and painful," one FDA medical officer confessed.

"You have to defend why you are holding up the drug to your bosses ... You cannot imagine how much pressure is put on reviewers."[56]

There are many FDA success stories, but they get little or no press because the default assumption is that the agency will do its job: protect the public. For the most part it does so extremely well, despite being a huge under-resourced agency with an almost impossible task. But near misses are like non-sightings of the black swan. It is very difficult to assess and give credit for averted disasters.

The gold standard in clinical testing are randomized, double-blind, multi-site, placebo control studies, which were completely absent from the thalidomide NDA. Half the individuals get the new drug, and the other half do not. People who are not in the study get nothing, though exceptions can be made by the FDA and other regulators worldwide on a compassionate basis. How long will dying people continue to participate in clinical trials and possibly take a placebo when the developmental drug under scrutiny might save them? We are not talking about drugs like thalidomide that provide a good night's sleep, but the possible difference between life and death. For the privilege of participating in a science experiment, the fact that they die while others live provides cold comfort to most. *Dallas Buyers Club* is a Hollywood movie, but it may be the future in a connected world where people identify the drugs they believe can help them and obtain them whether they are FDA-approved or not. No drug is without side effects, and the entire issue is about balancing risks. Dying people will do whatever is necessary, within their means, to obtain developmental drugs that are denied to them if they think those drugs might save their lives.

What makes the situation so confounding and difficult to fix is that, even when legitimate criticisms are addressed and changes made, things seem sometimes to get better and sometimes worse. For example, following legitimate criticisms from the AIDS Coalition to Unleash Power and other HIV activist organizations, Congress passed the 1992 Prescription Drug User Fee Act. It was designed to speed up regulatory review to get needed drugs to market fast. And it worked: median drug-approval time dropped by about 50 per cent. More importantly, lives were saved. So far so good. But the background political story is troubling and suggests that motivations may have been mixed.

As president for two terms in the 1980s, Ronald Reagan generally denounced regulation, without regard to the facts, and when Republican Newt Gingrich was speaker of the House of Representatives from 1995 to 1999, he referred to the FDA as "the leading job killer in America" and suggested it be abolished. Instead, its funding was cut. Maybe the president and the speaker thought that regulation slows progress, impedes innovation, and denies choice, all of which are true, but regulations also protect the public and save lives. One is left wondering whether critics of the regulatory regime, for all its failures, are motivated not by the public interest, and saving lives, as the speed-up on the release of AIDS drugs surely did, but by ideology and private profit.

The thalidomide scandal did not just lead to regulatory reform, imperfect though it be. Paradoxically, it gave ammunition to one of the most powerful protest movements of all time – pro-choice. *Roe v. Wade*, the 1973 landmark US Supreme Court decision that struck down most state laws prohibiting abortions, was more than a decade away. The court ruled in that case that a woman's right to privacy under the due process clause of the 14th Amendment extended to her decision to have an abortion. Before that decision, American women could, mostly, obtain an abortion only if their own lives were in danger.

In 1962 Sherri Finkbine was the host of a popular television show called *Romper Room*. Her husband purchased Distaval while on a trip to England, and she took it while pregnant with her fifth child. When news broke about the side effects of this drug, she had an X-ray, which established that her fetus was severely compromised; no legs and only one arm. She sought official approval for a hospital abortion in Phoenix, Arizona, but was refused and threatened with five years in jail. Instead, she went to Sweden, where the doctor confirmed the damage; the fetus was too badly deformed even to determine whether it was a boy or a girl.

This story got Americans thinking, and opinion about abortions began to change slowly, though Finkbine lost her job (Sissy Spacek played her in the 1992 HBO film, *A Private Matter*). Even so, and even as the death threats piled in, she insisted that it was *her choice* and she was glad she made it.

An Apology Fifty Years Too Late

Thalidomide did get a second life when American authorities approved it as a treatment for a severe and debilitating complication of leprosy. At the time, Kelsey was still on the scene: "We felt that was a reasonable use since there was such a great need for such a drug in this depressing disease," she said.[57] The drug continues to be tested and shows some promise in the treatment of bone cancer, Kaposi's sarcoma, solid tumours in the prostate and brain, Crohn's disease, rheumatoid arthritis, macular generation, and graft-versus-host disease. It may be a wonder drug after all.

When it is prescribed now, the mandatory precautions inspire confidence. The System for Thalidomide Education and Prescribing Safety (STEPS) requires women who might become pregnant to use two acceptable forms of birth control for prescribed periods before, during, and after treatment or simply to abstain from sexual intercourse. Capsules carry a diagram of a pregnant woman with a red line drawn across it.

In 2012, fifty years after the tragedy, thalidomide's manufacturer, Grünenthal, finally apologized – sort of – to the parents and children who had been affected by the drug: "We apologize for the fact that we have not found the way to you from person to person for almost 50 years. Instead, we have been silent and we are very sorry for that. We ask that you regard our long silence as a sign of the silent shock that your fate caused us."[58]

Grünenthal was shocked? It had been suffering and that was why it had taken fifty years to apologize? Imagine how the traumatized parents and victims felt. According to Harald F. Stock, the chief executive of the family-owned pharmaceutical business, who delivered the apology as he unveiled a bronze statue of a limbless child, his company did all the tests possible at the time. To say that was true would be to lie. To say that people were incensed would be an understatement.

In Germany, thalidomide victim Thomas Quasthoff was disgusted. His only previous communication from Grünenthal was when they once asked him to sing at their Christmas party. In Canada, thalidomide victim Paul Murphy described the apology as an "insult" and a "joke." Freddie Astbury, a Liverpool, England, victim, agreed: he called the apology "a disgrace."[59] Wendy Rowe in Australia gave birth to her daughter Lynette on 2 March 1962. The attending doctor told her that he had some unfortunate news. Their daughter was born without arms or legs. Wendy did not miss a beat: "We'll just have to look after her very well then."[60] And that's what she did for the next fifty years. This is what she had to say when she learned of the apology: "We had to get up and face every day, every day, and cope with the incredible damage that Grünenthal did." The drug company, she told the *London Telegraph*, had no idea what shock was. "Shock is having your precious child born without arms and legs. It's accepting that your child is not going to have that life that you wanted for her,"[61] she said sobbing as her daughter watched from her wheelchair. Berrisford Boothe, one of the remaining American victims, lashed out: "They've had 50 years to make billions of dollars while we struggled and our parents committed suicide. And now, they're apologizing for not saying anything. How dare they do that and think it is going to be enough."[62]

One Brave Dissenter

What was it about Kelsey that made her so special? The fact that she was a woman was a big part of it. She went to university at a time when few women did, and, even more unusual, she studied science. When she went on to get her academic doctorate and then her medical degree, she became a pioneer, one who inevitably faced structural barriers on her path.

Was there something about making her way in the male-dominated world of science and medicine that strengthened her resolve, or did she have it from the beginning? She stood up to bullies and refused to follow the path of least resistance, displaying fortitude, independence, and intellectual and moral courage. She was willing to take abuse, though her resistance was always quiet and informed. She made an attempt to see things from Merrell's side, but when she asked for something to substantiate their claims, there was nothing to see but a cover-up. When she knew that something was wrong, she would not rest until she got it right. She was also an outsider – a Canadian who was not part of any club in Washington. She also was not a kid; she was forty-six years old when the NDA arrived, and with a lifetime of professional accomplishment behind her, she was experienced and confident. The more Merrell pushed, the harder she pushed back.

Kelsey had no idea in the beginning that thalidomide caused birth defects, that a single pill taken at the wrong time could destroy lives, but she asked the right questions as she considered whether to approve the drug. When Merrell responded with bluster and bullshit, Kelsey realized she had to stand her ground until she got to the bottom of it. Once she read Dr Florence's letter, she recognized the link between thalidomide and neurological disorders. The drug could be taken at any time during pregnancy, and she would not approve it until she was convinced it was safe for the mother and her fetus. Her questions were basic, persistent, and scrupulously scientific.[63]

Kelsey was also an important transitional figure. The old world of regulation and inspection, where the big public enemies were the hucksters, snake-oil salesmen, and cancer quacks, was giving way to a new and burgeoning reality: a chemotherapeutic revolution in pharmaceuticals and the rise of molecular drugs for chronic conditions. Increasing attention was being paid to toxicology and clinical pharmacology at medical schools and within the FDA. Kelsey, scientist, pharmacologist, and physician, was at the right place, and it was the right time to lead the regulatory revolution. Geiling's assistants who went on to the FDA offered a "combination of basic medicine, up-to-date pharmacological training, specialty knowledge in toxicology, and professional esteem."[64] Although Geiling described Kelsey as "brilliant," she always shared credit with her colleagues and was consistently modest: "I only did what I thought was right," she said.[65]

The thalidomide tragedy was averted in the United States because Kelsey, alone and in the face of fierce opposition, did her job. Her perspective was educated, fresh, and unique. If there had been no thalidomide crisis, the United States, with the rest of the world following, would still at some time have brought pharmaceutical regulation into the twentieth century. But thalidomide created one of those moments when something had to be done. It could not be ignored in 1961–62, and it led immediately to a better and stronger regulatory system. Maybe someone else would have stopped thalidomide in the United States had Kelsey remained in South Dakota, but, interestingly, no one else stopped it anywhere else until it was too late. Kelsey was the only person in the entire world who said no. She said no to a bad drug application, she said no to an overbearing pharmaceutical company, and she said no to vested interests who put profits first. She was one brave dissenter. In the end, the question is not what made Frances Kelsey, but why aren't there more like her?

In 1995 a British Columbia high school in Mill Bay, just north of Victoria, was named after her. Twenty years later, in June 2015, she was named to the Order of Canada, Canada's highest civilian honour. On 6 August 2015 the lieutenant governor of Ontario – the queen's representative in the province – travelled to London, Ontario, where Kelsey was living with one of her daughters. Although she was nearly deaf and barely mobile, she received the insignia at a private ceremony. The next day, at the age of 101, Frances Oldham Kelsey passed away. To cite her own words, "it has been an interesting career."[66]

Chapter 4

Rachel Was Right: Rachel Louise Carson

"Before there was an environmental movement, there was one brave woman and her very brave book."[1] The woman was Rachel Carson, and her book was *Silent Spring*. Some books shake the world (Charles Darwin's *Origin of the Species*, 1859), others change the world for the worse (Adolf Hitler's *Mein Kampf*, 1925), but few make the world a better place. In American letters, Harriet Beecher Stowe's *Uncle Tom's Cabin*, 1852, and *Silent Spring*, 1962, top the list. The title of Rachel Carson's most famous book was deliberately apocalyptic: nature is noisy; silence is terrifying. *Silent Spring* suggested no future for planet Earth.

"Government Girl" Sounds the Alarm

Rachel Louise Carson was born on 27 May 1907 on a small family farm in the hamlet of Springdale, Pennsylvania. Her father, Robert Warden Carson, was a travelling insurance salesman, and her protective mother, Maria Frazier McLean, a trained teacher who followed the popular nature studies movement and its mantra, "study nature, not books."

The family was poor and the house had no indoor plumbing, but there were animals – pigs, cows, chickens, and horses – and it was surrounded by an orchard, woodlands, and rivers. Carson, the youngest of three children, began writing stories when she was ten and was published almost immediately. She loved the outdoors, learned the names of everything she saw there, and never lost her curiosity about the unknown. "If I had influence with the good fairy," she wrote years later, "I should ask that her gift to each child be a sense of wonder so indestructible that it would last throughout life."[2]

In September 1925 Carson entered the Pennsylvania College for Women (now Chatham University). She enrolled first in English but switched to biology after meeting an inspirational professor. After graduating magna cum laude in 1929, she accepted a position – "beginning investigator" – at the Marine Biological Laboratory in Woods Hole on Cape Cod (and saw the sea for the very first time). Three years later, she earned a master's degree in zoology from Johns Hopkins University – it took so long because she ran out of money and could study only part-time. A doctorate and an academic career was planned, but it was financially impossible.

When her father died suddenly in 1935, her mother needed help, as did her sickly and recently, and, for the second time, divorced sister, Marian, a mother of two. All of this meant that Carson had to find work: everyone was now dependent on her for support. Her brother, a judgmental and unforgiving Baptist, offered no assistance (and was actually a bit of a mooch). The only position available was low-paying part-time work with the US Bureau of Fisheries. There she wrote the script for *Romance under the Waters* – a national weekly radio program designed to attract public interest to the bureau's work. The series became a huge success.

This job, and the ones that followed after Carson took the civil-service exam and scored well, prepared her for her career to come. She was a generalist, not a specialist, and she learned how to synthesize scientific information from a variety of sources and disciplines and make it exciting. Moreover, because she stayed in publishing and public education, where women were more readily accepted than in many other government positions, she made steady progress. In the late summer of 1936, Carson became the second of two women working for the bureau in a full-time professional position paying $2,000 a year. Small and solemn, she now had the title of junior aquatic biologist, assigned to the Division of Scientific Inquiry.[3]

The family financial pressures increased when Marian died in early 1937, leaving two pre-teen girls, Virginia and Marjorie, for Carson to support. She moved to Silver Spring, Maryland, and began looking for part-time freelance work to augment her small government salary. She sometimes signed her articles "R.L. Carson," believing her readers would take her more seriously if they thought she was a man. Her big break came when the *Atlantic Monthly* published "Undersea," a beautifully written article about life in the ocean and the interrelationships between sea creatures and their environment. Simon and Schuster gave her a contract to turn it into a book.

Under the Sea-Wind, published in November 1941 – it took three years of nights and weekends – brilliantly told the stories of the sea creatures and birds that lived along North America's eastern seaboard all the way to the Arctic, in the open sea and along the sea bottom. It outlined their migrations and mating, their struggle to survive, and the variety and interconnectedness of all living things. Scrupulously scientific, it mixed prose with poetry and appealed to adults and children alike.

There was a theme to the book: all living things are interdependent, part of a delicate, intricate balance of nature. "To sense the ebb and flow of the tides ... is to have knowledge of things that are as nearly eternal as any earthly life can be," Carson wrote. They continue "through the centuries and the ages, while man's kingdoms rise and fall."[4] The reviews were positive, but gender mattered: some critics referred to her as a "government girl," "woman naturalist," or "mermaid." The sales – around 1,400 copies in the first year despite being a Scientific Book Club monthly selection – were not very good. "The world," Carson wrote, received her book "with superb indifference."[5]

Fortunately, the bureau, now the Fish and Wildlife Service, promoted Carson, and by 1945 she was supervising a small staff. At the end of the decade she was in charge of everything that the service published. She also kept writing in her own time, and her second book, *The Sea around Us*, appeared in 1951. It is as fresh and compelling today as it was half a century ago.

The book begins by describing the birth of the planet and the beginnings of life in unforgettable images. First, a fiery ball of hot whirling gasses tore away from the sun and liquefied as a molten mass. Next, the newly formed earth cooled beneath an endlessly overcast sky. As the earth's barren surface took shape, powerful solar tides tore away part of the planet and sent it flying off into space, creating the moon. After centuries of rain dissolved the continents and filled the oceans, a bewildering abundance of life appeared. It was evolution, but Carson was prepared to acknowledge the possibility that God was the architect of it all. While volcanic action created underwater mountain ranges and deep canyons, giant squids battled immense sperm whales. She depicted the underwater world and the fascinating creatures to be found in it in stunning lyrical detail – complete with great noise: there was an "extraordinary uproar," with "strange mewing sounds, shrieks and ghostly moans."[6]

While *Under the Sea-Wind*, almost without exception, told the stories of sea creatures, and largely from their point of view, in *The Sea around Us* Carson paid attention to mankind's impact on the planet by describing, for example, what happened when humans invaded previously unique and pristine island environments. Wherever man "set foot … he has brought about disastrous changes." To "species after species … the black night of extinction has fallen."[7] Instead of treasuring nature's "precious possessions, as natural museums filled with beautiful and curious works of creation, valuable beyond price,"[8] humans laid waste – a theme Carson would return to soon enough. Carson accurately observed that "we live in an age of rising seas," although she believed it was part of the natural order of things; no one then knew that it was the result of anthropogenic activity.

Nine of the chapters were condensed and serialized in a three-part *New Yorker* series, which generated huge mail traffic. Within days of publication, the *Sea around Us* was featured in the *New York Times Book Review* and later abridged by *Reader's Digest*, the largest-circulation magazine in the United States (and also conferring the ultimate badge of middle-class approval and respectability). It spent eighty-six weeks on the *New York Times* best-seller list – well ahead of J.D. Salinger's *Catcher in the Rye* – and the first edition sold over 1 million copies and was eventually translated into more than thirty foreign languages.

Americans love the unexplored frontier, and Carson was their increasingly trusted guide to the unknown mysterious sea. The spiritual but not quite religious sensitivity in her writing made it even more compelling. And there was something rather comforting about a history of the planet that spanned billions of years. Certainly, it tended to put current events in perspective. As one reviewer enthused, "once or twice in a generation does the world get a physical scientist with literary genius. Miss Carson has written a classic."[9] Carson bought back the rights to *Under the Sea-Wind*, and soon she had two books on the *New York Times* best-seller list. She no longer needed a day job: she moved to Southport Island, Maine, where she built a plain cottage on the rugged coast.

The Edge of the Sea came next (1955). "The edge of the sea is a strange and beautiful place," the book begins, and it goes on to describe the living things found off Maine's rocky shoreline, on the mid-Atlantic's sandy coast, and in Florida's mangrove swamps and coral reefs – perhaps the most diverse ecosystems on the entire planet. This masterful account displays encyclopedic knowledge about the creatures that inhabit the intertidal world, their relationships with each other, and "the intense, blind, unconscious will to survive, to push on, to expand."[10] It completed her

Rachel Carson, in the field. Although she could barely swim, Carson's knowledge of the undersea world was encyclopedic. (Credit: US Department of Agriculture)

sea trilogy, was another best-seller, and was also serialized in the *New Yorker*. "She's done it again," the legendary editor William Shawn wrote to Carson's literary agent.[11] Carson's descriptive powers are even more amazing given that she spent almost no time on or under the sea and could barely swim.

Then, in 1957, Carson's niece Marjorie died at the age of thirty-one, leaving a needy and unhappy five-year-old son, Roger. The forty-nine-year-old Carson adopted him. The next year her mother died – the two had been unusually close – and in 1959 Carson herself got sick. But something else was troubling her: the future of the planet.

Carson knew that humans, with their ingenuity and arrogance, had the power and the potential to destroy the physical world.[12] The atomic bomb had changed everything, followed by the Cold War arms race. The doomsday clock was moving closer to midnight, as would soon be vividly illustrated by the Cuban Missile Crisis in October 1962. "We still haven't become mature enough to think of ourselves as only a tiny part of a vast and incredible universe," Carson wrote. "Man's attitude toward nature is today crucially important simply because we have now acquired a fateful power to alter and destroy nature."[13] Carson insisted that humanity come to understand ecology – the relationship of living creatures to the environment and their interconnectedness with each other: "So delicately interwoven are the relationships that when we disturb one thread of the community fabric we alter it all," she cautioned.[14]

Conservation was essential – the controlled and systematic use and protection of natural resources, of water and of earth, and not just because they were beautiful but because they sustained all life. "The mistakes that are made now," Carson wrote, referring to radioactive waste in the sky, on land, and in the sea, "are made for all time."[15] Carson knew that was not necessarily true – after all, she had published a book that measured the life of the earth in hundreds of millions of years. But she chose to exaggerate to make her point. Even though Carson was a shy, private, gentle person, someone who was completely and genuinely averse to the spotlight and public attention, she was about to sound the alarm.

The proximate cause was a letter from an old friend, Olga Owens Huckins, who lived in Duxbury, Massachusetts, just north of Cape Cod. Owens loved birds and had an established a small sanctuary for them. When the state sprayed fuel oil laced with DDT to rid the area of mosquitoes, some birds died overnight.

Carson had been worrying about DDT for years: in 1945 she proposed to *Reader's Digest* a story on how it might upset the delicate balance of nature, but the editor there turned her down. In 1958, however, the *New Yorker's* Shawn, a talent spotter second to none, responded enthusiastically and commissioned 50,000 words on the dangers pesticides posed to people and animals. She already had a book project underway – her "poison book" as she called it. "There would be no future peace for me if I kept silent," she told her friend Dorothy Freeman.[16]

It turned out to be a race against time – and, as things turned out, there was little left. Roger needed attention, Carson suffered bouts of pneumonia, and she was diagnosed with breast cancer. She had a radical mastectomy, but the cancer had metastasized. There was one setback after another – blood poisoning, phlebitis, iritis (a painful eye inflammation). Finally, in 1962, Carson finished *Silent Spring*. She had three goals for the book – to warn the public about the dangers of pesticides;

to force the American government to enact an effective regulatory regime; and to create a book for the ages – and she achieved each one. In the big picture, people were destroying the planet and making it unfit for everyone and everything. And the enemy was DDT.

The Wonder Pesticide

DDT – Dichloro-Diphenyl-Trichloroethane – was first synthesized in 1874. Once applied, DDT remained lethal to pests much longer than any of its competitors – it was persistent, meaning that it did not break down easily in the environment, and as an insoluble chemical, it was not washed away by rain.

All of this made it extremely efficient as well as cost-effective. DDT was a true war hero. It killed insect enemies – mosquitoes and lice – soon after contact, saving troops in the Pacific from malaria and yellow-fever and concentration-camp survivors, displaced persons, and refugees in Europe from typhus. When Paul Müller, the scientist who discovered that DDT was very good at killing insects, received the 1948 Nobel Prize in Medicine, his citation read: "Thanks to you, preventative medicine is now able to fight many diseases carried by insects."[17] DDT saved lives. It was a miracle almost too good to be true: harmless to mammals, deadly to insects. Carson, however, had a very different story to tell:

> There was once a town in the heart of America where all life seemed to live in harmony with its surroundings ... Then a strange blight crept over the area and everything began to change ... There was a strange stillness ... The few birds seen anywhere were moribund; they trembled violently and could not fly. It was a spring without voices ... no chicks hatched ... no bees droned among the blossoms, so there was no pollination and there would be no fruit ... Even the streams were now lifeless ... all the fish had died.
>
> In the gutters under the eaves and between the shingles of the roofs, a white granular powder still showed a few patches; some weeks before it had fallen like snow upon the roofs and the lawns, the fields and streams.
>
> No witchcraft, no enemy action had silenced the rebirth of new life in this stricken world. The people had done it to themselves.[18]

The town did not actually exist, but every one of those disasters had happened somewhere in America. The white granular powder was DDT, and Americans, along with many in the Western world, were in love with it, and with good reason. It killed insects that ate crops and threatened the forestry industry, it removed unwelcome visitors from homes, and it was, without any doubt, a fabulous boon to public health. Indeed, DDT had eradicated malaria in the United States.

Malaria used to be a huge problem in the southern United States (and, at one time, reached as far north as Montreal), but the US Public Health Service eliminated it by massively spraying DDT in the fifteen years after the Second World War. In 1955 the World Health Organization (WHO) endorsed DDT as one of the pillars in its global anti-malaria campaign. Unfortunately, over-spraying for agricultural purposes, together with vector control, began to reduce some of its effectiveness. It was no longer working well.

The mistake lay not in using DDT on farms and in forests, cities, and towns to increase agricultural and forestry yields and save lives, but in abusing it, the consequences of which Carson would soon explain. It became part of the post-war chemical revolution. DuPont, a leading pesticide manufacturer, coined a slogan to promote its products: "Better Living ... through Chemicals." American ingenuity was seen as a reflection of American exceptionalism, and as a reason for optimism. However, long before Carson published *Silent Spring*, danger signs began flashing.

In 1944 Public Health Service researchers warned that the "toxicity of DDT combined with its cumulative actions and absorption through the skin place a definite health hazard in its use."[19] The next year, the prestigious journal *Nature* published an article warning that pesticides might be harmful. The director of the Fish and Wildlife Service urged caution, observing that more needed to be known about pesticides in general, and DDT in particular, and their effects on living things.

That was the conclusion of Brigadier-General James Stevens Simmons, the head of preventative medicine for the US Army. DDT, he wrote in the January 1945 *Saturday Evening Post*, may be a double-edged sword: "Its unintelligent use might eliminate certain valuable insects essential to agriculture and horticulture. Even more important, it might conceivably disturb vital balances in the animal and plant kingdoms and thus upset various fundamental biological cycles."[20]

When sprayed on water, DDT seemed to kill a lot of fish, and it was definitely toxic to many kinds of birds. In some laboratory experiments, a wide variety of animals got sick and some died. In 1948 the American Medical Association expressed concern: the chronic toxicity of many new pesticides, including DDT, was entirely unexplored. Two years later, the Food and Drug Administration concluded that it "is extremely likely the potential hazard of DDT has been underestimated."[21] That year, DDT got on the congressional radar, and the Delaney Committee (the House Select Committee to Investigate the Use of Chemicals in Food Products) held hearings. It was especially concerned when representatives from Beech-Nut, one of America's largest manufacturers of baby food, testified to the difficulty of sourcing pesticide-free vegetables. Nevertheless, a Public Health Service toxicologist assured the committee members that, while DDT caused liver damage in rats, it was reversible. Besides, there was no risk to people.[22] These and many other reports raising concerns about chemicals leaching into the system were far from confidence-inspiring.[23]

When Americans gathered around their tables for Thanksgiving in 1959, something was missing: cranberries. A herbicide, aminotriazole, used to kill weeds in the cranberry bogs, was carcinogenic to rats and had been found in some samples sent in for testing.[24] Industry spokesmen claimed that there was no cause for concern. The pesticide had been mistakenly applied before instead of after harvest. But for this mistake, there would be no problem at all, and certainly not any reason to throw out the baby with the bathwater. On the campaign trail, presidential candidates Richard M. Nixon and John F. Kennedy tried to give the industry a boost by publicly eating the targeted fruit: Nixon ate four helpings of the sauce, Kennedy drank two glasses of juice. Consumers were not convinced, especially after a number of states banned their sale. Some people began to look at their food a little differently.

Once one red flag was raised, others appeared, especially as more disturbing results were published about pesticides. People heard about Minamata, a faraway fishing village in Japan, where children were being born deformed and disabled because of mercury poisoning. First, the residents observed waterfront cats convulsing; then the symptoms spread to dogs and birds and finally to people, causing paralysis, slurred speech, loss of hearing, and sometimes agonizing deaths. (Meanwhile, in northern Ontario two pulp and paper companies continued to dump tons of mercury waste in the English-Wabigoon River system between 1962 and

1970. Not to put too fine a gloss on it, the way of life and culture of the Grassy Narrows First Nation was destroyed. Eventually, a settlement was reached providing woefully inadequate compensation for a lucky few – about 75 per cent of the applications were denied. Four decades later, people are still getting sick. In 2016 the Ontario government continues to look into the situation, but it "has not yet committed to a specific course of action to clean up the river."[25])

In the late 1950s, Robert Cushman, a world-famous ornithologist, assembled a group of like-minded Long Island, New York, bird lovers, including former president Theodore Roosevelt's son Archibald and Dr Benjamin Spock's unusual sister Marjorie. (Marjorie was a devotee of a guru named Rudolf Steiner, who, among other things, advocated biodynamic agriculture, which included burying ground quartz stuffed into the horn of a cow to attract cosmic forces to the soil.) They went to court, spending $100,000 (about $800,000 in 2016 dollars) to obtain an injunction halting a government plan to spray DDT on millions of hectares of land in three states to eradicate the gypsy moth, a real threat to forests. The commercial arrangements were unusual: the pilots were offered financial incentives to over-spray, and the area earmarked for spraying included large swaths where there were no gypsy moths. Some places were sprayed up to fourteen times in a single day. The injunction application failed, so Cushman's group came back asking for compensation and pointing out that the spraying not only did not work but caused significant collateral damage.[26]

This case came right on the heels of another public controversy: the American government was spraying millions of hectares of land in the south and southwest to eradicate the fire ant, using chemicals far more toxic than DDT. The fire ant was a nuisance but not a danger, yet the deadly broadside had caused huge damage to all sorts of living things and the environment. In some places there were more fire ants after spraying than before.

In another example in 1956, the US Forest Service sprayed many hundreds of thousands of hectares with DDT to eradicate spruce budworms. The spraying worked, sort of, but the ladybugs and pirate bugs – the natural predators of the spider mite – also disappeared as DDT was completely indiscriminate, killing friends and enemies alike. What followed was "the most extensive and spectacular infestation of spider mites in history," not to mention the defoliation of countless Douglas fir trees.[27]

Long before Rosa Parks, a brave Canadian woman, Viola Desmond, challenged segregated seating. (Photo courtesy of Wanda Robson)

At the Long Island trial, quite possibly the first environmental lawsuit launched by citizens in the United States, evidence was tendered that DDT killed both fish and birds and made food from farms and gardens unsafe to eat. A hematologist from the Mayo Clinic was one of more than fifty expert witnesses. He told the court about links between the pesticide and aplastic anemia and other disorders including, quite possibly, cancer. There was nothing, the plaintiffs argued, that justified the spraying, certainly no national or health emergency.

The Forest Service countered with its own epidemiological studies and also drew attention to the results of an experiment in which "volunteer" convicts were fed large doses of DDT and experienced no ill effects. The trial judge sided with the government, concluding that mass spraying was justified to combat the gypsy moth, even though the evidence established that the spraying did not work. Moreover, the judge found that DDT was not harmful to man, beast or insect, if properly applied.

The case ended up at the US Supreme Court, where leave was denied. Justice William O. Douglas, a well-known environmentalist, dissented:

"The need for adequate findings on the effect of DDT is of vital concern not only to wildlife conservationists and owners of domestic animals but to all who drink milk or eat food from sprayed gardens." He observed that the evidence before the lower court indicated that DDT adversely affected birds and animals and that it was associated with cancer and other illnesses. Further examination was of "public importance."[28] But none of his colleagues agreed, so the lower court decision stood.

Defeated, the Long Island group was down but not out, although in a way it no longer mattered. The case had been closely watched. If the courts would not provide redress, the fight had to move to the public sphere, and the timing was perfect, coinciding as it did with the birth of the civil-rights movement.

The Montgomery Bus Boycott (1955–56) began after another brave woman named Rosa Parks refused to give up her seat on a public bus to a white person. (About a decade earlier, an extraordinary African Canadian and Nova Scotian, Viola Desmond, challenged separate seating at a New Glasgow movie theatre. When she refused to give up her seat on the main floor, reserved for whites, local police roughed her up and tossed her in jail. A true Canadian hero, Desmond hired a lawyer and fought back.) Parks's act of defiance was an opening shot in the fight for civil rights that would consume the American nation and draw the attention of the world, and as Black Lives Matters eloquently attests, it continues to this day. People were waking up to many troubling things going on right around them. Smog permeated the atmosphere over Los Angeles, and green scum choked large parts of Lake Erie (in just a few years, the Cuyahoga River, which flows into Lake Erie and is a long-standing toxic-dump site, actually caught fire). Grassroots groups began to emerge everywhere, but even though the scientific evidence was accumulating, no one was connecting all of the dots. Then Carson published *Silent Spring*.

The Interconnectedness of Life

Chemicals are the sinister and little-recognized partners of radiation in changing the very nature of the world – the very nature of its life …

Since the mid-nineteen forties, over 200 basic chemicals have been created for use in killing insects, weeds, rodent and other organisms described in the modern vernacular as pests …

These sprays, dusts and aerosols are now applied almost uni-
versally to farms, gardens, forests and homes – non-selective chemicals that have the power to kill every insect, the "good" and the
"bad," to still the song of birds and the leaping of fish in the
streams – to coat the leaves with a deadly film and to linger on in
soil – all this, though the intended target may be only a few weeds
or insects.

Can anyone believe it is possible to lay down such a barrage of
poisons on the surface of the earth without making it unfit for all
life? They should not be called "insecticides" but "biocides."[29]

Carson explained how the indiscriminate use of pesticides and other
chemicals polluted everything, poisoned living creatures, and, she argued,
threatened all life. The Delaney Committee hearings and the Long Island
lawsuit had produced reams of documents and anecdotes, and Carson
gathered more from scientists across the country and overseas. Her entire
career had prepared her for this task. If she did not know where to find
a research report, or an expert to buttress her points, she knew how and
whom to ask.

It was nonsense to suggest that any one chemical concoction could
target a single species. DDT and other pesticides killed all insects, and
most of them – bees, for instance – were necessary to sustain life. Pesticides were also harming all sorts of living things – birds, mammals, rep-
tiles, amphibians, fish, and shellfish. DDT and other chemicals were visible
when first sprayed but then disappeared, making their way into the food
chain, where they could be found and measured everywhere around the
world from the Arctic to the Antarctic, as far as you could get from where
spraying had taken place – in water, plants, food, and all living things.

DDT's persistence was extraordinary. In one experiment DDT was
applied to hay, the hay was fed to cows, the cows were slaughtered and
fed to pigs – and, when the pigs were tested, DDT's metabolite (DDE) was
found intact.[30] The same transference was observed when alfalfa sprayed
with DDT was fed to hens and their eggs were eaten by people. DDT could
be tracked all the way up the food chain, but the higher it advanced, the
more concentrated the residue. In some experiments, pesticides freely
crossed the placental wall – just as thalidomide did.

Groundwater, lakes, rivers, and streams were being polluted from aerial spraying. When DDT was sprayed on millions of hectares of balsam

forest in New Brunswick to protect it from the spruce budworm (and assist the pulp and paper industry), it also killed the aquatic insects in the Miramichi River that baby salmon depended on for their food. "A whole year's spawning had come to nothing," Carson wrote in her chapter titled "Rivers of Death."[31] DDT was bad for birds because it caused some species to produce eggs that would not hatch or had extremely fragile shells.

Dead eggs. Fragile eggs. What could be more imbued with meaning? Peregrine falcons, bald eagles, brown pelicans, white pelicans, sparrows, and ospreys were all threatened with extinction. To this day we still don't know why some bird species were seriously affected and others were not. What we do know is that Carson got it right about wildlife, as was acknowledged in a 2012 book published by the right-wing Cato Institute: "Virtually everyone now agrees that DDT can harm certain bird species: its magnification up the food chain does cause thinning to occur in the eggs of raptors (including the bald eagle, the peregrine falcon, and the osprey), resulting in a decline in the numbers of those birds."[32]

Just like radiation, pesticides were unseen but deadly, travelling through time and space.[33] All life on earth was interconnected, Carson stressed. If some rats died from DDT poisoning, no one would have cared less. The loss of the Norway rat would be a cause for celebration (the province of Alberta has been rat-free for more than fifty years and everyone wants to keep it that way). But robins were dying after eating exposed earthworms. Birds were different: the silence in the spring. Carson knew exactly how to best make her case. "Who," she asked, "has made the decision that sets in motion these chains of poisonings, this ever widening wave of death that spreads out, like ripples when a pebble is dropped into a still pond?"[34]

Pesticides were making their way into people. They "bioaccumulated" (absorbing more quickly than they dissipated) and "biomagnified" (increasing in concentration as they passed from one species to the next up the food chain). They were found in human body fat and in breast milk, and perhaps could be transmitted generationally – the same problem that concerned Frances Kelsey. In the most quoted section of her book, the Introduction, Carson implied a link between DDT and radiation. Everyone knew radiation caused cancer. Subtle at first, this connection tapped into pre-existing public anxieties – and it worked. Radiation and pesticides: invisible, insidious, and life threatening.

Carson set out to awaken Americans from their slumber and frighten them out of their minds. People were worried about radioactive fallout, especially since a moratorium on atmospheric testing came to an end in September 1961 and both superpowers resumed exploding nuclear weapons in the atmosphere. Early results from the St Louis Baby Tooth Survey were published in *Science* in the fall of 1961. Strontium 90, a cancer-causing radioactive isotope, was appearing in significant and growing amounts in baby teeth – and in mothers' and cows' milk too. People were worried: about 50,000 American women in cities across the United States took to the streets on 1 November 1961 demanding a ban on nuclear testing. President John F. Kennedy watched from a window at the White House.

DDT and radiation both operated slowly, eventually causing disease and perhaps death. Carson did not know for sure, but she suggested that pesticides might very well cause cancer. In laboratory tests conducted by FDA scientists, DDT "has produced suspicious liver tumors," quite possibly "low grade hepatic cell carcinomas." Dr W.C. Hueper of the National Cancer Institute labelled DDT a "chemical carcinogen."[35] Carson presented the evidence she had gathered and appropriately and modestly observed that it was "a matter that warrants the most serious concern."[36] At the time, American authorities were annually spraying more than 80 million pounds of DDT on cities, farms, and forests.[37]

An Instant Best-Seller

Carson was an extremely demanding author and savvy businessperson with definite views on book production and promotion. She micromanaged the book's launch, determined to make her case effectively. At one level she was an unlikely person to write this book: the chronicler of shore, sea, and sky self-consciously and deliberately taking on the chemical industry – one of the most powerful and entrenched interests in the United States. But she was also the best person to write it: the foremost nature writer of her generation, with a deep reservoir of public goodwill. Carson had what all writers crave: fame, respect, money. But she wrote about what she loved, first the sea and now the planet earth, and that fierce commitment shone through. She was the ideal person to absorb the scientific information buried in academic journals and government reports, synthesize it with supportive media accounts, and interpret it all for an increasingly anxious public. Her years of experience in translating scientific jargon into accessible, often poetic, and always popular prose now paid off.

It was a pioneering accomplishment even if, as her critics claimed, she had no laboratory herself and conducted no experiments. She was a master at telling a gripping story; now she told a horror story. Just as *Silent Spring* was being published, news emerged that Frances Kelsey had prevented a true American tragedy. One woman had already saved the country, and here was another. The American people like the lone gunslinger, and Kelsey and Carson actually knew each other; both belonged to the Chevy Chase chapter of the Audubon Society, the organization dedicated to watching and protecting birds.

Carson's town was imaginary – a composite sketch – but the disasters it described were very real. Her narrative was compelling. An investigative journalist at the start of his career, Robert Caro (later the biographer of Lyndon B. Johnson and winner of two Pulitzer prizes in biography), was intrigued and wrote about the book and the issue in *Newsday*. Caro blamed the federal government for years of inaction, threatening "man with cancer, leukemia and abnormal gene development." He was among the first to draw the parallel to thalidomide: "Scientists say," Caro wrote, "that pesticide-affected genes could deform generation after generation, rather than just one generation, as in the case of thalidomide."[38] He made it clear that the pesticide and agricultural industries were in bed with the government: the Department of Agriculture was an active propagandist on behalf of the industry that was determined to spray even in the face of a growing body of evidence that these practices were unsafe.

Silent Spring struck a chord – the entire first printing of 100,000 copies was sold in the first two weeks. It revealed an even larger truth: humans had the means to destroy the planet not just by nuclear war but with pesticides too. The atmospheric testing of nuclear weapons, supposedly to prevent war by demonstrating the capacity to wage war, posed an existential threat. Carson made a similar case by combining laboratory toxicology data with epidemiological and ecological data, and augmenting both with anecdotal evidence. Yet she accepted some form of insect control as necessary, and in the book's final chapter she provided a buffet of possible solutions to the problem.

Carson never ruled out the proper use of pesticides. She knew they saved human lives. Insects and insect-borne disease could not be ignored:

"It is not my contention that chemical insecticides must never be used," she wrote. But "I do contend that we have put poisonous and biologically potent chemicals indiscriminately into the hands of persons largely or wholly ignorant of their potential for harm ... [and] we have allowed these chemicals to be used with little or no advance investigation of their effect on our soil, water, wildlife and man himself."[39] The question was how best to attack the problem, and Carson had a lot of ideas on how to make things better – for example, by diversifying agriculture.

Even more alarming, Carson warned, we were making insects stronger by our efforts. Because of the massive agricultural and pest-control spraying, insects were developing resistance to pesticides (just as today's massive abuse of antibiotics in beef and chicken production is leading to an increase in bacterial resistance in humans). The way it works with insects is that a large population is killed, but genetic composition is changed because of those few individuals that survive as a result of random mutation. Lickety-split, the susceptible population is replaced by the resistant one. Carson counselled prudence and caution for the "sparing, selective and intelligent use of chemicals."[40] She called for targeted, not aerial, spraying. Just like Kelsey, Carson wanted to be sure. When President Kennedy awarded Kelsey her medal, Carson told the *New York Post* that "thalidomide and pesticides ... represent our willingness to rush ahead and use something new without knowing what the results are going to be."[41]

In the beginning of June 1962 the *New Yorker* ran three long excerpts from *Silent Spring*. With its circulation of over 400,000, the magazine was read by almost everyone in the American elite, including President Kennedy and his wife, Jackie. Both Kennedys knew Carson: Jackie had invited her to join the Women's Committee for New Frontiers and, before the election, they had entertained Carson at their Georgetown home. The book was also the October selection for the Book-of-the-Month Club, which printed an exceptional run of 150,000 copies. Prominent people came forward to endorse it: Supreme Court Justice Douglas declared that Carson's book was "the most important chronicle of this century for the human race."[42] And Agnes Meyer, owner of the *Washington Post*, worked behind the scenes to promote it. On 2 July 1962 the *New York Times* published the first of its pro–*Silent Spring* editorials. Carson declared herself "deeply and quietly happy,"[43] but the roller-coaster ride had just begun.

On 28 August 1962 President Kennedy appeared at his forty-second press conference since taking office. The main news was Felix Frankfurter's overdue retirement from the United States Supreme Court. At the end there was an obviously planted question: "Mr. President, there appears to be a growing concern among scientists as to the possibility of dangerous long-range side effects from the widespread use of DDT and other pesticides. Have you considered asking the Department of Agriculture or the Public Health Service to take a closer look at this?" Kennedy told the reporters he had already instructed his officials to launch an investigation because of "Miss Carson's book" (though publication was still a month away).[44] The next day he announced that he had established a special panel of the President's Science Advisory Committee to look into pesticide use. Kennedy was definitely on side – "We must restore our own woodlands as a source of strength for the Nation's future ... set aside shoreline recreational refuge, and ranges"[45] – and he followed through by creating new national seashores at Cape Cod, Padre Island in Texas, Point Reyes in California, and Prime Hook in Delaware, one of the nation's most important stopover sites for migratory shorebirds.

The Chemical Industry Response

To be fair, Carson's evidence was curated: selectively scientific and highly anecdotal; grounded in cherry-picked literature but also illustrated by one-offs. Her list of "principal sources," though fifty pages in length, was hardly neutral or objective and the book itself was polemicized with anger and outrage for deliberate effect. Accordingly, the scientific world was split over *Silent Spring*: some saw no danger in the current pesticide use, while others saw danger everywhere or were at least willing to consider that possibility. The popular press, however, could not get enough. The book was making for a noisy summer, the *New York Times* observed in July 1962.[46]

Even before it was published, the chemical industry had prepared its response. It was the insects and rodents that were bad, not the chemicals that eradicated them, it declared. Left unchecked, these myriad small creatures would despoil the earth, denude the forests, eat the crops, cause destitution and famine, spread disease and death. Carson had got it all wrong, the spokespeople claimed: she did not know what she was talking about. "Any harm that is caused by the use of pesticides is greatly overcompensated by the good they do," Parke C. Brinkley, the chief executive officer of the National Agricultural Chemical Association, told the *New York Times*.[47] But telling the other side of the story was not Carson's objective or point. That story had already been told, leaving, in Carson's view, a gullible, credulous, stupefied, and misinformed public.

The Velsicol Chemical Corporation, a pesticide producer, leaned on the publisher, Houghton Mifflin. It was not a good idea to publish the book, it warned threateningly; there could be "unfortunate consequences." Anticipating a lawsuit, the publisher had a legal opinion in hand: everything Carson wrote could be defended in court. One pesticide company lawyer gave a speech in which he explained that the industry's opponents were "misinformed or mentally unbalanced ... driven by obscure sexual urges."[48] The giant Monsanto Company, a manufacturer of DDT, insecticides, chemicals, and plastics, published a parody of *Silent Spring*. Titled *The Desolate Year*, it told a completely different story: a world overrun by insects.

Trade journals were especially vicious in their response to the book. A review published in the *Chemical and Engineering News* in October 1962 under the title "Silence, Miss Carson!" stated that the author was biased and criticized her for something she never said: "For example, she indicates that it is neither wise nor responsible to use pesticides in the control of insect-borne diseases." A Harvard professor called *Silent Spring* "baloney." Industry organizations hired public-relations firms and raised money – rumoured to be $250,000 – to sponsor various initiatives to undermine Carson and her book, including the mass mailings of unfavourable reviews and the brochure *Fact and Fancy: A Reference Checklist for Evaluating Information about Pesticides*.

Ultimately, all this industry pressure was counter-productive. Whenever there is a large, well-financed, and organized campaign against a person or an idea, it is time to pay attention. The very fact of Carson was revolutionary. She challenged key social pillars. Men ran science. Men ran business. Men wanted to do all the talking and make all the decisions. Unlike her earlier books, there was no appeal to wonder, mystery, or primal longing in *Silent Spring*. It was a cautionary tale delivered with a sledgehammer.

The campaign against Carson intensified. "The result was more publicity than Houghton Mifflin could possibly have afforded."[49] As things turned out, *Silent Spring* was on the best-seller list for thirty-one months.

If the National Agricultural Chemical Association and its allies had been smart, they would have showered Carson with love, thanked her for raising some important points, illustrated some of the obvious benefits of pesticides such as fighting malaria and feeding the world's hungry, and outlined how they were working diligently to provide safe and effective pesticides. Or they could have just ignored her and waited for the news cycle to move on, as would inevitably occur. Instead, the controversy – their attacks – became the story: Carson, the main protagonist, was an underdog who was sticking it to The Man.

There was some fair-minded criticism, mostly in academic journals such as *Science*. "No attempt is made by the author to portray the many positive benefits that society derives from the use of pesticides," it complained. "No estimates are made of the countless lives that have been saved because of the destruction of insect vectors of disease ... No consideration is given to the important role played by modern pesticides in the production of food and fiber ... Modern agriculture ... could not exist without the use of pesticides."[50] That was all true, but most reviewers were barking dogs, unleashed to attack, their assessments completely devoid of balance. Most were men, offended, it seemed, by this uppity woman challenging the status quo – corporatist and capitalist – and doing so with verve. Even worse, she was attracting a growing following. *Silent Spring* not only attacked chemical companies, established institutions, and the government but questioned obedience to authority itself.

A Duel with Cold War Conformity

The misogyny in the criticism levelled at *Silent Spring* became explicit. Some reviewers were astonished that the book was written by a woman – and an attractive one to boot – but others called Carson a hysteric, as they often do when a woman says something that men do not want to hear. As the response became more aggressive, Carson was variously described as a peace nut, pantheist, health quack, food faddist, shrill fanatic, bird and bunny lover, anti-fluoridationist crank, priestess of nature, and wildlife bureaucrat. The book was a fraud – hoax, hogwash, and science fiction.[51]

"*Silent Spring*, which I read word for word with some trauma," a William B. Bean, MD, wrote in the *Archives of Internal Medicine*, "kept reminding me of trying to win an argument with a woman. It cannot be done."[52] A former secretary of agriculture and prominent Mormon Church leader, Ezra Taft Benson, asked: "Why is a spinster with no children concerned with genetics?"[53] (For Benson and his cronies, "spinster" was crude code. It was quietly whispered that Carson's closest relationships were with women. If they had known the truth, the reaction would have been even more ferocious: they would have gone mental.) In the early 1960s, any woman who threatened powerful vested interests and the established order – including prevailing and ironclad gender norms – had a bull's-eye on her back. Even the adoption of Roger was held against Carson: her nephew had been "born out of wedlock."

For good measure, Benson also told former president Dwight Eisenhower that Carson was "probably a communist." Today the adjective sounds laughable, but not so in 1962. "A post-World War II consensus dominated American society. At its core lay a profound anti-Communism that meant both containing Soviet expansionism abroad and fighting subversives at home. The consensus encouraged social and political conformity, respect for government and community authority, uncritical patriotism, religious faith, and a commitment to a vague notion of an American way of life ... A person did not have to be a Communist to come under suspicion as a subversive. One only had to dissent against commonly accepted values ... to be considered disloyal."[54] The Federal Bureau of Investigation (FBI) opened a file on Carson and began an investigation.[55]

Carson had instigated a battle for hearts and minds: "As seen from the point of view of the pesticide makers, her embryonic new idea – environmentalism – was, by definition, un-American."[56] The deadliest sin in the 1950s, William Manchester wrote, was to be "controversial."[57] Velsicol considered Carson to be a communist dupe who attacked the chemical industry with two goals in mind: to create the false impression that American business was grasping and immoral, and to reduce American food production to behind–Iron Curtain levels. But Carson was no propagandist in the employ of Mother Russia: she was the real deal, a true American patriot. It was her critics who threatened the American way of life. "It is one of the ironies of our time," she wrote the *Washington Post*, "that, while concentrating on the defense of our country against enemies from without, we should be so heedless of those who would destroy it from within."[58]

In October 1962 the popular weekly magazine *Life* concluded its profile of Carson with the suggestion that, once she was pacified, "the real dangers to public health could be evaluated, and then controlled by skilled medical *men*." The photographs accompanying the text were telling: Carson with a cat, Carson in the woods with some small children, Carson on a walk with other birders, and just one of Carson with a microscope.[59] The overall effect, as intended, was to undermine her authority. No male scientist would have been depicted that way. With every attack, however, Carson got stronger.

On 3 April 1963 CBS Reports aired an hour-long special, *The Silent Spring of Rachel Carson*, going ahead even after three major corporations withdrew their advertising support. Most American homes had television by then, and at least 10 million people, including President Kennedy, tuned in. They saw two key presentations: a quiet, plausible, and dignified Rachel Carson knowledgeably, clearly, and calmly explaining the hazards of pesticide use; and the wild-eyed Dr Robert H. White-Stevens, an employee of American Cyanamid clad in a white lab coat, denouncing the book so loudly that he seemed more a mad scientist than a clinical researcher (even to the "slight sibilant hiss" he added every time he uttered "Miss Carson").[60] When he suggested that man, to his credit, had undone the balance of nature, Carson let him have it with a knockout punch. Man could no more repeal the law of nature, she said, than he could repeal the law of gravity: "The balance of nature is built on a series of relationships between living things, and between living things and their environments. You can't just step in with some brute force and change one thing without changing many others. This doesn't mean we must never interfere, never tilt the balance of nature in our favor. But when we make the attempt we must know what we're doing. We must know the consequences."[61]

A Fight to the End

Right from the start, Carson knew she had a tough sell with this topic, and she consciously wrote the book as propaganda. Had she forecast a world with no snakes or spiders, *Silent Spring* would have sunk without a trace. But birds are different: people watch birds, and they know that the loss of the American bald eagle would be a national tragedy.

In some respects, Carson was not saying anything new: in the decade before *Silent* Spring, four other books on this very same subject were published in the United States. One of them, by American anarchist Murray Bookchin, *Our Synthetic Environment*, came out several months before Carson's and was drawn from similar sources. However, it was framed as a radical denunciation of capitalism and recommended a popular uprising against corporations and government.[62] Carson's critique, though forceful, avoided direct discussion and denunciation of the economic and political system and threats to the status quo. Moreover, as Shawn at the *New Yorker* said, it was "full of beauty and loveliness and depth of feeling."[63] Quite possibly, because of the end run, and because Carson was a woman, her message may have been more readily received.

Instead of revolution, Carson tapped into the American conservationist tradition already established by Theodore Roosevelt and Franklin Roosevelt. She wanted to connect her book with a modern environmentalism that accepted the interdependence of life and called for the protection and preservation of all living things, together with the earth, air, and water. Regulating DDT was part of that mission: it was being massively sprayed and over-sprayed on farms and in forests, cities, and towns. "Darwin himself could scarcely have found a better example of the operation of natural selection ... Spraying kills off the weaklings," she argued. "The only survivors are insects that have some inherent quality that allows them to escape harm. These are the parents of the new generation ... a population consisting entirely of tough, resistant strains."[64]

Vindication

On 15 May 1963 the President's Science Advisory Committee, chaired by Dr Jerome B. Wiesner, issued its report. Although it acknowledged the many social benefits of pesticides, it recommended that the use of persistent insecticides be restricted "except for necessary control of disease vectors" like malaria. The committee also called for reproductive studies "through at least two generations in at least two species of warm blooded animals. Observations should include effects on fertility, size and weight of litter, fetal mortality, teratogenicity, growth and development of sucklings and weanlings." It urged federal agencies like the FDA and the Department of Agriculture to cooperate with each other and recommended further investigation of pesticide toxicity and research into alternatives. "Elimination of the use of persistent toxic pesticides should be the goal." Carson had recommended the same course, and the committee credited her work and effectively endorsed it: "Until the publication of *Silent Spring* by Rachel Carson, people were generally unaware of the toxicity of pesticides."[65] The administration was now clearly on side. "Rachel Carson Stands Vindicated!" was the headline in the *Christian Science Monitor*.

Although she was dying from cancer – her pelvis was pocked with tumours – and the ongoing radiation treatments left her nauseous and weak, she carried on. In October 1962 she travelled across the country to give a speech and arrived at San Francisco's Fairmont Hotel in a wheelchair. She read her address to an obviously rapt and appreciative overflow audience. In one of the newspaper accounts that followed, she was described as a "middle-aged, arthritis-crippled spinster."[66] But Carson was no "cripple" – a derogatory and ridiculous word. She was a person of uncommon courage, bravery, and heroism – and her conclusions were valid: *Scientific American* reported that the few errors of fact in the book were infrequent, trivial, and irrelevant.[67]

A work of hooey would have been debunked years ago; instead her book has sold millions of copies and continues to sell well even though much of its science is out of date. Carson knew, because of her long experience in government, what was achievable and what was not. Her recommended reforms were within acceptable limits and, accordingly, led almost immediately to regulatory reform. By the end of 1962, more than forty bills had been introduced in various state legislatures to regulate pesticide use. In Washington, one environmental bill followed another for years to come. All because of her.

Weakened by years of radiation, wracked by pain, and almost completely invalided by the spread of her disease, Carson died of a heart attack on 14 April 1964, one month shy of her fifty-seventh birthday. Through it all, her intimate friend Dorothy Freeman, her neighbour on Southport Island, stood by her. "I have had a rich life, full of rewards and satisfactions that come to few, and if it must end now, I can feel that I have achieved most of what I wished to do," she wrote to Freeman, knowing time was short.

When Carson was accused of becoming too emotional about the destruction of the natural world, she replied that there was something wrong with people who did not become upset about nature's destruction. "It seems reasonable to believe, and I do believe," Carson wrote, "that the more clearly we can focus our attention on the wonders and realities of the universe about us the less taste we shall have for the destruction of our race."[68] Ultimately, she knew she had made an impact: "I have felt bound by a solemn obligation to do what I could. But now I can believe that I have at least helped a little."[69] Carson ushered in a paradigm shift, possibly less male, certainly more human.

Hailed as a writer, scientist, ecologist, conservationist, and dissenter, she was posthumously awarded the Presidential Medal of Freedom by President Jimmy Carter. Schools and buildings, bridges and ships, conservation areas, wildlife refuges, and prizes have been named after her, stamps have been issued with her image in the United States and around the world, and her childhood home has been listed on the National Register of Historic Places (with a foundation established to manage it). There is a statue of her at the Woods Hole Oceanographic Institution. Novelist Margaret Atwood even turned her into a saint: in *The Year of the Flood*, Carson is worshipped by God's Gardeners.[70]

We now believe what Carson believed: we are part of nature, and we destroy the natural world at our peril. Carson alerted the world to the dangers of pesticides, but she also got people to rethink their attitude about the environment. Yes, there would have been an environmental movement without Carson; the Sierra Club (1892), the National Audubon Society (1905), the Conservation Foundation (1947), and the Nature Conservancy (1951) were already up and running before the appearance of *Silent Spring*. But her singular vision inspired and shaped that movement – – and still does. To cite just one example, Greenpeace, founded in Vancouver in 1971, clearly owes much of its worldview to Rachel Carson.

A Contested Person – A Contested Legacy

In the years after her death, grassroots advocacy organizations continued to spread across the country and around the world. Everywhere, it seemed, legislation was passed to protect the environment – just as Carson had requested when she testified before Congress twice in the summer of 1963. The Clean Air Act followed in the United States, and, in 1965, the Water Quality Act. In 1967 the Environmental Defense Fund was founded with the unofficial motto: "sue the bastards." It began small with a fight to ban DDT in Suffolk County, Long Island, and then expanded its activities across the United States, first Michigan, then Wisconsin. Two years later, the National Environmental Policy Act was passed, requiring that environmental assessments be conducted in advance of major construction. In 1970 the Environmental Protection Agency (EPA) was created, building on a number of recent legislative reforms and establishing an environmental regulatory regime. Before long it launched an official inquiry into the use of DDT.[71]

Over seven months, the examiner heard from some 150 expert witnesses – the evidence was disputed – and he quickly determined just one month after the proceedings were completed that DDT was not either a mutagenic or a teratogenic hazard to people, did not kill birds, fish, or other wildlife. (This was the exact opposite of the result reached in Wisconsin following an even more exhaustive inquiry.) He recommended that it remain available for use given its evident benefits – to agricultural production and human health. Apparently, just because there was evidence of carcinogenicity and mutagenicity in animals did not mean that humans were at risk.

EPA Commissioner William D. Ruckelshaus, however, disagreed: he found that the evidence demonstrated compellingly that DDT threatened fish and wildlife and was a possible human carcinogen. Indeed, just before the hearings began, the National Cancer Institute concluded a study it had begun soon after *Silent Spring* was published; this study established that mice exposed to low levels of DDT over an extended period of time had an increased incidence of liver tumours. This did not mean that DDT would have a similar effect in humans, but it was better, the commissioner concluded, to be safe than sorry.

Accordingly, in 1972, DDT was banned. This was hardly a great victory for the environmental movement, although it was billed as such and did have some symbolic value. But the truth was that DDT was, year over year, losing market share, the result of "decreased effectiveness in an ecosystem that had been subjected to millions of pounds of the pesticide in the previous twenty years."[72]

Almost 100 insects were now resistant to its charms, including 19 species of mosquitoes capable of transmitting malaria. Its replacements were actually worse, more specific to be sure, but more poisonous too. In a happy coincidence, the new pesticides were more expensive, and more profitable. DDT could no longer be used to spray agricultural crops, but it could be used for emergencies such as a renewed outbreak of malaria (and has been used in the United States for public-health emergencies in the years since: for instance, for rabid-bat control in Texas and to suppress typhus-carrying fleas in Louisiana, both in 1979). Inevitably, however, the ban spread worldwide – decisions made in America carry weight – unfairly blemishing Carson's posthumous reputation.

The critics have had a field day: "Rachel Carson Lied, Millions Died," proclaimed one,[73] while another catalogued "the Lies of Rachel Carson,"[74] and a third, from the Ayn Rand Institute, reported on "Rachel Carson's Genocide."[75] *Forbes* magazine published "Rachel Carson's Deadly Fantasies,"[76] and entire websites, for example, rachelwaswrong. org, are devoted to attacking her. Run by a right-wing think-tank in Washington, the Competitive Enterprise Institute, it claims that millions of people suffer and die "because one person sounded a false alarm."[77] Novelist Michael Crichton compared her to Hitler, a common meme: "There has not been a mass murderer executed in the past half-century who has been responsible for as many deaths of human beings as the sainted Rachel Carson," Hoover Institution economist Thomas Sowell wrote in 2001.[78]

Carson has not only been blamed for tens of millions of deaths from malaria over the last five decades but, because malaria disproportionately kills Africans, she has also been accused of racism.[79] The Junk Science.org webpage features a Malaria Death Clock, and the accompanying text claims that Carson's bad science, which it exposes, led to the ban on DDT. All we need to do is spray, spray, spray, it implies, and Africans, South Americans, and Asians will be rid, once and for all, of malaria (as the United States is today).

It's true that the Americans banned DDT in 1972. But banning it for agricultural use and widespread pest control was the right thing to do in the United States, and providing an exception for public health was the smart thing to do. The "ban" spread to other countries only after the United States Agency for International Development (USAID) announced it would no longer pay for DDT and would cut off malaria-funding programs for countries that continued to use it. That policy was understandable, but it might have been a mistake, and it was compounded by the 1969 decision by the WHO to end support for malaria-spray programs overseas because mosquito resistance to DDT was making the pesticide pointless.

As a result, malaria deaths grew in the developing world: UNICEF estimates that about 1 million people a year, mostly children under the age of five, die from malaria – others say the number is much, much higher – and hundreds of millions more suffer from it. Carson gets the blame for this, accused of eco-imperialism or eco-colonialism (although it is not entirely clear what either is, what the differences are between them, and which is worse). "What the World Needs Now Is DDT," was the headline of a recent feature in the *New York Times Magazine*. The author, Tina Rosenberg, identified the problem: "DDT killed bald eagles because of its persistence in the environment. *Silent Spring* is now killing African children because of its persistence in the public mind." The United States and Europe used DDT irresponsibly to wipe out malaria, she continued: "Once we discovered it was harming the ecosystem, we made even its safe use impossible for far poorer and sicker nations."[80]

That statement is a little misleading: the international treaty that banned DDT and related pesticides, the 2001 Stockholm Convention on Persistent Organic Pollutants (which came into effect three years later), included an exemption for DDT to fight malaria. Regulating and restricting DDT actually made it more effective when it was put to targeted use.

Moreover, Carson's book was published in 1962. Four decades later, 152 countries decided to phase out DDT, except to fight malaria, based on forty years of scientific research. It was the mismanagement and promiscuous use of DDT, just as Carson warned, that led to the natural selection that undermined the pesticide's effectiveness. Massive overspraying was a demonstrable threat to the future of planetary life.

The right-wing think-tanks and their allies who blame Carson for malaria deaths are entitled to their opinion, but Carson was no murderer – she revered life. On this issue they are just plain wrong, as is the World Wildlife Federation, which still calls for a complete DDT ban.[81] And there's another point too: in many countries, the anti-malarial programs failed not because of Carson, who was responding to the proven environmental consequences of DDT's massive abuse in the United States, but because of the failure of a medicine-based approach, inadequate funding, corruption, complacency, ineptitude, wars, and natural disasters, most of which had nothing to do with DDT. In all of this, Carson is no more than an imagined and versatile scapegoat: most recently she has been blamed for the Zika virus.[82]

More balanced policies are now coming into place. In 2006 the WHO reversed its earlier position opposing DDT and recommended its use indoors to combat malaria, concluding that the health and environmental risks were offset by the benefits to public health. It continues to endorse DDT to fight malaria until a better alternative is developed.[83] If DDT, extraordinarily persistent as an insoluble chemical, is sprayed lightly on interior walls, around windows, and on ceilings, it can combat mosquitoes for up to one year. If DDT is sprayed on bed netting and interior walls by everyone in a village, malaria disappears. About seventeen countries around the world now use it in a limited and specific way. That is exactly what Carson called for.

Almost everyone, including Greenpeace, in a complete reversal of its earlier opposition, now believes that DDT is an important anti-malaria weapon, provided it is carefully and intelligently applied. "If I were a decision maker in Sri Lanka, where the benefits from use outweigh the risks," Ruckelshaus, the man responsible for the American ban, told the *New York Times*, "I would decide differently."[84] And that is what he always said: "I would have approved the use of DDT ... in a country struggling with malaria."[85] Carson would have agreed: she made that clear in *Silent Spring* and in every speech she ever gave. Today, no informed expert truly believes that DDT is a silver bullet, just a tool in the chest. It must be used with extreme caution, however. Even today, "pockets of resistance to DDT in some mosquito species in Africa are already well documented."[86] Over-spraying produces insect resistance. This has been proven time and time again.

Carson knew that pesticides save lives, and she repeatedly recommended their use where they were focused, necessary, and effective. She acknowledged right at the beginning of her book that insects were competitors for food and carried disease, and that they had to be managed appropriately. As she said in a speech before the book was published: "I criticize modern chemical control not because it controls harmful insects, but because it controls them badly and inefficiently."[87]

Just like thalidomide, DDT has its legitimate uses. Frances Kelsey did not stand in the way of using thalidomide to treat leprosy, and Carson did not oppose limited DDT spraying to save lives. "The real wealth of the Nation lies in the resources of the earth – soil, water, forests, minerals, and wildlife," she wrote. "To utilize them for present needs while insuring their preservation for future generations requires a delicately balanced and continuing program, based on the most extensive research."[88] *Silent Spring* called for that research.

The Long-Term Effects of DDT on Humans and the Environment

DDT proponents often refer to a mid-1950s experiment in which the subjects ate the pesticide over eighteen months with no documented adverse reaction, then or since; to San Jose State University Professor J. Gordon Edwards, who, to make a point, would pull out a jar of DDT and swallow a mouthful (providing proof that whatever its benefits, DDT does not cure stupidity); to the employees at the Montrose Chemical Company, a DDT manufacturer, who, unbelievably, never developed a single case of cancer; and to the tens of millions of people who have lived in village homes that have been sprayed with DDT and never got sick.[89]

But Carson's purpose was different from the subjects in any of these examples: she documented the immediate effects of DDT on birds and fish, and she was especially concerned about its long-term effects on humans. On the birds and fish, she proved her point. In the mid-1960s, for example, there were fewer than 500 nesting pairs of bald eagles in the continental United States. By 2012, according to *Scientific American*, "thanks to the DDT ban and other conservation efforts, some 10,000 pairs of bald eagles inhabit the lower 48."[90]

Bald eagles are at the top of their food chain. They were accumulating DDT and other pesticides at an exponential rate, and the very future of this species hung in the balance. Once the DDT was gone, they returned. The same was true about a really interesting bird, the peregrine falcon. The fastest bird in the world, its pairs nest in the same eyrie year after year, with some eyries in continual use for centuries. Its stable population began to decline with the reproductive failure conclusively linked to the introduction and widespread use of DDT. Once that stopped, the stock recovered.

The fish did not fare so well. In the fall of 1963, Velsicol, the company that tried to thwart publication of Carson's book, was the cause of an enormous pesticide-poisoning disaster. One of its factories in Memphis leaked a deadly chemical that made its way down the Mississippi River, causing massive marine death and entering the New Orleans water supply. Five million fish were found floating belly-up while others were in convulsions, bleeding from the mouth and fins, because of endrin – an insecticide and rodenticide. It was a clear-cut case. Highly toxic and potentially deadly to all forms of life, endrin was finally banned in the United States in 1991.

On the effects of DDT on extended human exposure, we still don't have the answer. The respected medical journal *The Lancet* reported in 2000 that there was "no strong evidence for any associated cancer risk among people."[91] As the WHO observed in 2011: "While a wide range of effects [was] reported in laboratory animals, epidemiological data did not support these findings in humans."[92] Just as with global warming, the scientific debate on DDT rages on. Amir Attaran, a controversial Canadian legal academic (and a serious dissenter in his own right), estimates that the volume of DDT required to protect the entire at-risk population of a country like Guyana is equivalent to what only one farmer might spray on a large cotton farm.[93] The professor also points out that there is "not even one peer reviewed independently replicated study linking exposure to DDT with any adverse health outcome."[94]

It is worth noting that DDT is the most studied industrial chemical in the history of mankind. And not everyone agrees that it is harmless to humans. The American government says that DDT may be a carcinogen which persists in the environment, travels long distances in the upper atmosphere, and builds up in fatty tissues.[95] *National Geographic* reported in 2015 that women who were exposed to DDT while in the womb had a quadrupled risk of developing breast cancer.[96] Soon after, *Time* reported that the International Agency for Research on Cancer had concluded that DDT was "probably carcinogenic to humans."[97] (To be fair, many commonly eaten foods, like bread, would fall into that category. Bread contains naturally found acrylamide, a suspected carcinogenic. The world is filled with naturally occurring killer chemicals.) A study of more than 14,000 New York City women found that, on average, those diagnosed with breast cancer had 35 per cent more DDE in their blood than healthy women.[98] We may never know for sure if DDT causes cancer: it can be found in the fat tissues of every single person on earth. There is no uncontaminated population against which to measure its cancer-causing effects.

Clinical research and studies from all over the world have linked DDT to a wide range of medical problems: damaged reproductive systems and increased miscarriages, premature births, and low birth weights; disruptions in semen quality, menstruation, gestational length, and duration of lactation; greater chances of developmental problems, decreased cognitive skills, and babies with retarded psychomotor development; cancers of the liver, pancreas, and breast and contributions to leukemia, lymphoma, and testicular cancer; high blood pressure; and Alzheimer's disease. Some of these studies have not yet been replicated and published in double-blind peer-reviewed journals – the gold standard for scientific research. But when the *President's Cancer Panel Report* for 2008–09 was released, it could have been cribbed from Carson's book: it concluded that a growing body of evidence linked environmental exposures to cancer, and that "efforts to inform the public about such harmful exposures and how to prevent them must be increased."[99]

After *Silent Spring*, aesthetic environmentalism was no longer an option – concerned people united in their demands for effective regulation. And they did so, now understanding that chemicals were like radiation, that poisons did climb the food chain and became more concentrated on their journey, that chemical contamination can last a very long time and might even affect the genetic composition of the human race.

In response, the chemical industries organized against Carson, worried about the effect a vigorous regulatory regime would have on their marketing freedom and their profits. One company official admitted that if the public became "frightened," then "governments at all levels [would] push for unnecessarily increased regulation."[100] Keeping the government out of their business was their true agenda, and Carson was simply a convenient target. The Competitive Enterprise Institute "hopes that tarring an icon will help diminish support for future green laws."[101]

The truth is that many of Carson's enemies pretend to be interested in malaria victims in Africa. They are actually a stalking horse for a more important fight right at home: against a regulatory regime that constrains their activities and profits. There is also a collateral benefit. By discrediting Carson and her followers, and blaming them for millions of deaths, they are effectively painting all environmental concerns with the same wide brush, especially climate change (which like almost everything is a legitimate subject of debate and dissent). After Ronald Reagan became president of the United States, the entire regulatory apparatus designed to protect people from pesticides and other chemicals began to be rolled back, ostensibly to promote economic growth. In setting "safe" levels for a pesticide, the regulator now seeks to balance toxicity with economic benefit.

To say that President Reagan was uninformed about environmental issues would be something of an understatement. "Trees cause more pollution than automobiles," the president seriously claimed.[102] Once he occupied the Oval Office, the ties between regulator and regulated began to raise more questions than answers. "Essentially, what we have inherited," Vice-President Al Gore wrote in his introduction to the fiftieth anniversary edition of *Silent Spring*, "is a system of laws and loopholes, deadlines and delays, facades that barely disguise a wholesale failure of policy."[103]

Silent Spring definitely did not stop pollution. Pesticide use in agriculture has substantially increased since Carson's death, and the petrochemical industry is bigger and more profitable today than ever before. Too many increasingly toxic pesticides continue to be widely applied, hurting and injuring people (especially agricultural workers), insects, plants, and animals. (Many are less persistent than DDT, however.) Industry's response has not dramatically changed from the one given in 1962: "Industry men insist that that any damage to wildlife and humans has been a matter of 'accidents' or failure to follow directions on the label."[104] Ironically, while Carson was worried about the indiscriminate use of a few hundred products, there are now tens of thousands.

The United States exports pesticides that are illegal at home to other countries, and chemical spoliation is worldwide in extent: not only does Dow Chemical's napalm burn the flesh of our enemies in war but we've seen the blight of Love Canal in New York, Sydney Tar Ponds in Nova Scotia, the *Exxon Valdez* in Alaska, Agent Orange in Vietnam, and Bhopal in India – an endless list of indignities against people as well as the earth, ocean, and air. One of the most common herbicides for home use, 2, 4-D, has been linked to lymphoma. Dandelion-free lawns versus lymphoma?

"Future historians may well be amazed by our distorted sense of proportion," Carson wrote. "How could intelligent beings seek to control a few unwanted species by a method that contaminated the entire environment and brought the threat of disease and death even?"[105] When we poison the planet we poison ourselves, and we have no other planet to go to if we destroy this one.

Mutagenic agents were another issue that concerned Carson. In the early 1960s pesticide manufacturers were not required to test their products for genetic effects, but she was among the first to state that chemical toxicity infiltrated biology at cellular and molecular levels, bringing immediate and possible generational harm. Here, too, she may yet prove to be prophetic: speculative research indicates that DDT "has trans-generational effects in progeny and generations never directly exposed."[106]

Millions may have died because DDT was not properly used to fight mosquitoes carrying malaria, but it is not because of Carson (who would have welcomed targeted spraying to save lives alongside a search for non-toxic alternatives). Her central claim was that mass spraying was destroying the planet and many living creatures. This has been proven repeatedly. Carson deliberately linked radiation and pesticides for polemical purposes even though she knew both had their appropriate uses. Hospital X-rays and radiation treatments save people – and quite possibly prolonged Carson's own life. *Silent Spring* may have been wrong here and there, but Carson was right to demand that pesticides not be used without proper research and without appropriate safeguards in place. DDT was banned in the United States because it had become a public menace. Rachelwaswrong.com is wrong. Rachel was right.

In a world where entire fisheries collapse, where toxic wastes are dumped and wash up on our shores, where coral reefs – living organisms providing shelter and food for perhaps one-quarter of all ocean species – are dead and dying, where giant dead zones proliferate and expand in the oceans – the oxygen is gone and *nothing* lives – and where global warming threatens just about everything in its wake, Carson's message rings stronger and more true than ever before. Carson actually anticipated what is now referred to as the precautionary principle: in common parlance, it is "look before you leap." There is a social responsibility to protect the public and planet from harm from plausible risk with careful testing and informed use. But, like everything, this too is complicated.

Do some benefits outweigh theoretical or small risks? What to do about scientific uncertainty? Should the litmus test really be the worst-case scenario? How best to handle low-probability events, remote events, and speculative ones? A standard of "any risk" will never work, but what constitutes a negligible or even an acceptable risk? What is a safe standard, and by whom and how is it determined? By industry, by regulators, by environmental groups? The devil remains in the details.

Carson was truly subversive, but in a good way: she demolished the accepted consensus that industrial progress should be accepted unquestioningly, consequences be damned. Governmental officials and chemical-company spokesmen had all assured the public that DDT and the other pesticides in common use were safe. At the time, people trusted government; they believed that, when a regulatory authority approved a chemical or a drug, it was safe. After the thalidomide near miss, however, a lot of people came to realize that government and industry could not be relied on to be truthful. The general respect for authority – corporate and government – evaporated. Even Dwight D. Eisenhower, as he ended his term as US president, warned against the unwarranted influence by "the military-industrial complex" and urged all citizens to remain knowledgeable and alert – just as Carson did.

Without any doubt, Carson was an important and prescient democratizing force. She did not believe that science belonged to scientists; rather, scientists had an obligation to share what they knew directly with the public. She understood intuitively, perhaps because she was a woman challenging entrenched scientific and business interests dominated by men, that public education and engagement were the way to go. Once people had the facts – which they were entitled to – they could decide what was best.[107] Who, she asked, had the right to decide? Certainly not "the control men" or an "authoritarian temporary entrusted with power."[108]

The relationship between industry and government was another matter she criticized. "Who speaks? And why?"[109] Carson understood all too well that special interests with money often get their way. She expressed concern that industry did not just fund research but directed it too, corrupting the search for truth.

Still, because of what they do, scientists can see warning signs before anyone else, and they are the ones with the competence and expertise to identify problems, pitfalls, and solutions. Scientists, researchers, academics, policy institutes, and think-tanks all provide the evidence that society needs to make the very best public-policy decisions. Governments need to fund that work, but as we shall see, not control it for highly politicized and partisan purposes. Carson was, undoubtedly, one of the first in the 1960s to call for power to the people, although she never used those exact words.

When the editor of the *New York Times Book Review* asked Carson to explain what had made her book so popular, she pointed to delay: *Silent Spring* had been published two years later than planned, but the timing – writer, topic, audience – could not have been better. Public concern over thalidomide and atmospheric nuclear weapons testing had made it clear that humans were not the masters of the universe, or even of our planet. Carcinogenesis, mutagenesis, and teratogenesis actually threatened the human race, a triple whammy of radiation, pesticides, and dangerous drugs – none of these threats was hypothetical, they were all demonstrably real. In 1946 the *New Republic* published a story about a town sprayed with DDT: "Not a bird call broke the ominous quiet."[110] But no one was listening, not yet.

The year 1962 was the right time and right place – it was the start of a decade of huge social unrest and dissent. Carson caught a wave and she had help, including her publisher and the *New Yorker*, both "caretakers of the traditional American ideals of free expression and dissent."[111] Some saw *Silent Spring* as a book about death, but it was actually about life, and it contained a hopeful message: people can live peaceably with nature. Humans had unleashed a chemical barrage that threatened the fate of the earth, but there were other imaginative and creative approaches to the problem of sharing the planet with all living things. Observing that the easy way is not always the best, Carson pointed to a different future: Integrated Pest Management, for example, which she advocated, has become a serious alternative to chemical controls. She was open-minded to her core, and asked the same of the rest of us. And that is one of the reasons why her book has remained so relevant and so popular to this day.

There are striking comparisons between Frances Kelsey and Rachel Carson – an uncanny synchronicity in their lives, careers, courage, clearsightedness, and contributions. They were women, close in age, who pursued a scientific education and professional path at a time when few women did and the barriers were real (and continue to this day). Both were forged by the Depression and the need to support themselves, and they became respected public servants. Both were brave and stood up to bullies as they challenged received wisdom and authority – about a wonder drug and a wonder chemical. Kelsey, a Canadian, did it the old-fashioned way – understated, calmly, deliberately, confidently; Carson, an American, chose a muckraking route. Both called industries to account when, motivated by profit, they were not properly testing their products. Both believed that people were entitled to know about the risks of these products – and, for that, they faced fierce opposition, some of it downright ugly. We are forever changed because of Kelsey and Carson. They each proved that one lone dissenter can make a real and lasting difference.

Chapter 5

Dissenting Juries and Judges

Dissent really matters. Juries and judges can save lives – or try to – and sometimes they change our world.

Juries

The American constitution guarantees federal criminal defendants a jury trial. The Framers liked juries and the role they played in exonerating those who resisted English authority before the Revolution.[1] In Canada the situation is somewhat different. Under the Charter of Rights and Freedoms, a criminally accused is entitled to a jury trial only if the maximum punishment for the offence is five years or more. In both countries the evidence indicates that, in general, juries understand the facts and get things right – except, of course, when they do not. But very few cases in either country go before a jury. Most end up in some sort of plea.

In their landmark though now somewhat dated study, *The American Jury*, Harry Kalven, Jr and Hans Zeisel observed that, by and large, American juries are no longer at war with the law, as they were in the eighteenth century when they refused to convict in prosecutions for seditious libel, and in the 1920s when they were disinclined to enforce the Volstead Act – Prohibition.[2] Still, juries remain unlikely to vote to convict where they believe that prosecutions are selective or where widespread law-breaking is tolerated if not outright condoned by the authorities. They avoid convictions if they believe that the accused has already been punished enough, such as where the pre-conviction incarceration is sufficient for their crime, or if an apparent and significant discrepancy exists between the offence and the sentence.

Something like that happened in a case in Saskatchewan when canola farmer Robert Latimer killed his twelve-year-old daughter, Tracey, on 24 October 1993, while his wife and the other children were at church.

Tracey, a quadriplegic who functioned at the level of a three-month-old child, was born with cerebral palsy, could neither walk nor talk, and endured unrelenting, excruciating pain. She had five or six seizures a day, had to be spoon-fed, and needed round-the-clock care for every single activity of daily living. Her prognosis was hopeless, and heart wrenching.

Latimer placed her in the front of his truck and ran a pipe from the exhaust into the cab. He was criminally responsible for her death, and that is what the jury found, but it also recommended that he be eligible for parole after a year. The judge, however, had no discretion under the Criminal Code once Latimer was found guilty, and he imposed the minimum sentence of twenty-five years with no chance of parole for ten years (the mandatory sentence was Parliament's quid pro quo when the death penalty was abolished in Canada). The jury in the Latimer case wanted to do what it thought was the right thing – recommending a short sentence – but the law wouldn't allow it. The disposition was appealed and upheld. However, Chief Justice Edward Bayda dissented: he found the long sentence "cruel and unusual punishment."[3] Latimer was released on day parole in March 2008, to widespread public approval, although not everyone agreed. He had, after all, murdered his disabled child.

Juries do not like it when one co-accused appears to be receiving preferential treatment compared to a partner in crime, the beneficiary of a more lenient outcome. Improper police and prosecution tactics like entrapment often do not end well. It used to be that game-law crimes – hunting out of season, hunting with a flashlight, hunting without a licence – would rarely, and in some places never, result in a criminal conviction. The same is true with gambling. The conservation movement changed public attitudes to hunting somewhat, and tolerance for gaming violations is now of mostly historical interest, while legalized gambling brought an end to the numbers racket. Instead of being run by and for organized crime, gambling is now an important profit centre for the state (and First Nations).

Empirical jury research is impossible in Canada, where it is against the law for jurors to disclose anything about their deliberations. Research from other common law jurisdictions reveals, however, that jurors pay careful attention during trials and that their sequestered deliberations are a critical part of the process of reaching a verdict. The first vote usually predicts the final one, even though all jurors must come to their own verdicts. If most of them initially vote to convict, the jury usually ends up convicting; if most initially vote to acquit, an acquittal is almost always the final result. American social-studies research suggests that lone stand-outs eventually conform to the majority view.[4] But some don't.

In general, dissenting jurors have two options: they can convince the others or hang the jury.[5] When the latter happens, something interesting occurs. Faced with a deadlocked jury, the judge issues an "exhortation," the clear message of which is that the dissenters should reconsider. The pressure become enormous.

Many individual dissenters end up conforming (and making it home in time for dinner). It is hard to reconcile a juror's obligation to vote by conscience – disagreeing with the majority – and then acquiescing. Ultimately, only a small percentage of criminal juries are hung – unable to reach a final verdict – and the judge must then declare a mistrial.[6] To paraphrase Kalven and Zeisel, the hung jury is the jury system's second most interesting phenomenon: "In one sense it marks a failure of the system since it necessarily brings a declaration of mistrial in its wake. In another sense, it is a valued assurance of integrity, since it can serve to protect the dissent of a minority."[7]

Jury Nullification

The most interesting jury phenomenon is jury nullification – when the jury unanimously decides not to enforce the law, which jury members might have done in the Latimer case had they known they could. American juries do it regularly to avoid third-strike convictions that would lead to disproportionate and absurdly long custodial terms. The Supreme Court of Canada has made it clear that, although juries have that power, no one is allowed to tell them about it. Nevertheless, juries have been exercising this right since medieval times in all sorts of cases, and the practice came into stark relief in the early nineteenth century.

At that time England had more than 200 capital offences on the books – crimes where the penalty was death. The death penalty was one way of managing the social disruption that accompanied the Industrial Revolution. But juries refused to convict or convicted on a lesser offence until the capital list was reduced to murder and treason (and eventually the death penalty was abolished in the United Kingdom). Jury nullification, a completely conscientious repudiation of the death penalty, left the British Parliament with no choice but to change the law.[8]

The jury's job description is straightforward: listen to the evidence and arguments; apply the law as described by the judge during the instructions; and, after discussing the evidence, arguments, and the law, arrive at a unanimous decision. But everyone knows that jurors do more than that: they sometimes convict for the wrong reasons. Atticus Finch in *To Kill a Mockingbird* begged the jury to do their duty, yet they found Tom Robinson guilty when it was clear beyond a reasonable doubt that he was not. Harper Lee's Pulitzer Prize-winning novel was obviously make-believe, but the story she told was anything but. Race mattered then, and still does. Since the founding of the republic, American juries have frequently acquitted white defendants for racially motivated crimes even when faced with irrefutable evidence establishing their guilt.

Unjust Laws Will Not Be Enforced

In the predominantly French-speaking Roman Catholic province of Quebec, no jury would ever convict Dr Henry Morgentaler for performing abortions that were clearly illegal. Under Canadian law at the time, abortions had to be done in hospitals following approval from a special committee. Morgentaler was repeatedly arrested and brought to trial for owning and operating a private abortion clinic in Montreal – and each time he was acquitted. The last time, in 1976, it took the jury only an hour to file back into the courtroom and declare "not guilty." Jury nullification is an important form of dissent: juries will not enforce a law they consider unjust, and there is nothing anyone can do about it. Morgentaler was scheduled for a fourth trial but the government finally threw in the towel.

The rules in Canada and the United States are straightforward: lawyers and judges cannot tell jurors they can ignore the law. If it happens, it is spontaneous. A lawyer in one of the Morgentaler cases was criticized by the Supreme Court for mentioning the possibility. While not exactly a dirty secret, it is a secret nonetheless because most jurors do not know they possess the power to acquit even where all the legal elements of the offence have been established. Acquittals cannot be appealed in the United States, where the system of double jeopardy prevails, but they can in Canada if "legal errors" can be established.

That is what led to Dr Morgentaler's imprisonment in March 1975. The Court of Appeal sent him to jail. The law was later changed to prevent

Dr Henry Morgentaler. He repeatedly broke the law, and juries repeatedly refused to convict. (Credit: Chuck Mitchell/Canadian Press)

this from ever happening again by requiring appeal courts to order new trials, not custodial terms, in cases where they overturn a not-guilty jury verdict. The Supreme Court of Canada has instructed trial judges to take steps not just to avoid jury nullification but to ensure that the law is properly applied. The practical reality, however, as the court observed in a 2006 decision, is that juries have the power to refuse to follow the law "when their consciences permit no other course."[9] Jury nullification is said to be the citizen's ultimate protection against arbitrary government, overreaching legislators, oppressive laws, and selective enforcement of the law by overzealous law enforcement, ambitious prosecutors, and callous, partial judges. *The Camden 28* is a classic case on point.

It was the height of the Vietnam War – and the bad news kept on getting worse. President Richard Nixon promised peace with honour, but the deaths mounted as the war expanded into Cambodia. American college kids took to the streets, and when four of them were shot dead and nine wounded by Ohio National Guardsmen at Kent State University in May 1970, protests erupted across the country. By the end of December 1970, there were still 280,000 American troops in Vietnam, and when the president announced that the end was in sight, no one believed him. Public opinion had turned decidedly against the war as the casualties increased. (From beginning to end, more than 2 million civilians and about 1.5 million soldiers on both sides, including 57,939 Americans, lost their lives.[10])

A majority of Americans believed that the war in Vietnam was morally wrong, and dissent against it was made even more urgent after details of the massacre of Vietnamese civilians at My Lai emerged during the trial of Lieutenant William Calley, Jr in Fort Benning, Georgia. On 16 March 1968 Calley and most of his men – twenty-six soldiers in all – raped, mutilated, and murdered as many as 500 men, women, and children in a bloody rampage that the army promptly covered up. Still, President Nixon referred to the protestors as "bums blowing up campuses."

There was a little truth to that: in March 1971 the Weather Underground (or Weathermen) – a Marxist offshoot of the Students for a Democratic Society – ignited a bomb in the Capitol building to protest the American invasion of Laos. (The previous year they had issued a "Declaration of a State of War" against the US government.) That same month, Lieutenant Calley was found guilty of murdering twenty-two civilians and sentenced to life imprisonment with hard labour. In April, President Nixon ordered Calley released pending appeal, and he was eventually pardoned. Just like the five lepers who tried to stop the *Challenger* launch, the three servicemen who tried to halt the rampage were shunned and denounced.

In early April 1971 John Kerry, a decorated Navy veteran opposed to the war, testified before Congress. Forty-five thousand Americans had now died in Vietnam. Nationwide protests continued. Later that month, the Vietnam War Out Now rally on the National Mall in Washington attracted 200,000 peaceful protestors. In May, civil disobedience replaced peaceful protest. If the government would not stop the war, the protestors would stop the government. At least that was the plan: to shut down Washington by blocking major intersections and bridges. The government called in the troops, who began tear-gassing and arresting everyone in sight. So many were taken into custody that an emergency detention centre had to be set up next to the RFK Stadium for the more than 10,000 protestors placed under arrest in the largest mass apprehension in American history (less than 100 were eventually convicted of very minor crimes and misdemeanours).

In June the *New York Times* began publication of the "Pentagon Papers." Americans learned that four presidents – Harry S. Truman, Dwight D. Eisenhower, John F. Kennedy, and Lyndon B. Johnson – had lied to them about US intentions and actions. And then, very early in the morning on Sunday, 22 August 1971, twenty-eight men and women gathered outside the federal office building in Camden, New Jersey.

They were a rag-tag group of mostly left-wing Roman Catholic blue-collar workers, hippies, students, nuns, and priests. Their plan was to break into the draft-board offices, search for Class 1-A status records (the lists of young men next to be drafted for overseas military service), and destroy them. But one of the conspirators was on the FBI payroll, and soon enough FBI agents swooped in as the group went about its work. Facing more than forty years in jail, the twenty-eight chose to be tried together, determined to turn the proceedings into a public referendum on the war.

The informer, however, had a change of heart. His deal with the FBI was that no one would face jail time. Instead of cooperating with the government, he went to work for the defence. His evidence conclusively established that it was the FBI that encouraged, funded, and helped to plan the operation, even providing the two-way radios the group used to communicate with each other. With obvious encouragement from the judge – "If you find that the overreaching participation by Government agents or informers in the activities as you have heard them was so fundamentally unfair to be offensive to the basic standards of decency, and shocking to the universal sense of justice, then you may acquit the defendants"[11] – the jury knew exactly what to do. Even though the twenty-eight had committed multiple crimes, acquittals were awarded in every single instance despite incontrovertible evidence that they had done most of the very unlawful things they were accused of.

Juries are sometimes like that. They will stand up to the prosecution and the state for things big and small and, simply put, ignore the law. In Britain, Stephen Owen's twelve-year-old child, Darren, was killed by a degenerate career criminal named Kevin Taylor in a hit and run – he ran over the child's head before speeding off in his lorry. He received an eighteen-month sentence for his crime and served twelve months. At his trial, Taylor swore at the family and, following his release, he vandalized Darren's grave. Owen, driven to the brink of suicide after losing his business and probably his mind, took matters into his own hands and wounded Taylor with a sawn-off double-barrelled shotgun. He was charged with attempted murder. But when the jury delivered a not-guilty verdict, hundreds of well-wishers cheered outside the court.

Likewise, a 1962 jury in Belgium took matters into its own hands when Suzanne Vandeput-Coipel killed her week-old daughter, Corinne. Suzanne had taken thalidomide during her pregnancy, and Corinne was born with misshapen hands growing from her shoulders. Dr Jacques Casters had prescribed the thalidomide; now he prescribed a strong dose of barbiturates, and Suzanne mixed them with milk and honey and fed them to the newborn. Mother, doctor, and several others were charged with murder. No one denied anything. After less than two hours of deliberations, the jurors were back with their verdict: not guilty. The acquitted emerged from the courtroom to be greeted by cheering from a huge crowd.[12] Sometimes the jury just does what it wants, regardless of the law and the evidence heard, and reflects community values.

But Sometimes Community Values Are a Problem

In reflecting community values, many juries have, and continue to, dispense injustice. An all-white jury convicted the Scottsboro Boys – nine African American youth falsely accused of raping two white women in 1931 – in an absolute rush to judgment. Another all-white jury, after an hour's deliberation, found Roy Bryant and J.W. Milam not guilty after they abducted, brutally tortured, and murdered fourteen-year-old African American Emmett Louis Till, dumping his body in the Tallahatchie River. He had dared to speak to a white woman, Bryant's wife, and perhaps even flirted with her. After the acquittal, Bryant and Milam sold their story to a journalist. They had never meant to kill the boy, only to frighten him, they explained, knowing they could never be retried for their crime. But they had to kill him when he refused to beg for mercy.

Viola Liuzzo was a white woman who answered Dr Martin Luther King's call for people of all faiths to help the civil-rights movement in the American South. In March 1965 she was shot dead by the Ku Klux Klan. Even eyewitness testimony from an FBI informant who was there was insufficient to secure a guilty verdict. The first trial ended in a mistrial, and the second in an acquittal from the all-white jury. Meanwhile, J. Edgar Hoover, anxious to divert attention from the FBI's bungling and conniving, leaked lies to the press that Liuzzo, a thirty-nine-year-old married, church-going mother of five, was actually a drug addict who was having sexual intercourse with the nineteen-year-old African American man who was with her when she was murdered.

The one common denominator in these three cases was that the juries were entirely white men and, to them, race governed their verdicts. Almost certainly, these verdicts reflected prevailing community values too – of their white community. As jury mix began to change, so did outcomes. But not necessarily, as the trial of Orenthal James "O.J." Simpson vividly demonstrated.

There is no question that on 12 June 1994 O.J. murdered his ex-wife and her friend Ronald Goldman. The evidence was incontrovertible and irrefutable. The DNA evidence directly linking Simpson to these crimes could not have been planted, and O.J., a serial wife beater, as they used to call it, with motive, opportunity, and no alibi, was, on the evidence tendered in court, the man responsible. The defence team – half celebrity, half talent – had no choice but to construct an alternative reality that pandered entirely to race – a narrative they pitched to a jury composed almost entirely of African Americans. O.J., they argued, was the victim of a massive, detailed, far-ranging conspiracy to frame the former football star for a crime he did not commit.

True, there was ample evidence of racism in the Los Angeles Police Department (LAPD), and one known racist police officer had been involved in the O.J. investigation. Detective Mark Fuhrman had been caught lying when he denied on the witness stand that he referred to African Americans as "niggers." For good measure, he was also caught on tape bragging about planting evidence, administering beatings, and harassing female police officers. Even the prosecutor, Marcia Clark, condemned him. "Is he a racist?" she asked the jurors in her final address, then answered that question and others: "Yes. Is he the worst LAPD has to offer? Yes. Do we wish the LAPD had never hired him? Yes. In fact, do we wish there were no such persons on the planet? Yes."[13]

It might have been more productive if she had focused her attention on the compelling evidence proving that O.J. was the killer. The prosecution, while committed and well meaning, was beyond inept, and the defence succeeded in turning the tables – it was a classic end run – and putting the police on trial.

In his final summation, the talented O.J. attorney Johnnie Cochran told the jury it was time to bring the LAPD to account. Fuhrman, he told the jurors, was a "genocidal racist, a perjurer, America's worst nightmare, the personification of evil." Something had to be done. "Who, then, polices the police?" he asked. "You police the police. You police them by your verdict."[14]

The jury began their deliberations at 9:16 a.m. on 2 October 1995. The first straw poll was ten for acquittal, two for conviction. There were nine African American jurors, one Hispanic, and two Caucasians. One of the two white jurors, Anise Aschenbach, a sixty-one-year-old retired Southern California gas clerk – the defence team called her "The Demon" – spoke up and criticized Cochran: "He wants us to send the LAPD a message. Does he think we're so stupid that we're going to send a message rather than decide based on what we heard in this case? I hope I was not the only one offended by his remarks." Well, that is exactly what Cochran thought, and, as it turned out, she was indeed the only one offended.

After "deliberating" for less than two hours, the standout caved despite her reservations, and the jurors unanimously voted to acquit. After their verdict was announced, and they were filing out of the courtroom, one of the African American jurors turned to O.J. and raised his fist in a Black Power salute. Another African American juror openly admitted what had happened: "We've got to protect our own," Carrie Bess announced. The same result had happened – the guilty went free – when in 1992 the almost all-white jury acquitted four accused and guilty LAPD officers who had mercilessly beat Rodney King, even though their crimes were captured in living colour on video. Days of riots followed.

The Ideal Juror

Mostly, though, juries try to do the right thing, although, like other groups, they sometime get it badly wrong. They say yes or no but never give reasons why until, in the aftermath of the more famous trials, they sell their stories and write their books – except in Canada. The ideal is "Davis," juror number 8 in *Twelve Angry Men*, the classic film noir where the architect played by Henry Fonda turned a hung jury into one that acquitted a young man on trial for the murder of his father. "What do we do now?" one of the jurors asks after the first vote, 11–1 to convict. "I guess we talk," juror number 8 responds. The imaginary jurors then begin to assess the evidence – and each other. As some of the underlying motivations unrelated to the case are hinted at and others exposed, and as the evidence is thoroughly reviewed, a consensus of not guilty beyond a reasonable doubt is achieved – and they acquit.

The jury is here to stay, but social media presents its challenges. Even when instructed otherwise, jurors Google their case. That is what people do when they are looking for information. In addition to creating opportunities for mischief, this reality – only in exceptional cases are juries sequestered throughout the trial – may also lead to a complete rethink of publication bans and *voir dires*. It will, inevitably, lead to jurors finding about nullification. What happens when information about that gets out – long advocated by some criminal law reformers – is anyone's guess.[15] The Fully Informed Jury Association, established in the United States in 1989, seeks to increase public awareness of the jury's nullification powers. It is inconceivable that it will stay secret for long. In the meantime, social media is already having an impact.

In one widely publicized incident, a juror sent a Facebook friend request to a witness. Others have been caught tweeting, blogging, and texting each other during the proceedings. The Brooklyn schoolteacher who wanted to get to know the firefighter witness expressed regret: "I should not have done that."[16] But no one should be surprised that she did. Social media has disrupted social barriers. The very idea that someone sitting on a dais gets to decide what you see and hear, and what you don't, sounds ridiculous to a generation accustomed to looking into things for themselves, and that can mean reading the news story, watching the video, and, if really interested, taking a look at all the source documents. Besides, how reasonable is it really, in this day and age, to expect people to sit still for days and just *listen*?

Dissenting Judges

Jeannette Vivian Corbiere was a Canadian "Indian," a registered member of the Wikwemikong band, until 11 April 1970, when she married David Lavell, a non-Indian. On 7 December of that year, Canada's Department of Indian Affairs sent Mrs Lavell, as the courts invariably referred to her, a notice. She was no longer an Indian, and her name had been deleted from the register. She protested. Loss of status had many meanings for her, some intangible, some not. She could no longer reside on her northern Ontario Manitoulin Island reserve or inherit family property, and her children would not be Indians. She could not receive treaty benefits, participate in band council, and be buried in a cemetery with her ancestors. This change in status was completely unfair for all sorts of reasons immediately obvious to us today. Even back then, it made no sense. It was completely discriminatory. When a male Indian married a non-Indian, he not only retained his Indian status but could confer it on his spouse.

When Mrs Lavell took the case to trial, Judge B.W. Grossberg could not seem to understand any of the issues before him (Grossberg knew every single rule of civil procedure and nothing else). Surely she had been *advantaged* by the administrative action? the judge suggested. The case eventually made its way to the Supreme Court of Canada, where in 1973 the majority dismissed the appeal. It also considered a parallel case where an Indian band had expelled an Indian woman from her reserve because she had married a non-Indian. Equality before the law, in the majority view, meant equal application of the law, and that law, providing for loss of status for Indian women who married non-Indians, had been on the books for a hundred years. Accordingly, the judges ruled, nothing was amiss.

There was a dissent. One judge in particular, Bora Laskin, had a different view about equality before the law. The 1960 Canadian Bill of Rights prohibited discrimination on the basis of race, national origin, colour, religion, and sex. As far as Laskin was concerned, one could not "leap over" these words in order to explain away and justify discrimination by invoking other words – "equality before the law" – and assigning them a narrow, technical meaning. He could not and would not countenance either the "statutory excommunication of Indian women" or their "statutory banishment."[17] Appeals to history, of always doing things this way or that, were of no assistance.[18] Laskin managed to persuade two of his colleagues to sign on to his dissent.

Being on the outside looking in was nothing new for Bora Laskin – a most unlikely judge on the Supreme Court of Canada. Born on 5 October 1912 in what is now Thunder Bay, Laskin was a brilliant student – a gold medalist at both Osgoode Hall and Harvard Law School. When he returned to Toronto, he could not find a job. Toronto was Orange,

intolerant, and WASP, and Jewish law students had a tough go. He per-
severed, obtained a teaching post, became a distinguished academic, and,
in 1965, was appointed to the Ontario Court of Appeal. Five years later,
Prime Minister Pierre Elliott Trudeau appointed him to the Supreme
Court of Canada, the first Jew on that court, and three years after that
Trudeau shocked the legal establishment when he named Laskin, the second most junior judge on the bench, as Canada's chief justice. Only the
second Supreme Court judge with a public profile (after Ivan Rand), he
was not only the court conscience but a liberal, a loner, and a civil libertarian. Laskin's most famous dissent – one where he stood alone – was
in *Murdoch v. Murdoch*.

Times were changing in Canada, the United States, and all through
the West as the woman's movement found legs. In Canada the Divorce
Act was amended to allow no-fault divorce after a three-year separation.
The divorce rate skyrocketed as both men and women escaped their
unhappy unions. In 1967 – Canada's centennial, when gender equality
and everything seemed possible – the government appointed a Royal Commission on the Status of Women. Celebrations were centred in Montreal,
the coolest city in the country and the logical location for a world fair,
Expo '67. Canadians were proud of their country and optimistic about
their shared future.

Pierre Berton, the popular and populist historian, called 1967 the "Last
Good Year." He was wrong about that – Canadian progress continues –
but troubles were brewing as the country adjusted to massive social
change, some peaceful, some not, especially bombings by the Front de
libération du Québec throughout the decade and the 1970 October Crisis, when separatist terrorists kidnapped the British high commissioner
and murdered a provincial minister. The federal government invoked the
War Measures Act, flooding Montreal with Canadian soldiers. It succeeded in crushing the separatists, bringing an end to their apprehended
insurrection, and forcefully demonstrating once again that the Canadian
state will never tolerate violence in support of political change.

Across the country in Alberta, a different battle was under way. After
Irene Florence Nash and James Alexander "Alex" Murdoch married in
1943, they built a large ranching operation. Irene raised their son, worked
the ranch, and, with an inheritance, may have monetarily contributed to
its expansion. The marriage proved rocky, probably because Alex was a
wife beater. One day they were arguing over property and he broke her

jaw in three places, causing permanent paralysis to her lip and jaw. When she was discharged from hospital, she found the ranch locked and her credit at the local store cut off. She took work as a cleaning lady to supplement the paltry monthly stipend a local magistrate ordered. In 1968 she reluctantly went to court and demanded her half of all their property.

At the time, the doctrine of "separate property" was in force. The ranch was in Alex Murdoch's name. Irene could get her share only if she could prove that she had made a contribution to its acquisition or maintenance, and that the title holder had agreed she shared in the assets. At the Supreme Court of Canada, all of the judges but one readily agreed with the trial judge's finding that Irene's contribution was just "what the average farm wife did."

But the evidence before the court established that Irene did much more than average "wife's work." She raised their son, worked in the fields, operated farm machinery, helped build the farmhouse, and operated everything while Alex was away for about five months a year. Whether Irene had financially contributed at all to the purchase of the property was somewhat sketchy. The majority dismissed her application. Their view was that possession was ten-tenths of the law. As such, she got nothing – not a knife, not a spoon, not even a kitchen fork. The eight old men on the court would not take away property from Mr Murdoch and give it to his Missus.

Once again, Justice Laskin dissented.[19] "The wife's contribution, in physical labour at least, to the assets amassed in the name of the husband can only be characterized as extraordinary," Laskin's dissent began.[20] For about twenty-five years until things fell apart, Alex and Irene worked together to accumulate everything they had, everything that Alex now claimed exclusively for himself on the basis that there was no proof of any formal agreement otherwise. However, according to Laskin, no written document was needed to create a "constructive trust" – a legal superstructure that the court could impose where justice required it, one that operated to prevent unjust enrichment by the husband. Why should Alex benefit exclusively from Irene's labour? The legislature, Laskin observed, should act to ensure the fair distribution of marital assets.

Although that was the "better way," it was not the "only way." As Laskin's biographer observed, "the decision illustrates both Laskin's creativity and his sense of restraint. By employing an existing doctrine in a new context to redress a perceived injustice, Laskin innovated within parameters well understood in the common law."[21] He might have looked across the pond as he struggled to find a solution. At the same time as *Murdoch* was before the Supreme Court, the English Court of Appeal was looking at a factually similar case and had no difficulty in unanimously agreeing to apply a constructive trust.[22] On closer examination, Laskin's dissent had embodied within it some serious limitations. It applied only to extraordinary labour, not "housekeeping," and that considerably narrowed its general application. But it was, nevertheless, a major step forward.

Sometimes a judge just cannot stand by. The constructive trust, easily understood by anyone, had (limited) practical effect but significant symbolic power as a remedial instrument for the redress of injustice. The fact that a judge of the Supreme Court valued a woman's labour was, for the time, a breakthrough. It also inspired a generation of feminist academics: "It was the Murdoch case that brought paid versus unpaid work, productive and reproductive labor and their value (or lack thereof) to the forefront of scholarly attention."[23]

In a democracy, judges do have something to add to the development of public policy. As Alexis de Tocqueville perceptively observed in 1835, "there is hardly a political question … which does not sooner or later turn into a judicial one" and vice versa. Within a decade of Laskin's dissent, every single jurisdiction in Canada declared marriage a partnership with deemed equal contributions by husband and wife, no matter who had done or paid for what. On dissolution, then, there should be an equal distribution of the matrimonial assets acquired during the marriage. Laskin's dissent would, in a few years, be adopted by the Supreme Court as the majority point of view. (For speed, nothing beats *Cary v. Curtis* where Justice Joseph Story's dissent was enacted into law by Congress in *36 days*.[24])

Paradoxically, Irene Murdoch regretted going to court. When she eventually received a divorce settlement representing about 25 per cent of the value of the ranch she had worked so hard to build, she told *Chatelaine* magazine: "I am sorry to have started it. It did more harm than good." She foresaw "three-generation farms falling into the grasp of greedy teenage brides who might win half their husband's land in a divorce settlement."[25] These fears were completely unjustified, and Irene later repudiated the remarks.

By any measure, however, she helped launch a sea change in Canadian attitudes about the role and rights of women. Her story took on a life of its own, coming at the right time and in the right place. The Canadian people could identify with the plight of this white woman who had worked so hard, in complete contrast, of course, to the injustice meted out to Mrs Lavell that barely registered on the middle-class radar but was increasingly a topic of conversation in the emerging feminist community. The legitimate aspirations of Canada's First Nations would have to wait many more years to be acknowledged and still remain unfulfilled.

Sometimes being brave pays off. Laskin believed that his dissents in *Lavell* and *Murdoch* were major factors in his appointment as chief justice. They pointed presciently to the future, which gradually took shape on the foundations he had laid. Laskin cared about context and recognized that law was a living and purposive social force – an approach that was completely in tune with Canadian Prime Minister Pierre Trudeau's vision of a just society.

An Appeal to the Future

One of the most famous dissents of all time is found in an 1896 case called *Plessy v. Ferguson*. In 1890 the state of Louisiana passed the Separate Car Act: it provided for "separate but equal" white railway cars and black railway cars. It was all part of a pattern throughout the southern states to separate and subordinate African Americans in all aspects of their lives.

Louisiana was a racial hodgepodge, and a group of concerned citizens had no difficulty in finding someone to challenge the law (something the railway company did not even want on economic grounds because it forced them to purchase additional cars). This group called Homer Plessy an "octoroon" – he was of seven-eighths European descent and one-eighth African – and government officials classified him as black. When he went to take his seat in the first-class section of a white car, where he had bought a ticket, he was arrested.

The American constitution guarantees equal protection under the law. The question to be answered by the US Supreme Court was whether segregated railway cars could be equal. Relying on precedents – notably the 1883 civil-rights cases where the Supreme Court gutted remedial

legislation prohibiting discrimination by individuals and organizations
– the majority said yes. Whatever equal protection meant, it was never
"intended to abolish distinctions based upon color, or to enforce social,
as distinguished from political, equality, or a comingling of the two races
unsatisfactory to either." The words "separate but equal" appear nowhere
in the majority judgment, but the "Court's ruling approved legally
enforced segregation so long as the law did not make facilities for blacks
'inferior' to those of whites."[26] Needless to say, while the railway cars
were definitely separate, they were in no way equal. One judge, John
Marshall Harlan, disagreed.

> ... in view of the Constitution, in the eye of the law, there is in
> this country no superior, dominant, ruling class of citizens. There
> is no caste here. Our Constitution is color-blind, and neither knows
> nor tolerates classes among citizens. In respect of civil rights, all
> citizens are equal before the law ... the destinies of the two races,
> in this country, are indissolubly linked together, and the interests
> of both require that the common government of all shall not per-
> mit the seeds of race hate to be planted under the sanction of law.
> What can more certainly arouse race hate, what more certainly
> create and perpetuate a feeling of distrust between these races,
> than state enactments, which, in fact, proceed on the ground that
> colored citizens are so inferior and degraded that they cannot be
> allowed to sit in public coaches occupied by white citizens? That,
> as all will admit, is the real meaning of such legislation as was
> enacted in Louisiana.

Justice Harlan, an immense Kentuckian, standing 1.9 metres and
weighing over 109 kilograms, was a former slaveholder. Although he
was a creature of his time and place and would remain a racist his entire
life, he was capable of real personal growth. Slavery, he came to believe,
was an enemy that had to be vanquished. When he became a Supreme
Court judge, he swore to uphold the constitution. The majority's ruling,
he said, put "the brand of servitude and degradation upon a large class
of our fellow citizens, our equals before the law." It was sure to stimu-
late brutal aggression toward African Americans and worsen conflict
between equal Americans.[27] Simply put, segregation statutes were "en-

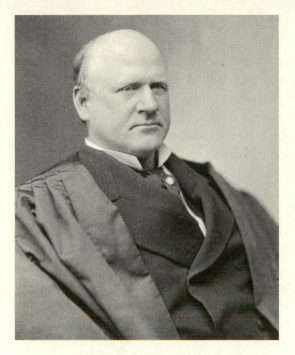

John Marshall Harlan. The American constitution, he wrote, was "color blind." His was a lonesome dissent, but one that accurately predicted decades of brutality against African Americans. (Credit: Brady-Handy Collection, Library of Congress)

acted for the purpose of humiliating citizens of the United States of a particular race."[28] They should not stand. But Harlan's opinion was a lonesome dissent.

Everything Justice Harlan predicted in *Plessy* came to pass – although no one could have foreseen the full extent of the brutality that was to follow – and the loser was the American people. Jim Crow, with all its meanness and cruelty, soon entrenched racial discrimination in American life, legitimized by the country's highest court.

Separate can never mean equal, and the *Plessy* decision encouraged the worst individual and community instincts and manifestations of private and state racism, in employment, segregated schools, housing, water fountains, and every aspect of daily life for African American citizens across the land. "Great Supreme Court dissents lie like buried ammunition for future generations to unearth when the time comes," Kathleen Sullivan, Stanford Law School's distinguished dean, once wrote.[29] Harlan's dissent stayed largely forgotten until the middle of the twentieth century, when the Supreme Court "began to undo the legacy of apartheid … against which Harlan had protested."[30]

Ironically, Harlan's simple phrase "our Constitution is color-blind, and neither knows nor tolerates classes among citizens" became the rallying cry for conservatives fighting affirmative action.[31] Harlan, of course, knew that the United States and its constitution were not colour-blind – the words were entirely aspirational and affirmative-action pro-grams would have been as foreign to him as man landing on the moon. Still, as the pre-eminent legal historian Melvin Urofsky observes, "few, if any, dissents in the Court's history, and few phrases, have had an impact on the constitutional dialogue comparable to that of Justice Har-lan in *Plessy*."[32]

In 1954 – more than sixty years later – the issue came back before the US Supreme Court. The courts can hold out for a while, but eventually judges have no choice but to make peace with society. When Oliver Brown unsuccessfully attempted to enroll his eight-year-old daughter Linda in the nearby public school, the answer was a categorical no. Instead, Linda had to leave home at 7:40 each morning, walk through a dangerous rail-switching yard, then wait for a bus to drive her to a seg-regated school.

Brown's case, along with a number of others, proceeded together to the Supreme Court, where the separate-but-equal doctrine was sure to be reversed because it was demonstrably untrue. Earl Warren, the chief justice, was determined to cobble together a unanimous opinion and resis-ted pressure from President Dwight Eisenhower to do otherwise. When the president invited him to a private dinner at the White House to explain that southern whites, rather than being bad people, were simply con-cerned about "their sweet little girls" being required "to sit in school alongside some big overgrown Negroes,"[33] Warren took a different view. Segregation was harmful to the republic, he argued, and unanimity on the issue was critical.

He was right: it was imperative that the court speak with a single voice as it moved to right a social evil. Unanimity has its place, provided all the judges truly agree. But they are not given independence to be lazy, timid, or fall into line. The job of a judge is to decide the case as each one thinks fit and it is critical in a democracy that the public see them doing exactly that.

Warren was no legal genius – but he had something much more impor-tant: excellent judgment. He also knew the difference between right and wrong, and he had sufficient respect and leadership ability to close the ranks and send a clear, unified message to the country and the world. He insisted that his colleagues take another look at Harlan's dissent: sepa-

Linda Brown. She had to take a bus to a segregated school far from her home, instead of attending the local school four blocks away. In *Brown v. Board of Education*, the US Supreme Court ruled that separate can never be equal. (Credit: AP Photo)

rate-but-equal institutionalized racism hurt the American people, white and black, he argued. "To separate [African-American children] from others of similar age and qualifications solely because of their race generates a feeling of inferiority as to their status in the community that may affect their hearts and minds in a way unlikely ever to be undone."[34]

This was not stirring prose, and it was far from poetry, but even the hardest heart could not help but be moved. Warren's heroic efforts to achieve unanimity, another famous US Supreme Court judge, Antonin Scalia, later observed, "helped to produce greater public acceptance."[35] *Brown v. Board of Education* was actually a two-part decision. In part one, the court held that separate can never be equal, and in part two it ordered segregated public schools to desegregate "with all deliberate speed." Compliance was another matter, and the decision set the stage for truly epic civil-rights battles to come. Notably, as Warren regretfully observed in his memoirs, "no word of support for the decision emanated from the White House."[36]

Judicial dissents are controversial. "A dissent in a court of last resort," US Chief Justice Charles Evans Hughes wrote, "is an appeal to the brooding spirit of the law, to the intelligence of a future day, when a later decision may possibly correct the error into which the dissenting judge believes the court to have been betrayed."[37] Not all dissents embody great wisdom or refute the errors of fellow judges. Most of the time the majority has got it right, and the dissenter is wrong. Still, as Benjamin Cardozo, a truly meritorious judge elevated by Herbert Hoover to the US Supreme Court, observed about dissenters: "Their eyes are fixed on the eternities."[38]

Justice Oliver Wendell Holmes, though he was among the greatest of all modern-day dissenters, called dissents "useless" and "undesirable," and Justice Potter Stewart said they were "subversive literature."[39] The current chief justice of the United States, John G. Roberts, has declared that dissents are a symptom of judicial dysfunction and that the court should speak with one voice. Many judges agree with him. Moreover, in civil-law legal systems, disagreement among appellate judges is never mentioned. Cases are always decided with one voice. That is also true under tyrannies of both the right and the left.

Why Judges Dissent

Judicial dissents serve many purposes. Judges dissent for the same reasons that Joan Didion wanted to write – to say listen to me, see it my way, change your mind, and do the right thing.[40] In previous years, formalism reigned in our courts: judges searched for the correct answer by applying established legal principles to the facts (and courts of equity were developed to help undo some of the damage). This doctrine of precedent, called *stare decisis*, delivered predictable results.

Of course, the law is not always determinate, and the right answer is sometimes elusive. Even so, society expects courts to settle controversy, not create it. Judicial disagreement reflects social division. As Justice Louis Brandeis explained, "In most matters it is more important that the applicable rule of law be settled than it be settled right."[41] He allowed, though, that in some cases precedent was insufficient: "In cases involving the Federal Constitution," he wrote, "where correction through legislative action is practically impossible, this Court has often overruled its earlier decisions. The Court bows to the lessons of experience and the force of better reasoning."[42] The Framers never intended that the US constitution be frozen in 1787 – after all, they provided for an amendment process. Whether that is a job for a judge is, of course, an entirely different matter.

Accordingly, the battles seeking constitutional change are the most hotly contested in the courts, the ones where dissent matters most.

The role of a supreme court in a democracy is to resolve authoritatively major questions of national law, all the while providing legal leadership to the lower courts. Supreme court judges in Canada, the United States, at the House of Lords in the United Kingdom, and throughout the common law world caucus after they hear a case. This deliberative process – a dialogue between equal individuals – confers legitimacy on the court. Unlike in the House of Commons or other legislative bodies, where votes are "whipped," judges are bound by their oath of office to reach their own independent decisions. Every member of the panel hearing a case is expected to participate in determining its outcome. In this way the judicial function is a reflection and extension of the democratic process. When judges do not agree, they can dissent.

While the deliberations take place in secrecy, dissents open a window on what occurred and how the final result was reached. They provide political legitimacy, lending authority to the court by demonstrating that the judges have considered different ideas and a wide range of possible outcomes. Dissents are a form of accepted disobedience: judges are protesting within their institutional roles. Moreover, dissents connect judges and judicial dialogue over time, allowing new generations to see how earlier ones grappled with similar problems.

Harlan's dissent in *Plessy* was, however, more than that. It served as the court's conscience, calling out to future generations that would, eventually, respond to ethical principles of fairness and equality. Dissenters attempt to persuade their colleagues that there is a better way. While the conversation about the particular case is generally rooted in something that happened in the past, the purpose of the exercise is to grapple with the future. Brandeis usually knew when to dissent and when not to. His dissents were often tactical, to secure ameliorating amendments and alterations in a majority's draft. If the majority opinion was narrowly confined and unlikely to cause future harm, Brandeis would discard his dissent (although a volume of his "unpublished" opinions was published posthumously).

Judges argue, cajole, attempt to persuade, and, if on the losing side, do whatever they can to limit the damage. Dissents stir debate: they make the majority more accountable by requiring them to address concerns and, in doing so, show the world how they got to a particular result. Smart and conscientious judges like it when their colleagues dissent: there is nothing better, US Supreme Court Justice Ruth Bader Ginsburg wrote, than an impressive dissent. By engaging with it, a majority opinion is clarified and refined.[43] Inadequacies and inaccuracies are exposed as the majority's view is strengthened. "You never see the best points the dissent makes," US Supreme Court Justice Stephen Breyer observes, "because they've been written out of the majority opinion, so there is no need to make that dissenting point anymore."[44] Judges look at their colleagues' dissents and address them, making them moot. Even the prospect of a possible dissent makes the majority drafter more amenable to reasonable revision.

Unanimous judgments raise questions. Because only the most difficult and troubling cases come before courts of last resort, there is something inherently suspect when every single judge at a supreme court agrees. The exceptions are those occasional cases of overriding national importance where it is imperative to have no ambiguity about the decision reached. Occasionally judges change their minds and a dissent morphs into a majority. That happens rarely, and for good reason. The majority usually gets it right, and the dissent is wrong – it has little impact and is soon forgotten. We venerate the great dissenters because they were vindicated in the end. For the most part, though, the majority blazes the law's trail, securing and advancing basic rights and fundamental freedoms. At least in Canada, judicial majorities have ensured that the constitution remains purposeful, alive, and responsive so it can change over time while still acknowledging and remaining faithful to its original intentions.

In the famous *Persons Case* of 1929, for example, the Judicial Committee of the Privy Council in the United Kingdom, then Canada's highest court of appeal, ruled that the word "persons" in Canada's constitution, while originally limited to men, should be interpreted to include women. The ruling opened the door to women being appointed to the Canadian Senate, and was justified because the constitution was "a living tree capable of growth and expansion within its natural limits."[45] Times change, and the Supreme Court usually keeps up, reflecting contemporary moral and social realities. But when it doesn't, when it fails to deliver, dissent matters.

Correcting Mistakes

In November 1935 two well-behaved Jehovah's Witness children were expelled for insubordination from their Minersville, Pennsylvania, public school for refusing to salute the American flag. The salute in question was exactly the same one used by the Nazis – a straight arm out. Lillian Gobitis was taunted and assaulted by her classmates; her little brother Billy's teacher grabbed his arm and tried to force him to salute.

Jehovah's Witnesses put conscience first, regarding themselves as members of God's Kingdom, not man's. They pay taxes but refuse to vote. They will not salute national flags, bow down to graven images, or serve in armies. As the Jehovah's Witnesses describe it, they "live in this world, but are not a part of it."

When the Gobitis case got to the Supreme Court in 1940, their counsel argued that the flag-salute requirement violated their constitutional rights, including freedom of religion. At all the previous trials the different judges had concluded that prescribing patriotism was hardly a reasonable approach to instilling loyalty and teaching civics. It served no public purpose. The majority of the Supreme Court, however, took a different view.

Felix Frankfurter, a former Harvard law professor and civil libertarian, had recently been appointed to the court by Franklin D. Roosevelt. He was assigned the task of writing the majority opinion, and he was determined to make an immediate impact. Although he privately conceded that the Minersville authorities were "foolish and perhaps worse" in imposing flag saluting, he held to his belief in judicial restraint unless there was a clear constitutional violation and concluded that the local school authorities were legally entitled to act as they did. The court, Frankfurter believed, should defer to the wisdom of the legislature (the school). The Supreme Court had previously validated compulsory flag salutes – and it did so again here. Justice Harlan Stone disagreed. Precedent is important, he said, but not when core values, constitutional values, come into play.

A conservative and former Republican, Stone, as a member of the presidential board of review for conscientious-objector status during the First World War, had been deeply disturbed about the treatment meted out to true religious objectors. In his sole dissent, he observed that options other than expulsion had been available which did not infringe on the religious liberties of this "small and helpless minority." No government could compel public affirmations that violated the religious conscience of these children. If the court had subjected the local ordinance to a searching judicial scrutiny, it would have become apparent that very minor adjustments could have been made to allow the children to continue to attend school, and there was no justification for the expulsions. Religious faith had, after all, "been thought worthy of constitutional protection."[46]

Once mandatory flag saluting had been countenanced by the country's highest court, the way was opened to persecute Jehovah's Witnesses everywhere. Unless you compel your children to salute the flag, one judge told other parents, I will take them away from you "and place them in an institution where they would be taught to understand what Americanism really is." Numerous children were actually removed from their homes and sent to state reform schools for further instruction. Even after the attorney general of the United States took to the airways to counsel restraint, violent mob attacks against Jehovah's Witnesses continued unabated.

The American flag, a deservedly beloved symbol of liberty and justice, had become an instrument of terror and oppression, directed mostly against children. In June 1942 a handful of judges who had signed on to Frankfurter's majority sent out a strong signal that they had made a mistake and were now ready to correct it. Following some effective and ingenious judicial staging by lawyers for the Jehovah's Witnesses, *Barnette v. West Virginia Board of Education* was quickly scheduled for hearing. Local West Virginia authorities had copied their counterparts in Pennsylvania, introducing even more stringent flag-salute requirements, with predictable consequences.

A newly appointed member of the court, a pragmatic former US attorney general named Robert Jackson – later to serve as a chief prosecutor at the Nuremberg Trials – wrote the majority opinion released on Flag Day, 14 June 1943. Almost three years after *Gobitis*, the court reversed itself, relying on Justice Stone's dissent, in some of the most moving and memorable pleas for tolerance of diversity and human freedom in American legal literature: "If there is any fixed star in our constitutional constellation, it is that no official, high or petty, can prescribe what shall be orthodox in politics, nationalism, religion or other matters of opinion, or force citizens to confess by word or act their faith therein." Accordingly, Justice Jackson concluded, "the action of the local authorities in compelling the flag salute ... transcends constitutional limitations on their power and invades the sphere of intellect and spirit which it is the purpose of the First Amendment to our Constitution to reserve from all official control." The actions of "village tyrants" could not be "beyond the reach of the Constitution."[47]

Barnette did not just overrule *Gobitis* but completely rejected the rationale on which it had been based. National unity and symbols were important, but restrictions on constitutional freedoms could be justified only to prevent a clear and present danger. Frankfurter, personally implicated, dissented, claiming again that judges should not pass on the wisdom of legislation deemed desirable by their elected representatives, but he was out of step with court and country.[48] *Gobitis* was not his only majority judgment that was overturned, and today his 251 dissents are studied "only for their futility."[49] Laskin's dissents in *Lavell* and *Murdoch* set him up for appointment as chief justice, but any hopes Frankfurter had of leading the court "vanished after the second flag salute case."[50]

Unfortunately, he did not have the benefit of future US Supreme Court Justice William O. Douglas's advice: "The court that raises its hand against the mob may be temporarily unpopular; but it soon wins the confidence of the nation. The court that fails to stand before the mob is not worthy of the great tradition."[51] Or as Benjamin Cardozo put it, "the prophet and martyr do not see the hooting throng."[52] An opponent of many of the path-breaking decisions of the Warren court, Frankfurter became increasingly isolated and reactionary. While he had, in 1948, hired the first African American clerk at the court, when the dean of Harvard Law School in 1960 recommended one of his brilliant students for a clerkship, Frankfurter said no to Ruth Bader Ginsburg, who is among the most outstanding justices in the court's long and rich history.

Seeing Things Differently

Research indicates that Canadian Supreme Court of Canada judges dissent at about half the rate of their American colleagues[53] and that outsiders tend to dissent more than insiders. Women judges at the Supreme Court of Canada dissent more than men, particularly when interpreting cases on equality rights[54] (although they are as likely to disagree with each other as with their male judges).

One study found that two judges with significantly high dissent rates were Jewish, while one was the first "ethnic" judge (of Ukrainian Canadian background, he was also a high-profile lawyer from a blue-chip Toronto firm). "What the women seem to have in common is an increased tendency to see something differently from the majority, whatever the majority happens to be."[55] Their tendency was to vote in dissent and to write, disproportionately, in dissent. The possibly underrated and definitely controversial Supreme Court of Canada judge Claire L'Heureux-Dubé observed that dissents are "rich sources of all that is potential and possible in law."[56]

Why do judges dissent? To "record prophecy and shape history,"[57] according to Judge Frankfurter, although that was not his legacy. William Brennan, another leading dissenter and influential judge of the US Supreme Court for more than three decades, offers another reason: "When a Justice perceives an interpretation of the text to have departed so far from its essential meaning that Justice is bound, by a larger constitutional duty to the community, to expose the departure and point toward a different path."[58] Dissents are written at some social cost. In the cloistered confines of any supreme court, it is much easier to concur than dissent.

Dissents are hard to write and often serve no immediate purpose. Not all dissents point the way ahead, but strong dissents point out what is wrong with the majority's view and contribute to the marketplace of competing ideas.[59] "A dissent challenges the reasoning of the majority, tests its authority and establishes a benchmark against which the majority's reasoning can continue to be evaluated, and perhaps, in time, superseded."[60] Dissents serve a serious purpose. They focus the law and the conversation. They prevent the process from becoming mechanistic by requiring the judges to engage with a different point of view. Each time the court revisits an issue, a dissent forces the judges to go back to basic principles and re-engage. As they do so, there must be an overriding recognition that the conversation is with the past, present, and future.

At the US Supreme Court, when decisions are announced from the bench, only the majority opinion is summarized. Usually, brief mention is made of concurrences and dissents. But from time to time a dissent is orally presented. It is the judicial equivalent of the shout-out: not only to record that something terrible has happened but to broadcast that message loud and clear.

"When history demonstrates that the court got it badly wrong, it is comforting," Justice Antonin Scalia wrote, "to look back and realize that at least some of Justices saw the danger clearly, and gave voice, often eloquent voice, to their concern."[61] Given the law's overwhelming progressive and liberal arc, it is unlikely that anyone will resurrect any Clarence Thomas dissent; at least it has not yet happened yet, although there are lots of opinions to choose from. (Thomas is a strict constructionist judge who goes years without ever asking a question in open court.) For someone who dissents more often than anyone else, it is noteworthy that Thomas has no interest in clerks who would have the temerity to disagree: "I won't hire them," he said. "It's like trying to train a pig. It wastes your time, and it aggravates the pig."[62] On the other hand, Justice Sonia Sotomayor brings a completely different experience and approach: open-minded, compassionate, curious, and willing to listen. Born in a public-housing project in the Bronx, she has emerged as the future conscience of the court.[63]

But today that mantle belongs to Ruth Bader Ginsburg, who joined the court in 1993 after a lifetime of hard work teaching and fighting for equality for everyone. She understands the importance of dissent and now leads the court's liberal wing. Ginsburg has turned her reading of dissents into performance art: serious, soft-spoken, and shy, she delivers a huge wallop through her stinging prose.

Everyone knows it's a big-news day when she arrives in court wearing her dissent jabot: black with gold embroidery and faceted stones. With her strong rhetoric on behalf of the poor, the marginalized, and the dispossessed, Ginsburg takes aim at the powerful, at entrenched interests, and at defenders of an unacceptable status quo and demands they be held to account. "It's like pulling the fire alarm, a public shaming of the majority that you want the world to see."[64] Or more gently, and to paraphrase another one of her biographers, she puts her dissents in a bottle and floats them to an unknown future court.[65]

We turn now to just that type of case – in Canada.

Chapter 6

Sentenced to Death

A Girl Goes Missing

On Tuesday, 9 June 1959, twelve-year-old Lynne Harper disappeared. A slim, friendly, and bright girl with dark hair and eyes, she was a student at Air Vice Marshal Hugh Campbell School on the Royal Canadian Air Force station just outside Clinton – a small southwestern Ontario town in the middle of farm country just eighteen kilometres from Bayfield. Lynne, like most of the other "air force brats," lived on the radar-training base, and she was also a Girl Guide and regularly attended Sunday School.

Two days later, Lynne's body was found in Lawson's Bush – the wooded area of Bob Lawson's sixty-hectare farm next to the base. She had been raped and strangled to death with her blouse. Her clothes and shoes were carefully arranged beside her swollen corpse, which was partially covered with branches. Maggots and insects moved in and out of her ears, nose, mouth, and genitals.[1]

Once Dr John L. Penistan, the county pathologist, made some cursory observations, the body was taken to a nearby funeral home, where he performed an autopsy. There was some potential evidence at the scene: old bicycle-tire marks and fresh tire skids. "These marks appeared to have been made quite sometime previous," Ontario Provincial Police (OPP) Corporal Harry "Hank" Sayeau observed, but the tire skids indicated that someone had recently "gunned it."[2]

The Investigation

Steven Truscott, age fourteen, was the last person known to have seen Lynne alive. Tall and popular, he attended the same school and was with her between 7:00 and 8:00 p.m., more or less, the night she disappeared. They left the school grounds together on his bike, and Steven either dropped her off at the side of the highway at the intersection of County

Lynne Harper. Her killer has never been found. (Credit: London Free Press Collection, University of Western Ontario Archives)

Road and Highway 8, when she told him she wanted to visit some nearby ponies, or he took her into Lawson's Bush, where he raped and killed her.

At first the police believed Lynne had run away: her parents reported she might be hitchhiking to Port Stanley, where her grandparents lived. When Lynne's father began a search around the base, Steven told him that he had dropped her off and that she then hitched a ride on Highway 8. The police decided to question him. With Steven's father in tow, they picked him up at school on Wednesday morning, 10 June, and over the next three days in seven separate police interviews, Steven would calmly, courteously, and helpfully repeat this story: after he left her at the corner, he saw her get into a grey, late-model Chevrolet with a lot of chrome and a yellow licence plate.

The pony story checked out. Just up the road from where Steven said he dropped Lynne off, Edgar Hodges lived in a shack with a couple of Shetland ponies in his stable. He told the police he knew Lynne – she had visited before, but not the night she went missing. On Thursday afternoon, 11 June, a search was finally organized. About two hundred and fifty airmen began looking for Lynne – one group went straight to Lawson's Bush, where they discovered her body.

Inspector Harold Graham was assigned to the case. At thirty-three, the youngest inspector at the OPP's Criminal Investigations Branch, he had rocketed through the ranks. It was just before 8:00 p.m. on 11 June when Graham arrived in Clinton to take charge. A General Information Broadcast (GIB) was issued. The police were looking for a late-model Chevrolet, white or grey, with yellow plates. Their initial assumption, plucked out of the air, was that Lynne had been murdered around 9:00 p.m., and both the police and the public were asked to be on the lookout for a killer with scratches on his face, neck, hands, and arms. The Ontario government offered a reward. It was not a modest amount for information leading to the arrest and conviction of the guilty person, but $10,000 for the killer, "dead or alive."[3]

Inspector Graham demanded the autopsy results. Dr Penistan was a graduate of Britain's University of London and had served as regional pathologist for a decade. The autopsy took just two hours to complete, and the doctor concluded that Lynne had been murdered, along with a "blind, violent, rape." Strangely, there was no bleeding and no sperm, although in the "vagina, hymen destroyed."[4]

Lynne had eaten dinner at 5:45 p.m. After pumping Lynne's stomach contents into a glass jar and holding the contents up to a light bulb for examination, and following discussions with the police, Penistan would, in due course, fix Lynne's time of death at between 7:15 and 7:45 p.m. The original estimated time of death of 9:00 p.m. would have ruled Steven out, but now it was pinpointed in the exact half-hour the two were together. For all intents and purposes, the investigation was over.

At 10:45 a.m. the next morning, Friday, 12 June, Inspector Graham interviewed Steven, who was again accompanied by his father. Graham pretended that Steven was a witness, but he was actually a suspect and entitled under Canadian law to a warning: that anything he said could be used against him. Steven repeated his story. There were lots of other kids to interview: 9 June had been a bright, warm summer night – around 32° – and they were out in droves in the schoolyard, on the County Road, and en route to the local swimming hole. Two of them – Dougie Oates and Gord Logan – had seen Steven and Lynne make their way across the bridge on the bike toward the highway. Gord also saw Steven return alone. But another two had quite different stories to tell.

Arnold "Butch" George said Steven and Lynne "were in the Bush, but he didn't know what they were doing." That was one of many versions he told police. The others were that he "heard" Steven had taken her into the Bush (though he never disclosed his source), that Steven planned to take her into the Bush, that he "saw" Steven take her into the Bush, and – more than fifty years later – that he saw Steven's bike immediately adjacent to the Bush. There were reports of other conversations between Steven and Butch – for instance, Butch's claim that Steven asked him to lie to the police.

The other talkative youngster was Jocelyne Gaudet, age thirteen, who told the police various versions of events during multiple interviews both before and after Steven was arrested. Each one was increasingly embellished with improbable detail, replete with logical gaps, but in the end she stuck to the story that she was supposed to meet up with Steven that night. They had made plans to go to Lawson's Bush to see some newborn calves, but Steven told her to keep it a secret. As it turned out, when he swung by on his bike at Jocelyne Gaudet's home around 6 p.m., she could not keep their date.

In the meantime, Corporal Sayeau had arrived at the forensic laboratory in Toronto with the glass jar. Sayeau called Graham with the lab report: the stomach-content examination established that Lynne had eaten dinner not more than two hours before her death. It had established no such thing – the official written report did not even address time of death – but this information was exactly what Inspector Graham was looking for. Under huge pressure to make an arrest, he ordered his men to pick Steven up.

Generally, the police ensured that a parent or a social worker was present when they were questioning a juvenile, though in 1959 it was not the law. Graham wanted a confession and, as he explained, "I chose to disregard those guidelines."[5] The police did not even tell Steven's frantic parents that they had taken their son into custody until later on Friday evening. Under interrogation, Graham, a bear of a man, challenged Steven's account and called him a liar. Then he left the room and another police officer repeated the performance.

This Keystone cops routine went on for about ninety minutes. When Steven did not budge, they changed course. By this point Steven's father had been notified, and they asked him to agree to a medical examination of his son. As a military man, he obeyed the rules. Dr John Addison, who had previously treated Steven and his brother, was called and arrived around 10:30 p.m. Friday. In the meantime, armed with a search warrant, three OPP officers went to the Truscott home.

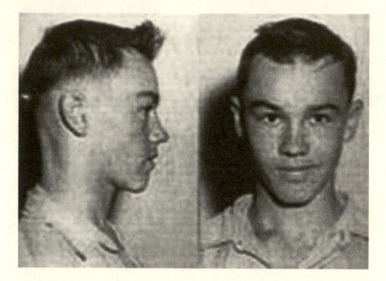

Steven Truscott. The fourteen-year-old was the last person known
to have seen Lynne alive.

"You don't need a search warrant," Doris Truscott told them – like
her husband, she deferred to authority. They gathered various items of
clothing from the house and Steven's red pants from the clothesline – the
pants Steven was wearing the day that Lynne went missing. Meanwhile,
Dr Addison was conducting his examination. There was one thing of
note: "a very sore penis"[6] with two lesions on the shaft. Have you been
masturbating? the doctor asked. No, the teenage boy replied initially, but
then admitted he had about a week before. Addison reported the results.
He also asked the police if he could play detective and privately question
Steven. Sure, they said. At 1:00 a.m., 13 June, an obviously exhausted
and demonstrably incoherent Steven continued to profess his innocence.
At 3:00 a.m. he was charged with first-degree murder and asked to hand
over his underwear. The pressure was off. So far as the police were concerned, the murderer had been caught.

Steven was a juvenile, but the law allowed for transfer to adult court
so long as a few conditions were met: the offence had to be indictable
under the Criminal Code; the accused had to be at least fourteen years
old; and the transfer had to be in the interest of the community and for
the good of the child. The authorities gave them all a check mark, though
it is not immediately apparent how the last point held.

The Preliminary Inquiry

In short order, Steven's father was transferred to Ottawa – the fact that Steven was the son of an enlisted man and Lynne the daughter of an officer was not lost on acute observers. Mr Truscott would now have to travel eight hundred kilometres each way to attend the proceedings, beginning with the preliminary inquiry, held one month after the transfer to adult court. The task was now to determine whether there was sufficient evidence to proceed to trial.

A junior judge, Dudley Holmes, was presiding. In those days, pretrial disclosure of the Crown's case was primitive. The preliminary hearing offered a preview, albeit incomplete, of what was to come. For the most part it was matter of fact: Lynne went missing; Steven was the last person known to see her alive; he behaved completely normally the night of the crime, the next day, and every day since; he cooperated with the police; his story never really changed; and he had an alibi of sorts in Dougie and Gord.

As was the practice, the defence called no witnesses. Steven's lawyer was Frank Donnelly – he was the go-to guy for the criminally accused in Huron County, his office just across the street from the imposing courthouse in the middle of the Goderich town square. With almost thirty years of experience under his belt, Donnelly had saved four men from the gallows, and he had a reputation for thoroughness. At the preliminary inquiry, however, he was merely gathering evidence, hearing what the Crown witnesses had to say and testing their accounts on cross-examination. It was a fishing expedition, pure and simple. Dougie and Gord, with their exonerating evidence, would be saved for later.

It was up to Crown attorney Glenn Hays to convince the magistrate that the case should proceed to trial, and he had exactly the evidence he needed: Steven's penis and the time of death. Dr Addison had "never seen as sore a penis in twenty-two years of practice."[7] The pathologist elaborated: "I think," Dr Penistan explained, "it is the sort of lesion which might well have been made by a blind, furious thrust of the male organ in the direction of the entry to the vagina."[8] It was fiction, but nothing compared to his evidence about time of death.

Although not known at the time (and not established for decades), the rigor mortis and insect infestation was consistent with a time of death as late as 7:00 a.m. on Wednesday, 10 June, but he testified that Lynne actually died between 7:15 and 7:45 p.m. on 9 June. An expert from the provincial laboratory called to give evidence about the contents of the glass jar had no idea when Lynne died, even though corroboration of time of death from the lab had supposedly convinced the OPP they had their boy.

The evidence of the various children out playing that summer night was equally confusing. Butch and Jocelyne failed to convince with their mixed-up stories. No one ever saw Steven and Lynne go into the Bush, and there was no physical evidence linking Steven with the crime – no blood on his clothes, no significant scratches. But the magistrate was in a hurry – suffering from terminal cirrhosis of the liver – and after two days he had heard enough. He remitted the case to trial.

The Trial

The trial began on 19 September 1959. The judge was Robert Ferguson, first appointed to the High Court of Justice in 1950. A local boy who studied at the University of Toronto and Osgoode Hall, he was well acquainted with Crown attorney Hays, who regularly tangled with defence attorney Donnelly. Hays had been called to the bar in 1938 and served in the Royal Canadian Naval Volunteer Reserve (1940–46). Two years later he was appointed the local Crown attorney and moved to Goderich, the county seat. Twelve men – farmers, merchants, a barber, garage mechanic, bowling-alley operator, and milkman – were called for jury duty.

The Crown had a very straightforward story to tell. When Steven failed to lure Jocelyne to Lawson's Bush, his attention turned to Lynne Harper. There was no bike ride to Highway 8, and no grey Chevrolet with lots of chrome. How did the police know that? Because they had taken Steven to the spot where he said he dropped Lynne off and to the place where he claimed he could see her get into a car. But no one, they said, could see that far: as proof they introduced some photographs they took, though they hadn't tested Steven to determine what *he* could see. Nor did they disclose other evidence that would have bolstered his statement. The Crown also led evidence that Lynne never hitchhiked – which the police at least knew to be untrue. The Crown's theory was that Steven's story was an elaborate hoax, fabricated by a sex fiend who was determined that June night to rape and kill.

Then there was the matter of that sore penis with its "large oozing sores." Could these lesions have come from masturbation? Absolutely not. A too-confident Donnelly allowed the Crown to get away with just about everything, including the readily disprovable evidence of Dr Penistan. By relying on his visual examination of the contents of the glass jar held up to a light bulb, he had no scientific clue about when death occurred.

It was actually impossible to determine time of death by stomach contents. Rigor mortis and insect infestation would have provided a much better but still inconclusive guide, but Penistan tailored what little he did know to point in Steven's direction.[9] Various children called by the Crown claimed to remember this and that, but in some cases their memories had improved in relation to the number of interviews they had had with the police. Butch was proven to be either an incorrigible liar or hopelessly confused.

Donnelly did mount a defence. Dr Berkely Brown, an internist, told the jury that caution was needed in using stomach contents to fix the time of death. All sorts of things affect digestion, including fear and death. When he looked at the glass jar, he concluded that Lynne's stomach had been digesting its contents for at least three or four hours before she died. If so, she was alive for a long time after Steven returned to the schoolyard around 8:00 p.m. Dr Brown had also served a five-year stint in the army and examined thousands of penises. Steven's sores were consistent with masturbation: Canadian soldiers overseas, "deprived" of their wives and girlfriends, were likely to "indulge in abnormal practices,"[10] the doctor told the scandalized court.

Donnelly also called Dougie Oates and Gord Logan. They both testified that they saw Steven and Lynne cross the bridge and head to the highway, and a little while later Gord saw Steven return alone. Gord had reported this information to the police before Lynne's body was found, well before Steven became a suspect.

Closing Arguments

At the end of the eleven-day trial, having heard from seventy-four witnesses, there was no evidence proving that Steven had taken Lynne into the Bush, and plenty of reason to conclude he had not. If the Crown was correct, Steven was a sex fiend who suffered from psychological disorders including fetishism. How else to explain the folded clothes and the arranged branches over the corpse? The killer had also taken a souvenir – a piece of Lynne's blouse. Yet no one had previously noticed that Steven was a bit off, and Jocelyne's and Butch's stories raised more questions than answers. Butch even admitted he had given several false statements to the police. (The full extent of his multiple, contradictory, and evolving statements would not emerge for years.)

All told, it was up to the Crown to prove guilt beyond a reasonable doubt, and Donnelly argued it had not. At best, all the prosecution ever established was that there were various children on the road to the highway and out and about that hot summer night who might have seen Steven but did not (leaving it for the jury to infer that was because he was busy in the Bush raping and killing Lynne instead of drawing the more likely conclusion that no one would have had any reason to notice or care when Steven and Lynne rode by on Steven's bike). Moreover, the timing of different kids in different places did not easily add up.

The defence established that two kids saw Steven on his way to the highway with Lynne, and one of them saw him return moments later without her and that one of these witnesses said so before Lynne's body was found and before Steven was identified as the person of interest. The medical evidence was challenged and the jury invited to believe Dr Brown that it was almost impossible to predict accurately the time of death and that the available evidence indicated that Lynne died long after 8:00 p.m. The sores on the penis could be easily explained, and certainly understood by anyone who knew teenage boys (or perhaps once was one). Steven even admitted to masturbating when pressed. It was up to the Crown to prove guilt beyond a reasonable doubt and Donnelly argued that it had not.

The Crown had a tough case to make, but Hays explained that the jurors had a choice: they could believe the well-respected local pathologist, Dr Penistan, who had examined the body, performed the autopsy, and studied the stomach contents, or they could believe Dr Brown, who only got to look at the glass jar during the trial. Penistan spoke not just with certainty but with an English accent, a crowd pleaser in class-conscious Canada. He was also a bit dashing, definitely debonair; and in most of the photographs from the time he was shown sucking pensively on his pipe.

Hays had a few problems. One of the big ones was that Butch was a proven liar. That called for a classic pivot with a dash of redemption added to the mix. Butch had seen the error of his ways, and Hays now explained to the jury he should now be believed, especially his claim that Steven had asked him to mislead the police. Hays couldn't do much about Dougie and Gord other than to reject their evidence and denounce them, asserting they could not see what they said they saw. They were "liars," he said. However, Dougie's story had been confirmed by another kid, Karen Daum. She was with Dougie at the time, but the defence did not appreciate that she was a witness too. She also saw Steven and Lynne on the bike well beyond the Bush on the way to the highway and told the police as much. Even though she was just a kid, she got the definite feeling that they were not interested in her specific recollection of events.[11]

It is inconceivable that Donnelly would not have called Karen Daum had he known about her written statement exculpating Steven, and it would have been major prosecutorial misconduct to keep quiet about it – Hays's job was to ensure that justice was done, not to secure a conviction. But the police certainly knew. They did not agree with it, so they suppressed it. As Corporal Sayeau explained, "she was a cute little girl, but she had to be wrong."[12]

Hays even arranged for Jocelyne Gaudet to enter the court in the middle of his jury address. Pointing to her, he said that, but for the grace of God, she would have been lying dead in the Bush. Instead, Lynne went there with Steven – "and to her doom."[13] It was a twist that could easily have been modelled on the popular television series *Perry Mason*. Emotional and dramatic, Hays's unethical stunt had an effective impact on the jury.

Evidence that was clearly not evidence was put before the jury and attributed with importance – for example, the bicycle tracks. Even though the testimony established that the bike tracks were not a match for Steven's bike and had been there for many days, the Crown told the jurors that they presented "fairly strong evidence that that bicycle was down there,"[14] leading to the inevitable conclusion that so was Steven. The judge buttressed this suggestion by his irrelevant observation: "The bicycle is not a common one."[15] This conclusion that the sum of the evidence was incontrovertible was reinforced by numerous exhibits establishing nothing: hair taken from Steven's head after he was arrested; clothes taken from his room that were not the ones he was wearing the day Lynne went missing.

Giving the Crown the benefit of the doubt, and this is admittedly a bit of a stretch, Hays may not have been deliberately taking advantage of the jurors but that was the result. Steven's underwear – seized from him after he was arrested – had traces of sperm and feces. The medical evidence was conclusive that sperm could not date from the rape, and it was unlikely that Steven had not changed his underwear in four days. The dirty shorts really served only one purpose: to prejudice Steven in the eyes of the jury.

Judicial Misconduct

After a short recess, Justice Ferguson gave his instructions. He was an experienced trial judge, and his explanation of the law was adequate. He told the jurors that Steven was presumed innocent and that the Crown had to prove beyond a reasonable doubt that he was guilty. Circumstantial cases were always difficult. The jurors had to find the facts: in particular, did Steven kill Lynne?

From the first day of the trial, however, Ferguson had made clear whose side he was on. Now, in his appraisal of the testimony, he went out of his way to endorse the case for the prosecution. In reviewing the evidence, a judge is entitled to indicate what evidence he or she prefers but must be scrupulously fair-minded throughout. Not Judge Ferguson. He also made factual mistakes, barely canvassed Dr Brown's testimony about time of death, and invited the jury to prefer the testimony of Dr Penistan, "an Attorney General's pathologist of many years standing."[16] He referred to the dirty underwear, advising the jurors to ignore the feces and focus on the semen: "It is consistent with an attack on this girl."[17] He even introduced a new theory about how Steven might have ridden with Lynne to the highway, then brought her back to the Bush, where he raped and killed her. That explained, the judge observed, why Steven could so calmly claim that he had given Lynne a ride to the highway.[18] He even suggested that some adverse inference ought be drawn because Steven chose not to testify, as was his right.

After the jury left the courtroom, Donnelly objected. What you did, he told the judge, was completely improper. "The jury listening to your charge could not help but get the impression that you consider a verdict of guilty was warranted on the evidence." The judge did not disagree: "What is wrong with that?" he angrily asked.[19] Canadian law actually forbade a judge from directing a jury to convict, "taking the case away from the jury" as it's called, but Ferguson had done exactly that.

As it turned out, the only point the jurors were troubled about was the evidence of Dougie and Gord. After three hours of deliberation they asked the judge about it, and he reiterated his pet theory that Steven might have taken Lynne to the highway and brought her back to the Bush. What really mattered, he repeated, was who killed Lynne. Donnelly again strenuously objected – it was the complete destruction of the defence case, and the judge had no choice but to recall the jury once more.

This time he could not contain himself: he told the jurors they should prefer the evidence of the Crown witnesses. Donnelly again objected, and when the jurors returned yet again, Ferguson made it clear that the defence was causing a fuss. Even the local police were shocked by the unfolding spectacle, one observing to another: "He didn't have to go that far, not that far."[20] Final deliberations took all of ten minutes to reach the verdict: guilty. Justice Ferguson then pronounced the words required by law: "I sentence you to hang by the neck until dead."

Even though Canadian jurors are not permitted to disclose their deliberations, it is very difficult to stop people from talking. "I knew by the third day," one of the jurors later admitted, "no one was going to prove that young monster innocent. If we'd had to stay there all winter to convict that fiend, I'd have stayed."[21] Another had a simple explanation: "I didn't like his look."[22] The judge and his theory had been persuasive: "Steven got Lynne into that Bush somehow and killed her, so it didn't really matter where he'd ridden her first,"[23] another juror said.

The press had been reporting all summer long that Steven had done it. The *London Free Press* told its readers that the two left the schoolyard between 7:00 and 7:10 p.m.: "According to medical evidence the girl died between 7:15 and 7:45."[24] No one needed any help in connecting the dots long before the trial began. Indeed, some of the evidence from the preliminary inquiry, although later ruled inadmissible for being nonsensical, was still reported in the press and, presumably, read and discussed by the jurors. When the trial was over, when the twelve men met in the jury room to consider Steven's fate, only one argued for Steve's innocence "until those last ten minutes."[25]

The date with the gallows was set: 8 December. However, when the Ontario Court of Appeal agreed to hear the case, the death sentence was postponed to 16 February 1960.

The Appeal

When the lawyers assembled at Toronto's Osgoode Hall on 12 January 1960 to argue Steven's appeal, there was an entirely new cast of characters. This time Steven was represented by John G.J. O'Driscoll, a prominent Toronto lawyer. The former junior for the legendary Arthur Maloney, O'Driscoll was a leading criminal barrister and, like most of the lawyers in this story, a future judge. Donnelly had by any measure fumbled the case, though, as Steven put it, "I guess he tried hard enough."[26] His lacklustre performance was not entirely his fault.

The police had buried some inconvenient exculpatory evidence that might very well have made conviction impossible – whether the Crown attorney knew about it is another matter. A Mr and Mrs Townsend, out for a drive the night Lynne went missing, reported having seen a young girl hitchhiking exactly where Steven said he left Lynne. Might it have made a difference if the jury knew that Lynne often hitchhiked, there were problems at home, she left when she wanted and went where she wished, and was seen hitchhiking the night she was killed? It would be years before Steven's lawyers learned what the police actually knew at the time – Karen Daum's statement for example – and chose not to disclose either at trial or before the appeal.

In the meantime, there would be no more local counsel for the Truscotts: "I felt that had we had a big-time lawyer, he could have done better," Steven's mother readily concluded.[27] The family's savings were long gone, and O'Driscoll was the man, with the Ontario Legal Aid Plan footing the bill. The attorney general also called out the heavy ammunition and assigned William C. Bowman, a career government lawyer and the director of public prosecutions, to the file.

There are errors in every criminal case, and this one had several grounds for appeal. In his opening jury address, for instance, the Crown attorney had referred to a statement Steven signed, planting the suggestion that there was a something inculpatory in it. It is an ironclad rule that, before any statement can be presented to the jury in a criminal trial, the judge must rule on its admissibility. This one had not been approved. Donnelly immediately objected, but the judge decided against calling a mistrial. When the statement was introduced a few days later, Donnelly protested again, and the jury was excluded for hours as the lawyers wrangled. They were never explicitly told that the signed statement was not a confession and they formed the impression that Donnelly was trying to keep something from them – a conclusion that was reinforced on numerous other occasions.

The evidence provided another ground for appeal. According to the Crown timeline, Steven had at most forty-five minutes, and possibly fifteen minutes less, to do the following: leave the schoolyard sometime after 7:00 p.m. with Lynne on his bike, ride quite some distance to Lawson's Bush, escort her down a long tractor trail, take her into the Bush, rape her, kill her, arrange her clothes neatly, break off thick branches from a nearby tree and arrange them on her corpse, return down that tractor trail to his bike and ride back to the schoolyard, hang out with some friends, and go home, acting perfectly normal all the while. He had no scratches, no stains on his clothes, and it all happened in broad daylight on and off a well-travelled road and trail (the crime scene could be seen from the trail). It was all a bit of a stretch, though the fact that Steven had cooperated and acted normally (which some observers may have found remarkable in a fourteen-year-old boy) was advanced as proof of cunning and culpability.

A conviction required proof beyond a reasonable doubt and, O'Driscoll argued, the evidence was at least as consistent with innocence as it was with guilt. Still, if it was not Steven, then who was it? At trial, the Crown focused on the old bicycle tracks but ignored the recent tire tracks – the one where the police concluded the driver must have "gunned it." And what about the local sex offenders? Generally recidivist, in any sex crime they are the obvious first suspects. There were several possibilities, but the police, thinking they had their boy, had not investigated any of these possible perpetrators.

Who Killed Lynne Harper?

What follows is speculative, but there were many possible local persons of interest who could have and should have been considered at the time, beginning with thirty-five-year-old Alexander Kalichuk. Just three weeks earlier, the air force sergeant had tried to entice a ten-year girl on her way home from school into his car in nearby St Thomas. He showed her a bag of panties, and invited her to choose a pair.

Nancy Davidson was one smart girl: "His eyes were bulgy and he had that glassy look ... and I knew he was drinking and I just wanted to get away."[28] As the encounter was unfolding, Nancy's father happened to drive by. She got in his car, told him what happened, and the police quickly captured Kalichuk. He denied any wrongdoing, but they found the bag of panties and a bottle of liquor.

Kalichuk was charged with contributing to the delinquency of a minor. He was posted at the nearby Aylmer military base but had worked at the Clinton base (1950–57) and still lived just outside of town. With his long record – indecency, exposure, drunkenness – he should have definitely been brought in for questioning. Some credulous magistrate bought Kalichuk's absurd account that it was all a big misunderstanding and that the panties were to be given out as gifts for some fishermen friends. The charges were dismissed just eleven days before Lynne Harper was raped and murdered. Kalichuk did not own a late model Chevrolet, but it was at least curious that he sold his brand new car a few weeks after Lynne was killed. His psychiatric state, tenuous at best, began to deteriorate further and he was in July 1959 confined to a mental hospital.

Clayton Dennis, age thirty-seven, lived in Seaforth, only fourteen kilometres away. A rapist who had served time, he told some local residents that Lynne "had it coming to her" and was "asking for it." The police never interviewed him. Same with Matthew Meron, a nineteen-year-old airman at the Clinton base who made extra money working as a lifeguard at the pool where Lynne swam. He was later apprehended attempting to rape his own daughter in some woods. When she resisted, he tried to strangle her.

Additional suspects emerged over the years – the daughter of a local sex fiend informed the authorities she saw her father carrying the limp body of a young girl out of the trunk of his car; an ex-serviceman from the Clinton base was found with a large collection of child pornography and a transcript of Steven's trial; and a local salesman and convicted sex offender confessed to his doctor on his deathbed that he had "done the murder that Steven Truscott went to jail for."[29] And there was the career criminal and sex offender Larry Talbot, who carried his "rape kit" everywhere and owned a late-model pale-blue Chevrolet with a lot of chrome.[30] And so it went with many possible leads – yet not one was ever investigated.

Appeal Denied

The judge's final address to the jury was another ground for appeal. Ferguson had it in for Steven. As he wrote to Justice Minister E. Davie Fulton several weeks after the trial, the incident was the act of a "monster." Although the jury recommended mercy, he knew of "no reason, other than the youth of the prisoner, to recommend commutation of the death penalty to life in prison."[31] But any criticism of judicial conduct is a high-risk proposition on appeal. The misconduct has to be blatant before the herd will abandon one of its own. And the protective instinct won here.

In short order, the five-person panel headed by Chief Justice Dana Porter (a former attorney general, decent man, and good judge) dismissed the appeal on 20 January. Under the rules only legal issues could be addressed on appeal. But the lawyers still had a lot to talk about, with nine hours of argument over three days. The basic question was whether the accused – Steven – had had a fair trial on proper evidence. Just one week later, the appeal was dismissed in a brief decision almost entirely bereft of reasons. Nothing was amiss.

The day after the Ontario Court of Appeal ruled, the federal cabinet gathered in Ottawa to discuss the Truscott case, with Prime Minister John G. Diefenbaker – previously a good defence lawyer – taking the lead.[32] There was almost no bandwagon "the Chief" would not climb on, but on the rights of criminally accused, and in his lifelong opposition to the death penalty, he was completely principled. Steven's death sentence was commuted to life in prison. Over Diefenbaker's term in office, more than fifty other death penalties were similarly commuted. In February the Supreme Court of Canada refused to hear the case because, it said, no issue of public importance had been raised.

Steven was sent to the Ontario Training School for Boys in Guelph, Ontario. When he turned eighteen, he was transferred to the Collins Bay Penitentiary in Kingston. Normally, rapists are given a rough go by the other prisoners and end up in protective custody and segregation. Steven was left alone. The other inmates clearly concluded that he was an innocent man. Small solace, to be sure, as he settled in for the long haul.

A Journalist Comes to the Rescue

Isabel LeBourdais, the daughter of Toronto lawyer Frank Erichsen-Brown, came from a socially prominent and wealthy family. Her mother, Isabel Russell McCurdy, was a suffragette who had helped to organize the Equal Franchise League and later joined the League of Women Voters. Her younger sister, Gwethalyn Graham, was a two-time winner of the Governor General's Award for Fiction and the first Canadian to have a book reach the top spot on the *New York Times* best-seller list. Educated at Toronto's Havergal College, Isabel was a liberated woman; her second marriage was to Donat Mark LeBourdais – a journalist and founding member of the Co-operative Commonwealth Federation, the precursor to today's New Democratic Party. She was active in all sorts of social movements; for instance, she was pro-choice and wrote about her own illegal abortions to secure support for decriminalization of the procedure.[33]

LeBourdais knew nothing about Steven Truscott until the fall of 1959, when she read in a newspaper that a fourteen-year-old boy had been sentenced to hang. Her first thought was that it was barbaric for the state to kill a child. "Does Canada really hang fourteen-year-olds?" she asked.[34] The more she thought about it, the more incensed she became. She began an investigation that would consume five years of her life (even as she lost her parents, her husband, and her sister, looked after two of her four children, and began a day job when she became a widow). No one involved in the case would cooperate, including Frank Donnelly (who had become a rude and tyrannical judge – his only saving grace was that he treated everyone equally badly). The Canadian military did what it could to impede her investigation, issuing a routine order on the Clinton base forbidding any military personnel from assisting her. That made the feisty LeBourdais even more determined to find out what had really happened.

LeBourdais approached the eminent Canadian publisher McClelland and Stewart, but Jack McClelland was surprisingly unenthusiastic in his response. Although he agreed that Steven had not received a fair trial, he insisted on "substantial control" over the project.[35] He seemed to be concerned that LeBourdais's indictment of the justice system might land back on him – especially since in one version of the manuscript she identified the person she thought was the real killer. M & S gave LeBourdais a publishing contract but the relationship between author and publisher was troubled from the start. In meeting after meeting, McClelland urged LeBourdais to tone it down, so much so that she eventually realized that what was left of her story when McClelland put away his pruning shears was a mealy-mouthed, wishy-washy embarrassment and disgrace.

On 1 January 1964 LeBourdais wrote McClelland: "From the beginning you have shown no confidence in me and no respect for my experience and knowledge. You have consistently taken the opinions of any Tom, Dick, Harry or Jane who was a reader, or lawyer, or editor or stooge … Anyone can take the easy road and play safe."[36] That was the path chosen by the to-the-manor born Jack McClelland, who, in this particular instance at least, had little interest in riling the establishment notwithstanding his reputation as a maverick. The other big Canadian publisher, Macmillan, also turned LeBourdais down. Fortunately, in London, England, the leftist crusader and publisher Victor Gollancz promised to flood Canada with copies of the book even if he lost money. Only then did McClelland agree to publish a Canadian edition – not the version he had originally urged but the real book, the one that pulled no punches.

The Trial of Steven Truscott was a Canadian publishing sensation. Word began to leak long before the book appeared on store shelves. "If there seems to be any merit in it [the case]," Ontario's attorney general told the *Globe and Mail*, "I'll look into it at once."[37] It was no even-handed account but, rather, a polemical attack on established institutions. LeBourdais was withering in her criticisms of accepted practices that made a mockery of the presumption of innocence. She examined every piece of evidence and pointed out the flaws, and explained trial procedure in easily understood terms. It is impossible to read the book and conclude that Steven was guilty beyond a reasonable doubt. There was doubt, in spades.

LeBourdais poked so many holes in Dr Penistan's evidence that it was remarkable he was allowed to continue his medical practice. She proved that whatever took place in that Huron County courthouse bore no resemblance to a fair trial: it was a kangaroo court. "Her book exposed for the first time some of the glaring problems with Steven's conviction: the constant changing of Butch George's stories, the improbabilities in Jocelyne's tales, the contradictions in the medical testimony, the dubious police tactics and the bias of the presiding judge," wrote Julian Sher, who would later write the definitive history of the Truscott case.[38]

Another one of the jurors from the trial commented on the growing brouhaha: "I am getting sick and tired of it. You'd think we were the guilty ones."[39] Justice Ferguson agreed: he urged the federal and the provincial governments to prosecute LeBourdais for public mischief.[40] But their complaints were ignored. To this day, no one has identified a single important factual error in LeBourdais's book. Across the province, student, community, and church groups began to mobilize. In just a few weeks, *The Trial of Steven Truscott* sold more than 60,000 copies and was attracting approving attention in both the United Kingdom and the United States.

There were calls inside Parliament for an inquiry. John Diefenbaker, now leader of the Official Opposition, demanded a royal commission. When LeBourdais appeared on television she spoke about Steven's penis. No one had ever used that word on live television in Canada before. The book was published in the midst of a parliamentary debate: the House of Commons was about to vote on the abolition of the death penalty. In a cliff-hanger vote, Parliament voted to restrict the death penalty to killers of police officers and prison guards, before abolishing it entirely on 14 July 1976.

Prime Minister Lester Pearson sent his parliamentary secretary, the distinguished Canadian war hero John Matheson, to offer Steven Truscott a secret deal that would settle the matter quietly: accept parole in lieu of an official inquiry. But there was a catch: admission of guilt. No, Steven replied, "I want the hearing, I deserve it."[41] And so the matter dragged on.

Complacent Canadians had been confident in their belief that the police always acted properly and that the courts not only symbolized justice but delivered it. Now LeBourdais challenged received wisdom – and a decidedly docile media – by offering up some disturbing but compelling ideas: that the police did not always tell the truth, that the justice system had flaws, and that an innocent person could be found guilty of a crime he did not commit. This was truly path-breaking in a country like Canada where, at the time, white middle-class people almost unreservedly believed in their public institutions (First Nations, racialized persons, poor people, and new Canadians often had a different experience and view).

As the pressure mounted, Pearson, heading a minority government, decided that something had to be done. LeBourdais insisted on a full-scale royal commission, with special attention paid to the conduct of the judge, the prosecutor, and the government witnesses, all of whom should be held to account. Instead, Ottawa chose the safe course: sending the case to the Supreme Court in a reference. "There exists widespread concern as to whether there was a miscarriage of justice in the conviction of Steven Murray Truscott," the government announced, "and it is in the public interest that the matter be inquired into."[42]

One author can change the course of history or at least come close. Rachel Carson's book *Silent Spring* fuelled the modern environmental movement. Isabel LeBourdais's book should have saved Steven Truscott – but it fell short.

To the Supreme Court

The judicial inquiry at Canada's highest court was a difficult task, complicated by the fact that some of the judges now hearing the case were among those who refused to hear Steven's appeal in 1960. If they changed their minds now, what would that say about their decision back then? The government should have followed LeBourdais's advice and referred the case to an independent inquiry. At the Supreme Court, Chief Justice Robert Taschereau had become a raging alcoholic and sometimes disappeared for days at a time. Moreover, the process itself was more than a little out of the ordinary. The court was asked to assume that Steven had been granted leave to appeal, and, unlike every single other appeal in its long history, the reference allowed the court to receive new evidence – and that meant hearing from Steven. He would be the first live witness ever to testify before the Supreme Court of Canada.

The Truscotts had no trouble in assembling another legal dream team: Ted Joliffe, a Rhodes Scholar, social democrat, and accomplished lawyer, joined by the legendary G. Arthur Martin, an outstanding criminal lawyer who had never lost even one of his sixty murder cases. On the opposite side, William Bowman again led the legal team for the Crown. The hearing began on 5 October 1966, but, unfortunately, the Supreme Court justices did not hear all the vital evidence.

In the original trial, Dr Penistan had pinpointed the time of death, and that, more than anything else, had sealed Steven's fate. But the doctor now realized he had got it wrong. He was now ready to admit that he had no idea when Lynne Harper died – it could have been within two hours of eating dinner, twelve hours, or even longer. He didn't have a clue.

About three weeks after the reference was announced, Penistan wrote to Inspector Graham and explained his "agonizing reappraisal." The intervening years had been good to Graham, his reputation enhanced by this most famous collar – Steven Truscott – and he had risen through the ranks to become assistant commissioner of the Ontario Provincial Police. The top job was well within his grasp. When he read the doctor's letter, Graham recognized it as a bombshell: it vindicated Steven. The rules were clear: they required that it be immediately disclosed to the defence. However, no one said boo. Penistan was not asked to testify before the Supreme Court. The letter was buried, and it would remain hidden for years.

Instead, for the medical evidence, a hodgepodge of experts testified and contradicted themselves and each other about what stomach contents could and could not reveal about the time of death. The Crown, for instance, called Dr Keith Simpson, the chief pathologist of the United Kingdom, to confirm what Penistan had told the trial court: that Lynne definitely died between 7:00 and 7:45 p.m. When G. Arthur Martin had his turn, he eviscerated the physician by quoting to him from his own authoritative books that stomach contents were "wholly unreliable" as a tool for estimating the time of death. Simpson even admitted that in one of his own cases, when nine hours had elapsed since her last meal, the stomach contents of the deceased were exactly the same as those found in Lynne.[43] This evidence alone established reasonable doubt.

Decomposition and rigor mortis were two other factors that could help determine time of death, but here, too, the experts disagreed even as they all testified with complete certainty. The police investigation was held up to scrutiny, for example, about who could see what from the intersection of Highway 8 and the County Road. The evidence led at trial was complete claptrap – if not deliberately cooked. The photographs the police showed the jury, the ones that purported to show that Steve could not see a car picking Lynne up, as he had claimed, were completely misleading.

In a way, though, all that really mattered was Steven Truscott, now a twenty-one-year-old man, and what he had to say. But Steven had been a prisoner for more than six years. He had changed. Prisoners do not speak up; rather, they look down when addressed and answer quietly. Now, when Steven had the opportunity to tell his story, he fumbled it badly. He came to court completely unprepared – his lawyers were focused on the new medical and other evidence and forgot about their client –

and his incoherent and unpersuasive meanderings actually undermined his central narrative.[44]

After five days the court recessed. The written briefs were filed in November and in January 1967 the lawyers gathered to begin their submissions. On 4 May 1967 the court issued its one-hundred-page decision.[45] A majority – eight of the nine judges – determined that there was no miscarriage of justice.

They went on at some length about who was where and when, what the different experts had to say, and how the trial judge behaved, but their deconstructed words left no room for ambiguity. Lynne was dead by 7:45 p.m., and Steven was the liar who took her into the Bush and raped and killed her: "There were many incredibilities inherent in the evidence given by Truscott before us and we do not believe his testimony."[46] The trial judge acted properly, and the jury got it right – Steven raped and killed Lynne, a conclusion confirmed by the fresh evidence the Supreme Court heard. Steven's evidence "simply cannot be believed."[47]

One judge, however, saw things differently.

The Dissenter

Emmett Matthew Hall was appointed to the Supreme Court of Canada in 1962 (he was sworn in on 10 January 1963), but his judicial career had begun five years earlier when a law school classmate – John Diefenbaker – became prime minister of Canada. Diefenbaker named Hall, a prominent lawyer in Saskatoon, chief justice of Saskatchewan's Court of Queen's Bench, the provincial trial court. In 1961 he promoted him to be chief justice of the Court of Appeal and the province before summoning him to Ottawa the next year. By any objective measure, Hall was an impressive man.

Born on 29 November 1898, Hall grew up on a dairy farm in Quebec. After his family moved west, he attended Saskatoon's College of Law and was called to the bar in 1922. A leading criminal and civil litigator, Hall had a well-deserved reputation for fearless advocacy, taking on the Ku Klux Klan in 1928 and, in 1935, representing some radical Bolsheviks possibly implicated in the death of a police officer during the Regina Riots.

A staunch Progressive Conservative, he had a fondness for the underdog, particularly in a battle against the state. In particular, he had a deep suspicion of police tactics, which he knew often resulted from tunnel

Emmett Hall. A Conservative appointee to the Supreme Court, his dissent in *Truscott* was, without doubt, the most powerful in the history of Canadian criminal law. (Credit: Duncan Cameron/ Library and Archives Canada)

vision. He became a stickler for due process, insisting it was the duty of the Crown to prove beyond a reasonable doubt that the accused was guilty. Innuendo, inference, and most circumstantial evidence did not cut it.[48] (To be fair, most cases turn on circumstantial evidence: stolen goods in the garage or DNA evidence left at the scene, to give two of the most common examples. The most undependable evidence is witness testimony). Until convicted, an accused was presumed innocent. "Every accused," he insisted, "has an inherent right to a fair trial by an impartial court."[49]

In his best-known work, the 1964 report of the Royal Commission on Health Services, Hall had recommended that the publicly funded "medicare," introduced in Saskatchewan by the socialist government of Tommy Douglas, be extended to the whole country and that it should be further improved to cover medical and dental care as well as prescriptions. By then, the Liberal government of Lester B. Pearson had replaced Diefenbaker, and Hall had been appointed to the Supreme Court. Still,

Hall's basic medical plan was implemented, to the overwhelming satisfaction of most Canadians: it has become a defining feature of Canadian identity, a source of national unity and pride.[50]

When the Truscott reference came to the Supreme Court, Hall stood alone. "Having considered the case fully, I believe that the conviction should be quashed and a new trial directed," he wrote in dissent. "I take the view that the trial was not conducted according to law."

Hall gave no opinion about whether Steven was guilty or whether the Crown had proven its case beyond a reasonable doubt – that was a matter for a properly instructed jury to decide "following a trial conducted according to law."[51] That had not happened here. "The law has formulated certain principles and safeguards to be applied in the trial of a person accused of a crime." In cases like this one, however, "a crime which calls out for vengeance, then comes the time of testing. It is especially at such a time that the judicial machinery must function objectively, devoid of inflammatory appeals, with the scales of justice held in balance."[52]

Justice Hall then began a point-by-point demolition of the Crown's behaviour and the trial judge's conduct of the case. It was all a complete sham. Dishonest. Disgraceful. Disreputable. While Hall did not use another expression – house of cards – he might as well have. In the medical evidence, the Crown's own expert before the Supreme Court, Dr Simpson, had testified that stomach contents could not establish time of death, yet the majority of the court concluded that "the weight of the new evidence supports Dr. Penistan's opinion."[53] The majority decision was seeking to justify a result, gathering what evidence it could, twisting it out of shape to support a finding that could not be justified on either the facts or the law. What had happened in the courts below was unfortunate, but what was taking place at the Supreme Court was an outrage. Steven had a right to a fair trial, and "the only remedy for a bad trial is a new trial."[54]

Speaking confidently, and with his fury barely concealed, Hall outlined a complete miscarriage of justice. The Crown attorney led prejudicial non-probative evidence, and the trial judge permitted it by allowing in, for example, the Crown's reference to Steven's intended imaginary rape and murder of Jocelyne Gaudet: "Crown counsel was pursuing a planned course of action that included the subtle perverting of the jury to the idea that Truscott was sex hungry that Tuesday evening and determined to have a girl in Lawson's Bush to satisfy his desires, if not Jocelyne, then Lynne."

Although the trial judge later told the jury to disregard some of the Crown's observations, it was too little and too late. The damage, Hall found, had been done. Likewise, the evidence about the bicycle tracks should never have been put before the jury. The tracks predated Lynne's murder and could not even be conclusively linked to Steven's bike, but that did not stop the judge in his address from adding some innuendo of his own: "The bicycle is not a common one." Not to put too fine a gloss on it, the trial judge and the Crown attorney were in cahoots.

In reviewing the evidence of Dr Penistan and Dr Brown, the trial judge made it clear whose evidence was to be believed: " "It will be for you to say whether you accept Doctor Penistan's theory, an Attorney-General's Pathologist of many years' standing, or do you accept Doctor Brown's evidence."55 This was, Hall wrote, a complete misdirection to the jury: "The jury should have been told that as between Dr. Penistan and Dr. Brown, if the evidence of Dr. Brown left a reasonable doubt in their minds as to the time of death, they must acquit. No jury can be told that they have to accept the evidence of one witness or that of another. The burden is on the Crown to satisfy the jury on every material aspect of the case beyond a reasonable doubt."

There is no magic about reasonable doubt: it is based on reason and common sense, and it arises logically from the evidence or the absence of evidence. Many things cannot be proved with absolute certainty, and an accused person cannot be found guilty by a jury unless the jurors believe him to be guilty. Not likely guilty. Not probably guilty. Not looks guilty. But guilty beyond a reasonable doubt.

If the prosecutor has not established proof beyond a reasonable doubt, the jury must acquit. In circumstantial cases, the evidence is "built piece by piece until the final evidentiary structure completely entraps the prisoner in a situation from which he cannot escape."56 The evidence, Hall continued, must conclusively point to the accused as the perpetrator of the crime and exclude any reasonable hypothesis of innocence. Did the evidence against Steven meet that test?

The medical evidence, Hall observed, was "contradictory in the extreme."57 The evidence before the trial court about time of death was simply wrong. Dr Addison's testimony that the sores on Steven's penis resulted from an "inexpert attempt at penetration" was inadmissible because the family doctor was, well, a family doctor not a sexologist. It was also extremely prejudicial because it tied Steven's sore penis to Lynne's rape and murder without any scientific foundation. The evidence about the dirty underwear and its vestiges of sperm was also inadmissible: the clothing was collected four days after the crime and was introduced for one purpose only: to prejudice and convict Steven. There was no proof that Steven had worn the same underwear for four days in a row, and even if he had, any trace of sperm connected to the Tuesday evening would have been unidentifiable by Saturday. Yet the judge told the jurors: "It is consistent with an attack on this girl."[58]

Justice Ferguson's theory that Steven took Lynne to the highway and then brought her back to the Bush, where he raped and killed her, was, Hall wrote, completely offside. "This introduction of the idea or theory that Truscott may in fact have taken Lynne to Number Eight Highway and brought her back to the Bush had not the slightest foundation in the evidence or in any inference which could be drawn from the evidence. It came wholly out of thin air. The Crown's case was that Truscott had not taken Lynne to Number Eight Highway at all."[59]

Hall stated that Judge Ferguson's reference to Steven's "calmness and apathy" to support his theory was gratuitous and highly damaging. It did not follow from the evidence showing that Steven appeared completely normal at 8:00 p.m. on the night Lynne went missing and every day thereafter. There were no mussed clothes, no blood or scratches – just a regular kid tooling around on his bike, going to school, politely answering all the questions he was asked. Also untenable was the evidence from the trial about what Steve could and could not see from the highway where he said he left Lynne. During the reference, the Crown had not even contested its unreliability. Hall pointed out that, had reliable evidence been introduced at trial, the jury could easily have reached a completely different view about Steven's credibility.

And on it went, with Hall finally concluding that there had to be a new trial. "I appreciate that after nearly eight years many difficulties will be met with if a new trial is held both on the part of the Crown and on the part of the accused, but these difficulties are relatively insignificant when compared to Truscott's fundamental right to be tried according to law."[60]

Hall did what he could to persuade his colleagues to take another look, but it was hopeless. Justice Douglas Abbott, whose own appointment to the court directly from the federal cabinet was controversial, dismissed Hall's dissent as "grandstanding." Really? As Steven's lawyer, G.

Arthur Martin, observed years later: "Here you had in a book, edited by
the [Crown] witness, a case where the stomach contents, similar to those
that existed in the case of Lynne Harper, were proved to have existed
notwithstanding a lapse of nine hours since the last meal." But Abbott
and every other judge except Hall concluded that "the weight of the new
evidence supports Dr. Penistan's opinion."[61] Hall was not grandstanding. He was honestly doing his job. To his dying day, Hall was furious
about his colleagues' behaviour in this case: "Not one of them had any
substantive criminal law experience." He was especially scornful of
Abbott, previously but never more a friend.[62]

Hall's dissent, without a doubt, is the most powerful in the history of
Canadian criminal law: it called everyone to account – the police, the
medical profession, the trial judge, the Crown attorney, the Court of
Appeal, and all the other judges on the Supreme Court – and every point
he made has since proved to be true. Hall never wavered in his view that
"Steven Murray Truscott received a bad trial and the [Supreme Court]
ought to have admitted that it erred in not accepting the appeal seven
years earlier."[63] As one of Hall's biographers observed, "It was a rare
case of a lone dissenter wagging the majority."[64] Hall's dissent was that
classic appeal to a future day, to other judges, and to history. "We didn't
lose," LeBourdais told reporters when the decision was announced, "we
were defeated, and there's a difference."[65]

As things turned out, Hall's dissent did matter.

Aftermath

After ten years in prison, on 21 October 1969, Steven, just twenty-four
years old, was paroled. He moved to another Ontario small town, changed
his name to Steven Bowers, found a job, married, had a family, and never
got into trouble with the law. But, as one year passed to the next, it just
did not sit right. When DNA evidence began exonerating other men who
had been wrongfully convicted, that got Steven thinking.

Toronto lawyer James Lockyer used DNA to secure the freedom of
Guy Paul Morin and David Milgaard – both convicted by juries but both
vindicated (1995 and 1997) after genetic tests proved that the murderer
was another guy – and he also established the Association for the Defence
of the Wrongfully Convicted (AIDWYC), now called Innocence Canada.[66]

Isabel LeBourdais and Steven Truscott. The intrepid journalist wrote a withering, path-breaking attack on Canada's justice system. (Photo courtesy Julien LeBourdais)

When Steven approached the lawyer, Lockyer told him he "was very confident we could find DNA samples. [He] made it very clear that the perpetrator would have left behind his DNA." Actually, Lockyer had no idea whether any DNA could be retrieved, but he was testing his potential client. Truscott did not hesitate: "Let's go for it," he said, "I have nothing to hide."[67] Lockyer could not find anything to test – most of the exhibits were long gone, and when Lynne's body was eventually exhumed no usable DNA could be recovered.

What he did discover was almost as helpful: there were thousands of pages of withheld evidence – some of it exculpatory – much of it pointing to a complete miscarriage in the administration of justice and with details of actual police and prosecutorial misconduct.

It was the perfect story for the CBC's *fifth estate*, the public broadcaster's flagship investigative newsmagazine. "His Word against History: The Steven Truscott Story" was broadcast on 29 March 2000 and garnered an audience of 1.4 million Canadians. The "science" that had put

Steven in jail – that he was with Lynne when she died – had been thoroughly debunked for years. All the experts agreed that time of death could not be determined by stomach contents. But without DNA or a confession, there could be no vindication.

An Application for Ministerial Review initiates a procedure in the Criminal Code that allows a closed case to be reopened. Many applications are made but few are granted, and relief, as an exercise of the ancient royal prerogative, is extraordinary. This time round the wheels of justice moved quite slowly after the application was filed in November 2001. The federal Department of Justice had to be persuaded that there was evidence that, if earlier available, could have affected the outcome. And it wasn't just any evidence, but significant evidence establishing that a miscarriage of justice had likely occurred.

The Cover-Up Uncovered

Working alongside the CBC's *fifth estate*, AIDWYC investigated further. It learned about Dr Penistan's "agonizing reappraisal" and about how Mr and Mrs Townsend saw a young girl hitchhiking exactly where Steven said he left Lynne and at the very time he was supposedly in Lawson's Bush raping and killing her. It also learned about witnesses who changed their stories after they were interviewed and re-interviewed by the police, and others like Karen Daum who corroborated – in a signed statement witnessed by Inspector Graham – Steven's alibi.[68] All of this evidence had been buried by the police.

The threshold for initiating a review was met – and this time it was the evidence that especially mattered, not the unfairness of the prosecution and trial. The government appointed Fred Kaufman to advise it on how best to handle the situation. A retired judge of the Quebec Court of Appeal, Kaufman had presided over the ministerial review of what turned out to be the wrongful conviction of Guy Paul Morin, who had also been sent to jail for murdering a young girl. After looking into the Truscott case, he recommended a brand new appeal. Steven was a poor witness – after hearing directly from him, Kaufman agreed with the majority of the Supreme Court of Canada about that – but he was not a deceitful one. Steven's story, he wrote, was not "incapable of belief."[69]

Hindsight, while not perfect, is often improved, especially when there is new information. In 1959 and in 1966 there was no legal obligation for the prosecution to disclose all the evidence to the accused, but there was a duty to be fair. Ivan Rand, perhaps Canada's most outstanding Supreme Court judge, had set out the obligation in a 1955 case: "The purpose of a criminal prosecution is not to obtain a conviction ... The role of prosecutor excludes any notion of winning or losing; his function is a matter of public duty than which in civil life there can be none charged with greater responsibility. It is to be efficiently performed with an ingrained sense of the dignity, the seriousness and the justness of judicial proceedings."[70]

Many defence attorneys scoff at the notion that their Crown counterparts are anything other than committed adversaries seeking to build a case and secure a conviction.[71] To be sure, there was nothing fair about the Truscott trial. The undisclosed evidence might very well have affected the outcome. Following a two-year review and a four-volume report, Kaufman concluded that a miscarriage of justice had likely occurred. That did not necessarily mean that an innocent man had been convicted.

On 28 October 2004, against the wishes of the Truscott family, who wanted the justice minister to order a new trial, the federal government referred the case to the Ontario Court of Appeal. A new trial would have been impossible as, after almost fifty years, there was no evidence to call, and an acquittal would have to be entered. It was far better to ask the Court of Appeal to try to get the bottom of what the *Globe and Mail* called the case "that haunts the Canadian imagination."[72]

It would take two years for the case to get back to court. There were four possible results: the court could dismiss the reference, order a new trial, enter an acquittal, or make a declaration of innocence. Every single court and every single judge but one who had looked at the matter – at trial, at appeal, and at the Supreme Court of Canada – had upheld Steven's conviction. Only one judge – Hall – pointed in a different direction. This appeal would be Steven's last chance for vindication. In preparing for the proceeding, the AIDWYC lawyers had some help: a road map from the Supreme Court of Canada reference – "the dissenting judgment of Justice Emmett Hall."[73]

Beginning in June 2006, a five-person panel began hearing the case and, for the first time in Ontario history, there were cameras in the court. Chief Justice Roy McMurtry was presiding, joined by four Court of Appeal colleagues, three of whom were experts in criminal law. This time Truscott had another dream team of Ontario's top criminal counsel in his corner: James Lockyer, Philip Campbell, Marlys Edwardh, Hersh Wolch, and Jenny Friedland. Seventeen witnesses testified that summer, though not Steven.

Facts matter, and the first witness emphasized the need for an "evidence-based approach." That meant not focusing on one item in isolation but looking at the whole picture. Assuming for the sake of argument, as Dr Penistan testified and as the government argued during the 1966 Supreme Court reference, that one could determine the time of death by stomach contents, was there other evidence that could corroborate or contradict Penistan's precise finding that Lynne died between 7:00 and 7:45 p.m.? There *was* other evidence to examine.

It was a hot summer night when Lynne disappeared, and two days before her body was found lying in the woods. On any measure, advanced putrefaction would have set in had she been left dead in Lawson's Bush between 7:00 and 8:00 p.m. on Tuesday. But there was remarkably little decomposition – "nil" was the way Penistan described it. Even though he testified that the degree of decomposition was consistent with his evidence about time of death, it was just not possible. In the 2006 appeal the experts testified that, if she had died at the time suggested, the rescuers would have discovered a different corpse from the one they stumbled on that Thursday afternoon. At the very least, there was *no* scientific basis to conclude that Lynne died between 7:15 p.m. and 7:45 p.m.

For the first time too, Penistan's "agonizing reappraisal" saw the light of day. The court readily concluded that the doctor's original evidence had been tailored to coincide with Inspector Graham's case. At the Supreme Court, the majority had paid special deference to Penistan's opinion because he was the one who examined the body at the scene of the crime and performed the autopsy. At the Court of Appeal, other evidence was also considered, including a detailed review of the testimony of all the children and some of the adults who were out that evening, along with the documents that had recently been disclosed, such as the statement taken by Inspector Graham from Daum. She testified for the first time, along with entomological experts from all over the world.

When the eighty-four-year-old former OPP officer Hank Sayeau was called to the witness stand, he was asked by one of the judges whether the police had considered interviewing any of the many well-known neighbourhood perverts/predators/sex offenders. "I don't recall that," he told the court. Bob Lawson told the court about a strange car he observed

Steven Truscott. He was never exonerated by the justice system – but the Ontario Court of Appeal eventually determined that a properly instructed jury would have likely concluded that there was reasonable doubt whether he killed and raped Lynne Harper. (Credit: Michael Stuparyk/Getty Images)

by the Bush that June night, but when he brought it to the attention of the police at the time they were just not interested. In January 2007 the lawyers and judges reassembled at Osgoode Hall for another three weeks for the final legal submissions.

On 28 August 2007 the Court of Appeal quashed the conviction: "Based on evidence ... we are satisfied that Mr. Truscott's conviction was a miscarriage of justice and must be quashed."[74] The medical evidence that Lynne died sometime before 8:00 p.m. did not stand up, and the court completely rejected Dr Penistan's evidence as "scientifically unsupportable."[75] The penis evidence was similarly dismissed: it had no probative value and should never have been allowed in the first place.

The court could not find that Steven was innocent – before that could happen, he would have to demonstrate his factual innocence, and that was almost impossible without definitive forensic evidence such as DNA or a believable confession by another party. Steven was the last person to see Lynne alive and was with her at a location close to where her body was found, so there was no way the court could categorically rule him out. Still, all five judges determined that if a jury had had the opportunity to hear all the evidence, and if it had been properly instructed by the trial judge, it would have likely concluded that there was a reasonable doubt.

In due course the Ontario government apologized to Steven Truscott and, after receiving the recommendation of a retired judge, the truly dis-tinguished Sydney Robins, paid him $6.5 million (and $100,000 for his wife, Marlene, whose dogged determination to achieve justice for her husband was nothing less than astonishing) for "the hardship caused by the wrongful conviction and the public recognition of the seriousness of the wrong" he had suffered.[76]

Bad People Who Do Bad Things and Other Reasons for Skepticism about Legal Outcomes

There will always be people ready to do the bidding of authority. Dr Penistan was on that list, but he was not the first nor would he be the last. The 2008 report of the Inquiry into Pediatric Forensic Pathology in Ontario, headed by Stephen Goudge, a judge of the Ontario Court of Appeal, found that one forensic pathologist, the soon to be completely discredited Charles Smith, was actually making stuff up to assist Crown attorneys in securing convictions.

In one case, based on Smith's evidence, a man was put in prison for twelve years for sodomizing and murdering his four-year-old niece when in fact she had died of natural causes. There had never been any crime even though the doctor testified that the girl died while being anally raped. Justice Goudge concluded that Dr Smith "lacked basic knowledge about forensic pathology." People suffered because of Smith. Whole families were destroyed because of Smith. Not because the science was unreliable, or had evolved, but because Smith was a bad man who did bad things.

As the chief justice of Ontario, George Strathy, has said, "there is growing recognition of the responsibility of the trial judge to exercise a more robust gatekeeper role in the admission of expert evidence."[77] The Court of Appeal in the Truscott reference endorsed this view and effec-tively directed trial judges not to accept expert evidence on its face but to analyze it critically.

Law enforcement must also up its game. In their haste to find the cul-prit in high-profile murder investigations, police forces often succumb to tunnel vision, which, like groupthink and racial profiling, impedes fur-ther consideration and investigation. "Tunnel vision ... is generated by a police and prosecutorial culture that allows the subconscious mind to rationalize a biased approach to the evidence. Moreover, it is mutually reinforcing amongst police officers, amongst prosecutors and in the interaction between these groups of professionals. It may even affect judges."[78] The presumption of guilt is alive and well, while some police practices – the Reid Technique, for instance, a trademarked method of police questioning – has an established track record of producing false confessions.

In the Truscott reference, the Ontario Court of Appeal did not have to reach any findings about the inadequate police work, but it could not help observing that police tunnel vision was "a feature found in many miscarriages of justice."[79] It is just one more cognitive impairment getting in the way of the truth and again illustrating the importance of dissent.

In the years since Truscott's original trial and appeal, new Crown disclosure rules have made a difference. The Supreme Court of Canada ruled in a 1991 case, *Stinchcombe*, that the Crown must, at an early opportunity, disclose any and all relevant information, inculpatory and exculpatory, to the defence (except for a very narrow range of privileged materials[80]). "The fruits of the investigation which are in the possession of counsel for the Crown," Justice John Sopinka wrote for a unanimous court, "are not the property of the Crown for use in securing a conviction but the property of the public to be used to ensure that justice is done."[81] However, Crown prosecutors always had the obligation to put justice first – and in the Truscott trial, and on countless occasions since, they did not. Prosecutorial error, like police misconduct, is a problem that plagues us still – and just about every other country in the world.

Isabel LeBourdais, the dissenter who came to Steven's aid when he was all alone, died at the age of ninety-three in 2003. She thus did not live to see the long fight for justice in the Truscott case succeed. Sadly, too, she had been a resident in a nursing home for the last eight years of her life and did not realize that her efforts had been continued by others. Yet she never doubted Steven's innocence. What made her alone take up his case, confront her publisher, the establishment, and seek justice? It can't be the money, or the glory. So what is it? What is it that motivates so very few to leave their comfort zone and fight for what is right?

We will probably never know who killed Lynne Harper. We do know that the Crown never came close to proving, beyond a reasonable doubt, that it was Steven. If there had been a proper police investigation, or a Crown counsel who cared about his ethical obligations, or a judge who did his duty to ensure that Steven got a fair trial, or a Court of Appeal and a Supreme Court that paid attention to the actual evidence, there would likely have been different outcomes all along the way. But as badly as the system failed, a small handful of individuals did not.

Dogged. Determined. Resolute. Courageous. Independent. LeBourdais was a hero, and Justice Emmett Hall too. So too were the young boys Dougie and Gord, who never wavered in their stories of seeing Steven riding his bike along the highway with Lynne and then returning alone. "I did what my mother and father taught me to do," Dougie, by now a grown-up man, wrote in 2012. "I told the truth. I told it over and over … Several times the police asked me to change my story. I stuck to what I knew to be the truth."[82]

Truth matters.

Chapter 7

Occupy Wall Street – and This, That, and the Other Place

Beginning at the end of 2010, and gaining steam throughout 2011, there were uprisings, big and small, throughout the Arab world: in Algeria, Bahrain, Egypt, Jordan, Iraq, Libya, Morocco, Oman, Tunisia, Saudi Arabia, Syria, and Yemen (but oddly not Palestine). These were mass popular movements involving hundreds of thousands dissenting against dictatorship and the status quo. These were people who actually had a lot to lose – their freedom, even their lives – by publicly protesting. And with one exception, the end result was more of the same: in varying degrees, terror, torture, dictatorship, and social suffering.

Tunisia was where the "Arab Spring" actually began. In mid-December 2010 Tarek el-Tayeb Mohamed Bouazizi, a street fruit-and-vegetable vendor, set himself on fire on the steps of City Hall to protest his never-ending mistreatment by local police and government. Tunisia is where, against all odds, a transition to democracy succeeded. Elsewhere, sadly, the Arab Spring was followed by an Arab Winter.

The protest at Tahrir Square in downtown Cairo was a partial success. It began on 25 January 2011, inspired by a brave young woman named Asmaa Mahfouz who posted a video on YouTube: "We just want our human rights and nothing else. This entire government is corrupt – a corrupt president and a corrupt police force."[1] Fifty thousand people responded, demanding the resignation of Egyptian dictator Hosni Mubarak. He had been president since Anwar Sadat was assassinated by Islamic fundamentalists in 1981. By the end of the month, there were 250,000 demonstrators in the historic square, followed soon after, *Al Jazeera* broadcast, by 1 million or more.

On 11 February Mubarak was removed – he nominally resigned but was later arrested, charged with corruption, and put on trial, caged despite being in a sick bed. In a little bit of "be careful of what you wish for," when the people had their say in Egypt's first and only truly free vote on 30 June 2012, they elected Mohamed Morsi, the Muslim Brotherhood candidate, to office. But Morsi was no democrat: he enthusiastically adopted some of his predecessor's policies, including abduction and torture of political opponents and journalists, and in November 2012 granted himself unlimited power. That was not what the Egyptian people had in mind. On 29 June 2013 Egyptians began to reassemble in Tahrir Square and across the country to demand his resignation. Within days, the military took over. It could not abide government by ignorant, barbaric fanatics, even if they had been democratically elected. Soon enough the streets were empty and the prisons full. It was, and remains, business as usual in Egypt.

The Protest Moves to Spain

At the beginning of 2011, however, the promise of the Arab Spring had not yet been dashed. People everywhere were excited about the transformative potential of a genuinely authentic pro-democracy movement, with its promise for fundamental progressive change, spreading through traditionally democracy-averse societies. But long-established democracies were hardly immune.

Spain, for instance, was in deep economic difficulties, with a recorded unemployment rate north of 20 per cent: 5 million people who wanted to work had no jobs. Youth unemployment was over 40 per cent, the highest rate by far in the European community. Although Spaniards were frustrated, they had little political choice in a country polarized between parties of the centre-right and the centre-left, a choice between Tweedledum and Tweedledee.

No one had anything new to say about the structural changes Spain desperately required. There was also a curious consensus in the political establishment that transcended political stripe: agreement to impose the austerity and budget cuts demanded by global finance and international regulators, while the homegrown banking industry benefited from taxpayer-funded bailouts. It was a race to the bottom, with the human and social wreckage of failed public policies on everyday display. No matter who was in power, unemployment increased and home foreclosures accelerated while the rich increased their wealth.

Many believed that the system had completely failed and the only way out was by starting over again. What better way than by meeting in public squares and, without leaders or agendas, coming up with real solutions to the pressing problems? Instead of choosing between the traditional alternatives of right and left, they reasoned, "with consensus, we take an issue, hear the range of enthusiasm, ideas and concerns about it, and synthesize a proposal that best serves everybody's vision."[2] Without hierarchy, "revolutionary energy" would flow. Since everyone got to speak – this would be a true democracy – everyone would, in theory, benefit from the ideas and insights of others. This was the narrative on sale, and it attracted buyers.

At the beginning of 2011, Democracia Real YA (Real Democracy NOW) took to social media with the motto "We are people, not commodities, in the hands of politicians and bankers," and called on youth, the unemployed, and the poor and poorly paid to take to the streets on 15 May, just one week before the scheduled municipal elections. Almost fifteen thousand *indignados* (the outraged) assembled at Madrid's Puerta del Sol, and more than 100,000 people throughout Spain joined the protest in the days that followed, bringing sleeping bags and tents to public squares across the land. When truncheon-wielding police removed the Madrid *indignados* in the early hours on 17 May, the protests spread farther. Old-fashioned police brutality is a sure crowd generator.

The hashtag #spanishrevolution began trending on Twitter as the protests continued from one day to the next. A Madrid webcam broadcast the events from Puerta del Sol to the world – 11 million views by July 2011. *Der Spiegel*, *Le Monde*, the *New York Times*, and the *Washington Post* all compared this revolution with the one that had successfully concluded in Cairo. Everyone marvelled on how well organized it was – the protestors had even created an assembly (more on that shortly). An edict issued by the Regional Electoral Board banning the Madrid rally was ignored. Demonstrations continued throughout the summer.

There was definitely something appealing about the Spanish movement, and it began to travel. At the end of May, Greek protestors gathered in Syntagma Square in Athens as their government came to terms with the austerity measures imposed by the European Union and the International Monetary Fund in response to the country's huge debt, bloated public sector, and general reluctance to pay income tax. In Tel Aviv in June, hundreds of thousands of Israelis took to the streets to protest the high cost of living – their protest was sparked by yet another increase in the cost of cottage cheese – and to demand economic justice.

What was interesting about the Spanish protest (15-M, they called it) was not just its longevity and broad appeal. It rejected politicians, partisan politics, and labour-union support and experimented with something different – the assembly. It was time to "take back democracy." Spanish youth and the middle class concluded that the system was rigged against them. "We need a new idea of how we can make society, to build another system," a Puerta del Sol protestor told the *Huffington Post*, adding, "We can build it together. We rely on the collective intelligence of the people."[3] That was, in any event, the party line.

Crowds know some things, as James Surowiecki's *The Wisdom of Crowds* proved, but experience teaches other things. There was a definite disconnect between "Real Democracy NOW" and real democracy now. When the ballots from the municipal election were counted, it was a landslide – for the right wing. When national elections were held in November, the Spanish Socialist Workers' Party was shown the door. The new boss was just like the old boss, as Prime Minister Mariano Rajoy's economic agenda immediately demonstrated.

In March 2012 Spain's Central Bank declared that the country was back in recession. In the meantime, 15-M was long gone from Puerta del Sol: the police cleared everyone out in August 2011. In response, the *indignados* decided to do something different: in January 2014 they formed a new political party, Podemos (We Can), which is now Spain's third-largest. It took a handful of European Union seats in Strasbourg and then won 20 per cent of the popular vote and 69 (out of 350) seats in Parliament in the 2015 general election, possibly ending Spain's traditional two-party system. This anti-corruption and anti-austerity party has obvious public support, but, as the *New York Times* observed, its platform is little more than a half-baked "wish list."[4]

The Origins of Occupy Wall Street

Meanwhile, in Vancouver, Canada, and in Berkeley, California, two people – Kalle Lasn and Micah White, the co-founder and senior editor, respectively, of *Adbusters* – were paying careful attention. Born in Estonia on 24 March 1942, Lasn, along with his family, fled the advancing Soviet Army toward the end of the Second World War and ended up in a West German refugee camp before being resettled in Australia when he was seven. A graduate of the University of Adelaide in theoretical and

Kalle Lasn. One of the founders of *Adbusters*, Lasn believed that revolution was within reach. (Credit: Grant Harder)

applied mathematics, he worked for four years writing code in the Australian military. After a sojourn in Tokyo (where he started a market-research company), he travelled the world, arriving in Paris just in time for the May 1968 student and worker protests against capitalism. The attempted insurrection was suppressed and, after an election, everything returned to normal, but not for Lasn. Paris 1968 was a transformative event for him, and he began to dream of a global revolution. In 1970 he moved to Vancouver and began producing award-winning documentaries for Canada's National Film Board (NFB).

One day when Lasn went to a supermarket and found he had to insert a coin before he could release a shopping cart, he deliberately jammed his quarter into the slot so hard that the cart became inoperable. He called it a "culture jam," an act deliberately designed to make a statement and subvert society. He went on to write a book titled *Culture Jam* (1999), and although he did not invent culture jamming, he definitely helped to popularize it.

Lasn expresses his mission in five words: "We will wreck this world."[5] He is against a lot of things: war, corporations, lobbyists, consumerism, television, branding, globalization, and Israel, to list just a few examples. He is in favour of the environment, feminism, and Palestinians. Culture jamming is the objective of the magazine *Adbusters* that Lasn co-founded in 1989 with Bill Schmalz, a colleague from the NFB and wildlife photographer. It challenges consumerism and its assorted real and imagined evils by ridiculing it, in the rich tradition of other culture jammers ranging from *Mad Magazine* to Abbie Hoffman (playing himself) and Sacha Baron Cohen (playing Borat). *Adbusters* purports to expose concealed realities as it raises big questions about the true human and environmental costs of consumer consumption.

In the same way that Rachel Carson called attention to pesticides in the soil, culture jammers point to the mental environment, "increasingly polluted with toxins."[6] "We are," Lasn observes, "constantly being hyped, suckered and lied to."[7] Resembling pollution rather than information, these "messages" are "infotoxins," irrelevant to basic human needs yet occupying inordinate space in the human brain to the exclusion of authentic information necessary for the sustainability of ourselves and the planet. If we don't resist, Lasn believes, a "dark age [will be] coming for humanity."[8] Culture jamming points the way: people must be shocked out of their consumerist trance. That's what *Adbusters* has tried to do, albeit sometimes with a heavy and judgmental hand.

By 2011, *Adbusters* had thousands of paid subscribers and accepted donations but never advertisements. It describes itself as "a global network of artists, activists, writers, pranksters, students, educators and entrepreneurs who want to advance the new social activist movement of the information age." Opposed to capitalism, the magazine has encouraged many anti-consumerism campaigns, including Buy Nothing Day, Buy Nothing Christmas, and TV Turnoff Week (which morphed into Digital Detox Week). None of them had great success, but there was an underlying genius. While people could have wildly different reasons for supporting anti-consumerist activity, their specific motivations did not matter if they shared the same goal. Punk rockers and fundamentalist Christians could find common ground.

In 2006 Micah White, age twenty-four, came on board. The *San Francisco Chronicle* called him "one of the most fascinating people in the Bay Area," and in 2014 *Esquire Magazine* included him in its list of "most influential under-35-year-olds in America." The child of a Caucasian mother and an African American father, in middle school he refused to

Micah White. Described Occupy Wall Street as "beautiful and inspiring." (Credit: Eugênio Goulart)

stand for the national anthem, and in high school he formed an atheists club, soon gaining, and enjoying, national media attention. After graduating from Swarthmore, he moved to Vancouver to work with Lasn – and the collaboration continued even after White settled in Berkeley.

Both Lasn and White believed that "a revolutionary moment was within reach,"[9] but their campaigns kept failing. "Rather than be discouraged," White recollected, "I became convinced that our idea for a contagious action spread through a hashtag was simply ahead of its time. We failed because we were too early." He was confident, though, "that if we tried again the people might catch up."[10] In 2011 events in Egypt and Spain, and mass protests around the globe, including student protests in White's Berkeley backyard, suggested that the timing might be right. Seizing the moment, *Adbusters* called for the occupation of Wall Street.

"Are you ready for a Tahrir moment?" the magazine asked in a mass e-mail to its 90,000 "culture jammers" in early July. It proposed a peaceful occupation of Wall Street and selected Saturday, 17 September. Calling for "a shift in revolutionary tactics," it encouraged people to converge on lower Manhattan, "set up tents, kitchens, peaceful barricades and occupy Wall Street for a few months. Once there, we shall incessantly repeat one simple demand in a plurality of voices."[11]

But what demand? "We talk to each other in various physical gatherings and virtual people's assemblies ... we zero in what our one demand will be, a demand that awakens the imagination and, if achieved, would propel us toward the radical democracy of the future." The one demand would be determined by the protestors not by leaders – there weren't going to be any. The post was signed "Culture Jammers HQ," and it formally introduced the #occupywallstreet hashtag.

Adbusters called for parallel protests all over the world. A poster posing the question "What is our one demand?" soon gained iconic status and became the emblem of Occupy Wall Street (ows): it pictured Wall Street's bronzed Charging Bull with a ballerina on top, and armed hoody-wearing protestors (or police?) with gas masks emerging from the background ready for the battles ahead.

ows gathered more steam than Lasn and White ever imagined as a variety of groups began meeting in New York throughout the summer to coordinate the September occupation. One of them, a coalition of activists, artists, and students – the New Yorkers against Budget Cuts – had just concluded an occupation outside City Hall after thousands of public-school teachers received pink slips. They set up a tent city they called Bloombergville for three weeks of protests against deep spending cuts to education and other public services. They packed up only after City Council passed a budget that avoided most of the layoffs.

Anxious for a repeat performance, many of New York City's most committed social activists and anarchists, along with veterans of Tahrir Square and the Spanish 15-M, held a meeting at the beginning of August. Among the advertised purposes of this meeting were holding a "People's General Assembly on the Budget Cuts" and planning the 17 September occupation of Wall Street. Over the days and weeks that followed, the organizers assembled on the fourth floor of 16 Beaver (an artists' space in lower Manhattan not far from Wall Street), at the Irish Hunger Memorial near Battery Park, and at the south side of Tompkins Square Park.

With anarchists, Marxists, social democrats, and assorted true believers representing all known equity-seeking groups and every imaginable political stripe, the conversation was always heated.

The Issues

Wall Street has been the target of many protests over the years. Depending on your point of view, it is the epicentre of American capitalism or, as White calls it, "the financial Gomorrah of America."[12] After the 2008 financial crisis, people had a lot to be angry about. Millions of Americans lost their homes after being force-fed predatory mortgages. These were the NINJA loans (no income, no job, no assets). Too good to refuse, bankers had suckered ordinary Americans who were unaware, or willfully blind. Soon enough, there would be a day of reckoning and payments that could never be met. People who should have been protected by the system, and from themselves, lost everything as bailiffs threw their

Across the United States millions of Americans were evicted from their homes and their possessions tossed on their front lawns. Here one such 2008 scene in Waco, Texas. (Credit: Larry Downing / Reuters Images)

possessions on front lawns. In the years after 2008, 5 million home fore-closures displaced more than 10 million people, and millions more were straining to keep afloat.[13] In 2005 two people, Warren Buffet and Bill Gates, had a combined wealth equivalent to the total owned by 120 million Americans – the bottom 40 per cent. Four hundred Americans owned 50 per cent of everything. This disparity was a global phenomenon: by 2015, the world's richest 62 people had more wealth than half the world's population counted together, down from about 388 people just five years earlier.[14] In 2008 the Organisation for Economic Co-operation and Development (OECD) ranked the United States higher in income inequality than any country in Europe. Canada followed, and follows, suit. On 15 January 2017 the *Globe and Mail* reported that the two richest Canadians – worth some $33 billion – had more wealth than about twelve million Canadians, the bottom 30 per cent.

As more riches flowed to the top 1 per cent, their tax rates declined – on the prevailing theory of "trickle-down" or supply-side economics. It was all part of a neo-conservative deregulation movement that was enthusiastically promoted by the right and acquiesced to by virtually everyone else. As Buffet observed, he paid proportionately less income tax than his assistant. The average income of the top 1 per cent in the United States in 2011 was around $1 million a year. For the top one-hundredth of the top 1 per cent, it was $24 million a year. In contrast, the average income for the bottom 90 per cent was just under $30,000 annually. Income, of course, only told part of the story. The other part was wealth and here the spread here was even greater.

In Canada, the top 1 per cent had average incomes of about $381,000. The median income in the rest of the country: $29,000.[15] Year after year, income inequality in both the United States and Canada continued to increase. The Conservative government of Prime Minister Stephen Harper cut corporate tax rates and the rich got richer. In 2007, on the eve of the financial meltdown, a *Wall Street Journal* columnist, Robert Frank, published *Richistan*, which revealed, among other things, that there was a worldwide shortage of butlers. On the other side of the ledger, about 45 million Americans relied on food stamps just to survive. In 2011 the federal American minimum wage was $7.25 an hour – the price of a foot-long sub or a burrito from Chipotle. In some states the minimum wage was even less. People were working like dogs and living in abject poverty. Approximately one in seven Americans was being hounded by a debt-collection agency. People were finding it impossible to get ahead – ordinary people, that is.

The wealthy had clearly captured the political process, and their reward was low taxes and a regulatory environment that permitted their vast accumulation of wealth. The biggest and most profitable companies in the world arranged their affairs so they paid little or no tax. Corporate citizenship was passé. Compensation for chief executive officers increased while working peoples' wages remained stagnant or declined. In 2011 American CEOs, who used to earn about thirty times more than the average worker, were earning 100 times more. In Canada, the top 100 CEOs earned 189 times the compensation of their average employee.

Henry Ford had some odd ideas, but he understood that for his company to succeed, the people who built his cars had to be able to afford to buy them. Otherwise, the American Dream was just that, a dream. By the early twenty-first century, Horatio Alger stories had become a cruel hoax. Only 6 per cent of Americans born at the bottom now make it to the top. Add in long-standing and growing disparities for African Americans and other racialized persons, and it was clear that huge structural problems were contributing to growing income inequality. The male-female wage gap, in contrast, was decreasing (and the trend suggested further narrowing, especially as women become better educated than men).

In the meantime, unemployment in many areas skyrocketed into the double digits as technology took its toll and increasing numbers of jobs were automated or outsourced to low-paid people in the poorest parts of the world. Students graduated with no jobs on offer but with debts they had no possibility of paying off, ever. Intern Nation, McJobs, the "gig" economy, and working for chump change became facts of life. In Washington, cutting the budget and trimming social spending only made a bad situation worse. How did legitimate, fair-minded worry about the growing public debt come to be more important than equally compelling concerns about the victims of the economic collapse?

Corporate-governance scandals at Enron, Tyco, and WorldCom, to give just three examples, further eroded confidence in the system while the big-bank bailouts destroyed what was left. The banks were too big to fail, the government said, and money flowed to them. Among all the G7 countries, Canada was the only one that did not need to bail out its banks. When management was caught out, it apologized and paid fines, but the costs were relatively trivial and internalized as a part of doing business. Behaviour became less reckless but as remunerative as ever.

Soon enough it was back to normal: record corporate profits and big bonuses for the richest Americans. As economic recovery took hold after 2008, the incomes of the top 1 per cent increased by 11.6 per cent. For the 99 per cent, the increase was 0.2 per cent.[16] Public-opinion polls at the time showed that most people believed that government did nothing for them, and far too much for the 1 per cent. In 2010 the poverty rate was at its highest point in twenty years.[17]

No one was held responsible for this neglect of the poor and the middle class, but the writing was on the wall. In March 2011 the Nobel laureate economist Joseph E. Stiglitz made a dire prediction in *Vanity Fair*:

> In recent weeks we have watched people taking to the streets by the millions to protest political, economic and social conditions in the oppressive societies they inhabit. Governments have been toppled in Egypt and Tunisia ... The ruling families elsewhere in the region look on nervously from their air-conditioned penthouses – will they be next? They are right to worry. These are societies where a minuscule fraction of the population – less than 1 percent – controls the lion's share of the wealth ... As we gaze out at the popular fervor in the streets, one question to ask ourselves is this: When will it come to America? In important ways, our own country has become like one of these distant troubled places.[18]

Two months later, 20,000 people marched on Wall Street protesting bank bailouts and budget cuts. Like so many protests before and since, it had nothing but local impact, mostly because it disrupted traffic, and was forgotten within days. During the planning meetings for OWS, some of the 15-M veterans suggested a different approach: not the usual cookie-cutter protest but a general assembly, where all of the decisions, including the setting of demands, would be made by consensus. This idea even had North American roots, including the Longhouses of the First Nations as well as Quaker meeting practices that had been modernized by anti-nuclear protestors in the 1970s. Once the New York General Assembly was formed, its purpose, according to Professor David Graeber, one of OWS's leading theorists, a committed anarchist, and the likely creator of the slogan "We Are the 99%," was to create "a body that could act as a model of genuine, direct democracy to contrapose to the corrupt charge presented to us as 'democracy' by the US government."[19]

This protest was going to be different – and it was.

The Occupation

People of a certain age and experience have a narrow and linear view of protest, informed by the sit-ins, marches, and boycotts of one stripe or another since the mid-twentieth century: the great civil-rights movement of the 1960s, for instance, or, at the local level, various activities led by community organizers such as the young African American from Chicago with a Harvard law degree named Barack Obama.

These kinds of protests are termed vertical: they have a hierarchy of leaders as well as specific issues and demands. OWS, however, was horizontal – as the politically progressive American magazine *Mother Jones* put it, "a leaderless group of people who get together to discuss pressing issues and make decisions by pure consensus."[20] "We are our demands," occupiers would chant. The General Assembly "was a horizontal, autonomous, leaderless, modified-consensus-based system with roots in anarchist thought."[21] *Adbusters* was definitely the inspiration, but, although it would provide unsolicited "tactical briefings" over the course of the occupation, its work was largely done.

At the end of August 2011, the hacktivist, anarchist Internet group Anonymous issued an open invitation to "Fellow Citizens of the Internet" to come to Wall Street and peacefully protest.[22] It used its Twitter feed to promote the OWS demonstration, bestowing on the new "movement," or whatever it was, instant street cred: Anonymous could not be bought. The police knew the occupiers were coming and blocked off preferred sites.

On 17 September the protestors – banging drums, shaking tambourines, blowing horns, and chanting "bring justice to the bankers" – mustered at the Charging Bull and then moved to nearby Zuccotti Park. Named after Brookfield properties chairman John Zuccotti, it was a small rectangular block of granite adorned with fifty honeysuckle trees surrounded by skyscrapers, around the corner from the New York Stock Exchange. The by-law that created the park required that it be kept open to the public twenty-four hours a day for "passive recreation."

The "occupation of Wall Street" had now begun. It was fine, at first, with the mayor, Michael R. Bloomberg. He told the *New York Times* that people have the right to protest, and that the city would make sure they had locations to exercise their right. Neither Lasn nor White ever visited the tent city, but White liked what he saw from afar: "From the beginning, Occupy Wall Street was a beautiful event," he wrote later.[23]

Others agreed: ows was a model democracy, model society, and model civilization: "You could meditate, change your wardrobe, update your blog, cook lentils, read a book, sweep up litter, bandage a wound, bang a drum, roll a cigarette, debate how best to challenge corporate hegemony, make art, wash dishes and have sex, usually in the company of others. The square teemed with friends and strangers, allies and antagonists; it was intensely public and interactive."[24] WiFi was indispensable, but service was interrupted when the police removed the power generators. Before long, power generated by volunteers pedalling bicycles at high speed filled the gap and everyone could blog and tweet, watched by thousands more who "liked" what they saw.

By and large, and especially in the beginning, the occupiers were white, mostly young (mid-thirties on average), well educated, and with time to spare. Many others who had nothing to do with the larger project came for the free food, medical care, kinship, and conversation. Society's dispossessed, actively encouraged by the police to "take it to Zuccotti,"[25] arrived in large numbers too, bringing with them drug dealing and abuse, petty theft, and sexual and other assault. Reports of public urination and defecation increased. Some people came because they were curious. Others believed that ows might be history in the making, the American equivalent of the October 1917 Russian Revolution. Who would want to miss that?

Many people, Lasn and White among them, truly believed that something big was in the air. As the days went by and nothing happened, however, mainstream media and political pundits began to ignore the whole disorganized mess. But American law enforcement took it seriously, especially as the protest began to spread to other cities. From August 2011 on, both the FBI and the Department of Homeland Security monitored the Occupy movement through the Joint Terrorism Task Force. Even though they knew that these were peaceful protestors exercising their First Amendment rights, they designated them as a "terrorist threat" and ramped up surveillance.

Occupy Wall Street. Powering up the generators at Zuccotti Park.
(Credit: Daniel South)

Over the next few months, intelligence streamed in from across the country. Milwaukee law-enforcement officials, for example, reported that the group intended to sing holiday carols at an undisclosed location of "high visibility." From Nevada came the information that the Reverend Al Sharpton – a prominent African American activist – would be attending a "rally for jobs and justice." Other events flagged for possible follow-up police investigation included a meditation led by Buddhist monks, yoga classes, and a march of students dressed like "zombie bankers." Protestors' "attitude toward retail" was of particular interest to the authorities.[26] For the rest of American society, OWS failed to engage – until the police came to the rescue.

A week or so into the occupation, on 24 September, a New York police officer was captured on video walking up to a group of women protestors who were following police instructions. He pepper-sprayed them in the face for no reason other than to hurt them.[27] This blatant act of male violence against women – women left screaming in pain – captured global attention. Twenty-four hours later, Anonymous revealed the perpetrator's identity: Anthony Bologna, a deputy inspector with the New York Police Department (NYPD), who was already facing lawsuits arising out of his actions at the 2004 Republican National Convention.

The police insisted that their officer, inevitably mocked on *The Daily Show* as "Tony Baloney," "acted appropriately," but that was demonstrably untrue. The video went viral, with over 1 million views in the first four days, and thereafter the mainstream media paid real attention. National Public Radio arrived, and the *Newark Star-Ledger* published an editorial: "The nation should listen to this small Wall Street encampment."[28] As Republican pollster Frank Luntz confided to GOP governors, "I'm so scared of this anti–Wall Street effort. I'm frightened to death. [OWS is] having an impact on what the American people think of capitalism."[29]

Back in Canada, former prime minister Paul Martin described OWS as very powerful: "I have yet to talk to anybody," he said, "who doesn't say that they aren't reflecting a disquiet that they themselves feel."[30] Others had a different take. They were "demonic loons," the conservative American political commentator Ann Coulter declared, proving once again that it takes one to know one.[31] Republican strategist Karl Rove described them as a "group of nuts and lunatics and fascists."[32] In the *New York Times*, columnist David Brooks called them "milquetoast radicals," a third of whom, according to a *New York Magazine* survey, believed that the United States was no better than Al Qaeda.[33] Brooks also suggested that the people behind OWS were anti-Semites.

Anti-Semitism allegations have dogged *Adbusters* for years. A 2010 photo essay comparing the situation of Palestinians in Gaza and Jews in the Warsaw Ghetto – pictures of Palestinians and Jews in both places fighting fires, smuggling food, being attacked by men in uniform – attracted immediate condemnation from Jewish groups as just more demonization of Israel.[34] One year later, in a February 2011 blog post, Lasn compared Israel to a drunk friend: "For over half a century, America has been Israel's bartender and enabler: each year dumping billions of dollars in military aid that is used to oppress Palestinians."[35] Nevertheless, the charge – anti-Semitism at OWS – was completely off base. The people in Zuccotti Park were running things, not a seventy-year-old in Vancouver. Regardless, the whiff of anti-Semitism in OWS would never quite leave the air even as some of the protestors openly celebrated the Jewish High Holidays at Zuccotti Park.

Anthony Bologna's unprovoked, deliberate, and sadistic police brutality attracted public sympathy for the protestors and the interest of celebrities: actor Susan Sarandon, hip-hop artist Kanye West, filmmaker

Michael Moore, politician Jesse Jackson, economist Joseph Stiglitz, and the activist academic Cornel West (who called President Barack Obama "a black mascot of Wall Street"). Joan Baez came to sing, but many in the crowd were too young to know who she was.

Organized labour showed up to demonstrate its solidarity, albeit with misgivings. Union leaders admired the vitality, commitment, and drive of the occupiers but were disturbed by their denunciations of the United States. The ambivalence was repaid in kind on the street: What are they doing here? OWS and organized labour were obviously mismatched. The union movement has clear goals, as Samuel L. Gompers, the one-time head of the American Federation of Labor, said: "We want more schoolhouses and less jails; more books and less arsenals; more learning and less vice; more leisure and less greed; more justice and less revenge; in fact, more of the opportunities to cultivate our better natures."[36] When asked what it wanted, all OWS could say was "stay tuned."

Doing nothing often requires the greatest discipline. If the authorities had been paying careful attention, they would have noted that, as the uproar over the pepper-spraying began to die down, so too did media interest in OWS. On Day One, several hundred people turned out, and, at the height of the event, between 200 and 300 occupiers stayed overnight and between 200 and 1,000 appeared during the day (more on weekends or for a big march). *Time* magazine reported 44 per cent public approval of OWS, *CBS/New York Times* put the figure at 43 per cent, and Rasmussen said 33 per cent. Gallup found that 22 per cent agreed with OWS's goals, even though it never had any.

The numbers at Zuccotti Park were small and would probably have begun to fall, but on 1 October the NYPD decided to arrest 700 protestors marching toward the Brooklyn Bridge and to "kettle" – confine to an enclosed place – and manhandle many of them in the process (the marchers were planning to blockade the bridge). That revived the dying news story, and fresh participants began the trek to Zuccotti Park. Four days later, OWS held its largest march ever. With organized labour in tow, 15,000 protestors went on a walk. OWS, the *New York Times* now reported, "has clearly tapped into a deep vein of anger ... bringing long-time crusaders against globalization and professional anarchists together with younger people frustrated by poor job prospects."[37]

Another unnecessarily provocative move was the mayor's musing, on 13 October, that the protestors would have to leave the park so it could be "cleaned." All that did was energize some of the couch potatoes monitoring events on their laptops to show up and bolster the ranks.

"We are the 99%," was the second most effective slogan in American political protest, and occupiers now appropriated the first: "Hell no, we won't go." "Banks got bailed out. We got sold out," was another OWS slogan that resonated. Lasn was ecstatic: "Without leaders, without demands, they've been able to launch a national conversation the likes of which America hasn't seen for a couple of generations. It doesn't get any better than that."[38]

Tumblr, an emerging image-based micro-blogging site, launched the "99 Per Cent Project," which featured "selfies" of regular people holding handwritten signs describing their circumstances. Thousands of these stories have been published there and elsewhere: "I did everything I was supposed to do! I worked hard, studied hard, got into college. Now I'm unemployed with no prospects and $80,000 in debt."[39] "I did everything they told me to, in order to be successful. I got straight A's and a scholarship. I went to University and got a degree. Now I'm sinking in student debt, unable to get a job. I have an eviction notice on my door, and nowhere to go. I have only $42 in the bank. I AM THE 99%." "I am a 37 year old who makes $8.00 an hour ... After paying Insurance, Federal & State taxes, Social Security, Medicare, I am left working for the gas money to get to work. I AM PISSED!"[40] Parallels emerged between the Tunisian Mohamed Bouazizi and the American 99 per cent – people who played by the rules but could never get ahead in an unfair system that conspired against them.

"The diversity of the stories and faces on display provides a pretty definitive rebuttal to anyone still naïve or malicious enough to claim that the movement is composed exclusively of hippies, anarchists, and other phantasms of the 1960s New Left." Rather, the Tumblr blog provides a portrait of an emerging American: often over-educated for the few jobs and salaries available, stripped of dignity, tormented by anxieties over how to care for themselves and their families, laid off from jobs, "clinging precariously to an idea of middle-classness that seems more and more to be chimera of the past."[41]

Not everyone could congregate at Zuccotti Park, but anyone with access to the Internet could tell the world what had happened to them. The American people were suffering, and this blog may, one day, share equal place with Walker Evans's iconic Depression-era photographs for

WE ARE THE 99 PERCENT

I have done *awful* things to make my mortgage payments…including selling my body.

But I am no longer willing to sacrifice my remaining shreds of dignity on the altar of a faceless institution that gave me an ill–advised loan to begin with.

Are you guys really *THAT* greedy?

Selfies. One picture is worth a thousand words, and there were thousands of pictures telling the ring-true story of the American experience. For many, playing by the rules no longer worked.

its authentic and honest account of a slice of the American experience. All told, ows had unquestionably unleashed a different kind of political protest.

"Inequality is back in the news largely thanks to Occupy Wall Street," *New York Times* columnist Paul Krugman wrote on 3 November 2011.[42] He reviewed the latest data from the Congressional Budget Office and, while he did not endorse ows, he agreed with the conclusion that the future of America was at stake. "Extreme concentration of income is incompatible with real democracy ... Our political system is being warped by the influence of big money."[43]

The mainstream media was now at Zuccotti Park every day and websites proliferated: We Are the 99 Percent, Occupy Together, Parents for Occupy Wall Street, to name just a few. "In the months leading up to the first occupation, and in the year afterward, Occupy established an online presence unmatched in the history of social action."[44] From 25 July to the end of August, four Occupy hashtags accounted for a handful of messages a day. On 15 November, volume peaked at just over 400,000 Twitter accounts. YouTube (72 million views of different Occupy videos), Vimeo, Flickr, Instagram, and Snapchat were deployed round the clock. Crowdmaps showed the spread of the movement around the world.[45] "ows and This, That and the Other Place," as the amusing P.J. O'Rourke put it.[46]

By year's end, there were Occupy protests in almost 1,000 cities in more than eighty countries, including Canada (from Newfoundland to British Columbia). Toronto's protestors, who set up camp in the park adjoining St James Cathedral, were beset by "white supremacy, patriarchy, and heteronormativity." Accordingly, the first challenge they faced was how best to deal with their "whiteness." They also needed to "address their level of privilege in relation to others."[47] Yet another urgent issue was the core contradiction that, in occupying the park, they were trespassing on land stolen from First Nations.[48] The camp came to an end on 23 November, two days after a judge upheld a municipal eviction order.

The Proceedings

What did ows want? An easier question to answer is what the protesters – and the other occupiers around the world – were against. That answer was fairly straightforward: just about everything. As things stood, though, there would never be any solutions on offer, just nostrums.

One year earlier, a huge rally called by organized labour and the National Association for the Advancement of Colored People (NAACP) in Washington, DC – One Nation Working Together – attracted 175,000 people and almost no media coverage. In February 2011 more than 100,000 people opposed to Governor Scott Walker's slash-and-burn budget cuts attended a protest in Madison, Wisconsin. This gathering topped weeks of mass protest – daily rallies with tens of thousands of people showing up.

ows would never reach numbers like these, yet it became the world's second truly international protest movement. The first produced the 15 February 2003 demonstrations in some 600 cities around the world against the Iraq War. (According to the BBC, between 6 and 11 million took part in the coordinated protests.) ows lasted longer and attracted far more attention. "A group of people started camping out in Zuccotti Park," Krugman observed, "and all of a sudden the conversation has changed significantly towards being about the right things. It's kind of a miracle."[49]

When President Obama was asked a question at a news conference soon after ows began, he expressed sympathy: "I think that the American people understand that not everybody has been following the rules; that Wall Street is an example of that; that folks who are working hard every single day, getting up, going to the job, loyal to their companies, that that used to be the essence of the American dream. That's how you got ahead – the old-fashioned way. And these days, a lot of folks who are doing the right thing aren't rewarded, and a lot of folks who aren't the doing the right thing are rewarded."

Did the White House not have something to do with that? Jake Tapper, CNN's chief Washington correspondent asked. "Your administration hasn't really been very aggressive in prosecuting." That was true, but the president had an explanation: "One of the biggest problems about the collapse of Lehmans and the subsequent financial crisis and the whole subprime lending fiasco is that a lot of that stuff wasn't necessarily illegal, it was just immoral or inappropriate or reckless … The financial sector is very creative and they are always looking for ways to make money."[50]

Could it really be true that the financial fraudsters – the people responsible for the 2008 meltdown – had done nothing illegal? Apparently, since no one was in jail. The president talked a good game: he didn't just say all the right things but had plenty of ideas about how to fix things. He had overseen the bank bailouts and pursued regulatory reforms, yet the latter were regarded as tepid at best. A week later, the White House announced that President Obama was working for the interests of the 99 per cent.

On 6 December in Osawatomie, Kansas, the president deplored the "breathtaking greed of the few." He insisted that restoring fairness was the "defining issue of our time."[51] In his January 2012 State of the Union Address, he said: "We can either settle for a country where a shrinking number of people do really well, while a growing number of Americans barely get by, or we can restore an economy where everyone gets a fair shot, and everyone does their fair share, and everyone plays by the same set of rules."[52] The president of the United States had hijacked the central message of OWS, but the protestors down at Zuccotti Park paid little attention: they were still trying to come up with just one big demand.

That was the job of the General Assembly, which met at least once a day. On 23 September the assembly issued its draft Principles of Solidarity, pointing to "the blatant injustices of our times perpetuated by the economic and political elites." It concluded: "Demands will follow." The Declaration of the Occupation came next, at the beginning of October, following tortuous and seemingly never-ending discussions. It took two weeks to arrive at a consensus for this second and last statement – and it listed numerous predictable grievances.[53]

It was not going to be easy to achieve consensus about just one demand in a group that straddled the political spectrum, including real extremes. There were truthers, birthers, lizardmen, feminists, environmentalists, conservatives, liberals, and people "shouting nonsense,"[54] some advocating affordable health care, free tuition, cancellation of student debt, animal rights, the environment, and legalization of marijuana, while others were opposing global warming, corporate personality, currency, capitalism, and the death penalty.

There were also people who wanted to get high, and people who had nowhere else to go. Everybody got to speak, and when they did it soon became obvious that some of them were not well (and that is not including the followers of Lyndon LaRouche who are truly one of a kind). When a Demands Group formed in October, the General Assembly voted them out of existence. They regrouped, giving themselves the task of "developing the concept of demands." That was the last anyone heard of them. There were people from New York, from across the country, and from the rest of the world: the obligatory anarchists (or were they romanticists?), a social activist named "Germ," and a genuine and appealing young woman with big red glasses and straight red hair named "Ketchup." They ranged from baristas and bicycle messengers to retired people, lawyers, clergy, students, the unemployed, and the homeless. Some people quit their jobs and travelled far to be part of it all.

The immediate practical problem was how to have a conversation among several hundred people without any microphone or sound system – which Mayor Bloomberg had banned to protect the neighbourhood from constant noise. Again, someone in the crowd came up with a solution they called the People's Mic – the "people's microphone." In meetings, all who wanted to speak raised their hands, and "stack keepers" selected who would have the floor and in what order. Amid complaints of "white skin privilege," women and racialized persons came to the fore, followed by white men. Whoever got the nod would begin to address the crowd, and the crowd would repeat it, a few words at a time, in a mass chant.

Obviously, this system was not the best means for communicating anything other than the most straightforward of thoughts, though proponents argued that it encouraged "deeper listening." Housekeeping items came first, sometimes followed by the real business at hand: the one big demand or where next to march. General Assembly meetings went on for hours. There was a lot to do: "On top of reforming global capitalism, they had to handle fights, thefts, drug use and sexual assaults, while operating under the strain of official hostility, police surveillance, constant interaction with supportive and hostile visitors, and weather."[55] Entire meetings were often wasted on trivial matters, such as where to buy fair-trade bins.[56] Working groups on sanitation, security, and the kitchen – there were about 100 of them – operated in the same way.

The General Assembly had more rules of order than *Roberts*. Holding palms upward and wiggling fingers (twinkling) signified approval; holding them down and wiggling (de-twinkling), disapproval. Hands at an even keel signalled uncertainty. Anyone with arms crossed in an x could block what was being discussed. All blocks had to be addressed, and consensus reached, before moving on. Anyone could at any time, with a different hand signal, bring up a procedural point – and it had to be dealt with right away. It was a time-consuming process, with the most unreasonable people and the most outlandish ideas dominating discussion.

And then there was the Drum Circle group. They banged their bongos day and night, demonstrating that they couldn't care less about the General Assembly other than to drive the participants "ape shit crazy."[57]

Occupy Wall Street Drum Circle. (Credit: David Shankbone)

When the General Assembly, bowing to community pressure, asked them to tone down the night-time drumming, the request was rejected and the person who made it beaten up. The drummers knew what was really going on: "They've turned into the government that we've been trying to protest." Some of the occupiers began to believe that the drummers were actually a police plant: "undercover cops unleashing their sacred masculine."[58]

The satirists had a field day, although normally hard-headed commentators of the American political scene, such as the *New Republic's* David Greenberg, admitted to a "frisson of excitement" about the inspiring events in Zuccotti Park.[59] He conceded that there was "something excruciating about watching the 'human mike' in action ... but the protestors are doing something very right and very important. They have gotten the nation to focus on the cost and injustice of inequality, on the need for financial regulation, on the problem of job creation, and on other urgent concerns that ... Washington has largely avoided addressing."[60] Others saw only the gong show.

There was controversy about coming up with even a single demand. "Demands are disempowering," one of the protestors observed, "since they require someone else to respond."[61] Another protestor agreed: "The process is the message."[62] By the beginning of October, the critics, and criticisms, were piling up. When Micah White was asked what he wanted, he replied, "economic justice."[63] A few days later he elaborated: "Of course the people in the general assemblies are still figuring out the issues. And yeah, the revolutionary process is difficult and beautiful, and exciting, and messy, but it is something we need to work through." We are, he said, "in an end time moment ... if we are smart, savvy and inspired, there's a real possibility we can overthrow the corporate power structures and change all the rules."[64]

Lasn was likewise unconcerned about how long the process was taking. Patience, he counselled in an interview with *Salon*. "We will get into specifics, just give us time." As demands emerged, he predicted, "we may well find millions of people marching around the world."[65] There was something to be said for not coming up with one demand: ows was "a blank screen upon which the grievances of a huge swath of the population can be projected."[66] By the middle of October, $450,000 had been collected and local pizza shops were among the very few neighbourhood businesses that welcomed the occupation. Some sympathizers did not just "like" what they saw but opened their wallets and phoned in orders sending "occupies," as they called them, to the protestors.

Fortunately, no one was in a hurry. "All great movements of the past started like this," Laurel, an elementary teacher from the Bronx, explained to reporters.[67] The common refrain was that "we are here for as long as it takes." ows protestors were planning on remaining in Zuccotti Park over the winter and possibly forever – or so they thought.

"After two or three weeks a good number of the sleepovers were vagabonds," Todd Gitlin, a former head of the Students for a Democratic Society, Columbia University professor, and chronicler of activities at Zuccotti Park, observed.[68] The police undoubtedly encouraged their arrival, part of an unfortunate tradition in American law enforcement to infiltrate, discredit, and disrupt protest movements. The park became a hangout for people with mental-health issues, hardened criminals, drug dealers, and the homeless as well as the true believers.

The General Assembly, unable to prevent sexual and other assaults, tried creating safe places "for people who identified as female" and offered training "around consent and other forms of assault awareness,"[69] but the end was clearly in sight. In the beginning, the authorities could either "allow activists to hold the space indefinitely, permitting a staging ground for continual protests against the area's financial institutions. Or police could act on behalf of the country's 1 percent and shut down dissent, a move that would perfectly illustrate the protestors' claims about what American democracy had become. It was a no-win situation for the state."[70] As time passed, however, there was no longer a stark choice.

The Canadian writer Grant Munroe was there from the beginning: "Here's the truth: those first two weeks in Zuccotti were exhilarating ... By November 15 ... the nightmarish inefficiency of horizontal power sharing and cliquish nature of those contesting power within various groups was intolerable. I never liked twinkly fingers; I liked getting things done. With nothing being done, my friends and I left."[71]

ows had become many things, but it was no model democracy, no model society, no model civilization. It was not even a Potemkin village: it was a dirty, disorganized eyesore. ows was a mile wide, but it was never even an inch deep. At its height, it did not come close to matching the numbers who made their way to Tahrir Square and Plaza del Sol. It was time to clean up the place.

On 15 November 15 at 1:00 a.m. the police began to clear Zuccotti Park, meeting mild resistance. "Whose park?" the occupiers chanted and replied, "Our park!" and "This is our home." Not for much longer: by 3:00 a.m. the occupation was over. Cleaners with power washers immediately descended on the space, while city officials packed up the protestors' tents and tarps. About 200 people were arrested.

The exasperated mayor had had enough and told the protestors that the eviction had nothing to do with the First Amendment: "It does not give anyone the right to sleep in a park ... it does not protect the use of tents and sleeping bags to take over a public space."[72] The protestors were informed they could come back anytime, but not for occupation and sleepovers. Locals breathed a sigh of relief: "I think my neighbors are very thankful that the mayor acted," a resident of a building overlooking the park commented, "but we remain completely outraged for having to endure this for nine weeks."[73]

Hours before the NYPD descended on Zuccotti Park, *Adbusters* had sent out another "tactical briefing" proposing that the occupiers pick an early date, declare victory, throw a party, and evacuate the park. "Although [the magazine's] scattershot advice had long since been ignored or ridiculed by most people in ows, the idea of such a shift had been coming up repeatedly in conversations among organizers."[74] The police action trumped that plan. "I cannot believe how stupid Bloomberg can be," Lasn told the *New Yorker*. "This means escalation. A raising of the stakes. It's one step closer to, you know, a revolution."[75] Not quite.

Within a week, most Occupy encampments around the globe were gone in what was almost certainly an internationally coordinated law-enforcement response. In most places, the police evacuated Occupy encampments with a minimum of fuss; in others – for example, Oakland, California – it was downright ugly as local law enforcement took revenge on the Black Bloc, looters, arsonists, and thugs who had hijacked that city's occupation and terrorized the city for weeks. They were, Chris Hedges, the popular American commentator, wrote in a widely circulated article, "the cancer in Occupy."[76]

Two days after the eviction from Zuccotti Park, the OWS website claimed victory: "This is the climax of a decades-long battle for the soul of humanity itself."[77] The protesters went their separate ways. "The protest continued, with one demonstration after another, but the fifty-nine days of rude, anarchic freedom on a patch of granite in lower Manhattan were over."[78] Bloomberg was ambivalent no longer: "You want to get arrested?" he told protestors making their way back to Zuccotti Park. "We'll accommodate you."[79] He also pointed to a problem that the protestors never quite addressed: "If you have something to say, really, to say, that would be a great contribution; nobody can hear you when everybody's yelling and screaming and pushing and shoving."[80] The occupiers periodically returned to Zuccotti Park for reunions, but they never occupied it again. When they do get together, the police are always there waiting.[81]

OWS Mattered. Really.

"I am a free radical now," White announced in a "Letter to The People" two years after OWS came to an end. "My allegiance is with The People alone. I believe we are less than four years away from a decisive people's victory in one or more nations. If our leaderless revolution can survive through mutation, innovation and escalation, then we stand a good chance of flanking the dinosaurs and taking legislative control of a State after a period of sustained unrest."[82] White called on The People to go underground and begin preparations for the coming struggle: "To sustain innovation in the long term, we must heed the warnings of Snowden and migrate from the clearnet (the monitored commercial Internet) to the darkweb (the anonymous and encrypted parallel Internet) ... Learning to navigate the darkweb ... is a survival skill for everyday people who are dreaming of democracy."[83] It is not quite clear what White had in mind. There has been no decisive "people's victory" anywhere since 2011 other than peaceful transitions of power in mature democracies.

There is no question that Lasn, White, and many others had oversized ambitions. They believed that OWS would change everything. "Without leaders," White wrote, "we all became leaders. Beautiful ideas did not have to wait for approval ... A better world seemed imminent and already manifesting."[84] Revolution "seemed within reach."[85] That was absurd. OWS could barely run a small village, and then not well. "This is what democracy looks like," the OWS protestors continually chanted. No thank you.

The way things work in a democracy is that people, not mobs, rule – through the ballot box. To this day, Lasn and White seem surprised that the government did not agree to dismantle capitalism and hand over the keys to the occupiers at Zuccotti Park. "Beautiful and inspiring," White wrote, OWS was "a social movement par excellence."[86] Uh, no. When the entire world was watching and listening, OWS had absolutely no idea what to say, how to move the ball down the field, and where to go from here. "People want to see, like, actual results," was the way one of the occupiers put it when it was all over.[87]

Many careful observers predicted trouble from day one. Andrew Potter, co-author of *The Rebel Sell*, warned that OWS's unstructured nature carried within it the seeds of demise. "Protests based on culture jamming must also adapt themselves to the very systems they hope to overthrow if they want to effect any meaningful change," he told the Canadian Press one month into the occupation.[88] "The left has consistently stayed outside the system, to see the system as part of the problem, not part of the solution. What you've seen is a lot of people who would much rather take to the streets and leave it in the streets."[89] Writing in the *New York Times* on the one-year anniversary of the start of OWS, financial columnist Andrew Ross Sorkin could not have been more dismissive: "It will be an asterisk in the history books, if it gets a mention at all."[90]

In a way, OWS was doomed from the start. Almost one year before, Malcolm Gladwell got it right. Networks do some things well, he wrote in the *New Yorker*: Wikipedia is the classic example. But no one uses a network to design a car. "No one believes that the articulation of a coherent design philosophy is best handled by a sprawling, leaderless organization system. Because networks don't have a centralized leadership structure and clear lines of authority, they have real difficulty reaching consensus and setting goals. They can't think strategically; they are chronically prone to conflict and error. How do you make difficult choices about tactics or strategy or philosophical direction when everyone has an equal say?"[91] As ows demonstrated, you don't.

"If you're taking on a powerful and organized establishment you have to be a hierarchy," Gladwell continued. "The Montgomery bus boycott required the participation of tens of thousands of people who depended on public transit to get to and from work each day. It lasted a *year*. In order to persuade those people to stay true to the cause, the boycott's organizers tasked each local black church with maintaining morale, and put together a free alternative private carpool service, with forty-eight dispatchers and forty-two pick-up stations."[92] It moved with "military precision." Dr Martin Luther King had a million-dollar budget and 100 full-time staff, all of whom had assigned roles. Discipline and strategy succeeded in Montgomery. The movement that Dr King led was hierarchical to its core.

ows was nothing like that. Horizontality and the General Assembly, fuelled by social media, created a glorious spectacle for a time, then an increasingly seedy carnival. "The problem with the Occupy movement was not that it lacked good slogans. The difference between the Tea Party and the Occupy movement is that the Tea Party's slogans were also its policies, and so the Tea Party had an easier time motivating its followers to get involved in the political process in order to make very specific demands of their representatives. The problem with Occupy is that they never got beyond slogans – and not for want of trying. It's because the type of changes its participants wanted were *intrinsically* more complicated, more controversial, and could not so easily be derived from slogans."[93] But it didn't have to be that way.

ows failed to follow any of Saul D. Alinsky's *Rules for Radicals*, a book that instructs people in how to change the world from what it is to what it should be.[94] The rules have one core message: talk issues, not ideology. Build organizations. Focus on concrete winnable goals. Immediate change in a democracy is impossible. Building organizations and achieving goals takes time. Alinsky would not even hire an organizer unless he had raised enough money in advance to cover two years' salary. He played the long game, worked with local community organizations, identified real problems, and proposed plausible solutions. Community organizers like Barack Obama, who followed in Alinsky's footsteps, had little interest in banging bongos.

There is no single recipe for dissent – consider Frances Kelsey's path, or Rachel Carson's – but whatever it is, it is definitely not culture jamming or dancing to the tune of a culture-busting meme. When Lasn sabotaged that shopping cart, he felt great. What about the people who came after him who could not liberate a cart for their own shopping? Or the store that had to pay someone to repair his vandalism?

Culture jamming may make people feel good, virtuous, and countercultural, but it will never, as Lasn aspires, "wreck this world." It won't even change it. It may get some people thinking about some things, such as, for instance, "who is the asshole who jammed his quarter into the cart?" Of this, revolution is not made. Every single successful movement for social change has been disciplined, centralized, and hierarchical in direct proportion to its ultimate success. Then came OWS. Convincing people not to buy clothing and shoes made by children in sweatshops is relatively easy. Fomenting revolution is a bigger, more serious, project.

OWS did not lead to a revolutionary upheaval. Political democracy was not reinvented with the General Assembly as a model for anything except what not to do. OWS did not lead to much in terms of legislation, nor can it claim responsibility for either electing or defeating politicians. OWS veterans can point to ad hoc victories here and there, preventing home foreclosures and pressuring politicians and banks. But all of that happened before OWS and would have happened without it, although many Occupy hands did learn new skills, and life lessons, the most important being to fight for defined, clearly stated, attainable goals. Even White came to belatedly realize that it was the ballot box that really mattered.

Yet, for all of its many faults, OWS was organic: it gave expression to something legitimate, authentic, and true. The challenge is in combining short-term uprisings like OWS and turning them into sustainable vehicles for achieving social change. In this OWS failed, but in itself it was no failure. It was a different expression of dissent, one that forever changed the conversation. People began talking about the huge gulf between rich and poor. OWS gave us a brand new vocabulary: the 1 per cent and the 99 per cent. Every year the World Economic Forum in Davos identifies the top five global risks so the big brains can figure out solutions. Before OWS, income inequality was never among them, but in 2012 it ranked first. *Time* magazine named the "Protestor" the Person of the Year in 2011.

We always sort of knew what the occupiers were demanding, and that goes a long way in explaining its appeal: "If hope is an impossible demand, then we demand the impossible. If the right to shelter, food, and employment are impossible demands, then we demand the impossible. If it is impossible to demand that those who profit from recession redistribute their wealth and cease their greed, then yes, we demand the impossible," the singular Judith Butler declared when she addressed the occupiers on 23 October.[95]

Many of the occupiers had no detailed grasp of the financial system, but no one needed an advanced degree to know that something was wrong with the distribution of wealth in American society and the world. They knew, as did the 15-M in Spain, that anti-deficit rhetoric was built on the backs of the poor, the unemployed, and the middle class. They knew that the 1 per cent ruled. It is easy to dismiss OWS as a bunch of disconnected malcontents with a never-ending list of complaints and no solutions, and that is partially true. To be sure, Lasn and White were delusional dreamers, completely disconnected from reality, but they were on to something.

OWS ingrained in the larger culture the now commonly accepted belief that extreme levels of economic inequality are untenable over the long term. Obviously, some income inequality is needed: to reward initiative, skill, and hard work. And some jobs appropriately attract higher compensation than others. "But to accept that *some* inequality is a fact of life in a capitalist economy is not to accept that *ever-greater* inequality is either necessary or desirable."[96] What makes the status quo corrosive is how immutable it has all become. In the aftermath of OWS, a Pew Research Center poll reported that 66 per cent of all Americans believed there were "very strong" or "strong" conflicts between rich and poor, a huge leap from the 2009 numbers.[97]

Over the course of the fall of 2011, the term "income inequality" appeared in the Nexis database six times as often as it had before the occupation of Zuccotti Park. The number of stories about income inequality in American newspapers quintupled after OWS, and coverage continues in the mainstream media. "This ragged group, living in tents and tarps for two months ... helped focus everyone's attention on the growing income inequality in this country. They made '99 percent' into popular language for the have-nots," the *New York Times* editorialized the day the protest was finally shut down.[98] This story is not going away. When Richard Nixon visited China in 1972, Chinese Premier Zhou Enlai was asked about the impact of the French Revolution. "Too early to say," was his still-quoted response.

ows's great strengths were its youth and enthusiasm, but they were also its weaknesses. The earliest arrivals at Zuccotti Park had commitment and drive, together with an obvious willingness to endure hardship in support of their cause, whatever it was. ows was able to expand around the globe and attract international attention to its message, no matter how inchoate it turned out to be. Paradoxically, ows created the best brand in the history of advertising: the 99 per cent became shorthand for income inequality and it is known around the globe. ows may prove to be more than a passing diversion.

The Roosevelt Institute's May 2015 report, *Rewriting the Rules*, began with the assertion: "The American economy no longer works for most Americans."[99] It goes on to recommend broad and sweeping reforms in just about every aspect of American economic life. Senator Bernie Sanders, the dishevelled, aging Vermont socialist, supported ows from the very beginning. When he ran for the Democratic Party nomination for President, ows veterans flocked to his campaign, bringing with them the fervour of true believers – so much so that the campaign of his competitor, Hillary Clinton, began cribbing from ows and Sanders himself (even though she was clearly the candidate from Wall Street). Donald Trump also signed up, sort of: the system, he told all and sundry, *was rigged against him!*

The Occupy movement never came up with its one big demand. "At first, the 'one demand' was simply hard to agree on," one of the early organizers recalled, "but gradually its absence seemed to make more and more sense."[100] Not really. In a linear world it is difficult to respond to generalized complaints. Removing Hosni Mubarak is straightforward and success is easy to assess. Complaining about the "system" makes sense in those parts of the world where taking it to the streets is the only option. In the democratic West, not so much. Convincing people to bang drums is not dissent. It is disruptive. Lasn and White succeeded in putting income inequality on the agenda in spite of themselves. One real demand might have made a real difference.

Imagine if ows had come up with one big demand, such as, for instance, a decent minimum wage? Now that was something that might have attracted real public support, as minimum-wage drives – The Fight for $15 campaign – in the years afterwards illustrated. Fast-food workers, retail employees, childcare providers, home-care aides, personal-service workers, and others at the bottom of the wage food chain have united together and have begun to achieve results across America.

The 1999 Battle in Seattle, on the occasion of the meeting of the World Trade Organization, is not a model for much, since Black Bloc criminals crowded out protestors with legitimate concerns about globalization and the widening of the socio-economic gap between rich and poor. That protest, however, had a plan: to disrupt operations and thwart globalization. In a 19 April 2002 interview, Lasn said, "One of the reasons I think the battle in Seattle was so successful is because there was a clearly defined goal: to shut the meeting down and stop those inside from passing the world trade rules … Everyone was focused on one goal: 'Let's create trouble and stop this meeting!'"[101] There is a lot to be said for emulating what works, for instance, identifying a specific and obtainable objective and then fighting for it.

Even so, there are no easy answers, and certainly no immediately obvious solutions to the problem of wealth disparity. To date, capitalism, with all of its destructive and immoral tendencies, is only the system that works. Increasing taxation has some immediate appeal, but government track records in spending public money wisely are nothing to write home about. We actually have no good ideas about how to distribute wealth more equitably, but plenty of bad ones, most of which have been thoroughly discredited by human experience. The political class has the responsibility to figure this out, but whether it has the aptitude is another matter entirely. This makes dissenting voices all the more important, although no one at Zuccotti Park had anything sensible to propose about anything, especially on how to respond appropriately to the unemployment that inevitably follows in the wake of technological advance. Creating more service jobs is not the answer.

Nevertheless, income inequality, the role and influence of money in politics, unemployment, student debt, barriers to mobility and equality, executive compensation and entitlements, corporate governance – will have to be addressed eventually. The American Dream need not be over, but it is on life support.

No serious person wants a hand-out society. Most people want a fair system, not a rigged one, where everyone has the opportunity for an education, a job, health care, a decent house, a good life, a future for their children. If these basic goals are not within reach, Lasn and White may be proven correct: people will rebel. Consider the words of Conrad Black, who, love him or hate him, is a very smart guy. Speaking of the presidential faceoff between Hillary Clinton and Donald Trump, Black argued in the summer of 2016 that this contest was the last stand of moderation: "One more debacle like the past four or five presidential terms, and the animals will be released."[102]

Clearly, one of them – Trump – has already been let loose. It is early days, but the indications are that the forty-fifth president of the United States is quite comfortable in using his pulpit, and Twitter account, to trash talk and bully anyone who has the temerity to dissent and disagree. Predictions are a mug's game, but here is one: the world is about to become extremely dangerous.

"Think of this simple analogy, of an increasingly fancy house in a poor and deteriorating neighborhood," Mohamed El-Erian, the former CEO of PIMCO, suggests. (One of the world's largest investment firms, PIMCO has about $1.5 trillion under management.) "The well-being of the house," he continues, "cannot be divorced from the neighborhood as a whole."[103] Or, as Joseph Stiglitz wrote six months before OWS: "The top 1 percent have the best houses, the best educations, the best doctors, and the best lifestyles, but there is one thing that money doesn't seem to have bought: an understanding that their fate is bound up with how the other 99 percent live. Throughout history, this is something that the top 1 percent eventually do learn. Too late."[104]

The only way our world works is if we look out for each other. We've been warned.

Chapter 8

How Not to Make Public Policy

Dissenters sometimes tell us what we need to know. So do scientists, researchers, academics, public-policy institutes, and think-tanks. As Rachel Carson showed, scientists often see things first – in her case, she spotted the warning signs of an impending environmental disaster. Scientists are the ones with the competence and expertise to identify, and then describe, problems and potholes. They can also help propose solutions. Frances Kelsey looked at the thalidomide New Drug Application. Kevadon had been approved by regulatory authorities in fifty countries, but she alone in the entire world could see that that the medical case for the drug had not been made. The more she looked into it the stronger her conviction became that it posed a dangerous threat.

Dissenting juries, for good and for ill, say no to outcomes they consider unjust. Whether it was capital cases in England during the Industrial Revolution, or the repeated criminal prosecutions of Dr Henry Morgentaler, if the law is out of tune with prevailing community values, juries will refuse to convict even if sometimes the results leave much to be desired. Courts of appeal must resolve society's most intractable problems. Sometimes, though, only one judge in nine can clearly see that a terrible mistake is being made. They will then launch an appeal to the intelligence and morality of a future day.

Public-policy institutes and think-tanks look at social, economic, environmental, and other problems independent of government. They are an important counterweight to entrenched interests, inside the government and out. They, too, can point in a different direction, and often do just that. We don't need to do what they say: ultimately the politicians get to decide; that is why they are elected. But we do need to provide them with institutional support so that they can provide us with the data we need to consider all of the options and alternatives.

Instead of ensuring that public policy was fully informed, the recent Conservative government in Canada took what steps it could to deprive the public-policy process of evidence – the information needed to make the very best decisions. The war on crime had little to do with making streets safer, while the war on science likewise had everything to do with the pursuit of political and ideological goals. From cancelling the indispensable long-form census, to muzzling scientists, to monkeying around with funding programs for basic research, not to mention trashing libraries, the federal government launched an all-out fight against dissent.

This is a cautionary tale.

Legislation with a Political Agenda

For almost a decade (9 years, 271 days), from 6 February 2006 to 4 November 2015, Canadians lived in the middle of a phony war, one that was almost entirely make-believe. Take Prime Minister Stephen Harper's "war on crime." It was designed to "tackle crime," "make communities safer," and "hold offenders accountable," but it was ineffective and counter-productive. Still, being tough on crime, real and imagined, was raw wedge politics, always a crowd pleaser for the Conservative Party base. These and other Harper policies helped ensure that the political contributions – in general, the Tories raised the most money from the most donors – continued to flow.

Much of the legislation came courtesy of omnibus bills that combined all sorts of unrelated legislative changes. Gathered together in one big package, these bills severely restricted Parliament – the House of Commons and the Senate – from scrutinizing, studying, and debating the proposed laws. When it came time to say yea or nay (usually after the government had used its majority to cut off debate), members of Parliament had to vote on the entire bill – hardly the best democratic practice. Omnibus legislation, Harper declared when he was in opposition, was "a contradiction to the conventions of the House."[1] When he assumed power, however, he quickly changed his mind.

Prison farms were closed, jails expanded, and parole opportunities reduced, while international prisoner transfers and pardons became harder to arrange. The strategy was simple: "Lock 'em up and throw away the key." Prisons will always have a place because some people just have to be removed from society, but they are no solution to the crime problem. In a 2008 speech, Harper explained that facts were immaterial: it was "your personal experiences and impressions" that mattered. Don't be fooled, he warned, by special-interest groups and their "statistics."[2] The statistics demonstrated that crime was down and declining, but none of them made any difference to Stockwell Day, the president of the Treasury Board, who told the *Globe and Mail* that there was an alarming increase in unreported crime.[3]

The whole approach was completely cynical, as Harper's chief of staff, a former academic, confessed: "Every time we propose amendments to the Criminal Code, sociologists, criminologists, defence lawyers and Liberals attacked us for proposing measures that the evidence apparently showed did not work. This was a good thing for us in that sociologists, criminologists, and defence lawyers were and are held in lower repute than Conservative politicians by the voting public. Politically it helped us tremendously to be attacked by this coalition of university types."[4] That was certainly Harper's view. "Another part of the problem for the past generation has been those ... who are not criminals themselves, but who are always making excuses for them ... the ivory tower experts, the tut-tutting commentators."[5] Evidence did not matter: "We're governing by what we told and promised Canadians," Justice Minister Rob Nicholson proudly proclaimed.

Completely devoid of any nuance, the Harper government offered a stark choice: criminals or victims. It is very difficult to calibrate a criminal-justice system to protect the citizenry, prevent and punish crime, and rehabilitate the offender. Balancing and respecting rights is never easy. Even the most aspirational people do not wish to coddle criminals or hug thugs. That said, the simple truth is that Harper's government had an obsession about a crime wave that was not sweeping the country. The numbers told the story: serious crime has been in decline for years. Use of guns? Down. Use of knives? Down too. The cases that crowd the courts are serious offences such as driving under the influence and common assault, along with less serious things such as violating terms of probation and minor property theft. The fact, however, is that violent crime in Canada is way down. According to the *Globe and Mail* in July 2016, it is at "fifty year lows."[6]

Regardless, more and more money was spent on a diminishing problem, one that preoccupied the government until the very end of its term. On its last day in office, government MPs were instructed to vote in favour of the Life Means Life Act, which required certain convicted murderers to be locked away for the rest of their lives with the possibility of parole, only in exceptional cases, after thirty-five years. This act was completely politically driven – to prove that the Conservatives were tough on crime and to further demonize criminals. During their governance, warehousing replaced rehabilitation, and overcrowded institutions made prisons even more dangerous for inmates and correctional officers alike.

The government deliberately went out of its way to offend the entire legal establishment when the peeved prime minister, unable to impose an unqualified semi-retired jurist on the Supreme Court, publicly denounced Canada's respected chief justice. The Harper government believed it could publicly attack a judge as well as one of the country's most respected and dignified institutions. Harper and a succession of servile and obedient justice ministers knew from warnings by senior bureaucrats that much of the proposed anti-crime agenda would not pass judicial muster, but the onslaught continued. The government set new records for losing cases at the Supreme Court of Canada where it proved almost impossible to defend its offside legislation.[7]

When the Prime Minister's Office (PMO) determined that the Department of Justice's research department was part of the problem – a secret report concluded that its research was "not aligned with government ... priorities"[8] – the response was sure and swift: the researchers received pink slips. Changes were made to ensure that the diminished research capacity "better supported" government objectives, whether sound or not. As intended, the terminations had a chilling effect on those researchers who remained employed. But they kept to the facts, and their subsequent research proved, for example, that mandatory minimum sentences – the government's favourite criminal-justice reform – had no deterrent effect. No matter: the government imposed sixty mandatory minimum jail sentences and severely restricted conditional sentences (a form of house arrest).

The evidence was conclusive, former Liberal justice minister and respected law professor Irwin Cotler told the House of Commons, that mandatory minimum sentences do not work. As several critics pointed out, if getting tough on criminals by locking them up were an effective approach, the United States, with about 2.2 million people in its penitentiaries (at an annual cost of over $80 billion), would be one of the safest countries in the world, which it is demonstrably not. Instead, it has one of the highest rates of recidivism, despite its Dickensian prisons where prisoners are brutalized daily by the conditions, other inmates, and the guards. Simply put, the evidence demonstrates that sentence severity "has no effect on the level of crime in society."[9]

Mandatory minimum sentences quiet social unrest and inspire confidence in some quarters, but they do almost nothing to deter crime. Some people need to be sent away for a very long time, and in some cases, forever. The point is to look at the gravity of the offence, the circumstances of the case and the offender, and then to determine what sentence would best punish and rehabilitate, deter others, and protect the public. There is a huge difference between a teenage first offender caught at the border with illicit drugs intended for personal use and organized criminals who are apprehended attempting to import vast quantities of drugs for sale to the public. Sexual offences run the gamut, and in some situations it is readily concluded, on the evidence, that a particular person is a persistent predator and should receive an indeterminate prison sentence – meaning that he will almost certainly never again be let loose.

But it is judges, not Parliament, who are uniquely and best situated to consider these individual cases and come up with appropriate outcomes within the legal framework established by Parliament. In a Charter of Rights and Freedoms world, judges are the ones most qualified to determine what penalty best fits the crime within a range set by Parliament, not by rote application of one size fits all (with appropriate safeguards to control any discriminatory effects of judicial discretion). Paradoxically, mandatory minimum sentences sometimes lead to innocent people pleading guilty to lesser offences in plea deals to avoid the risk of a custodial term.

As a practical matter, many defence lawyers anecdotally reported that jury nullification was alive and well as jurors did what they had to do to avoid the imposition of completely unjust mandatory minimum sentences. Notably absent in many of the reforms was any sense of proportionality. All of this was lost, or more probably ignored, by a government where public-policy decisions were excessively politically informed. Fighting crime, or appearing to do so, was popular with the public. It was as straightforward as that.

Scaring the Citizenry

The various pieces of law reform had provocative Orwellian names: the Zero Tolerance for Barbaric Cultural Practices Act (coupled with a "Barbaric Practices Snitch Line" promoted by cabinet ministers Kellie Leitch and Chris Alexander), the Faster Removal of Foreign Criminals Act, the Serious Time for Most Serious Crime Act, the Protecting Canadians by Ending Sentence Discounts for Multiple Murders Act, and the Respecting Families of Murdered and Brutalized Persons Act, to name just a few of the bills that dominated the legislative agenda. There were, of course, changes that made sense and received all-party support, but some of the reforms and new laws did not.

On three separate occasions, for example, the government introduced amendments to the Criminal Code modifying sentences for having sex with an animal in front of a youth. Given all the pressing problems in Canadian society, how this non-issue and extremely rare offence became a government priority is almost unfathomable, unless its real purpose was planting in the public mind the false belief that there was an epidemic of this nature in need of parliamentary, public, and police attention. Perhaps that was the point: to change perceptions by distorting reality. "No argument or evidence was ever provided for the need for these changes," criminologists Anthony Doob and Cheryl Marie Webster pointed out.[10]

The government's own lawyers privately and repeatedly warned that many of these laws violated the Charter of Rights and Freedoms. As predicted, the Harper government's legislative changes have been regularly set aside by the courts, especially the fetters imposed on judges to do their job and tailor the penalty to the crime and the criminal. As soon as the government of Justin Trudeau was elected, the new justice minister began her tenure by abandoning previously launched and impossible-to-win appeals. Still, for ten years, ideology triumphed.

Attacking the Vulnerable

We have known for a long time that marginalized people, especially First Nations and African Canadians, are over-represented in the prison system. That is still true, with aboriginal custodial rates rising year after year. While First Nations, Métis, and Inuit Canadians account for only

3–4 per cent of the Canadian population, they constitute about 25 per cent of the federal prison population, and far too often have ended up in jail for relatively minor offences. Racialized people are disproportionately represented as well, and not only in prison but also in maximum-security institutions and solitary confinement.[11] Many prisoners are sick and mentally ill – for example, about 30 per cent of female federal prisoners and 15 per cent of males have previously spent time in psychiatric institutions.

The federal prison ombudsman pulled no punches: "We are criminalizing, incarcerating, warehousing the mentally disordered in large and alarming numbers."[12] The changes legislated by the federal government, however, had a significant impact. By increasing sentences, reducing parole, making the victim surcharge mandatory and pardons harder to obtain, the government hurt a lot of people. How does imposing a fine on an impecunious criminal facilitate her reintegration into society? How does denying a pardon to an otherwise eligible former felon help anyone? It just makes it more difficult for them to turn around their lives. What about community supervision instead of prison? The government's agenda did not make anything better for anyone. So why the phony war on crime?

The intention had to be to change Canadian values, the way people think. Vince Li, for example, was actually psychotic in 2008 when he beheaded Tim McLean, a carnival worker, on a Greyhound bus. His crime was abhorrent. But he was not a monster, just an extremely sick man. In due course he got better, and the Manitoba Criminal Code Review Board determined that he could be safely released. The federal government responded immediately: it changed the law by allowing the courts to label some people high risk and provided a separate review process for these cases. Henceforth, applications could be made only once every three years, not once a year. Someone who was better, and was no longer a threat to society, might have to wait three years for a review. It was easy to turn Li into a poster boy for the legislative change, and challenging for most people to care about him or his fate, but that doesn't make it right.

In a fair society, people should be released when it is safe and appropriate to do so even if their crime was heinous, not subject to some arbitrary schedule set by Parliament. But that was never the point with the Harper government: it wanted to send a different message. Criminals are bad. The mentally ill are bad. So there is no need for Canadians to be concerned about them or for government to help them. Changing the role of government was Harper's Holy Grail: reducing it was part of the program; so too was changing attitudes and values. Between "them" and "us" there was no choice. Besides, a frightened population inevitably meant more Tory votes.

Who Needs Statistics?

The prime minister also launched a parallel war on information. It started with the abolition of the long-form census – a completely confidential form given to about 20 per cent of Canadian households every five years that asked questions about age, education, earnings, family status, language, housing, transportation, education, and cultural heritage. The accumulated answers provided a portrait of the Canadian people that was indispensable to researchers. It was replaced with a much costlier voluntary survey with a low take-up rate, especially among marginalized groups most in need of government services. If we do not know who they are, and where and how they live, how can we possibly appropriately respond to legitimate needs?

When the long form was abolished in June 2010 without any consultation, without any debate in the House of Commons, or even any discussion in cabinet, that decision was roundly denounced by most provincial governments and a wide swath of Canadian society that included the country's business leaders, academics, industry associations, and think-tanks of every political persuasion. They all needed reliable, comprehensive data about how Canadians lived and worked in order to make informed public-policy and business decisions – where to build hospitals and schools, locate police and fire stations, extend public transit, and other matters of civic importance.

Ever since 1086, when William the Conqueror compiled the Domesday Book, governments have relied on a regular census to collect taxation and gather vital information. They need to know who is out there and what they are up to. Yet in 2010 Tony Clement, the minister in charge, had the audacity to announce that chief statistician Munir Sheikh had approved the move to abolish the long-form census, which was the opposite of the truth.[13] Sheikh had actually told the government that the new voluntary approach would not produce reliable data: "Intelligent policy development is not possible without good data," he explained.[14] Amid the multiple layoffs at Statistics Canada, Sheikh resigned, following the tradition set by James Elliott Coyne, the governor of the Bank of Canada, who also resigned in principled protest over misguided political interference by the Diefenbaker government in the bank's operations. Honourable behaviour like this had been pretty rare around Ottawa for a very long time.

Clement justified the change by citing "privacy concerns" and arguing that no one should go to jail for failing to fill out the long form – although that penalty had never been imposed. The government, he seemed to be saying, had no business in knowing how many bedrooms were in a house. It turned out that after the previous census, when some twelve million forms were distributed across the country, there were fewer than 200 complaints. Making the whole thing even more dishonest was the fact that it remained unlawful not to fill out the short-form census. (After the Harper government was defeated, the perennially eager and ambitious Clement, with his eye on the Conservative Party leadership, which he eventually concluded was a complete non-starter, told reporters, "In hindsight, I think I would have done it differently."[15] What that might have looked like, Clement never explained.)

In due course, the *Globe and Mail* editorialized that "conducting a half-witted census turned out to be more expensive. The 2011 voluntary household survey increased errors, reduced accuracy, chopped the response rate by 30 per cent – and even cost an extra $22 million. Congratulations: The Harper government figured out how to spend more for less."[16] That revelation alone blew up the myth of good Conservative economic management. The day after Justin Trudeau's Liberals were elected in November 2015, the new government announced that the long form was back. "We are committed to a government that functions based on evidence and facts," the prime minister told the CBC.[17]

Why did the government of Canada kill the long-form census? It knew that the response to the new voluntary form would be low, especially by the marginalized people most in need. Although government personnel talked about privacy and principle, their real concerns were ideological, stemming from their contempt for the idea that the state could promote the public good. As former cabinet minister and Conservative MP Maxime Bernier, another leadership contender, remarked: "If some special interest group wants data on Canadians, they can do that, they can pay for that and they can do it."[18] The conclusion is inescapable that the abolition of the long-form census had nothing to do with privacy concerns and everything to do with the role of government in society and an administration intent on avoiding its responsibilities. The Harper government wanted to destroy the ability of a respected autonomous agency to collect information that could be used to reach informed public-policy decisions.

"Starve the beast of data, the theory goes," Harper's biographer John Ibbitson wrote, "and government will be less able to tax and intrude, because it won't know enough to justify the tax or the intrusion."[19] The cancellation of the long-form census was not an isolated event; rather, it was one among many by a government that had no intention of making decisions based on facts. It was, Ibbitson concluded, one of Harper's "most discreditable and puzzling acts."[20] The prize-winning journalist was half right. Discreditable, yes; puzzling, hardly. One would be forgiven for thinking that this initiative, too, was part of a larger plan: to deprive democratic institutions of a vital tool for good governance.[21] Plenty of other evidence also points in that direction.

The War on Science

The Great Lakes – Superior, Huron, Michigan, Erie, and Ontario – are the largest body of fresh water on the planet and vital to both Canada and the United States. Home to 150 species of fish, the Great Lakes support Canadian and American agriculture and a declining but still important fishery, and they provide drinking water to tens of millions of people. They were and are seriously polluted. In 1965 the International Joint Commission, the body responsible for managing and protecting these waters, recommended that research be carried out into trans-boundary pollution – especially the green scum choking Lake Erie. Three years later, the governments of Canada and Ontario set aside a large area southwest of Kenora as an Experimental Lakes Area (ELA) for that research – fifty-eight small, deep, and pristine lakes and their catchment areas covering some 900 square kilometres in the Canadian Shield. Housing and a field station were built, and scientists came from around the world to work there.

Over the years, cutting-edge research at the ELA made a huge contribution to knowledge about water quality, safe drinking water, and fish farming. The ELA helped hydroelectric companies design eco-friendly reservoirs. Real and prize-winning discoveries were made about the impact of human activity on the environment. What was learned at the ELA led in large part to the Canada-United States Air Quality Agreement (the "Acid Rain Treaty") and hundreds of thousands of Canadian lakes were saved from death. ELA researchers discovered that phosphates from household detergents caused algal blooms – Lake Erie's green scum – and that led to industry reforms. The research resulted in hundreds of peer-reviewed papers, doctoral dissertations, and important ongoing scientific experiments – truly game-changing research.

The ELA was unique in the entire world – the only place where scientists could perform controlled experiments within a freshwater ecosystem, such as whether the massive fish kills that Rachel Carson complained about were caused by pesticides or something else. What would happen to birds and animals, for instance, if DDT were properly applied?

All this valuable research was accomplished for an annual cost of around $2 million. Yet in May 2012 the Harper government decided to shut the place down. The ELA, the minister of fisheries and oceans announced, would close the following March, and, at the same time, approximately 200 Fisheries scientists were let go.

Money could not have been the reason for the closure or the mass termination of scientists. The government had just spent $50 million beautifying Tony Clement's northern Ontario constituency, including building parks, walkways, and a gazebo. They called it "investments in infrastructure to reduce border congestion," even though the nearest border was far away.[22] One particularly important set of experiments at the ELA brought to an immediate end by the closure announcement had to do with silver nanoparticles – the tiny anti-bacterial silver particles that are added to toys and clothing to kill odour and disease-carrying bacteria. When they ended up in watersheds and waterways, they seemed to be toxic to ryegrass, algae, and fathead minnows. Even more alarming, they could also move into the human brain, where they definitely did not belong. Scientists and the public needed to know more, but research time on the project had run out.

Nature, a prominent peer-reviewed scientific publication, condemned the closure, observing that it was hard to believe that money was the real reason.[23] In March 2013, without any notice whatsoever, Department of Fisheries officials began dismantling the cabins used by visiting scientists, a particularly heavy-handed move because the federal government was in talks with the International Institute for Sustainable Development, a Winnipeg-based think-tank that was trying to come up with a takeover plan. Researchers were barred from the site, and the long-term continuity in ongoing data collection was irreparably interrupted. Eventually a salvage program of sorts was cobbled together, thanks to the governments of Ontario and Manitoba, and Ottawa made a token contribution (in August 2016 the new Liberal government announced long-term funding commitments for the facility).

The closing of the ELA was part of another omnibus bill tabled in the House of Commons in the spring of 2012. In the previous year's general election, Harper had finally earned his "strong, stable majority," giving the Conservatives a virtual carte blanche. The title was promising – the Jobs, Growth and Long-term Prosperity Act – but the content of the legislation was not. More than 400 pages long, it amended seventy federal laws and made vast and deep financial cuts across the federal bureaucracy, with massive layoffs directed primarily at scientists, researchers, and statisticians. It also introduced significant changes in some of the country's most important environmental legislation. One of the amendments permitted previously prohibited pollution by allowing some toxic-water dumps, provided they killed less than 50 per cent of the fish within ninety-six hours (ignoring one of Rachel Carson's important cautions: take the long view with chemicals and pesticides that percolate up and down the food chain). Another provision cancelled almost 3,000 scheduled environmental assessments, including several pipeline reviews.[24]

The Jobs, Growth and Long-term Prosperity Act did, however, provide for some new spending: $8 million was allocated to the Canada Revenue Agency to audit various organizations that were supposedly overspending on political activities and violating their charitable status, including high-profile outfits like the David Suzuki Foundation, Amnesty International, and OXFAM. These harassing audits largely confirmed compliance with the rules under which the organizations were operating.

Firing Scientists/Muzzling Scientists

Scores of scientists lost their jobs during the Harper government's time in power. Some long-standing public servants were marched out of their offices by security. In 2011 the results of a major government research review were released. The Jenkins Report was the work of a blue-chip panel of experts. It recommended establishing priorities with industrial partners for applied-research institutes and building science capacity with universities that excel at basic research. Looking back some years later, one of the committee members, David Naylor, the former president of the University of Toronto and a distinguished doctor and medical researcher, recalled that the National Research Council (NRC) did follow up with a new priority-setting process: "This ended up being more or less the opposite of what we recommended."[25]

The NRC, at one time Canada's premier scientific agency, was "refocused" to become a "concierge service" offering "a single phone number to connect business to all their research and development needs."[26] The minister provided details: "It will be hopefully a one-stop, 1-800. 'I have a solution for your business problem,'" Gary Goodyear told a meeting of the Economic Club of Canada in Ottawa.[27] The idea that research innovation could be generated on demand by calling a 1-800 number was somewhat unrealistic.

Goodyear was a creationist chiropractor from Cambridge, Ontario. He was the minister of state for science and technology and became best known to the Canadian people when he refused to answer a reporter's question about whether he personally believed in evolution. The Harper government was certainly in favour of doing more with less. That would explain the its decision to reduce the ranks. In truly unfortunate timing, on their last day at work, and on the way out the door, some of the terminated employees, along with those that remained, were given a $3 gift certificate from Tim Hortons courtesy of NRC head John McDougall: "Thank you for the contribution you have made ... here is a token of appreciation: have a coffee and donut on me."[28] Under McDougall's leadership, during Harper's time in power, the NRC shed one-quarter of its PhDs.[29]

No matter who they were or where they worked, all Canadian government scientists were muzzled.[30] Within a year or so of taking power, the Harper administration – which had campaigned on a platform of accountability and transparency – took control of the communications apparatus across the entire federal government, including cabinet ministers and Conservative MPs. No government likes surprises, but this one took message centralization to new heights. Everyone, bureaucrat or elected official alike, had to fill out a Message Event Proposal and submit it to the PMO for approval. Environment Canada, probably the most tightly controlled of all the departments, ordered its scientists to refer media inquiries to media specialists. "Just as we have one department," the scientists were told, "we should have one voice."[31]

This directive had nothing to do with academic freedom (which government scientists may or may not possess) but everything to do with not allowing scientists to talk about their work, inform the public, and contribute to the conversation. The restrictions reportedly extended to conferences the scientists attended on their own time and dime. They were forbidden to speak about climate change, the environment, the health of wildlife and the fisheries – about everything in fact. The *Globe and Mail's* Lawrence Martin described it as "a muzzling operation of exceptional scope."[32] This veteran journalist had experienced the same treatment as a correspondent in Moscow under communist rule: "Never thought I'd see it in 21st Century North America," he observed.[33] Martin was not alone.

It was "an attempt to guarantee ignorance," according to the *New York Times*. *Nature* referred to the government's "startlingly poor behavior."[34] *The Economist* concurred, describing the suppression of scientific free speech as "comical excesses in communication control."[35] Research scientists were even required to obtain government permission to publish their papers in peer-reviewed journals.

Even the increasingly ignored national science adviser – the academically accomplished and preternaturally wise Arthur Carty – was let go. Important institutions were closed: to name but a few, the National Roundtable on the Environment and the Economy, providing information on sustainable development and economic growth; the First Nations Statistical Institute, providing information on First Nations communities; and the National Council on Welfare, providing information on poverty. The prime minister asked rhetorically: Why would we fund those agencies when they offer solutions that run counter to our policy?[36]

Scientific agencies such as the Canadian Foundation for Climate and Atmospheric Sciences ran out of money when its mandate was not renewed. The Canada Centre for Inland Waters, focused on the health of the Great Lakes, and the Global Environment Monitoring System Water Program, a research network that watched over the ecology of all of Canada's freshwater, were severely hurt by fiscal cuts, while many others such as the Centre for Offshore Oil, Gas and Energy Research, the agency responsible for assessing offshore oil projects, had their long-term funding gutted. Industry Canada did, however, find $15 million to invest in a new think-tank, the oil-industry-friendly Canada School of Energy and Environment. A former top aide to the prime minister – disbarred lawyer, convicted fraudster, and former bankrupt Bruce Carson – was placed in charge (with the support of the University of Calgary administration but over the objections of the faculty).

Changing the Rules

In 2012 a moratorium was imposed on the Major Resources Support program (MRS). It provided money to scientists to develop and operate large-scale equipment essential for the most advanced research. That freeze led to mothballed labs across the country. Also under threat was the Research Tools and Instruments Grants Program, the main equipment-funder for basic researchers. The National Sciences and Engineering Research Council (NSERC) saw its funding reallocated. Ottawa, just like a for-profit business, was looking for return on investment. That meant directing money to industry-centred research: "Canada's federal government will focus strategically on research in areas that are in the national interest from a social and economic perspective."[37] In practice, money for oil-sands and nuclear-energy research went up; funding for manufacturing processes and products, up; funding for aquaculture (fish farming), up; but funding in other areas went down – climate-change research, conservation and preservation research, and research on the environmental impact of economic activity– for example, the carcinogenic run-off from the oil sands and the impact on the surrounding boreal forest and in the atmosphere.

It was a similar story with the other main Canadian grant-awarding bodies: the Social Sciences and Humanities Research Council (SSHRC), the Canadian Institutes for Health Research (CIHR), and the Canada Foundation for Innovation (CFI).[38] By and large, new money was specifically targeted away from basic research, with the government's priorities made paramount. The result, according to the OECD, is that Canada is now the only developed country in the world with an intellectual-property deficit. We spend more to acquire technology developed by others than they buy from us. The Science, Technology and Innovation Council's most recent report is extremely dispiriting. We are not competitive, and we are falling farther and farther behind other developed nations. It appears that focusing on applied research, at the expense of basic science, may well lead to technological stagnation and economic suicide. As is well known, there is applied research and yet-to-be-applied research.

The government is entitled to ensure that its money is wisely spent – a goal most taxpayers share. Research that fosters industry and economic progress and that stimulates innovation with a practical payoff is valuable. Research collaboration among government, industry, and the academy should be fostered. The Harper government actually increased science and technology spending nearly every year it was in office, but the money was increasingly directed toward applied research. Economic progress is critical, but basic scientific inquiry that seeks knowledge for the sake of knowledge is important too. The government has a role – the invention of the Internet proves that – but not to the exclusion of other activity in the research ecosystem.

Unfortunately, just as in the elimination of the long-form census, we may have spent more for less because of the funding reorientation. Naylor lamented the change in focus to fettered research – match-funded, industry-facing research with an applied orientation. As a result, he said, there had been no improvement in "our industry and competitiveness indicators."[39] Naylor was that rare academic who knew what he was talking about and said what he thought. Although he had been invited to lead a task force on health-care innovation, the government was so furious with his recommendations that it denied him permission to hold a press conference when he released his July 2015 report *Unleashing Innovation: Excellent Healthcare for Canadians.*

The basic problem with the report was that it envisaged re-engagement with the provinces and territories and real federal leadership, not the disentangled unproductive federalism that Harper had adopted with increasing avidity during his time in power. When it got wind of some of the coming recommendations, the PMO's first move was to demand changes. These demands were summarily rejected.[40] Harper's bad behaviour then became the story, and piqued public interest. His government was at the end of its rope, and its self-destructiveness was reaching new highs. All it had to do was give the report a lukewarm reception, promise to study it carefully, and it would have been lost in the mist of time. It is currently being carefully reviewed by the new government.

Trashing Libraries

Government research libraries were targeted too, either closed or consolidated. Books were tossed, sent to closed stacks, or put away in boxes. Library and Archives Canada had its budget slashed and its staff reduced. On and on it went, and Harper's ministers either said nothing or, presumably, were in complete agreement. (The Hon. Dr Kellie Leitch, PC, O.Ont., MD, MBA, FRCS[C], co-creator of the Barbaric Practices Snitch Line, now known for telling students, "I'm not an idiot," is one example on point.) After the October 2015 election, the new government brought with it a different approach, reflected, for example, in Justin Trudeau's promise to "run a government that believes in science – and a government that believes that good scientific knowledge should inform decision-making."[41]

In June 2016 Liberal science minister Kirsty Duncan appointed Naylor chair of a top-notch panel to look at the federal government's support for fundamental science. "The nine-member panel," *Science* reported, "will examine the impact of a decade of policies under the previous prime minister, Stephen Harper, aimed at converting labs into tools for industrial development and commercialization."[42] Ultimately, it was all about the politicization of science. "Governments," *Nature* editorialized, "come and go, but scientific expertise and experience cannot be chopped and changed as the mood suits and still be expected to function. Nor can applied research thrive when basic research is struggling." The government, the editorial continued, had to smarten up, and fast: "There is a difference between environmentalism and environmental science … the latter is an essential component of a national science program, regardless of politics."[43]

Scientists, especially government scientists, are, by nature, a reserved, cautious, cloistered lot. When almost 2,000 protesters took to Ottawa's streets on 10 July 2012, making their way to Parliament Hill, their frustration was palpable. They carried placards with the words: "No Science, No Evidence, No Truth, No Democracy" and "Save ELA." One of them was dressed like the Grim Reaper, and pallbearers carried a coffin for the mock funeral service observing science's death. The usual suspects turned out, but this protest was different: among the crowd were hundreds of mature men and women, dedicated public servants, all wearing

Parliament gets to decide, but we need to listen to the experts, and they need to be free to speak out.

their white lab coats. The theatrics, as intended, attracted attention. But what was really behind the march – behind this rare expression of public dissent by government scientists – was something deadly serious: a disruption in a long-standing social compact.

Government scientists conduct research and gather the best evidence – observable, verifiable, and peer-reviewable reality – so that the politicians can make the best public-policy decisions. It seems so obvious. We need the facts, no matter what they are, to address the serious problems we face. When we inhibit science, by throwing away books, undermining the collection of data, closing research stations, firing scientists, and directing the research of the ones that remain, we inhibit knowledge and damage democracy. The Harper government did not reject the best evidence – as it was politically entitled to do – but sought to eliminate, suppress and censor it.

"This was no random act," Allan Gregg explained at the University of Ottawa, "but a deliberate attempt to obliterate certain activities that were previously viewed as a legitimate part of government decision-making – namely, using research, science, and evidence as the basis to make policy decisions. It also amounted to an attempt to eliminate anyone who might use science, facts, and evidence to challenge government policies."[44] Gregg, a pollster from the Brian Mulroney era, was an insider objecting from the outside, and he was not alone. Four former Fisheries ministers, two Liberals and two Conservatives, spoke out against changes in the Jobs, Growth and Long-term Prosperity Act. The ex-ministers knew from their time in office that these legislative changes would lead to irreparable damage to Canada's fish habitats.[45] Unfortunately, like the protesting government scientists, they were ignored.

The tone of it all, though, was contagious. It spread to the House of Commons where civility, not a strong suit for many years, continued to decline. Dissent and disagreement were treated like death in the Conservative caucus, and for some MPs that was the result of disagreeing with the boss. Just ask Michael Chong, one of the few Tories who had the temerity to disagree on a matter of real principle.

Instead of crafting the best-informed laws, Canada ended up with something much less. Knowledge and public policy go hand in hand. The Westminster tradition – with its independent, non-partisan, and expert civil service advising the executive and a Parliament where the opposition checks and prods – has suffered mightily. Every democratic government, regardless of its ideology or hunger for power, must ultimately respect "the baseline Enlightenment commitment to human progress – to the gathering, interpretation, dissemination, and use of knowledge in the pursuit of more equitable government and a higher quality of life."[46] The public-policy objective must always be to free scientists to conduct the most thorough and rigorous research in order to inform government and the public. Experience elsewhere demonstrates that evidence-based public policy is both effective and cost-efficient.[47]

The government still gets to choose what to do. For instance, at the end of 2011, Canada withdrew from the Kyoto Protocol on climate change. The government did not believe it made sense for Canada to spend billions buying carbon credits when the two biggest producers of greenhouse gas – China and the United States – had rejected the agreement. All that would do, the government reasoned, would reduce Canadian competitiveness. After all, Canada doesn't have much of a carbon footprint in the first place.

This may have been the right decision, but that's not the point even if it was informed by what Harper privately believed about global warming and climate change. It was a political decision, one the elected government was entitled to make. If the Canadian people did not like it, they had their options, which they exercised on 9 October 2015 when they turfed the Tories from power and gave Justin Trudeau's Liberals a majority government. Prime Minister Harper lost his job, but the Canadian people were the real losers from years of institutionalized ignorance.

The Age of Wilful Blindness

Making political choices is one thing. But this is a far cry from the Harper government's decade-long war against facts, evidence, and democracy. It was a war on dissent: not the usual kind of dissent, but objective nonconforming voices that had important things to say about Canadian public policy, voices with information that would have informed discussion and added to debate. At every opportunity, and in every way, the Harper government chose to squelch dissent, to dismiss any views other than its own and those that supported its highly politicized agenda, one that was directed at political gain in fast and dirty real time. Poor people suffered. Vulnerable people suffered. People who needed our help suffered. With its way cleared, the Harper government pursued its goals full steam ahead, the consequences be damned. The ten years of Conservative rule under Stephen Harper can rightly be called the Age of Wilful Blindness.[48]

Chapter 9

The Clock Is Ticking and It's 1973 All Over Again

When God spoke to Moses in 1311 (BCE), according to the Jewish calendar, he promised to rescue the Israelites from slavery in Egypt and bring them to a "good and spacious land, a land flowing with milk and honey."[1] Today, Israel has the highest standard of living in the region, great beaches, a fabulous nightlife in Tel Aviv, and really beautiful people. It stands for achievement, especially in advanced technology, and ranks fifth on the Bloomberg Innovation Index, just ahead of the United States. In *Start-Up Nation*, Dan Senor and Saul Singer called it the innovation capital of the world.[2] Israel leads the way in the percentage of the economy spent on research and development, and half the world's top technology companies have invested in myriad Israeli start-ups. The country is an economic miracle, the offspring of an entrepreneurial, innovative, and creative culture willing to take risks. The Israelis have a word for it – *bitzua* – which means getting things done.

It all makes sense. Israel is surrounded by loud enemies and quiet "frenemies," and its only true meaningful ally, the United States, is 9,000 kilometres away. It has no significant natural resources – although its ingenuity coaxed food from rock and it is tapping natural gas from the sea. Some Israelis have even figured out how to harvest drinking water from the air. But high technology is its economic future. Venture capitalists recognize its genius, and university professors come to study how it all came together. Compulsory military service provides some explanations: the Israeli Army values brawn but mostly brains, and the training and technical skills it provides to fight war and hunt terrorists are unparalleled. Real leadership, innovation, and entrepreneurship are hugely valued. The population mix also plays a part: Zionists from everywhere including about 1 million well-educated Russians who arrived through the 1990s. Together they have morphed into a multicultural Jewish mélange, all benefiting from the excellent educational system.

Palestinian citizens of Israel are denied these advantages. For example, despite government programs to recruit Palestinians, only a small fraction of the 100,000 and more people working in Israeli high tech are Palestinian Israelis. When one of the authors of *Start-Up Nation*, Dan Senor, was asked the reason, he replied, "Discrimination."[3] It was more complicated than that, of course, as Senor elaborated. But the bottom line is that Israel has built a magnificent civilization – for Jewish Israelis.

In October 1973 Israel came close to defeat when Egyptian and Syrian forces massed on the borders and overconfident Israeli officials, wedded to a concept of Arab intentions that was no longer true, did virtually nothing. The Yom Kippur War followed, and the losses were staggering. Forty-five years later, the same thing is happening again. History is repeating itself, but with a completely different kind of threat and a brand new cast of characters. Once again, the threat may well be existential. Once again, the nation's leaders seem woefully blind to an unfolding national-security disaster.

Today, there is no need for the Tenth Man. Dissenters in Israel are protesting loudly, and they are not alone. All over the world, increasing numbers of people, especially Jewish people, are taking a harder look at the received wisdom, the stereotypes, and the myths, and when they do they don't like what they see. The pushback is enormous and sometimes downright vicious.

Criticism of Israel in polite company has always been taboo, and critics, even those with Israel's best interests at heart, are often branded as anti-Semites when they deviate from the party line. Few topics are more passionately felt on all sides of the political divide. But dissent has emerged and it is growing, even though it is almost impossible to have a frank and civil discussion about Israel in North America. The situation in Israel is a little different; there everyone has an opinion about everything but the dissenters are often singled out for harsh treatment. No matter where in the world, though, dissenting Jewish voices, as we shall see, stand out.

Dissent is never easy, but dissenting about Israel is particularly fraught. There is no way to sugarcoat it. The only way to understand the current situation is to acknowledge what has happened since Israel was carved out of Palestine in 1947. Israelis need to take a hard look at their history and at the society they have built and to consider realistic peace options. The Palestinians, in turn, have a role to play and a huge amount of work to do, beginning with a complete change of leadership. Given the power imbalance, it is up to Israel to make the first move. There is risk in this, of course. But less risk than the perpetuation of the status quo.

The Changing Map

The September 2001 United Nations World Conference against Racism was supposed to celebrate the end of apartheid in South Africa. Instead, with hundreds of governmental and NGO delegations – some 5,000 participants from 163 countries – it quickly degenerated into an anti-Israel free-for-all with its closing declaration equating Zionism with racism. That declaration was later amended, but the message was clear: as far as the conference was concerned, Israel was an apartheid state just as South Africa had been.

The South African anti-apartheid campaign began with a consumer boycott in 1959 but soon turned into an international movement to isolate South Africa until the goal of ending apartheid was achieved. Amazingly, it worked. There was violence, but eventually a multiracial constitutional democracy with political equality for everyone was established in South Africa on 27 April 1994. From start to finish, it took thirty-five years.

Apartheid was the Afrikaans word for "apartness," but it was more than that. The systematic oppression of one group by another, something Jews know about, is a crime against humanity and is prohibited by international law. The Israelis have a different word for it – *hafrada*, meaning separation. That is what Israel does: in the occupied territories, it separates the Palestinian population from the Israeli (Jewish) population. In effect, the same thing happens within Israel itself: both the Jewish Israelis (Israelis) and the Palestinian Israelis (Palestinians) are citizens, but the Jewish Israelis are the privileged ones.

Nothing is simple in the Middle East, least of all the multiple histories. The Jews claim Palestine because, thousands of years ago, they had a kingdom in part of it and, ever since, have had a presence there. Besides, God promised it to them: the Chosen People in the Promised Land. Numbers are inexact, but in 1947, the year before Israeli independence, there were about 650,000 Jewish settlers in Palestine and about 1.3 million Palestinians. The Palestinians also saw themselves as a people tied to their land and had no interest in their country becoming a Jewish state. Palestine should, they argued, be for Palestinians, not for Zionists from around the world longing to establish a homeland in someone else's country.⁴ Not so, some of the Zionists claimed: Palestine was "a land without a people for a people without a land." One way of looking at Israel is to see it as one country consisting of two national movements with equal attachment and equal rights to the land. Another way is to see it as one country with an indigenous population that had lived there for millennia but was pushed aside to make way for a settler colonialist state.

In the immediate aftermath of the Holocaust, emotions ran high. Zionists were completely committed to the establishment of a Jewish state, and much of the world appeared to agree. But, as a Canadian diplomat named Elizabeth MacCallum asked at the time, why should the Jewish problem be solved on the backs of the Palestinians who had nothing to do with the cataclysm in Europe? Both Jews and Palestinians had the opportunity to make their case in 1947 before the United Nations (UN) Special Committee on Palestine (Ivan Rand, a judge of the Supreme Court of Canada, was a member).⁵ They got a second chance at the UN General Assembly. The Special Committee had recommended partition: one state for the Jews, one for the Palestinians.

Even though this particular recommendation was lopsided and unworkable, and the Palestinians and various Arab countries strenuously objected, the General Assembly accepted the partition plan on 29 November 1947. The UN did not just admit Israel to membership, it created the new state. The Zionists, who owned about 6 per cent of the land and constituted about one-third of the total population, were to be given more than half (56 per cent) of the country (although it was assumed that the new Jewish state would be absorbing huge numbers of European refugees). The hundreds of thousands of displaced persons from Europe were soon joined by tens of thousands of Jews expelled from Arab nations who had nowhere else to go.

In November 1947 the map of Mandatory Palestine (British-controlled Palestine) was as shown in Figure 9.1. The UN partition plan provided for two separate states shown in Figure 9.2.

At midnight on 14 May 1948, the British Mandate over Palestine came to an end and the State of Israel was proclaimed. The War of Independence – the continuation of a low-level civil war that began after the UN partition vote – started the next day when all of Israel's neighbours attacked. When that war was over in January 1949 and the first armistice

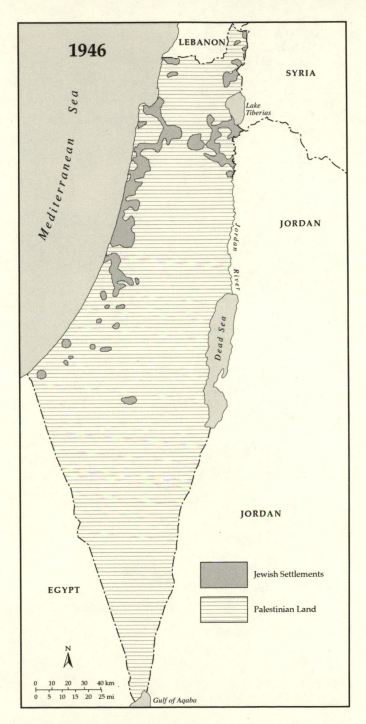

9.1 Credit: Adapted by Barry Levely from Palestine
Teaching Trunk

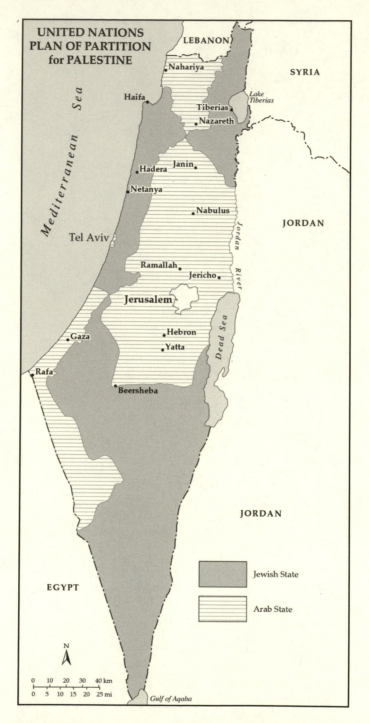

9.2 Credit: Adapted by Barry Levely from United Nations original

signed with Egypt on 24 February 1949 (Lebanon in March, Jordan in April, and Syria in July), Israel's borders had expanded considerably, as shown in Figure 9.3.

History vs. Reality

There are histories of Israel and histories of Palestine, completely different narratives competing for oxygen and attention. Israel's modern fabled past has dominated the discourse, cementing among Westerners a version of the country and its impressive accomplishments. But there is another version of events.

Israel's founding prime minister, David Ben Gurion, intended from the outset to accept any UN partition proposal, simply because it would confer international legal recognition of a Jewish state, and then to ignore it. He had much larger ambitions: to take control over as much of Mandatory Palestine as he could while expelling as many Palestinians as possible.[6] As early as 1938 he made his objective clear – "a transfer of the Arabs out of the Jewish state"[7] – though he must have known that Arab world, much less the Palestinians, would never agree. Zionist leaders called it Plan Dalet, or Plan D. Cast in military terms – to secure the interior for the impending battle for borders – the objective would be achieved through "depopulation and destruction of [Palestinian] villages that hosted hostile local militia and irregular forces," meaning just about all of them.[8]

This initiative began slowly after passage of the partition resolution at the UN and gathered steam with Israel's Declaration of Independence. It was soon amplified by the intense struggle for a Jewish state. Ben Gurion knew exactly what this project entailed and the impact it would have on the Palestinians: "We and they want the same thing: We both want Palestine,"[9] Ben Gurion remarked in 1936. Twenty years later, he confessed to Nahum Goldmann, the president of the World Jewish Congress, "We have taken their country ... we have come here and stolen their country."[10] The "New Historians," Israelis who are rewriting their country's highly romanticized past in light of documents from the recently opened state archives and other sources, have come to the same conclusion.[11]

One of them is Ilan Pappé. He describes what happened: "Military orders were dispatched to the units on the ground to prepare for the systematic expulsion of the Palestinians from vast areas of the country. The

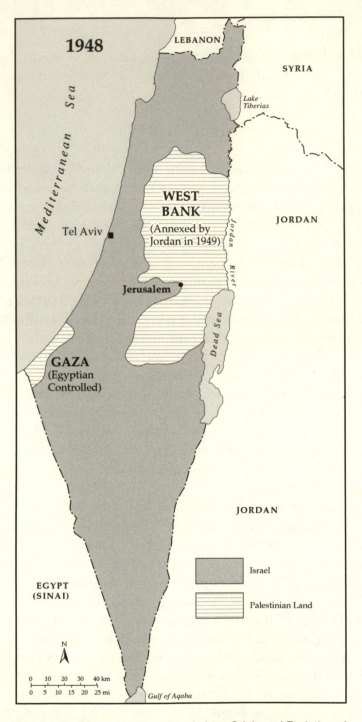

9.3 Credit: Adapted by Barry Levely from Origin and Evolution of the Arab-Zionist Conflict

David Ben Gurion. At the Declaration of the State of Israel on 14 May 1948. Note the portrait of Theodor Herzl, founder of Zionism. (Credit: Rudi Weissenstein/Israel Ministry of Foreign Affairs)

orders came with a detailed description of the methods to be employed to forcibly evict the people: large-scale intimidation; laying siege to and bombarding villages and population centres; setting fire to homes, properties, and goods; expulsion; demolition; and finally, planting mines among the rubble to prevent any of the expelled inhabitants from returning."[12]

Massacres, like the one carried out by the anti-Arab, some say terrorist, Zionist paramilitary organization, the Irgun, at Deir Yassin, a peaceful village on the western outskirts of Jerusalem, terrified the entire Palestinian population and encouraged further Palestinian flight. The details are disturbing. On 9 April 1948 Zionist forces entered the village. Soon enough, "Arab family after family were slaughtered," hundreds murdered, and "there were also cases of mutilation and rape."[13] It is a depressing story that runs counter to almost everything the world has been asked to believe about the founding of the Jewish state: "Jews expelled, massacred, destroyed and raped in that year, and generally behaved like all the other colonialist movements operating in the Middle East and

Africa since the beginning of the nineteenth century."[14] Deir Yassin was repaid in kind: on 13 May 1948 Arab fighters massacred about 150 defenders of Kibbutz Kfar Etzion south of Bethlehem after they surrendered.

Pappé is not some disloyal Israeli with an axe to grind. Other New Historians – Benny Morris, Tom Segev, Avi Shlaim, Hillel Cohen, Baruch Kimmerling, and Simha Flapan – have concluded that some of the key founding stories are myth. They don't agree on everything, but the destruction of the Palestinian community is unambiguous and the means employed are confirmed by Israelis and Palestinians alike.[15] "I'm shocked by the deeds that have reached my ears," Ben Gurion said at the time.[16]

Even though these unpalatable conclusions are based on papers found in Israeli state archives and wide-ranging historical research, they have not been welcomed in Israel. According to Segev, seventy years after the fact, key government documents have yet to be released – in particular, records of discussions between Israeli leaders on the decision to expel the Palestinian population and evidence of atrocities committed against the Palestinian population to encourage their departure.[17] The Palestinians and many others who investigated these events have been claiming as much for years.[18]

Israel and its supporters believe that the Jews are the indigenous population: they were there first and never left. Arabs, they say, came later via conquest, migration, and settlement. As first in line, the country belongs to them.[19] Some of them observe that Israel's pre-independence planning included peaceful co-existence with the Palestinians and point, for example, to the work of the Situation Committee and its blueprint for the government of a new country, including "integrating a large Arab minority into the Jewish state." Unfortunately, they continue, "events on the ground tipped the balance."[20]

According to this narrative, Israel never intended to expel the indigenous population – it was "unforeseen" – but, once it happened, chose to accept it, much like "an unexpected inheritance."[21] Defenders also point to the post-1948 mass expulsion of Jews from Arab lands and the confiscation of their property.

The Palestinians have a different perspective: they call Israel's 1948 Declaration of Independence and the war that followed the *nakba* (the catastrophe), an unmitigated national disaster. In its wake, a myth was propagated: that the Palestinians decamped on blanket orders from Arab leaders outside Israel.

In his landmark study *The Birth of the Palestinian Refugee Problem, 1947–1949*, however, Benny Morris observes that there is "no contemporary evidence" supporting that conclusion: "For decades the policy of the Palestinian Arab leaders had been to hold fast to the soil of Palestine and to resist the eviction and displacement of Arab communities."[22] The documentary record establishes that some Palestinians, especially the rich, left voluntarily (intending their departure to be temporary). But many were victims of a deliberate expulsion plan hatched long before the UN-approved partition.[23] Widespread looting and wholesale confiscation of property followed, and once the Palestinians were gone, none of them were allowed back. According to Morris, Zionist forces realized in the spring of 1948 that "a transfer of the prospective Arab minority out of the emergent Jewish state had begun, and that with very little extra effort and nudging on the part of the Jewish forces, it could be expanded."[24] The temptation to push the Palestinians out proved irresistible.

"Ben Gurion," Morris concludes, "clearly wanted as few Arabs as possible to remain in the Jewish state. He hoped to see them flee." Cannily, he "refrained from issuing a clear or written expulsion order" and relied, instead, on his generals *understanding* his wishes.[25] In short order, an estimated 700,000 men, women, and children, more than half the Palestinian population, were uprooted into exile – most by expulsion or threat of expulsion – largely to wretched refugee camps where, along with their millions of descendants, they remain to this day. Hundreds of thousands more joined them after the June 1967 Six Day War. The Israeli establishment made no secret of the long-term goal: "You shall," Defence Minister Moshe Dayan declared after the 1967 expulsions, "continue to live like dogs, and whoever wishes may leave, and we will see where this process leads."[26]

In the years following the 1948 War of Independence, more than 400 Palestinian towns and villages were bulldozed into oblivion and the land was appropriated by the state. Walid Khalidi's *All That Remains* provides an encyclopedic record of hundreds of once-vibrant villages that have disappeared. The Palestinian presence was erased, as village names and street names were replaced by Hebrew substitutes and, sometimes, Israeli settlements were built where they had been. International Jewry became an unwitting accomplice as its donated money was used to plant pine and cypress forests over the ruins of almost 100 former villages. It continues to this day. Ayalon Canada Park is an example.

No part of the park – some 700 hectares – is within the Green Line, Israel's 1949 internationally recognized borders. It was captured during the Six Day War. Thousands of Palestinians were expelled, and their three villages razed. The Canadian branch of the Jewish National Fund has been raising money for the project ever since. The road to the park is named for former prime minister John Diefenbaker, who officially opened the park in 1975.

Whether for military reasons (to secure the interior and the borders), political reasons (to prevent the return of refugees), or economic reasons (to turn over Palestinian property to Jewish settlers), by April 1949 more than 100,000 Jewish immigrants had taken up residence in "abandoned" Arab houses.[27] As several writers have observed, it was the deliberate and planned destruction of a people, their culture, and their society, accompanied by a massive cover-up, with a repeat performance after the Six Day War, and it continues to this day.[28] In Ben Gurion's words, "the concepts of 'ours' and 'not ours' are only for peacetime, and during war they lose all their meaning."[29]

By expelling the Palestinians, Israel created a time bomb. Aharon Cizling, an Israeli cabinet minister, knew that in 1948: "We still do not appreciate what kind of enemy we are now nurturing outside the borders of our state," he admitted. "Our enemies, the Arab states, are a mere nothing compared with those hundreds of thousands of [Palestinians] who will be moved by hatred and hopelessness and infinite hostility to wage war on us."[30] Ben Gurion and others in the Israeli leadership convinced themselves, however, that time was on Israel's side. That, Segev wrote in his path-breaking book *1949: The First Israelis*, "was an error."

Ben Gurion believed that Israel "could manage perfectly well without peace with the Arab states and without a solution to the Palestinian refugee problem."[31] When the Israeli Foreign Ministry was asked in 1949 what would happen to the refugees, one of its officials replied: "The most adaptable and best survivors would manage by a process of natural selection, and the others will waste away. Some will die but most will turn into human debris and social outcasts and join the poorest classes in the Arab countries."[32] Putting it a little differently, and more gently, Ben Gurion concluded that "the refugees would become absorbed wherever they happened to be, and thus the source of conflict would completely disappear,"[33] but the exact opposite occurred. The longer they remained in exile, the stronger their national consciousness grew. The Israeli prime minister "failed to take into account the unifying power of exile and home-sickness."[34] There were opportunities to resolve the refugee problem in 1949, but they were squandered, as has every opportunity for peace since, by both Israelis and Palestinians. The price of peace has only increased.

Israel's map stayed the same until the Six Day War when, once again, its neighbours mobilized en masse in a tragically miscalculated attack. When it was over, Israel was the unabashed superpower of the region and its borders had expanded even farther (see Figure 9.4)

Israel controlled the Sinai until it was returned in 1982 in exchange for peace with Egypt. Israel still controls parts of the Golan Heights – in violation of international law, it has annexed the seized territory – and has built more than forty civilian settlements on land taken mostly from Syria but also Lebanon.[35]

Today, the map of Israel had changed again, shown in Figure 9.5.

Israeli Apartheid?

Israeli forces evacuated the Gaza Strip in 2005, along with some decid-edly reluctant settlers they dragged away with them. While most com-mentators contend that the Gaza Strip is effectively occupied by Israel, given its degree of control over almost every single aspect of daily life, Hamas, the acronym for Islamic Resistance Movement, an offshoot of Egypt's Muslim Brotherhood, has governed there since 2006. There are 1.8 million people crammed into 362 square kilometres, compared to, say, Liechtenstein, with 38,000 people in 160 square kilometres.

But Gaza is no Liechtenstein: with little industry and virtually no econ-omy, Gaza is almost entirely dependent on foreign aid. The inhabitants live in abject poverty in a failed slum city-state,[36] one that seems to suit everyone but its miserable residents. Israel and Egypt decide what goes in and what goes out by air, sea, and land – or they try to. This blockade, Britain's former prime minister David Cameron said, has turned Gaza into a "giant open prison."[37] The Swedish foreign minister called it a "cage."[38] The people inside, victims of a medieval siege, are subject to a collective punishment of deprivation, subjection, and cruelty. And they are angry: Hamas, an implacable enemy of the Jewish state, has repudi-ated signed peace agreements and turned Gaza into a staging ground for missile and tunnel attacks against Israel (when it is not busy torturing and murdering its own internal enemies, real and imagined). It is a recipe

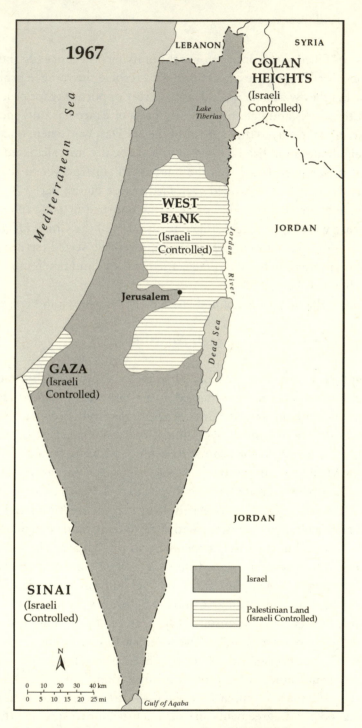

9.4 Credit: Adapted by Barry Levely from Origin and Evolution of the Arab-Zionist Conflict

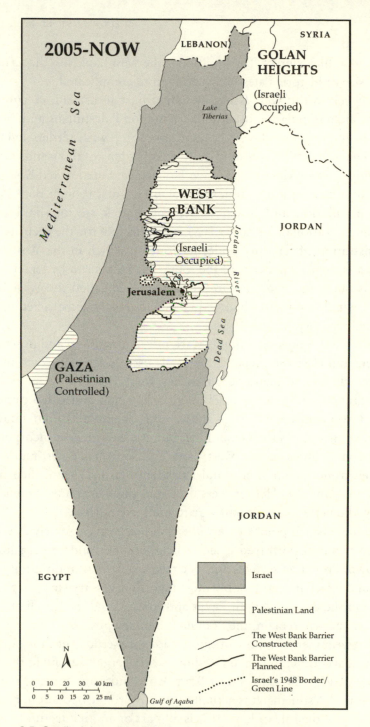

9.5 Credit: Adapted by Barry Levely from Origin and Evolution of the Arab-Zionist Conflict

for never-ending conflict. The situation in the West Bank, less than a quarter the size of historic Palestine, is even more complicated.

Israel seized the West Bank, including East Jerusalem, in 1967. In 2015 it had a population of around 2.8 million Palestinians and, in violation of international law,[39] at least 400,000 Jewish settlers living in more than 200 settlements (and quite possibly tens of thousands more). In addition, approximately 200,000 Israelis lived in annexed East Jerusalem, and 20,000 in the annexed Golan Heights, though both Palestinian population and Israeli settlement figures are unreliable. The Palestinian National Authority (PA) is responsible for the security and administration of territory under its control, which in the West Bank means less than 20 per cent of the total. The rest is run by Israel – and Israel is building a wall, a 670-kilometre fence called the West Bank Barrier, which is 9 metres high in places and mostly constructed within occupied territory.

As former US president Jimmy Carter describes it: "In addition to the concrete and electrified fencing materials used in the construction, the barrier includes two-metre-deep trenches, roads for patrol vehicles, electronic ground and fence sensors, thermal imaging and video cameras, sniper towers and razor wire – almost entirely on Palestinian land."[40] Sometimes it follows the Green Line, but at other times it incorporates settler communities on the West Bank and separates Palestinian communities from one another – and Palestinian farmers from their now-confiscated land. In places it veers deep into the West Bank, as much as twenty kilometres – about half way to the Jordan River.

From the Israeli point of view, the wall has been extremely effective, or at least it can be portrayed as such: suicide bombers and terrorist attacks are down. Providing security for its citizens is the paramount duty of a state, and Israel understandably must take all necessary steps to protect itself. But there is peace with Egypt and Jordan, and the Israeli Defense Force is, and will remain, the dominant military power.

Every year there are more outposts and more settlements, the purpose of which, according to Israeli Gershom Gorenberg, "is to fill in the gaps … to extend Jewish control over West Bank land, to fragment the territory left to Palestinians. It is actually a massive rogue operation, making a mockery of the rule of law."[41] It is all part of an architectural master plan, described by Israeli architect Eyal Weizman in *Hollow Land*, to expand permanently the borders of the Jewish state.[42] That it inflicts

The Wall. Built almost entirely on Palestinian land, in some places it veers deep into the West Bank, separating Palestinian communities from each other and Palestinian farmers from their now-confiscated lands. (Credit: Ahmad Gharabli)

misery on the local population is an intended by-product, especially welcome to the extent it encourages emigration.[43]

Other features of the occupation of the West Bank – now in its fiftieth year – includes diversion and monopolization of the watershed, separate and inequitable road systems, a complex and onerous permit system (one is required for virtually every single aspect of daily life), and parallel legal systems – the Israeli for the privileged settlers, and a controlling military justice for the Palestinians.

None of this is a secret, at least not in Israel. Michael Ben-Yair, Israel's attorney general in the mid-1990s, explained: "We enthusiastically chose to become a colonial society, ignoring international treaties, expropriating lands, transferring settlers from Israel to the occupied territories, engaging in theft and finding justification for all of these activities. Passionately desiring to keep the occupied territories, we developed two judicial systems: one – progressive, liberal – in Israel; and the other – cruel, injurious – in the occupied territories. In effect, we established an apartheid regime in the occupied territories immediately following their capture. That oppressive regime exists to this day."[44] Ben-Yair concluded that Israel had become an unjust society, one that had "turned the lives of millions into a nightmare."[45] In the years since 2002 when Ben-Yair spoke out, conditions in the occupied territories have only worsened.

Israel's respected human-rights watch dog *B'tselem* observed: "Different legal systems are applied to two populations residing in the same area, and the nationality of the individual determines the system and the court in which he or she is tried."[46] Close to 100 per cent of Palestinians charged with an offence are convicted, mostly for small crimes such as participating "in unauthorized processions." In contrast, close to 100 per cent of the investigations into military and settler violence against Palestinians never reach trial. On the rare occasion that a settler is convicted, only a light sentenced is imposed. As a result, fanatical settlers have licence to demolish homes, burn Palestinian crops, cut down their olive groves, and torch their mosques.

It is not just the settlers: according to *B'Tselem*, the IDF demolished more Palestinian homes in the West Bank in the first half of 2016 than in all 2015, leaving 740 Palestinians (including 384 children) homeless. In the last decade, more than 1,000 homes have been bulldozed.[47] The treatment of Palestinian children by the IDF, as successive UNICEF reports have clearly set out, should be an international human-rights scandal.[48] According to the *Jerusalem Post*, it took the personal intervention of the minister of justice to stop the military from confining arrested juveniles in outdoor cages in the middle of winter: "The Public Committee against Torture [in Israel] said that the practice was just one example of the torture and ill treatment of Palestinian children by law enforcement."[49]

When Israeli, Palestinian, and international human-rights organizations complain about these activities, "Israel trashes the reports as biased, distorted, and, inevitably, anti-Semitic."[50] But is that true? In Hebron, for example, a Palestinian city of about 120,000, some 500 "divinely" inspired settlers moved in and made it their mission to provoke and attack men, women, and children, embarrass and humiliate them, and defile their mosques. They are free to do so because, as *B'Tselem* and others report, the IDF does nothing.[51] Israeli soldiers also regularly use tear gas against Hebron's children – American-manufactured tear gas – and inflict beatings on young and old alike.[52] Israel has promised to "strengthen the Jewish settlement in Hebron."[53]

Israel's control of the security apparatus in the West Bank has resulted in a system eerily reminiscent of the worst excesses of the apartheid regime in South Africa: military brutality; extended "administrative" detentions, expulsions, and deportations; curfews, denial of due process, and restrictions on movement, free expression, and assembly; frequent and harassing military checkpoints and roadblocks (some 600 in all); seizure of privately owned land for the building of more illegal settlements; and house demolition, a form of collective punishment upheld by the Israeli Supreme Court.[54] The court has also approved "moderate physical pressure" in cases of "necessity." According to the Israeli organization the Public Committee against Torture in Israel, between 2001 and 2015, almost 1,000 complaints were filed with the Israeli attorney general against the Israeli Security Agency, better known as the Shin Bet or Shabak, and in response "zero criminal investigations were launched."[55]

Ben Ehrenreich's 2016 book, *The Way to the Spring*, describes life in the occupied territories in chilling detail. Israel's behaviour has become a lightning rod, attracting almost universal condemnation, in particular from the United Nations but also from Israel's most important and steadfast ally, the United States. As the left-leaning newspaper *Haaretz* editorialized, the regime that Israel has imposed "has a name – it's called apartheid."[56] In return, plenty of Palestinian violence is directed at Israelis, with the settlers as frequent targets. Where will the monstrous cycle end?

Systemic Discrimination

Records unearthed by the New Historians and others indicate that some of Israel's founders were crude racists,[57] and their attitudes undoubtedly set the stage for what was to follow. Israel's Declaration of Independence promises not only a Jewish state but a modern egalitarian and democratic one, with "complete equality of social and political rights" for "all its inhabitants irrespective of religion, race or sex." It hasn't happened. Palestinians inside Israel, representing about 20 per cent of the population, are able to vote, sit in parliament (the Knesset), and occupy high judicial and official positions, but Israel is a Jewish state and it accords Jewish citizens – the Israelis – privileged treatment. For example, Israel attaches important benefits to military service – housing, education loans, and public-sector employment. Palestinians (except for Druze and the Circassian) are not required to serve, though they can volunteer.

Legislation helps to preserve the distinction too. The Law of Return (1950) guarantees all Jews immediate citizenship in Israel: people who

Above and Opposite
Checkpoints (Credits: left, Emil Salman; right, Magne Hagesæter)

have no connection to Israel except their religion are granted citizenship on arrival, while under the Citizenship Law (1952) actual refugees and their children – the very people displaced from their homes in Israel – cannot even visit. The Nationality and Entry into Israel Law (2003) means that Palestinian citizens of Israel who marry a non-citizen are not allowed to bring their spouses into the country if the spouse comes from the occupied territories or an "enemy state."

Non-Jewish citizens of Israel, meaning Palestinians, are discriminated against in myriad ways. Adalah, the Legal Centre for Arab Minority Rights in Israel, has identified more than fifty laws that directly discriminate against Palestinians in their own country. The Israeli flag has a Jewish star, and the national anthem speaks of a "Jewish soul." Successive opinion polls indicate that the vast majority of Palestinians in Israel believe they are being discriminated against.[58] When asked the same question, only about 13 per cent of the Israeli population felt this way.

This systemic institutional discrimination has repeatedly been condemned in US State Department reports and acknowledged by Israel itself.[59] The 2003 report of the Or Commission, asked to investigate

conditions of Palestinians in Israel, concluded that the "government handling of the Arab sector has been primarily neglectful and discriminatory."[60] Significantly less money is spent on education for Palestinian citizens than for Israelis, for example, which means fewer opportunities in life.

A far greater imbalance is evident in employment, income, and the ability to buy land. More than 90 per cent of the land in Israel is reserved for Israelis (even though much of it was seized from Palestinians without compensation). True, while discrimination is rife, the condition of Palestinians in Israel is probably better than anywhere else. In recent years, Palestinian infant mortality rates have fallen, life expectancy has increased, and educational attainment has gone up: Palestinians currently hold 7 per cent of government jobs and, if they attend university, can become doctors and lawyers. However, no one seriously suggests that Palestinian citizens of Israel enjoy anything resembling political, social, and economic equality. About a third of all Israelis apparently believe that Palestinian citizens of Israel should not have the right to vote.[61] The treatment of Bedouins in Israel is especially shocking. To give just one example, under the Prawer Plan, 70,000 Bedouin living in the southern Negev faced forcible removal from thirty-five "unrecognized" villages, though Bedouin have lived there through recorded history.

The Israeli Supreme Court has upheld a Jewish-only housing complex in a Tel Aviv suburb, and the Admissions Committee Law, passed by the Knesset in March 2011, explicitly allows certain local community organizations to exclude Palestinians. "Imagine," a Palestinian Knesset member said at the time, "if Britain or France had made a law preventing Jews from living in certain communities."[62] The Israeli law was upheld by the Supreme Court in 2014. According to Amnesty International, Israelis regularly demolish homes of Palestinians – citizens of Israel – in Israel and sometimes entire "unrecognized" villages too.[63] Since Israel's founding, more than 1,000 new Israeli settlements have been established, yet the government has not authorized the building of one new Palestinian community.[64] Many Palestinians within Israel are considered "internally displaced," meaning that they are not allowed to return to their actual or ancestral homes. By and large, the property they owned in 1948 now belongs to the state. Martial law continued until 1966 (providing additional opportunities for Palestinian land confiscation), while the country remains under a state of emergency to this day. That classification provides legal justification for a variety of oppressive regulations, which are regularly used to control Palestinian behaviour in Israel and the occupied territories.

Every American president since 1967 has opposed building new settlements in the occupied territories, possibly until now. In September 2004 George W. Bush spelled out the US position: "Israel should impose a settlement freeze, dismantle unauthorized outposts, end the daily humiliation of the Palestinian people, and avoid any actions that prejudice final negotiations."[65] But construction continued, and the Israel lobby works assiduously to ensure that the United States provides billions of dollars in foreign aid by consistently conflating American and Israeli interests. Under the watch of every Israeli prime minister since 1967, the number of settlements and settlers in the occupied territories has increased. As Dayan said after the Six Day War when Israel captured almost everything, "this is not the end."[66] Andrew Sullivan, the former editor of the Zionist *New Republic*, has blogged about it: "Just keep giving them money and they [the Israelis] will give the US the finger in return."[67]

Boycott, Divest, Sanction

In July 2005 a conference was held in Ramallah, the PA capital on the West
Bank, where almost two hundred Palestinian organizations gathered to
represent Palestinian refugees, Palestinians living under Israeli occupation, and Palestinian citizens of Israel. Together, whether left, right, religious, or secular, they called for a worldwide BDS campaign – to boycott,
divest, and sanction Israel. They formulated four key demands: self-deter-
mination for the Palestinian people, an end to the occupation, equal treatment for everyone, and recognition of the right of all Palestinian refugees
and their descendants to return to their homes in Israel.

BDS arose out of frustration with the status quo, but, as might have
been expected, the final demand was non-negotiable from the Israeli
point of view. A Palestinian right-of-return has proven the major stum-
bling block in successive peace talks, although the subject of some "creative" proposals such as a token actual return, cash payments, and some
friendly nations, such as Canada, agreeing to help by admitting refugees.

While there has always been intermittent activity on the Middle East
peace front, no lasting accomplishment has been recorded since Egypt
and Israel signed their peace treaty on 26 March 1979, followed by Israel
and Jordan on 26 October 1994. Since then, traditional diplomacy has
floundered as conditions in the occupied territories – some Israelis call
them "disputed" – have deteriorated.

A BDS movement has emerged and grown because the Israeli-Palestinian peace process failed. The 1993 Oslo Accords, signed by Yitzhak
Rabin and Yasser Arafat on the White House lawn on 13 September 1993,
went nowhere. Neither side delivered on their empty promises and the
result was a dependent, landlocked parody of a Palestinian state. The
agreement did nothing for the original refugees and their descendants
(kept confined by their Arab hosts in camps from one generation to the
next) or for Palestinians inside Israel, and it created only uncertainty about
Jerusalem's fate (all "final status" issues to be determined "later"). This
"peace of the brave," as President Bill Clinton called it, was to conclude
within five years by Permanent Status Negotiations. The Oslo Accords
were a masterpiece of ambiguity: quickly diminishing sizzle and no steak.

Instead of peace, Arafat became Israel's enforcer in those large parts
of the West Bank it did not retain for itself – "the tinpot ruler of a Transkei
on the Mediterranean."[68] Under the guise of "security coordination,"

Arafat and his PA successors can be relied on, much of the time, to do Israel's bidding while the Palestinian people get more angry as their circumstances deteriorate daily. The ongoing Oslo negotiations were accompanied by accelerated expansion into occupied territories. For example, when Ariel Sharon, then minister of defence, returned to Israel from ongoing negotiations with the Palestinians at the Wye Plantation in Maryland in October 1998 – yet another meeting in the pointless Oslo discussions – he had a clear message for the settlers: "Move, run and grab as many hilltops as they can ... because everything we take now will stay ours. Everything we don't grab will go to them."[69]

His invitation was accepted: "Virtually not a week goes by without a new revelation, each more sensational and revolting than the previous one," *Haaretz* editorialized about the building spree.[70] Some of these settlements are actual cities with tens of thousands of inhabitants, schools, shopping and recreation centres, restaurants, theatres, hospitals, parks, synagogues, and adjacent industrial parks.

Peaceful Protest Not Terrorism

BDS is explicitly non-violent, making it even more compelling to many: it professes to be in the tradition of Mahatma Gandhi and Nelson Mandela. "We, representatives of Palestinian civil society, call upon ... people of conscience all over the world to impose broad boycotts and implement divestment initiatives against Israel similar to those applied to South Africa in the apartheid era."[71] It was a call for a political solution, not a call to arms.

For some, that means two states for two peoples, but for others, probably most of its adherents, it is nothing less than one state for all peoples, a Greater Palestine running from the Jordan River to the Mediterranean. "Separation can't work in so tiny a land, any more than apartheid did," the Palestinian intellectual Edward Said observed in 2001. "If we are all to live, we must capture the imagination not just of our people, but of our oppressors. And we have to abide by humane democratic values."[72] One thing is for sure: it is either marriage or divorce.

For Israelis, a one-state solution is seen as the end of Israel since it would be demographically swamped. That might have given rise to some urgency to negotiate a two-state solution, but it hasn't, at least not yet. BDS's focus on the rights of all Palestinians everywhere was a brilliant move. This time, no one was left behind. Because it unifies the Palestinian people behind common, interlinked goals, it's impossible to play one segment of Palestinian society against the others. BDS challenged the silos and political fragmentation, gathering the parts and turning them into a national movement. This all-encompassing nature makes BDS a formidable force.

BDS also did an end run around the corrupt Palestinian leadership, speaking directly to people in Israel, the occupied territories, the refugee camps, and all over the world. By divorcing the movement from any Arab government, the campaigners have kept their independence, and their official slogan – Freedom, Justice, Equality – has universal appeal. BDS operates under a secular umbrella, using the language of international law. (Israel, itself a creation of international law and a member of the United Nations, is, according to the International Court of Justice, in violation of international law for building both settlements and the wall in occupied territory.)

Because it is decentralized, self-funded, and volunteer-driven, BDS is playing the long game, and small symbolic victories suit it fine. The BDS leadership emphasizes "context sensitivity": local activists make the decisions about what to do, though everything is subject to a national steering committee with headquarters in the West Bank. Without a doubt, BDS is the smartest thing the Palestinians have ever done. It is classic Dr Martin Luther King. As he wrote in his "*Letter from a Birmingham Jail*": "Nonviolent direct action seeks to create such a crisis and establish such creative tension that a community that has constantly refused to negotiate is forced to confront the issue. It seeks to so dramatize the issue that it can no longer be ignored."[73]

BDS is growing, especially in North America.[74] Student groups back it, organizing Israeli Apartheid Week to raise awareness. After the University of Toronto provided space for the first such event in 2005, the university stated in response to furious objection: "To the extent that these events have engendered debate in the context of strongly held and widely divergent views, they have also reflected the fundamental social role of the University … Our openness to such activities reflects our institutional commitment to freedom of speech, a fundamental freedom that has been earned through many generations of struggle and sacrifice, and repeatedly championed by universities in democratic societies."[75] Culture-wars critic Barbara Amiel, writing in *Maclean's*, offered to "eat her hat the day they allow an anti-Islamism Week ... organized on campus by Jewish students."[76] Yet three years before Israeli Apartheid Week was even invented, the University of Toronto had hosted a series of lectures sponsored by a Jewish students' organization called Know Radical Islam. Free speech is free speech.

The University of Toronto no more sponsors Israeli Apartheid Week than it does any of the thousands of events that take place on campus every year. "On-campus groups that are registered with the university have the right to use meeting space for meetings of their members, while off-campus groups can also rent space – provided they obey the law," was the way University of Toronto president David Naylor explained it.[77] "We have," Naylor later wrote in response to some criticism that the university was demonstrating pro-Israel bias, "simply emphasized that the right of free speech on our campuses carries with it responsibilities to consider the weight of one's words, and to embrace discourse along with expressing dissent."[78] According to the *New York Times*, by May 2015 there were hundreds of BDS groups on American college campuses.

To be sure, casting the Israeli-Palestinian conflict as a struggle between oppressed and oppressor, the settler and the indigenous population, is simplistic, but it resonates, especially among the young. It also leads to the formation of alliances with other socially progressive groups seeking equality – for example, over local police brutality against African Americans. Dr Angela Davis, a former leader of the US Communist Party, socialist academic Cornel West, and Patrisse Cullors, the co-founder of Black Lives Matter, linked the riots in Ferguson, Missouri, to the treatment of Palestinians by Israel. "Blacks and Palestinians are dehumanized as a matter of institutional order," they said as they pledged solidarity with the Palestinian people and support for BDS.[79] One BDS supporter told students opposing the movement, "What you call conflation, we call solidarity."[80] Framed in this way, locating BDS within a continuum of socially progressive causes is an effective strategy.

In the University of California system, for example, nearly all the student government councils have come out in favour of BDS (though few of American university administrations have yet implemented the various resolutions). It is completely unacceptable that the fierce debates regularly spill over into anti-Semitic incidents, and the perpetrators must be held accountable. If universities serve any purpose, it is for the free exchange of all ideas, and there is no justification for Jewish students and professors being targeted, harassed, intimidated, and bullied because of their religion and their Zionism. When Jewish students were recently pushed out of a public lecture sponsored by Students for Justice in Palestine at Brooklyn College in New York, for example, the culprits were appropriately condemned by the administration.[81] That same group invaded a faculty council meeting demanding that "Zionists" be barred from campus. Someone should be barred: the students for "justice." By any measure, however, there is enormous activity around BDS on North American university campuses, including among the professoriate.[82]

The Asian American Studies Association came first, endorsing BDS in April 2013, and it was followed, among other groups, by the 5,000-member American Studies Association, the Native American and Indigenous Studies Association, the Peace and Justice Studies Association, and the National Women's Studies Association, all highly politicized organizations. In June 2016 the 9,000-plus members of the American Anthropological Association defeated a BDS resolution by only thirty-nine votes. When the American Association of University Professors rejected BDS on principled grounds, the response sparked a heated discussion among its 48,000 members. More than 250 universities and almost all the important academic associations have declared academic boycotts contrary to core values such as the free international movement of scholars and ideas.

BDS supporters see it differently: Israeli academic institutions – as distinct from individuals – must be boycotted, they say, because they are part of the institutional architecture that supports an apartheid state and, as such, are implicated in injustice (how to distinguish between institutions and individuals is never adequately addressed). According to BDS followers, Israeli universities provide military and other research that enables and perpetuates the occupation, and suppress historical study of the *nakba*. Some, such as Hebrew University in Jerusalem, have also expanded their footprint on occupied land.

Part of the purpose of the boycott is to send a message to Israelis that "their self-image of Israel as a democratic society is being questioned by people they respect and societies and associations to which they want to belong."[83] But boycotting academic institutions is completely contrary to academic freedom and the exchange of information and ideas. Moreover, academics are often the most vigorous critics of their own government policies as well as the most passionate advocates of human rights. For their part, Israeli academics are among the most vociferous defenders of the Palestinian people, although free speech is the real point.

Most of the BDS action in North America, however, is on the economic side, where church groups have been falling into line. In 2014 the Presbyterian Church (USA), with 1.8 million members, narrowly approved a divestment resolution, though it reaffirmed Israel's right to exist and insisted that the resolution was not an endorsement of the BDS movement or "our lack of love for our Jewish sisters and brothers."[84] In 2015 the United Church of Christ, with 1 million members, voted overwhelmingly to follow suit: "Our quarrel is with the policies of a government which has built massive settlements on occupied territory, constructed walls that inhibit the freedom of movement for Palestinians and steal their land, demolished homes, and erected a security structure that controls almost every aspect of Palestinian life."[85] The Episcopal Church, with 1.8 million members, however, turned down a BDS resolution, and the much smaller Mennonite Church postponed its decision, but not for long. In July 2016 the Mennonite Church Assembly Canada overwhelmingly passed a pro-BDS resolution. Earlier that year, the pension fund of the United Methodist Church blacklisted five Israel banks (and a construction company active in the occupied territories) from its investment portfolio because of Israel's violation of Palestinian human rights. It followed the exact same decision by a major Dutch pension fund, an important Danish financial institution, a Norwegian insurance giant, a Swedish fund, and others. Sometimes, these pressure tactics work.

There are plenty of examples to choose from. SodaStream is probably the best known and illustrates the competing narratives. This company, which sells its product in 70,000 stores in 45 countries, was one of about 1,000 Israeli companies that operated in industrial zones on the West Bank. At one time, it had about 900 employees. The factory in Mishor Adumim, east of Jerusalem, employed Israelis, Palestinians from Israel, and Palestinians from the occupied territories. It was a model employer, paying everyone the same rates, as well as transportation costs and health insurance. But it was located on occupied land – land that had been confiscated – a decision undoubtedly influenced by government subsidies. As such, SodaStream was seen to be supporting an illegal occupation.

In setting up shop in the occupied territories, SodaStream knew exactly what it was doing. In its regulatory filings before its NASDAQ listing, the company identified a number of risk factors, including that its manu-facturing facilities were located "on disputed territory sometimes referred to as the West Bank."[86] An effective boycott was organized against the company and its spokesperson, actor Scarlett Johansson, and it worked: revenues tanked and the stock tumbled. By February 2016, the plant had been relocated inside the Green Line (the company claims that BDS had nothing to do with this decision), and Bedouins in the Negev city of Rahat assumed the vacant positions.

SodaStream's CEO begged the Israeli government to provide its West Bank employees with work permits, but the request was refused. "These people had been on payroll for years," Daniel Birnbaum told the *Times of Israel*. "I mean these are human beings and they have families and they depended on us ... I must say that that the position of the govern-ment is absurd and even criminal."[87] In truth, SodaStream caved to BDS pressure, and the government seized the opportunity to punish the com-pany for moving back to Israel and, perhaps more importantly, to use it as an example of how BDS hurts the Palestinian people. Which in the case of these particular Palestinians, it did.

The organization Americans for Peace Now says that only a boycott of settlement goods will force Israel to stop expansion into disputed ter-ritories.[88] Other West Bank–based industries, along with companies that operate only inside the Green Line, are succumbing to BDS pressure: for example, Ahava, the cosmetics manufacturer now owned by a Chinese investment firm; G4S, a British security firm; Vitens, a Dutch water com-pany; and Veolia, a French infrastructure group. Orange, the mobile-communications giant, is scheduled to terminate its licensing agreement with Israeli Partner Communications in 2025.[89] The number of labour unions that have endorsed BDS is growing, as are the artists who refuse to perform in Israel. The Pulitzer prize–winning writer Alice Walker re-fuses to allow Israeli editions of her books.

There have also been moves to oust Israel from international sport. They have not yet succeeded, but the attempts themselves have an impact. In 2015 the Fédération Internationale de Football Association (FIFA) came very close to expelling Israel from international soccer, sending shock waves throughout Israeli society.

People Are Beginning to Pay Attention

Within Israel, Yair Lapid, the former finance minister, has been brutally frank. Israel, he said in early 2014, is reaching a tipping point – that same place South Africa found itself in the dying days of apartheid.[90] More than one-third of Israel's trade is with Europe, accounting for approximately 12 per cent of GDP. A true European boycott would be a disaster, and the consequential damage to the Israeli economy would be enormous: 10,000 Israelis would be fired immediately; the cost of living would rise; the education, health, welfare, and defence budgets would be cut; and Israel would be shut out of many international markets.[91] And that, Lapid warned, would be just the beginning. "If Chinese or Indian or Japanese companies come to believe that because of Israel they will lose their big markets in Europe, they won't hesitate ... before joining the sanctions so as not to lose business." BDS had to be fought, he said, but "let's not kid ourselves – the world listens to us less and less."[92]

A full-scale European boycott has not happened yet, but it cannot be ruled out. In 2013 the European Union cut off funding for Israeli academic institutions and companies operating in occupied territories – anything beyond the Green Line. The next year an important EU research and innovation program – Horizon 2020 – was reserved for projects inside the Green Line. Under EU guidelines, wine, produce, and cosmetics originating from occupied territories – East Jerusalem, the West Bank, and the Golan Heights – must be clearly marked as such. "The push reflects hardening political and public attitudes on the continent towards Israel's occupation of Palestinian lands, which are beginning to shape a tougher foreign policy."[93]

The Green Line matters. Products from Israel enter Europe mostly duty-free, but not the goods from the occupied territories. The UK's Trade and Investment Agency does not even attempt to disguise the underlying motivation: "We understand the concerns of people who do not wish to purchase goods exported from Israeli settlements in the Occupied Palestinian Territories."[94] Tesco, the British supermarket chain, announced in 2014: "We've axed fruit from Israel."[95] Denmark climbed on board, then Belgium. According to the non-profit Rand Corporation, "public opinion may be shifting" on BDS, and "the movement is growing."[96] And Canada's national newspaper, the *Globe and Mail*, reported in 2014 that foreign direct investment in Israel had dropped 46 per cent from the previous year: "Israel is increasingly concerned with the successes of the boycott and divestment efforts."[97]

Israeli Prime Minister Benjamin Netanyahu calls BDS a "strategic threat," one that is even more dangerous for Israel than Iran or terrorism.[98] Yet he refuses to refer to it by name, calling it instead the "delegitimization movement." "We are in the midst of a great struggle being waged against the state of Israel," he claims, "an international campaign to blacken its name."[99] Soon after coming to power as leader of the right-wing Likud party, Netanyahu announced that Israel had "no intention of building new settlements or of expropriating additional land for existing settlements."[100] But then he did the exact opposite, approving the construction of settlements on occupied land on the grounds that they are necessary for Israeli security.

Netanyahu is a force to be reckoned with. Israeli-born, American-educated (MIT), he served with bravery and distinction in the IDF, was wounded in battle, and left active service as a captain. He knows *his* history; "it was not the Jews who usurped the land from the Arabs, but the Arabs who usurped it from the Jews."[101] In and out of power since 1996, in March 2015 Netanyahu began his fourth term as prime minister, matching David Ben Gurion's record and well on his way to becoming the country's longest-serving leader. And quite possibly its most intransigent one too. Israeli historian Avi Shlaim described his approach: "Under his leadership, the confiscation of Arab lands proceeded apace and the right-wing settlers were given free rein to harm, to harass, and to heap humiliations upon the long-suffering population of the occupied territories."[102] Netanyahu was once secretly recorded on video explaining his approach to the Palestinian problem. It was necessary, he explained, "to beat them up, not once but repeatedly; beat them up so it hurts badly, until it is unbearable."[103]

In July 2011 the Knesset passed the Law for the Prevention of Damage to the State of Israel through Boycott, allowing anyone who was harmed by the call for an economic, cultural, or academic boycott because of their affiliation to Israel to sue for damages. It was a questionable legislative response and probably an unlawful one as well, though it was upheld by the increasingly compliant courts. Immediately it became the subject of ridicule: "Sue Me, I'm boycotting Settlement Products," taunted Peace Now, the most prominent peace group in Israel. Women for Peace, an Israeli group that supports BDS, put the law this way: "An illegitimate government passes an illegitimate law to protect an illegitimate occupation, while complaining about delegitimization. We will continue boycotting, protesting, demonstrating and resisting the occupation, and we call on everyone else to do so too."[104] A *New York Times* editorial published on 17 July 2011 said it all: "Not befitting a democracy."

Netanyahu, a rigid, uncompromising hawk who has jeopardized Israel's relationship with its most important ally and source of funds, the United States, fails to understand that international isolation and the economic consequences of BDS are a potentially more serious threat than territorial withdrawals or any Arab army. Unfortunately, he has a lot of help. Avigdor Lieberman, for example, the former foreign minister appointed minister of defence in June 2016 and a likely contender to succeed Netanyahu, talks of blowing up the Aswan dam, calls Peace Now "a virus," and wants to revoke the citizenship of Palestinians who refuse to swear a loyalty oath to the Jewish state. In 2015, when he was foreign minister, he publicly advocated "beheading" disloyal Palestinians: "Those who are with us deserve everything, but those who are against us deserve to have their heads chopped off with an axe."[105]

Even Israel's strongest defenders don't like what they see. In March 2016, after an IDF medic shot and killed a wounded Palestinian terrorist in Hebron, who was lying on the ground awaiting medical help, the *New York Times*'s Thomas Friedman observed that "for those of us who care about Israel's future, this is a dark hour."[106] But it got worse. Instead of being charged with murder – and the deed was captured in every detail on video – the best Israeli authorities could come up with was a manslaughter charge. In early January 2017, twenty-year-old Sergeant Elor Azaria was convicted by a military court. The presiding judges almost laughed out loud in response to his various defences. Two things happened in the immediate aftermath: first, Prime Minister Netanyahu called upon Israel's president to issue a pardon, and second, the presiding judges were accorded police protection – the threats to their safety came from fellow Israelis. An eighteen-month sentence was subsequently imposed. Palestinian children get longer sentences for throwing stones at cars and IDF troops. For Palestinians, it was another sign pointing to a conflict about to spiral out of control.

Peter Beinart, a former *New Republic* editor and professor at the City University of New York (CUNY), asked what Israel would have to do for the American people to scream no? One example may be Lieberman's

August 2016 "carrot and stick" announcement, reported by the *Jerusalem Post*, that he planned to reward the "good Palestinians" in the West Bank and severely punish the "bad ones."[107] He has also recently proposed legislation reinstituting the death penalty for convicted terrorists. As Nathan Hersh of Partners for Progressive Israel wrote in the *Toronto Star*, "Lieberman's proposed legislation is a sign of the disease of intractable conflict metastasizing."[108]

The Israeli prime minister is possibly the best friend BDS has ever had. "We've got to give credit to Netanyahu," BDS co-founder Omar Barghouti, a doctoral candidate at the University of Tel Aviv, told *Haaretz*, for "without him we could not have reached this far."[109] There is no denying that the end of the peace process, Netanyahu's attitude and approach, the situation in Gaza, and the continuing escalation of government-subsidized settlements, among many other factors, have "provided highly combustible gasoline to BDS propaganda."[110]

Still, Netanyahu continues to retain enough public support in Israel's proportional electoral system to govern, having successfully cobbled together a "coalition of the ascendant" – ultra-Orthodox, settlers, and immigrants, all right wing – which have kept him and Likud in power election after election. An Israeli public-opinion poll reported in June 2015 that 13 per cent of the respondents had never even heard of BDS, 20 per cent were "not worried" at all, and only 28 per cent were a "bit worried."[111] Yet all around them forces are mobilizing. Many groups in Israel, from virtually all strata of society, are bitterly opposed to the continuing occupation of Palestinian lands and are saying so. The goal of Breaking the Silence, a group of former IDF soldiers who served in the occupied territories, is to bring to the attention of the Israeli public the systematic abuse of Palestinians and the looting and destruction of their property.[112]

Tzipi Livni, a former foreign minister, justice minister, and leader of the opposition, is one of the most prominent Israeli voices warning of the dangers ahead: "Europe is boycotting goods. True, it starts with settlement goods, but their problem is with Israel, which is seen as a colonialist country ... it will spread to all of Israel."[113] Livni got a personal taste of Israel's future in January 2017. Expected to attend a conference in Brussels, she cancelled at the last minute after being tipped off that the authorities had an arrest warrant ready and planned to bring her in for questioning in an ongoing Gaza war crimes investigation.

Michal Rozin, a member of the secular social-democratic Meretz Party, asked the Knesset in the midst of a 2015 debate on BDS: "The government must internalize that the boycott is a wake-up call, not anti-Semitic propaganda. Is the continued support for settlements worth the demolition of Israel's standing as a legitimate nation in the world?"[114]

BDS has become an instrument for Israeli politicians to wage war against each other. "The right long ago realized that the BDS effort is an electoral boon. With its stridency, double standards and examples of openly anti-Semitic supporters and participants, it doesn't take much to depict the BDS movement to receptive Israelis as little more than ugly prejudice – and to depict the Israeli left, as it agonizes over the continued occupation, as its enablers."[115]

Some suggest that a "Jewish civil war" is in the offing and there is ample anecdotal and objective evidence illustrating a growing rift in the Jewish world.[116] Quite simply, more and more organizations within Israel and elsewhere – some call them post-Zionist – are protesting the excesses of successive Israeli regimes. Others are voting with their feet: as many as 1 million Israelis may well have left the Promised Land. *Yerida* – emigration – is the Hebrew opposite of *aliyah*, returning to Israel, and it's a derogatory word. Israelis cannot stop thinking about it, however, even if most, for the time being, are staying put.[117]

Not everyone is worried. If the West turns against us, some Israelis believe, there is always the East. And then there is that famous Israeli self-reliance. When Israel had difficulty purchasing arms, it started its own weapons industry and soon became the fourth-largest arms exporter in the world. BDS also touches a raw nerve for all Israelis who know their history, from the 1882 May Laws in Tsarist Russia, which imposed severe social and economic sanctions, to boycotts on Jewish businesses in Germany in the 1930s, a prelude to the attacks and mass murder that followed. The racist spillovers in the current campus debates, and increasing attacks on Jews and their businesses in parts of Europe, can only revive those memories and go some distance in explaining why positions are so ideological and entrenched.

The basic facts, however, are that Israel is occupying land belonging to others and mistreating its own citizens. Israeli industry is locating on occupied land, attracted by lower taxes, cheaper labour, and a more lax environmental regime. Some of the settlers want a nice house they can afford, and they also get subsidies and tax breaks, while others dream of a greater Israel: they call the West Bank Judea and Samaria, and claim that God gave it to them too.

The bigger message is that BDS is a non-violent fight for human rights sanctioned by international law. Despite the claims of the Israeli government, many BDS supporters are not anti-Semites: many of them are actually Jews in Israel and all over the world. Among them are Israeli soldiers and officers who have experienced the occupation first hand and want nothing more to do with it. If calling its critics anti-Semites is the Israeli government's strategy for countering BDS, that is not only unpersuasive and unproductive but doomed to failure. The most outspoken criticisms of Israeli actions, and the most vocal dissent attracting the greatest attention, come from Israelis themselves and from Jewish voices abroad.

The Generation Gap

If Israel thinks it can count on the Diaspora, the Jews who live in other countries, especially the United States, that's another mistake. A state created on religious and ethnic lines that discriminates against its own citizens has little appeal for many younger Jews who were born and bred in liberal democracies. Certainly, as conditions in the occupied territory and Israel itself become better known, this number will only increase. An apartheid state will attract almost no support among Jews in the United States. "For several decades, the Jewish establishment has asked American Jews to check their liberalism at Zionism's door, and now, to their horror, they are finding that many young Jews have checked their Zionism instead."[118]

Data indicates that American Jews under the age of thirty-five, except for the Orthodox population, are much less "comfortable with the idea of a Jewish state" than the older group.[119] In a landmark 2013 Pew Survey, 25 per cent of American Jews between the age of eighteen and twenty-nine believed that the United States gave Israel too much support. And in his study of attitudes within the American Jewish community, Northeastern University professor Dov Waxman concluded that "the age of unquestioning and unstinting support for Israel is over."[120]

When Hillel, a Jewish students group, refused to permit criticism of Israel, a new group actually willing to listen to dissenting views, Open Hillel, was established at American university campuses, including Harvard. "We believe," the group proclaims on its website, "that free discourse ... is essential in the context of an educational institution and a democratic society; and that open discussion and debate are core Jewish values."[121] The students are not alone: many American Jews are dissatisfied with Israel.[122] A 2014 Forum poll found that Canadians were almost equally split between support for Israel and for Palestine, but, significantly, Israel's numbers were decreasing.[123] Mirroring international results, support for the Palestinian side was highest among youth and in the province of Quebec. Public opinion in Europe has become increasingly negative about Israel. The EU has agreed, in principle, to recognize a Palestinian state, and a handful of its members have passed symbolic resolutions doing so.

Why Attitudes Are Changing

People all over the world are appalled by the proponents of ethnic cleansing in the Israeli political establishment. Brigadier General Effi Eitam, for example, a Yom Kippur War hero, Entebbe rescue veteran, cabinet minister, and one-time member of Netanyahu's government, called for stripping Israeli Palestinians of their political rights and expelling them from Israel. Like Lieberman, he calls them "a cancer." He had to resign from the military after news leaked that he ordered subordinates to beat a Palestinian prisoner to death. Yet this was the person Netanyahu tapped in 2009 to be Israel's special emissary for North American "campus engagement." In some countries, Eitam would have been arrested as soon as he got off the plane.

One of the options the Israelis talk about in their efforts to keep the Jewish state Jewish is "transfer." There is soft transfer – the steps Israel now takes to make life unpleasant for Palestinians in Israel and the occupied territories to encourage migration. And there is hard transfer – or forced expulsion. "An evil spirit is infiltrating public discourse: the spirit of exclusion," says Segev. "The danger lies when the possibility of transfer becomes part of the political discourse, when it seemingly becomes a legitimate subject."[124]

This is the Overton Window in action – the insight arrived at by Joseph Overton, a vice-president of the Mackinac Center for Public Policy, that the acceptable range of political thought in a culture at a particular time can be moved. The unthinkable becomes thinkable once an idea has been introduced, argued for, framed, and restated. It crosses from fringe thought to legitimate issue and soon enough to public policy.

Some of the vocabulary now being used by Israeli political leaders is extremely disturbing, but it is just one step in a longer-term process of domestic conditioning. "The window has moved, and rough beasts come slouching through it to be born."[125] Outside Israel, the transfer message is a harder sell, although it attracts customers. Eventually people will put together the pieces. For example, while Palestinians from Gaza and the West Bank are denied opportunities to work in Israel – as SodaStream learned – labourers from China, Thailand, and Romania, among other places, are warmly welcomed. "Israel reduces as far as possible its dependence on a Palestinian workforce and applies all means at its disposal to stifle the economy of the Occupied Territories with the intention of completely driving out the remaining inhabitants."[126] Slowly but surely, however, people have begun to question some of the received wisdom.

It is impossible to pinpoint exactly when attitudes began to change. Israel's 1982 invasion of Lebanon is one possible turning point: the world was repulsed and disgusted by the massacres in the Sabra and Shatila refugee camps as Israeli forces stood by, or worse. An official commission of inquiry concluded that the commander, Defence Minister Ariel Sharon, was "personally responsible"– yet he later became prime minister. The First Intifada – a popular uprising against the growing Israeli occupation in the West Bank and Gaza that began at the end of 1987 and lasted for years – left more than 1,000 thousand Palestinians dead, including children, with 106 recorded cases of "child gunshot deaths," as Israel responded with Operation Iron Fist. The Swedish branch of Save the Children concluded that between 20,000 and 30,000 Palestinian children required medical treatment for beatings inflicted by Israeli forces in the first two years alone.[127] Yitzhak Rabin's policy – he was the defence minister at the time – was "force, might, beatings."[128] Rabin evolved over time: he won the Nobel Peace Prize in 1994, along with Shimon Peres and Palestine Liberation Organization leader Yasser Arafat, in recognition of their negotiation of the Oslo Accords. Rabin was assassinated by an Israeli extremist in 1995.

The Second Intifada began in 2000 after Sharon, opposition leader at the time, made a deliberately provocative visit to the Temple Mount – a Muslim Holy site – accompanied by a huge security detail. The PA took full advantage of the opportunity Sharon presented. The result: an even higher death toll, for Israelis and Palestinians, military and civilian alike. Amid the skirmishes, the settlements continue to expand, as does their effective integration into pre-1967 Israel. Indeed, the Green Line has so thoroughly faded that it no longer appears on new Israeli maps. Israelis in Israel and in the West Bank share the same telephone system, road system, electricity grid, water supply, and bus and rail system. It is one country, for them, but not for the Palestinians who live in the occupied territories under completely different circumstances.

And then there is Gaza – year after year the world sees visuals of bodies scattered in rubble-filled streets. The end result is always more of the same: staggering civilian casualties and massive material damage. Images of murdered children and their wailing, furious parents crowd everything else out although there is always plenty of suffering to go around. While older North Americans and Europeans tend to sympathize with Israel, their children increasingly reject the Zionist dream.

The generational change is reflected in other ways too. BDS is drawing attention away from the institutional old-timers – the American Israel Public Affairs Committee, the powerful pro-Israel lobby group – and even the new kid on the block, J Street. Instead, dissenting Jewish voices have emerged, such as the Jewish Voices for Peace, which supports BDS. "It's not about destroying Israel," the spokesperson for the 8,000-member organization insists, "but full equal rights and a democratic society are more important than preserving the Jewish character of the state."[129] Israel has to be convinced, Rabbi Alissa Wise insists, "not by force, but by global consensus that something has to change."[130]

The response from the Jewish establishment has been ferocious, but the very existence of this group allows others, Jews and non-Jews, to sign on and express dissent because it allows them to protest Israeli policies without being branded as anti-Semites. Jewish Voices for Peace is pilloried by mainstream Jewish organizations with that old canard about self-hating Jews, but the message to get out of the occupied lands and ensure equality between all the citizens of the same country rings true for increasing numbers. BDS demands equal rights for everyone, including refugees and their descendants who fled or were forcibly displaced in 1948 and 1967 and left stateless. Undoubtedly, this is the number-one obstacle to a peaceful solution. Acknowledging that these people – and there are as many as 5 million of them – have rights – including quite possibly some of them returning to their villages and homes – threatens not just another one of the founding myths but Israel's entire reason for being: as a Jewish state.

Many Jewish BDS supporters are passionate in their Jewish identity but refuse to allow tribal allegiance to compromise their commitment to basic, universal human values. Democracy and diversity are the touchstones of our times and, like the rest of the society in which they live, increasing numbers of Jews have almost no interest in organized religion. Many younger Jews have little affiliation to what Beinart, himself an observant Jew, calls "the grand drama of Jewish victimhood."[131] Universal morality and common sense trump religious solidarity.

The pro-boycott Jewish Voices for Peace is perhaps the fastest-growing Jewish organization on campuses nationwide," CUNY professor Eric Alterman observes; "many liberal Zionists share the movement's complaints about the brutality and self-defeating nature of Israel's nearly 50-year occupation."[132] Add in the culture wars taking place within Israel itself – one of the biggest bus companies, Egged, conceded to an ultra-Orthodox demand for separate bus entrances and seating for women – and you have a state with even more fault lines.

For years, Israelis have asked, "Where is the Palestinian Gandhi?" In 2004 Mahatma's grandson Arun visited the West Bank and suggested that 50,000 refugees march home to Israel and force the Israeli government to decide "between yielding to a wave of people power and gunning the marchers down in cold blood."[133] Now that would have been interesting. "We don't do Gandhi very well," a former Israeli general confessed to the American ambassador.[134] In his report to Washington, disclosed by WikiLeaks, the ambassador pointed to Israel's Achilles heel: "Less violent demonstrations are likely to stymie the IDF."[135]

Former prime minister Ehud Olmert has asked what would happen if the Palestinians said, "'There is no place for two states between the Jordan and the sea' and 'All we want is the right to vote.'" That would be a complete non-starter: "The day they get it, we will lose everything," Olmert acknowledged. But how does Israel tell the world that, after half a century of occupation, Palestinians don't get to vote?[136] Friedman wrote in the *New York Times*, "If American Jews think it's hard to defend Israel today on college campuses, imagine what it will be like when their kids have to argue against the principle of one man one vote."[137]

It is not fair, Israel claims, that it is held to a higher standard than anyone else. Yet it doesn't matter that Morocco is occupying the Western

Sahara or that China is engaged in the brutal oppression of Tibet, or that all Arab countries are the worst place in the world for women or gays, that no Arab country comes close to Israel on any democracy index, or that Bahá'ís, Christians, Copts, Druzes, Ibadis, Ismailis, Jews, Kurds, Maronites, Sahrawis, Tuareq, Turkmen, Yazidis, and Zaidis are persecuted throughout the Arab world. Nor does it matter that the PA and Fatah in the West Bank, Hamas in the Gaza Strip, and Hezbollah everywhere torture and murder their enemies as often and as brutally as anything the Israelis ever mete out.[138] The only issue is that the West, which provides Israel with massive political, financial, and military support, is entitled to ask questions and insist on answers. Israel claims that it is the only democracy in the Middle East, and it cannot object when it is held to account as one and found to behave in ways inconsistent with democratic values. Israel's contradictions are becoming harder and harder to sustain.

As people learn about conditions in the occupied territories and in Israel, the attitude becomes less *Anne Frank* and *Exodus* and more *My Name Is Rachel Corrie*. Corrie was the young American woman who, in 2003, was peacefully protesting against yet another Palestinian home demolition – she was standing in front of the Nasrallah home in Gaza – when she was killed by an IDF armour-plated Caterpillar bulldozer. Weighing more than sixty tons, these bulldozers can demolish a house in minutes. Corrie was wearing a fluorescent orange jacket but the bulldozer still drove right over her.

The fact that Israel is the most inventive, entrepreneurial, creative, democratic, and open society in the entire Middle East and has Gay Pride celebrations – more than 200,000 people turned out to the June 2016 event in Tel Aviv – does not balance the ledger. It's all "Pinkwashing," critics say, part of a strategic branding exercise to position Israel as a relevant and modern liberal democracy, in contrast to every other Arab state. In fact, Israel is an ethnocracy, not a democracy like Canada or the United States. The only countries less popular than Israel, according to a 2013 BBC poll, are North Korea, Pakistan, and Iran.[139]

Israel has the most powerful army in the region, but this fight may be won and lost with words. In June 2015 a multibillionaire named Sheldon Adelson summoned leading Israel supporters from across North America to an emergency summit. The purpose of the meeting, held at Adelson's luxurious hotel, The Venetian, on the Las Vegas strip, was to

Rachel Corrie. This brave young American woman has become a symbol of peaceful dissent. (Credit: Denny Sternstein, Rachel Corrie Foundation)

organize and fund an anti-BDS fight, particularly on North American university campuses. Other wealthy people have also called for "donor strikes" against universities.

These attacks on dissenting voices may be toxic and counter-productive, although Adelson and others are completely entitled to try to counter speech they hate with speech they like, and we need to listen to that too. What Adelson and his peers, including the Israeli government, fail to understand, however, is that the broad brush doesn't work. It is pointless and untrue to call all of Israel's critics anti-Semites or to try to draw a red line between permissible and impermissible criticism, especially since the loudest critics of Israel's actions can be found in Israel and among Jewish voices elsewhere. A decentralized, peaceful, non-violent movement using social media – for example, Electronic Intifada or Mondoweiss – will not be easily fought or discredited, nor will people of conscience who no longer conform to communal norms be dissuaded from exercising their rights, although the pressure to conform is intense.[140]

McCarthyism Plain and Simple

Canarymission.org is a sophisticated website providing extensive profiles of student and professorial BDS supporters; its aim is to "expose
those who promote lies and attacks on Israel ... Canary Mission believes
that we all have the right to know if an individual has been affiliated with
movements that seek the destruction of Israel."[141] The profiles – pictures
and all – specialize in guilt by association, and critics point to an unstated
but evident objective: to punish the protestors economically by "jeopardizing their job prospects."[142] Similarly, in September 2002, the website
Campus Watch posted dossiers on suspect academics. Netanyahu claims
that BDS is on "the wrong side of the moral divide" and that the movement will "fail."[143] BDS proponents disagree, believing they are on the
right side of history.

At present, Israel continues to enjoy bedrock political support, especially in North America. In February 2016 the Canadian House of Commons passed a Conservative Party motion "condemning BDS" and its
supporters. The moderator of the United Church of Canada wrote to
Prime Minister Justin Trudeau in June 2016 asking him to vote against
it: "We do hold strong commitments to democratic rights and freedoms
... The United Church of Canada stands in solidarity with groups and
individuals exercising this right in nonviolent, peaceful ways. We urge
you to stand firmly for democracy and defeat this motion."[144] Trudeau
was not persuaded. Most Muslim MPs skipped the vote, and only the
New Democratic Party and the Bloc Québécois (with a trio of Liberals)
voted against it. In Ontario an anti-boycott bill, the Standing up against
Anti-Semitism in Ontario Act, introduced by a former Conservative Party
leader, was defeated by the legislature in May 2016. Premier Kathleen
Wynne, who was visiting the West Bank at the time, announced her opposition both to the bill and to BDS.[145]

In the United States, more than twenty states have passed or are considering passing laws to boycott the boycotters.[146] The extremity of the
response reflects the recognition that BDS presents a serious threat.

Activists can purchase a share in a company and create an uproar.
Rachel Corrie's parents, Cindy and Craig, took on Caterpillar – the manufacturer of the bulldozer that killed their daughter. They borrowed
shares owned by the Sisters of Loretto, a Catholic community of nuns,
so they could speak out against the company at a shareholders meeting

in Chicago. A lawsuit against the company was also brought on their behalf.[147] The Church of England divested from Caterpillar around that time. Even when efforts fail – Caterpillar still sells its bulldozers to Israel even though the company is well aware of how they are sometimes used – they make an impact.

In March 2016 some BDS activists in Calgary went into a No Frills supermarket and affixed labels on some products that read: "Made In Israel: A Country Violating International Law."[148] The labels were removed, but the protest got media attention. Demonizing BDS activists – Canary Mission, Campus Watch, and others – with bullying tactics may backfire. What kind of people publish photographs of kids exercising their right to dissent? (Although if some of the profiles are even half true, there are clearly genocidal maniacs at large who should be brought to the attention of the authorities.)

It is not as though Israel has not been warned of the harm it is inflicting on itself. Secretary of State John Kerry predicted in August 2013 that Israel would face an international boycott "on steroids" if it continued its construction of new illegal settlements.[149] He has reiterated over and over again that BDS will accelerate unless Israel makes peace with the Palestinians. There is only one answer to BDS, the US ambassador to Israel observed in March 2016: "The presentation of a political process, negotiations or some political horizon that gives hope for a two-states-for-two-peoples resolution to the Israeli Palestinian conflict."[150] The EU's ambassador agrees: "If [the Palestinian issue] were solved, there would be no BDS movement."[151]

In March 2015 the Israeli people returned to the polls. Netanyahu often gives comfort to the West when he is speaking English, but speaking in Hebrew during the election he assured Israelis that there would never be a Palestinian state and that he planned to build thousands of new housing units in East Jerusalem. What looked like a losing campaign turned around almost overnight into a winner. The opposition spoke about revitalizing the peace process, but insecure Israeli voters responded positively to Netanyahu's nativist, fear-mongering, and racist electioneering.

No Israeli leader has ever intended to make peace with the Palestinians. "But the bluff of the century," *Haaretz's* senior columnist Gideon Levy wrote in the election's aftermath, "was convenient for everyone."[152] It was always about playing for time, building more settlements, and consolidating rule. Public-opinion polls in the United States indicate that only a minority of Americans believe that Israel is serious about pursuing peace.[153]

Avraham Burg, who has been both speaker of the Knesset and head of the Jewish Agency (the group responsible for settling Jews in Israel), has said that little runway is left: "The world is still putting up with all this, but not for much longer, it will soon be over."[154] And, he warned, "we cannot keep a Palestinian majority under an Israeli boot and at the same time think ourselves the only democracy in the Middle East. There cannot be democracy without equal rights for all who live here, Arab as well as Jew."[155] Three former prime ministers of Israel have concluded as much.

Speaking to an overflow audience at New York's Central Synagogue in June 2016, Ehud Barak (prime minister, 1999–2001) had nothing good to say about his successor. As the *Jerusalem Post* reported his words, Netanyahu has "gone off the rails."[156] He amplified these comments at a prestigious policy conference at the end of June in the posh Tel Aviv suburb of Herzliya: Israel, he said, was well down the road of fascism, poised to become an apartheid state. "The entire Zionist project was in grave danger."[157] Ehud Olmert (prime minister, 2006–09) agrees: the occupation of the West Bank puts Israel at risk of becoming an apartheid state.[158] According to the late Shimon Peres, four-time prime minister and Israel's former president, BDS may become unstoppable, and Israel will become a "pariah," just like South Africa.[159]

The Beginning of the End?

Israel has had its way for a long time, but cracks are beginning to show. *The Israel Lobby*, a brave 2007 book by John J. Mearsheimer and Stephen M. Walt, called for a complete reassessment of America's special relationship with Israel. In March 2010, while US Vice-President Joe Biden was visiting Israel, the government announced that 1,600 more Israelis would be moving to East Jerusalem. "This is starting to get dangerous for us," Biden told Netanyahu. "What you're doing undermines the security of our troops who are fighting in Iraq, Afghanistan and Pakistan. That endangers us and it endangers regional piece."[160] Privately, US administration officials were furious: Secretary of Defense Robert M. Gates publicly described the Israeli prime minister as an ungrateful ally who was jeopardizing Israel's future by refusing to grapple with its growing isolation in the world.[161] Netanyahu refused to budge. At that point, Avi Shlaim, the eminent Israeli New Historian, wrote in the *New York Times*, "Israel needs to learn some manners."[162]

Israel, Shlaim continued, could not survive without American financial support: $118 billion in direct US government aid since 1949, or $3 billion a year now, not counting the tax breaks for donations to Israeli charities and loan arrangements with favourable terms. Nor could it survive without American military technology or diplomatic support. Since 1978 the United States has exercised its veto power in the UN Security Council to shield Israel from international condemnation more than forty times. Various American-sponsored peace initiatives, the Oxford professor continued, have been "all process and no peace while providing Israel with just the cover it needs to pursue its illegal and aggressive colonial project on the West Bank." None of it was in the US national interest; rather, America suffers because of its "blind support" for the Jewish state. "The fundamental problem with American support for Israel is its unconditional nature. Consequently, Israel does not have to pay the price for acting unilaterally in a multilateral world, for its flagrant violations of international law, and for its systematic abuse of Palestinian human rights."[163]

"We will," Netanyahu told the Knesset on 26 October 2015, "forever live by the sword." Israel, he added, "needs to control all of the territory [of historic Palestine] for the foreseeable future."[164] US Ambassador Charles W. Freeman agrees that Israel has no intention of ever ending its occupation:

> Israel has never been prepared to risk peace with those it displaced from their homes in Palestine. When faced with a choice between territorial expansion and advances toward reconciliation with Arabs, Israel always chooses land over peace. The now-defunct American sponsored "peace process" on which the United States staked its reputation in the Middle East and elsewhere, and which I labored to support, has been revealed to all as part of an elaborate diplomatic deception, intended to provide political cover for Israel's continued expansion at Palestinian expense ... Israel can enjoy neither diplomatic tranquility nor security from non-hostile neighbors and the world's Muslims if it continues to deal with its captive Arab population through the culling of their leaders by

targeted assassination, the tyranny of occupation, and the perse-
cution of checkpoints and separation walls, punctuated by sniper
attacks and occasional bombing campaigns against defenseless
Palestinian civilians ... It is a suicidal strategy for Zionism.[165]

What Netanyahu has never understood is that American Jews are
Americans first and hold the interests of the United States dear. The Israeli
prime minister thinks he can bully the American president and get away
with it, but support for his Israel is neither universal nor inevitable. His
3 March 2015 speech to the US Congress may mark the beginning of the
end of the consensus around Israel's special relationship with the United
States. He accepted an invitation from Republican Speaker John Boehner
to address Congress without even informing President Obama. In
response, sixty Democrats boycotted his speech, to the delight of the Arab
world. In fact, Palestinians were ecstatic. As Napoleon remarked, never
interrupt an enemy when he is making a mistake.

Still, and for the time being, most politicians on both sides of the American political divide continue to profess their unqualified support for Israel,
having either internalized a fairy tale or, as Friedman put it in the *New
York Times*, been "bought and paid for by the Israel lobby"[166] (he later
qualified these remarks). The lack of American empathy for the Palestinian people and their plight is surprising; however, while the condition
is chronic, it is not irreversible. The rote and ritualized affirmations of
fealty for Israel by all presidential candidates, and others vying for national
office, turn more and more Americans off. "The depressing truth is that
Israel's current behaviour," celebrated historian Tony Judt wrote in 2003,
"is not just bad for America, though it surely is. It is not just bad for
Israel itself, as many Israelis silently acknowledge. The depressing truth
is that Israel today is bad for the Jews."[167] In one of his last interviews
before he died in 2010, Judt predicted "that in decades to come America ... will abandon Israel as annoying, expensive and a liability."[168] The
American people appear increasingly to agree. In a spring 2016 Ipsos
survey, 33 per cent reported believing that it was legitimate to boycott
Israel. In the United Kingdom, the number is higher: 40 per cent agreed
that divestment was a legitimate measure.[169]

Some American Jews, along with Christians awaiting the End Times,
will support Israel no matter what. They will convince themselves, and

try to convince others, that Israel is a democracy and shares American values. In his book *Palestine: Peace Not Apartheid*, former president Jimmy Carter stated that "the policy now being followed" is apartheid.[170] The United States, he warned, was "squandering international prestige and goodwill and intensifying global anti-American terrorism by unofficially condoning or abetting the Israeli confiscation and colonization of Palestinian territories."[171] For his candour, Carter had to fight off allegations of anti-Semitism and the claim of a loudmouth celebrity lawyer that his book was "indecent."[172] Jimmy Carter can be criticized for many things, but he was the architect of the Camp David Accord that directly led to lasting peace between Egypt and Israel. He epitomizes decency. And he is in good company.

South African Archbishop Desmond Tutu said the same thing as Carter after his 2002 visit to Israel, adding, "Israel will never get true security and safety through oppressing another people."[173] The most recent Pew Research Center study, released in May 2016, found that sympathy among American millennials for the Palestinian cause had significantly increased: from 9 per cent in 2006 to 27 per cent.[174] Israel has a choice: "Grant citizenship to Arabs in the West Bank, or cease to call itself a democracy" is the way the *Atlantic*'s pro-Israel Jeffrey Goldberg describes it, adding that the Israelis are deluding themselves if they think that American Jews are going to sit idly by and allow the discrimination to continue. "I think," he continued, that "we're only a few years away, at most, from a total South-Africanization of this issue ... A non-democratic Israel will not survive in this world."[175]

"I envision a time that is not far off," Israeli author Amos Oz said in a February 2015 speech to the Institute for National Security in Tel Aviv, "when workers in Amsterdam, in Dublin or in Madrid will refuse to service El Al planes. Customers will boycott Israeli products, leaving them on the shelves. Investors and tourists will shun Israel. The Israeli economy will collapse. We are already at least halfway there."[176] Oz is no alarmist; he's been advocating the two-state solution for years. But he has his eyes open.

The Israeli commitment to a peace process has been proven a fiction. No single country or political party or politician bears full responsibility, but it is noteworthy that the settlement project in the occupied territories, and its horrible human toll, continues no matter what negotiations are held, what progress is made, what agreements are reached. As Beinart writes, the country is wasting its time trying to stop BDS by improving Israel's image: "Israel doesn't have a public relations problem; it has a moral problem."[177] No one has a crystal ball that works, but quite possibly arrest warrants will be issued for Israeli soldiers and politicians and the docket at the International Court of Justice and the International Criminal Court will be flooded (institutions where the United States cannot exercise a veto).

"Nowhere has a democracy of masters lasted over time," the well-respected Israeli political scientist Zeev Sternhell wrote in *Haaretz* in June 2016.[178] Israel as a free nation "will not survive the occupation."[179] For speaking out, Sternhell, a veteran of four Israeli wars, was injured when a settler set off a pipe bomb at this house. According to Noam Chomsky, "the people who call themselves supporters of Israel are in fact supporters of its moral degeneration and probably ultimate destruction."[180]

Israel is unlikely ever to be militarily defeated, but nor are the Palestinian people going away. In 1956 Moshe Dayan, completely out of character, and in a rare moment of clarity, predicted the future. He was speaking at the funeral of a farmer killed by Palestinian marauders:

> Let us not today fling accusations at the murderers. What cause have we to complain about their fierce hatred for us? For eight years now, they sit in their refugee camps ... and before their eyes we turn into our homestead the land and villages in which they and their forefathers have lived ... Let us not be afraid to see the hatred that accompanies and consumes the lives of hundreds of thousands of Arabs who sit all around us and wait the moment when their hand will be able to reach our blood ... This is the fate of our generation. The only choice we have is to be prepared and armed, strong and resolute, or else our sword will slip from our hand and thread of our lives will be severed.[181]

Dayan was not entirely without empathy for the Palestinian plight but could see no way out of perpetual conflict.[182] In his view, and this is the one embraced by Netanyahu, the conflict is irreconcilable and peace is impossible. This informs and explains Israeli policy in the occupied territories. Israel's prime minister actually believes that the status quo is sustainable. But, as Goldberg pointed out in the *Atlantic*, "it is not."[183]

What makes the situation even more tragic, Goldberg continued, is that Netanyahu "could, if he so chose, deliver 70 per cent of Israelis to a painful compromise."[184]

There Is Another Way

Israel has South Africa and Northern Ireland as models to choose from – two other settler colonial states that made peace with the past and charted a new course for the future. Apartheid ended in South Africa when the white rulers realized that their security could be assured only by sharing power with all peoples – Africans, coloured, Indians, and whites. "After a long process of deep introspection," South Africa's last apartheid leader, F.W. de Klerk, concluded that white rule, if continued, "would bring disaster to all the peoples of our country, including my own."[185] Pik Botha, South Africa's last apartheid foreign minister, elaborated: "We overcame our own fear of majority rule and began to realize that majority rule was something in our interest in the long term."[186] The country became a multiracial democracy and belongs to all those who live in it. It is not heaven, not even close. Economic inequality is as bad as ever, and, like every country, South Africa faces many serious challenges, but it is a democracy with political equality.[187]

Similarly, peace came to Northern Ireland in part because of British-led diplomacy, but mostly because the people of Northern Ireland were tired of the fighting. Exhausted and traumatized, they said "enough." The 10 April 1998 Good Friday Agreement that brought peace to Northern Ireland was negotiated by the political elites but ratified by a popular referendum. It enshrined democratic government – one person one vote, with the people deciding how they would be governed and by whom. Significantly, it was recognized that "it is essential to acknowledge and address the suffering of the victims of violence as a necessary element of reconciliation" and that "victims have a right to remember." The Northern Ireland Commission for Victims and Survivors was given that job.

In South Africa it was the Truth and Reconciliation Commission that took on the enormous task of trying to repair apartheid's terrible damage. Its mandate was to bear witness to the past and to deliver restorative, not retributive, justice. South Africa's Interim Constitution reads: "The well-being of all South African citizens and peace require reconciliation between the people of South Africa and the reconstruction of society ... There is a need for understanding but not for vengeance, a need for reparation but not for retaliation, a need for Ubuntu but not victimization."[188]

Ubuntu, a Zulu word, means human kindness, humanity toward others. The only hope for change in Israel is for both Israelis and Palestinians to begin by embracing this spirit and adopting this approach. "We in South Africa," Archbishop Tutu wrote, "had a relatively peaceful transition. If our madness could end as it did, it must be possible to do the same everywhere else in the world. If peace could come to South Africa, surely it can come to the Holy Land."[189]

Instead, in 2011 the Knesset passed a law – the Nakba Law – defunding any organization that commemorated the *nakba*. Israelis call these commemorations more delegitimization, but this war on their history will fail. In Pappé's words, Israeli Jews "have to recognize that they have become the mirror image of their own worst nightmare."[190] They must acknowledge and take responsibility for the past, and that means knowing the whole truth and addressing the legitimate entitlements of millions of refugees. Professor Raphael Cohen-Almagor, a moderate two-state supporter, writes that Israel needs to "honestly confront history, refute myths, and acknowledge the role it played in the creation of the refugee problem."[191] That won't be easy.

Israel's now decades-long march to the right has been accompanied by, in the words of Avi Shlaim, "officially instigated attacks" on the New Historians and their work. The debate about Israel's founding and history, Shlaim observes, continues, "and it is the kind of debate that never ends ... The more Israelis feel under threat, the more they retreat into nationalist narratives of the past and the less tolerant they become of dissenting voices. But it is precisely in such times of crisis that dissenting voices are most vitally needed. Xenophobic and self-righteous national narratives only fuel and prolong this tragic conflict. A more complex and fair-minded understanding of the past is therefore essential for preserving at least the prospect for reconciliation in the future."[192] Shlaim and his New Historian colleagues have pointed the way – but their voices are under official assault. As Ariel Sharon put it just before becoming prime minister, and this has been official policy ever since, the New Historians "must not be taught."[193]

Individual acts of terrorist violence have always grabbed the headlines and still do. Beginning in 2015 it was "Young Knife-wielding Palestinians" running wild in Israeli streets. "There is," the *Independent* observed, "a numbing repetition to the news" along with a sense that something unprecedented is occurring: "a shapeless rebellion of individuals driven by an unknowable combination of hatred and despair."[194] Palestinian violence against Israelis is definitely increasing, the result of years of hate education and indoctrination and actual community approbation and financial reward for "martyrs" referred to as Shahid/Shaheed. These are expressions of violence along a continuum that includes Israel's organized and systemic use of violence against Palestinians as a deliberate instrument of its public policy. After all these years, Israelis and Palestinians might want to try something new.

In both South Africa and Northern Ireland, peace came about, in part, because of "a dissenting view from the national consensus."[195] The Arabic word *sumud* means steadfastness – and both the Palestinians and the Israelis have it. But no one can seriously believe that either ratcheting up the terrorist attacks or building more settlements and continuing the immoral abuse of Palestinians in Israel and the occupied territories points the way to a peaceful future. Inevitably, since 1948, every act of violence has been repaid in kind – and there is no end in sight.

The Countdown

"The countdown to the end of Israeli society has begun," Avraham Burg wrote in Hebrew in 2003 in *Yediot Aharonot*, one of Israel's largest-circulation daily newspapers. His article was translated into English and French and widely republished. "The Jewish people did not survive for two millennia in order to pioneer new weaponry, computer security programs or anti-missile missiles. We were supposed to be a light unto the nations. In this we have failed." Burg is no anti-Semite, no self-hating Jew, no BDS dupe. He is a patriot. "The time for illusions is over," he wrote, and "the time for decisions has arrived. We love the entire land of our forefathers and in some other time we would have wanted to live here alone. But that will not happen. The Arabs, too, have dreams and needs."[196]

Israel has a lot to answer for, but it still needs to be a partner for peace, and needs to find one too. Gaza's last democratic elections were a decade ago. The situation is perhaps even worse in the West Bank. Abbas has been discredited beyond redemption as the Palestine Papers leaked to Al Jazeera and the *Guardian* in 2011 demonstrate.[197] To say he had become a little too cozy with Israel and the United States would be something of an understatement – not that it got him or the Palestinian people anywhere. The last time the Palestinian parliament convened was in 2007, and Abbas continues to rule as president even though his term expired in 2009. There is a huge leadership deficit – both Israeli and Palestinian – and that has to change before anything else will.

Countless people are asking the same question: Is this the Palestinians' South African moment? Israelis have to be convinced that they have an option other than apartheid – that democracy is not just for Jews but for everyone. In South Africa, once the struggle was reconceived as no longer a fight against whites but one against white power, and not against settlers but against the settler state, it was possible to plot a real road map to peace. Israel is not Northern Ireland, nor is it South Africa, but their lessons are still instructive.

The Yom Kippur War was a long time ago – in October 1973. Way back then Israel was blind to events taking place in plain sight, ignoring the few dissidents as alarmists. This time around there is no shortage of dire warnings, both from Israelis and from others outside Israel. There are dissenters everywhere. But the country and its political leaders remain impervious, bent on their destructive course. In 2011 hundreds of thousands of Israelis took to the streets to demand jobs, affordable housing, and economic opportunity, spurred to action by an increase in the price of cottage cheese. But what about the long-term survival of their country?

A recent Pew Center poll revealed that half of Israelis believe that Palestinians – citizens of Israel – should be expelled or "transferred."[198] True, the other half presumably disagreed, but those in favour were mostly religious Jews, the Israeli group with the highest birthrate. Most striking of all, 79 per cent of all Israelis believed that Jews were entitled to "preferential treatment." As an opinion piece published by the Brookings Institute noted, "so much for the notion of democracy with full equal rights for all citizens."[199] Eventually the West will choose democracy over Jewishness. In the meantime, the mad march to disaster continues.

The number of settlers in East Jerusalem and the West Bank is growing at the rate of 5 per cent per year. The amount of land they are occupying is increasing too. According to the Rand Corporation, "if the pace of settlements continues at the present rate over 20 years, the area in the West Bank and East Jerusalem available for creating a Palestinian state would be substantially smaller and composed of noncontiguous areas. The difficulty and cost of moving such a large number of settlers would be dramatically larger than the resources required to move today's settlers, and, thus, the ability to create a successful Palestinian state would be greatly eroded."[200]

It is no longer even clear that the Israeli Army, increasingly dominated by Orthodox Jews, settlers, and their supporters, would even obey orders to remove recalcitrant settlers, as was necessary when Gaza was evacuated.[201] There are hundreds of thousands of them in the West Bank, and they consider that land their own. Some will never leave willingly. Will Israel risk civil war?

A just two-state solution was possible once perhaps, and maybe it still is. Israeli actions, however, make it increasingly unlikely, no matter how much lip service some Israeli and most American politicians pay to the idea. This is Israel's tragic self-defeat. There is no longer a territorial basis for two states, and Israeli settlements and the wall make a contiguous Palestinian state impossible. Looking at the map (Figure 9.6), it is hard to imagine how the land between the Jordan and the Mediterranean can be peacefully partitioned. The "facts on the ground" – the settlements, security areas, closed military zones, "nature preserves," state land, and bypass roads – pockmark the entire West Bank, and hundreds of thousands of heavily armed true believers ensure that there will never be a viable Palestinian state. In 2007 Peace Now reported that more than 30 per cent of the land registered to West Bank settlements was *stolen* from its Palestinian owners. In its official response, the government rejected the finding, claiming that the settlements were built either on state-owned land or land "not registered in anyone's name."[202]

The problem is as old as the conflict itself: "What to do with the people when all you want is the land?"[203] In October 1973 a few dissenting voices pointed out the obvious, but no one listened. The situation today is completely reversed: dissenters are speaking up and their voices are loud and clear. They are pointing to an impending cataclysm, and they have the evidence to back up their claims. A quick look at a settlement map tells all we need to know:

The United States consistently opposes building new settlements – at least it did before Donald Trump was elected president – but the cash continues to flow. "Our American friends give us arms, money and advice," Dayan once cynically observed, adding, "We take the money,

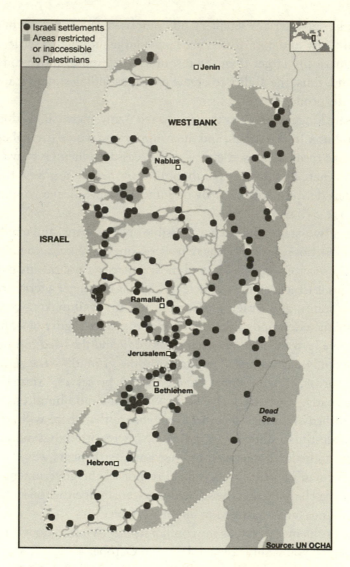

9.6 Israeli settlements in the West Bank. (Credit: UN OCHA)

we take the arms, and we decline the advice."[204] In July 2016 the Netanyahu government announced yet another expansion into the occupied territories. The following month, the *New York Times* reported that the Israeli government had begun to quietly legalize "pirate outposts."[205] When further settlement projects were approved, the US State Department objected: "We oppose steps like these."[206] Netanyahu brushed off the criticism: "We're familiar with the American position; we don't accept it."[207] In October 2016 Israel announced the construction of yet another West Bank settlement. A *New York Times* editorial dated 6 October 2016 summed it up: "If the aim of the Israeli government is to prevent a peace deal with the Palestinians, now or in the future, it is close to realizing that goal."[208]

The announcement of yet another settlement was actually flabber-gasting, coming as it did in the wake of an unprecedented US promise of $38 billion in military support over the next ten years. The State Department condemned the move: the new settlement of 300 homes would be "far closer to Jordan than Israel" and would "effectively divide the West Bank and make the possibility of a viable Palestinian state more remote."[209] It was also a complete betrayal of Israeli promises to American officials that the government would block new settlements.

Without consequences, Israel will continue on its self-destructive course. With President Donald Trump in power, the situation is sure to get even worse. Instead of listening to the international community, Israel thumbs its nose. UN Resolution 2334 was passed on 23 December 2016, with the United States abstaining. As important were the countries that voted in favour of it, including France, Japan, New Zealand, and the United Kingdom. For the first time ever, the United States did not use its veto in the Security Council to defeat an anti-Israel resolution, one that categorically condemned the settlement project and repeated some obvious truths: they are illegal, pose an obstacle to peace, and stand in the way of the two-state solution. Netanyahu and Israel's allies in Congress would have none of it, blaming and branding the American president, and his secretary of state, as unrepentant anti-Semites, the complete opposite of the truth. President-elect Trump tweeted in the aftermath of the UN resolution that things would change when he moved into the Oval Office, and they have; there are already rumblings that the US embassy in Israel will be moved from Tel Aviv to Jerusalem, and Trump's choice of American ambassador is a fervent supporter of settlements. Whether the United States ever actually moves its embassy to Jerusalem or not, Israel immediately began to act as if it has been given a free pass: even more settlements were announced in January 2017 and, more likely than not, some of the existing ones will soon be annexed to the Israeli state. On 26 January 2017 the Bulletin of Atomic Scientists moved their Dooms-day Clock thirty seconds closer to midnight.

Israel has to change its behaviour. The US can't or won't force it to, but BDS might. Under President Trump, the US is unlikely to become an honest broker, quite the opposite in fact. It is hard to imagine that the Trump administration has much to contribute in helping Israelis and Palestinians chart a peaceful future. Canada could, and probably should, reassert its traditional even-handed role in the Middle East as peace-keepers, but it must first undo a decade of blind, blinkers-on, uncritical Israel support. The time is right for a worthwhile Canadian initiative.

Anti-Semitism is not old news. Liberals and lefties can fantasize about a future where we are all equal, secular, smart, and tolerant, but ISIS, Brexit, and Trump, to give just three examples, point in a completely different direction. Anti-Semitism is alive and well. The Palestinian people includes the best (people who genuinely wish to live peacefully alongside their neighbours) and the worst (Jew haters and baiters who want to drive the Israelis into the sea). Clearly, many BDS supporters want nothing more than to destroy Israel and are merely masquerading as Mandela-pluralists or Canadian-style multiculturalists.

Israelis, for their part, are completely divided about the present, the future, and the legitimate entitlements of the Palestinian people. In the meantime, BDS is set to strike at the heart of Israel: its international relations, its foreign markets, its democratic legitimacy. This is a much more powerful force than the Egyptian and Syrian armies who launched their attack on Yom Kippur 1973. Then there was no Tenth Man to challenge the consensus. Now there are millions of dissenters in Israel and abroad, but no will to listen and no current capacity to rise to the challenge. One big jolly, happy, progressive, multi-sectarian, and multiracial state is a fantasy. But so too is the sustainability of the status quo. The problem, simply put, is that the Palestinians win on numbers, so the Israelis must secure the space. Out of this a solution must be found.

The situation is terribly complex and fraught with danger, but it need not end in tragedy. Huge changes are needed in both US and Israeli policy. Israel can choose to be a Jewish garrison state or a democratic state, but it cannot be both. Whatever opportunity is left to avoid unmitigated disaster will require farsighted political leadership and true Palestinian and Israeli partners for peace. At present, the prospects for either seem remote. Whether the epiphany comes, and what it will be, is impossible to predict. But if something does happen, it will present a brief opportunity to do something extraordinary.

Conclusion:
Further Reflections on Our Dissenters

People know what they know. They have little interest in knowing what they don't know, and often everybody is shouting. Groupthink almost led to the destruction of Israel in October 1973. Notwithstanding the accumulating and incontrovertible evidence that Egypt and Syria were preparing an attack, Israel could not see what was unfolding right in front of it. The cost – almost 3,000 Israelis dead – was tragic and preventable. Another tragedy is unfolding there today. History is repeating itself, although not exactly.

This time many dissenting voices in Israel are speaking up – too many to replicate the disciplinary action Israeli authorities scheduled for the young army officer on the Syrian front who tried to sound the alarm before the Yom Kippur attack. They are joined by more and more voices in the West, especially Jewish voices. BDS is having an impact. Two states for two peoples may still be salvageable, although the facts on the ground suggest otherwise. What is not sustainable is Israel's present course of non-stop colonization of the occupied territories, and the ongoing degradation of the Palestinian people no matter where they live. People are entitled to their views – but squelching or ignoring dissent is a recipe for disaster. The dissenters clearly have something important to say and their numbers are growing.

Reflecting on the experience of the Cuban Missile Crisis, Robert Kennedy observed that time was critical – to talk, argue, disagree, and debate some more. "But more than time is necessary," he wrote. "I believe our deliberations proved conclusively how important it is that the President has the recommendations and opinions of more than one individual, of more than one department, and of more than one point of view. Opinion, even fact itself, can best be judged by conflict, by debate. There is an important element missing when there is unanimity of viewpoint."[1] During the Cuban Missile Crisis, President John F. Kennedy went to great lengths to ensure that he cast the widest possible net. He demanded options.

In insisting that ExComm look at the situation from the Soviet perspective, Kennedy demonstrated that he had learned something from the Bay of Pigs. As his brother Robert continued: "During the crisis, President Kennedy spent more time trying to determine the effect of a particular course of action on Khrushchev or the Russians than on any other phase of what he was doing. What guided all his deliberations was an effort not to disgrace Khrushchev, not to humiliate the Soviet Union, not to have them feel they would have to escalate their response because their national security or national interests so committed them."[2] John Kennedy was determined not to stumble into war. "If anybody is around to write after this," he told Robert at the height of the crisis, "they are going to understand that we made every effort to find peace and every effort to give our adversary room to move. I am not going to push the Russians an inch beyond what is necessary."[3]

ExComm members were separated from their vested interests and redeployed in a common cause. They were instructed to look at all options, to hear and consider all points of views (especially the Russian), and to come up with alternative courses of action. Kennedy and his men were not the best and the brightest, as their follow-up act in Vietnam proved: a truly pointless war between 1955 and 1975, it left well more than 3 million people dead. But when the fate of the world quite possibly hung in the balance, by listening to different and dissenting points of view, the American president got it right.

Manufacturing Dissent

Good decision making is enhanced by putting together different pieces of information gathered from a wide variety of sources, in a setting where team members are truly encouraged to speak and where new information – information that might change everything – is welcomed, not suppressed. Disagreement, instead of being rejected as argumentative, should be encouraged and embraced. "Open door" policies are meaningless unless accompanied by an open mind and a real curiosity about how others see things, and skepticism about everything, especially received wisdom.

We need to consider whether the group is wrong, and whether the dissenters are wrong too. The point is not to ignore consensus – when smart people and experts agree on something after having looked at it carefully, their conclusions should not be readily dismissed – but to question assumptions and beliefs by examining all the evidence and trying to look at it in a different way.

At the very least, institutionalizing dissent provides a safe way to disagree with more powerful voices and entrenched interests. The devil's advocate, red teams, and independent directors are among a host of devices that can be deployed. But they are all role players, and their job is known by one and all. To be sure, they have something to add, but what they can never bring to the party is the fervour of a true believer. Only an authentic dissenter can do that: someone with courage, someone completely committed to making a point, regardless of the personal or career consequences.

That someone was missing before the *Challenger* blew up and when the *Columbia* was damaged on lift-off and information was badly needed to assess the situation and try to come up with a rescue plan. But the situation was different when Frances Kelsey was asked to approve William S. Merrell's application for approval for Kevadon. An authentic dissenter now stepped forward. To be sure, Kelsey was an uncommon dissenter. She was just doing her job, and doing it well, but she wouldn't take the path of least resistance. When the New Drug Application came to the FDA, it had already been approved in fifty countries around the world. She could easily have given it a rubber stamp. But she wouldn't be bullied or bamboozled – and she saved the American people from a true tragedy.

Rachel Carson also had courage to spare. She took on one of the most powerful economic interests in American society – the pesticide industry. Carson had an unusually broad view: she wasn't the first person to raise concerns about wanton pesticide use, and she didn't discover the damage that over-spraying was causing to plants and animals and quite possibly to humans. But she gathered the different jigsaw pieces and put them together in a picture that convincingly illustrated that the planet was in peril. Her work gave birth to the modern environmental movement, proving just how influential one dissenter can be.

Carson saw the future: science served the public and the public had a right to know. She was also a natural-born muckraker and marketer. She knew what to do to attract attention for her book and how to get her brand new idea about pesticides – new to most people, that is – into the public domain. Of course, it helped both Kelsey and Carson to have

Ron Ridenhour. He blew the whistle on the massacre at My Lai.
(Credit: Associated Press)

the president of the United States on their side and in their corner. But it was only after they had done their work that the accolades began to flow.

People who do the unexpected are especially interesting: both Kelsey and Carson studied science at a time when most women did not go to university, and few of those who did were enrolled in science or medicine. The fights they fought in what was then a man's world clearly strengthened their resolve, and they were ready to stand up when opportunity presented and it mattered most. Prescient and admirable, brave and steadfast, Kelsey and Carson saw things that everyone else missed.

A lot has to do with character. Either you have it or you don't. There are really remarkable people out there: people who risk their reputations, their financial security, and sometimes their lives in pursuit of principle and really big ideas – challenging and dangerous ideas. We need to know more about them, to try to figure out what makes them stand up while everyone else remains seated, and then to listen carefully to what they have to say. One thing is for sure: you don't have to be a doctor or a scientist or a judge to dissent bravely. Everyone matters.

Ron Ridenhour was a helicopter gunner serving in Vietnam when he heard about a massacre at a small village named My Lai. Instead of keeping quiet, he investigated and, when he returned stateside, he blew the whistle.[4] Even President Richard Nixon could not ignore his 1,500-word letter outlining the atrocity.

What was it about Ron Ridenhour that made him do this? "It all began when as an uneducated draftee he was lying in his bunk and overheard a group of fellow enlisted men planning a nighttime assault on the only black solider in the unit. Ron said that he sat up in his own bunk and heard himself saying, 'If you want to do that, you have to come through me.'"[5] Until that moment Ridenhour had no idea that he was going to step up. But having done it once, he was ready to speak up when he learned of a terrible crime committed by his countrymen. Doing good is habit forming.

Remember Tank Man? He was the pro-democracy dissenter who stood in front of a Chinese tank in Tiananmen Square on 5 June 1989. To this day, his identity and fate remain unknown, but his courage will be remembered forever. What about Ieshia Evans? She was the fearless twenty-eight-year-old woman who defiantly faced off against two heavily militarized police officers in Baton Rouge, Louisiana, in early July 2016 after yet another African American man, Alton Sterling, was killed by the police outside a convenience store. In an increasingly familiar story, the whole sad episode was caught on video and left little question about what had occurred. Evans, a New York City nurse, was among more than 100 protestors for Black Lives Matter who took to the streets. Both Tank Man and Evans made millions of other people consider the world as it is and how it might be.

Wolves fight in packs, but the lion (usually) fights alone. When the *New Yorker* and Houghton Mifflin stood beside and behind Carson and *Silent Spring*, they showed the world that independence, courage, and dissent still matter and that a word, a sentence, a paragraph, a chapter, a book, and ultimately an idea can change everything. Isabel LeBourdais, who first told the Truscott story, shows us how important journalists are to society, and what an intrepid investigator can reveal when motivated to discover the truth. LeBourdais dissented against everything and everyone in the legal establishment and in doing so set the stage for taking a courageous new look at the wrongful conviction of a teenage boy, Steven Truscott.

Tank Man. One person can captivate the imagination of the world.
(Credit: Jeff Widener/Associated Press)

That is the story of judicial dissent – a judge who sees it differently, and then does her duty and says so. Most judicial dissents deservedly go nowhere, but some save a person – Justice Emmett Hall tried to do that in *Truscott* – and a few seek to better our society. Jury nullification is a different story. There the record is decidedly mixed. As jurors discover they possess this power, however, things are going to change in the courtroom: prevailing norms and social assumptions are going to be put in stark relief.

Public protestors are the dissenters with whom we are most familiar – the ones that tie up our streets and impede our progress. The cranks and loony-tunes often steal the show, and poking fun at them is like picking low-hanging fruit. Nevertheless, ows had an important message: income inequality must be addressed. It has gotten completely out of hand, and the situation is getting worse. The system *is* rigged and needs reform. We have the same choice as the Israelis: bury our heads in the sand or address the problem head-on. Something remarkable happened when protestors occupied Zuccotti Park and a thousand other places around the world in more than eighty countries. ows was a shambles and, at times, a bad joke. But we ignore its dissenting message at our peril.

Ieshia Evans. Fearless. (Credit: Jonathan Bachman/Reuters)

Dissenters start with an observation: there is something wrong. That initial observation unites all dissenters, whether they are part of a mass movement like OWS or are acting on their own because circumstances leave them no other choice. BDS is much more complicated since motives are so hugely mixed. Partly right and partly devious, it is, nevertheless, not going away. There is definitely something extremely unseemly about the way that some people are fixated on Israel in a world filled with social injustice. But simply calling for balance, explaining that there is more to the story, saying that it is all so very complicated, and arguing that the Israelis are doing their best in a bad neighbourhood in a dangerous part of the world does not address legitimate and pressing concerns.

Without a doubt, much of the criticism of Israel is anti-Semitic. But some criticism of Israeli policies is honest and true. There are good people who accept Israel's legitimacy within the pre-1967 borders but reject its colonial project in the West Bank. One doesn't even have to be sympathetic to Palestinian aspirations to be worried about, and responsive to, their power. A solution has to be found, and no serious person believes that it is another fifty years of occupation.

In the meantime, it is easy to denigrate dissenters by calling them all sorts of names, and to dismiss the peace camp as useful idiots paving the way for Israel's destruction. But it is nonsensical to believe that the current course leads in any other direction. To quote the Apollo 13 astronauts, "we have a problem" in the Middle East, and it is one that truly threatens peace on the planet.

Frances Kelsey could see that Merrell's New Drug Application was hooey, and said so. That's what Rachel Carson did too. She noticed that pesticides were affecting the environment and she looked into it. She then published her results – and good public policy followed. Observation followed by inference. But you need the data first. That is what made Prime Minister Stephen Harper's phony war on crime and his attack on science and basic research so dangerous.

Depriving the public-policy pipeline of evidence, an exercise that was symbolized by the cancellation of the long-form census, left Harper free to pursue his other goals: attacking a crime wave that was *not* sweeping the country, demonizing criminals who are actually mostly broken and ill people who need help, muzzling and firing scientists, closing research stations, and trashing libraries. All these initiatives were done in pursuit of one goal: to curtail dissent by eliminating the evidence that was needed to make good public-policy decisions instead of the politicized ones that Harper avidly pursued.

Information is the only antidote to ignorance. Our political leaders get to make decisions – that is what they are elected to do. But we need them to make the best decisions based on the best evidence. The 2015 federal election was, in part, a democratic revolt against a government that repudiated the use of science and evidence in making public-policy decisions.

Even a broken clock is accurate twice a day. Everyone knows that. Just because a voice is raised in dissent does not make it more important than any other voice. As President Barack Obama told the 2016 Howard University graduating class, we have to speak out but also to listen to those with whom we disagree.[6] Although we want advisers aligned with our fundamental values, we do not want them looking alike, thinking the same way, saying the same thing, and following the same leader. We want different people: the weak and the powerful, the rich and the poor, the boss and the bossed, optimists and pessimists, and people who speak other languages, come from away, have another world view, and are not afraid to step out of line. The truth is that where you stand does affect what you see.

We know a lot about human behaviour. The social scientists teach us that diverse groups of people with diverse sources of information consistently generate better ideas than homogenous groups. There is huge value in different perspectives: we can draw lessons from nature, and the most stable community is a complex one. Monoculture, as most farmers will attest, is bad; diversity, however, is good because it creates a system of checks and balances – what Carson called the balance of nature.

The government's "eternal temptation ... has been to arrest the speaker rather than to correct the conditions about which he complains," Justice William O. Douglas observed.[7] Disciplining the dissenter is normative. Dissenters often have a rough go. Yet we pay a huge price when we suppress dissent, ignore it, or marginalize it. Dissent is not for the faint of heart. It is not easy; it never has been and never will be. But our problems are not going away. There will always be abuses of power to confront, wrongs to right, new challenges, new crises, and new opportunities for authentic dissenting voices to say, "Stop, listen to me."

Acknowledgments

I had a lot of help in writing this book from many people, including terrific research assistants and colleagues and friends who read and commented on successive drafts of the manuscript, or parts of it. I didn't always do what they suggested, but I definitely listened to what they had to say, even when the discussions were difficult. Because of Canary Mission, discussed in chapter 9, I am not publicly acknowledging any of them. I would, however, like to thank publicly Philip Cercone at McGill-Queen's University Press, quite possibly the bravest publisher in Canada and certainly the finest. He was immediately receptive to the idea of this book when I sent him the first chapter and provided great encouragement at every stage. Rosemary Shipton gave a completely unwieldy manuscript a thorough structural edit and improved it beyond measure. I first met Curtis Fahey more than thirty years ago when he shepherded the publication of *Moscow Despatches*. I could not have been happier when he took on the copy editing of this book.

Thank you everyone.

Notes

PREFACE

1 Naomi Klein, *This Changes Everything: Capitalism vs. the Climate* (Simon and Schuster 2015), 464.
2 "Times Will Begin Reporting Gay Couples' Ceremonies," *New York Times*, 18 August 2002.
3 *Obergefell v. Hodges*, 576 US (2015).
4 Charles Evans Hughes, *The Supreme Court of the United States: Its Foundation, Methods and Achievements: An Interpretation* (repr.; Washington, DC: Board Books 2000), 67–8.

CHAPTER ONE

1 Uri Bar-Joseph, *The Watchman Fell Asleep* (Albany, NY: SUNY Press 2005), 64.
2 "Sadat Peace Initiative of 1971 – English Text," *The Israeli-Palestinian Conflict: An Interactive Database*, n.d., http://ecf.org.il/media_items/542.
3 Ofer Israeli, "The 1973 War: Link to Israeli-Egyptian Peace," *Middle East Policy* 20, no. 4 (2013): 88–98.
4 Aryeh Shalev, *Israel's Intelligence Assessment before the Yom Kippur War* (Brighton, UK: Sussex Academic Press 2010), xvi. See also Bar-Joseph, *The Watchman Fell Asleep*, 46.
5 Uri Bar-Joseph, *The Angel: The Egyptian Spy Who Saved Israel* (New York: Harper 2016).
6 Sunday Times Insight Team Staff, *Insight on the Middle East War* (London: A. Deutsch 1974), 35.
7 Chaim Herzog, *The War of Atonement, October, 1973* (Boston: Little, Brown and Company 1975), 26.
8 Ephraim Kahana, "Early Warning versus Concept: The Case of the Yom Kippur War 1973," *Intelligence and National Security* 17, no. 2 (2002): 82.
9 Herzog, *The War of Atonement, October, 1973*, 41.
10 Bar-Joseph, *The Watchman Fell Asleep*, 75.
11 Shalev, *Israel's Intelligence Assessment before the Yom Kippur War*, 31–2.
12 Ahron Bregman, "Ashraf Marwan and Israel's Intelligence Failure," in Asaf Siniver, ed., *The October 1973 War: Politics, Diplomacy, Legacy* (London: Hurst Publishers 2013), 204; Anwar Sadat, *In Search of Identity: An Autobiography* (New York: Harper and Row 1978), 241.
13 Bar-Joseph, *The Watchman Fell Asleep*, 77.
14 Abraham Rabinovich, *The Yom Kippur War* (New York: Schocken 2005), 8.
15 Panagiotis Gatidis, "The Israeli Intelligence Failure at the Yom Kippur War 1973," Institute of International Relations, http://www.idis.gr/?p=3236.

16 Shaley, *Israel's Intelligence Assessment before the Yom Kippur War*, 54–5.
17 Ibid., 54.
18 Uri Bar-Joseph, "Last Chance to Avoid War: Sadat's Peace Initiative of February 1973 and Its Failure," *Journal of Contemporary History* 41, no. 3 (2006): 551.
19 Yigal Kipnis, *1973: The Road to War* (Charlottesville, VA: Just World Books 2013), 63.
20 Ibid., 25–6.
21 Bar-Joseph, "Last Chance to Avoid War," 549–51.
22 Hasan el-Badri, Taha el-Magdoub, and Mohammed Diael Din Zohdy, *The Ramadan War, 1973* (Dunn Loring, VA: T.P. Dupey Associates 1978), 17–18. See also Boaz Vanetik and Zaki Shalom, *Nixon Administration and the Middle East Peace Process, 1969–1973: From the Rogers Plan to the Outbreak of the Yom Kippur War* (Brighton, UK: Sussex Academic Press 2013).
23 Michael I. Handel, "The Yom Kippur War and the Inevitability of Surprise," *International Studies Quarterly* 21, no. 3 (1977): 490.
24 Edgar O'Ballance, *No Victor, No Vanquished* (New York: Presidio Press 1996), 25. On his diplomatic deception campaign, see Sadat, *In Search of Identity*, 232–70.
25 Galia Golan, *Soviet Policies in the Middle East: From World War II to Gorbachev* (Cambridge: Cambridge University Press 1990), 82–94.
26 See generally John Amos, "Deception and the 1973 Middle East War," in *Strategic Military Deception*, ed. Donald Charles Daniel and Katherine Lydigsen Herbig (New York: Pergamon 1982), 317–34.
27 Rabinovich, *The Yom Kippur War*, 74.
28 "Document 63," *The National Security Archive, George Washington University*, http://nsarchive.gwu.edu/NSAEBB/NSAEBB98/octwar-63.pdf.
29 Golan, *Soviet Policies in the Middle East*, 85.
30 This exchange is the recollection of Mordechai Gazit, director general of the Prime Minister's Office, who spoke English and attended the meeting. For this and other versions, see Shaley, *Israel's Intelligence Assessment before the Yom Kippur War*, 80.
31 Ofer Aderet, "Jordan and Israel Cooperated during Yom Kippur War, Documents Reveal," *Haaretz*, 12 September 2013.
32 Uri Bar-Joseph and Amr Yossef, "The Hidden Factors That Turned the Tide: Strategic Decision-Making and Operational Intelligence in the 1973 War," *Journal of Strategic Studies* 37, no. 4 (2014): 589.
33 On the detailed war preparations, see el-Badri, al-Majdub, and Zuhdi, *The Ramadan War, 1973*.
34 Doron Geller, "Israel Military Intelligence: Intelligence during the Six-Day War (1973)," http://www.jewishvirtuallibrary.org/jsource/History/intel73.html.
35 Rabinovich, *The Yom Kippur War*, 68.
36 Sunday Times Insight Team Staff, *Insight on the Middle East War*, 9.
37 Avi Shlaim, "Failures in National Intelligence Estimates: The Case of the Yom Kippur War," *World Politics* 28, no. 3 (18 April 1976): 353–4, doi:10.2307/2009975.

38 Mohamed Heikal, *The Road to Ramadan* (New York: Quadrangle Books 1975), 32.

39 Jacob Eriksson, "Israel and the October War," in Siniver, ed., *The October 1973 War*, 38.

40 Ibid., 37.

41 Kahana, "Early Warning versus Concept," 94.

42 Shlaim, "Failures in National Intelligence Estimates," 353.

43 Uri Bar-Joseph and Arie W. Kruglanski, "Intelligence Failure and Need for Cognitive Closure: On the Psychology of the Yom Kippur Surprise," *Political Psychology* 24, no. 1 (2003): 87.

44 Uri Bar-Joseph, "Israel's 1973 Intelligence Failure," *Israel Affairs* 6, no. 1 (1999): 19.

45 Henry Kissinger, *Crisis: The Anatomy of Two Major Foreign Policy Crises* (New York: Simon and Schuster 2015), 13.

46 See generally Saad El Shazly, *The Crossing of the Suez* (San Francisco, CA: Amer Mideast Research 1980).

47 Heikal, *The Road to Ramadan*, 27.

48 Rabinovich, *The Yom Kippur War*, 26.

49 "Saad El Shazly," n.d., http://el-shazly.com/ (domain expired but can be viewed at http://web.archive.org/web/20161004040103/http://el-shazly.com/).

50 Bar-Joseph, *The Watchman Fell Asleep*, 25.

51 Bar-Joseph, "Israel's 1973 Intelligence Failure," 11.

52 Uri Bar-Joseph, "Main Trends in the Historiography of the Yom Kippur War: A Thirty-Year Perspective," *Journal of Israeli History* 24, no. 2 (2005): 257.

53 Michael Russell Rip, "Military Photo-Reconnaissance during the Yom Kippur War: A Research Note," *Intelligence and National Security* 7, no. 2 (1992): 127; Michael Russell Rip and Joseph F. Fontanella, "A Window on the Arab-Israeli 'Yom Kippur' War of October 1973: Military Photo-Reconnaissance from High Altitude and Space," *Intelligence and National Security* 6, no. 1 (1991): 15–89.

54 Gabriella Heichal, "Perception, Image Formation and Coping in the Pre-Crisis Stage of the Yom Kippur War," *Israel Affairs* 6, no. 1 (1999): 214. Disciplining the dissenter is normative. In June 1941 Stalin was convinced that the Germans would not attack and he would not tolerate any information to the contrary. On the eve of the attack, four Soviet officers provided evidence that the invasion was imminent. Lavrentiy Beria, Stalin's chief of the secret police – conscious of "your wise conclusion" that there would be no attack – promised to have them "ground into labor camp dust." See Uri Bar-Joseph and Jack S. Levy, "Conscious Action and Intelligence Failure," *Political Science Quarterly* 124, no. 3 (2009): 479.

55 Rabinovich, *The Yom Kippur War*, 52.

56 Bar-Joseph, *The Watchman Fell Asleep*, 93.

57 Howard Blum, *The Eve of Destruction* (New York: Harper Collins 2009), 134.

58 Eriksson, "Israel and the October War," 38.

59 Gatidis, "The Israeli Intelligence Failure at the Yom Kippur War 1973."

60 Rabinovich, *The Yom Kippur War*, 74.

61 Bar-Joseph and Kruglanski, "Intelligence Failure and Need for Cognitive Closure," 88.

62 Sunday Times Insight Team Staff, *Insight on the Middle East War*, 55.

63 Blum, *The Eve of Destruction*, 137.

64 Bar-Joseph, *The Watchman Fell Asleep*, 93.

65 Shaley, *Israel's Intelligence Assessment before the Yom Kippur War*, 126.

66 Golda Meir, *My Life* (New York: GP Putnam's Sons 1975), 355–6.

67 "Document 7," National Security Archive, George Washington University, http://nsarchive.gwu.edu/NSAEBB/NSAEBB98/octwar-07.pdf.

68 Blum, *The Eve of Destruction*, 139.

69 Ibid., 140.

70 Shaley, *Israel's Intelligence Assessment before the Yom Kippur War*, vii.

71 Ibid., 98.

72 Uri Bar-Joseph, "The Intelligence Community during the Yom Kippur War (1973)," in *Israel's Silent Defender: An Inside Look at Sixty Years of Israeli Intelligence*, ed. Amos Gilboa and Ephraim Lapid (Jerusalem: Gefen Publishing House 2011), 84.

73 Bregman, "Ashraf Marwan and Israel's Intelligence Failure." On Marwan, see generally Ahron Bregman, *The Spy Who Fell to Earth*, 1st ed. (CreateSpace Independent Publishing Platform 2016).

74 Shaley, *Israel's Intelligence Assessment before the Yom Kippur War*, 123.

75 Bar-Joseph, *The Watchman Fell Asleep*, 191–6; Kipnis, *1973: The Road to War*, 276.

76 Herzog, *The War of Atonement, October, 1973*, 53.

77 Moshe Dayan, *Moshe Dayan: Story of My Life* (London: Weidenfeld and Nicholson 1976), 378.

78 Rabinovich, *The Yom Kippur War*, 93.

79 "Document 9," National Security Archive, George Washington University, http://nsarchive.gwu.edu/NSAEBB/NSAEBB98/octwar-09.pdf.

80 Blum, *The Eve of Destruction*, 149–50.

81 Heikal, *The Road to Ramadan*, 45.

82 6 October 1973, was the tenth day of Ramadan. On that day in 623, the Prophet Mohamed began preparations for the Battle of Badr, and ten days later he took Mecca.

83 Blum, *The Eve of Destruction*, 127.

84 Rabinovich, *The Yom Kippur War*, 28.

85 Uri Bar-Joseph, "Lessons Not Learned: Israel in the Post-Yom Kippur War Era," *Israel Affairs* 14, no. 1 (2008): 70.

86 Seymour M. Hersh, *The Samson Option* (New York: Random House 2013), 223.

87 Uri Bar-Joseph and Rose McDermott, "Personal Functioning under Stress: Accountability and Social Support of Israeli Leaders in the Yom Kippur War," *Journal of Conflict Resolution* 52, no. 1 (2008): 158.

88 Dayan, *Moshe Dayan*, 619.

89 Bar-Joseph, *The Watchman Fell Asleep*, 230.

90 Bar-Joseph and McDermott, "Personal Functioning under Stress," 166.

91 Bar-Joseph, *The Watchman Fell Asleep*, 231.

92 Undoubtedly, Israel ordered this alert for both military and political purposes:

to blackmail the Americans into providing supplies, and to put the Egyptians and Syrians on notice that they would be destroyed. See Hersh, *The Samson Option*. As Kissinger's aide at the time, National Security Council member William Quandt, later observed, "I did not know what kind of warheads they had, but it did not make much sense to me that they would be equipped with conventional ordnance. I assume others agreed." Adam Raz, "The Significance of the Reputed Yom Kippur War Nuclear Affair," *Strategic Assessment* 16, no. 4 (2014): 107.

93 Ari Shavit, *My Promised Land* (New York: Spiegel and Grau 2013), 193–4.

94 Kissinger, *Crisis*, 145.

95 Amir Oren, "Kissinger Wants Israel to Know: The U.S. Saved You during the 1973 War," *Haaretz*, 2 November 2013.

96 Hersh, *The Samson Option*, 227.

97 Kissinger, *Crisis*, 251.

98 Ibid., 248.

99 Kipnis, *1973: The Road to War*, 28.

100 Egypt and Syria lost approximately 16,000 soldiers, with countless more wounded. There are varying accounts of the numbers of tanks, artillery, and planes destroyed. See Geraint Hughes, "Britain, the Transatlantic Alliance, and the Arab-Israeli War of 1973," *Journal of Cold War Studies* 10, no. 2 (2008): 3; and Blum, *The Eve of Destruction*. The direct financial cost of the war was estimated at between $8 and 10 billion. See Israeli, "The 1973 War: Link to Israeli-Egyptian Peace," 3. See also Bar-Joseph, "Lessons Not Learned: Israel in the Post-Yom Kippur War Era," 70–83.

101 Herzog, *The War of Atonement, October, 1973*, 54.

102 Rabinovich, *The Yom Kippur War*, 489.

103 Gili Cohen, "I Couldn't Face up to Army Chiefs, Golda Told Inquiry Panel," *Haaretz*, 12 September 2013.

104 Pnina Lahav, *Judgement in Jerusalem: Chief Justice Simon Agranat and the Zionist Century* (Berkeley, CA: University of California Press, 1997), 228.

105 Susan Hattis Rolef, "The Domestic Fallout of the Yom Kippur War," in *Revisiting the Yom Kippur War*, ed. P.R. Kumaraswamy (London: Routledge 2000), 177–94; Michael B. Oren, "The Yom Kippur War Was 40 Years Ago. Everything You Thought You Knew about It Is Wrong," *New Republic*, 13 October 2013.

106 Uri Bar-Joseph, "The 'Special Means of Collection': The Missing Link in the Surprise of the Yom Kippur War," *Middle East Journal* 67, no. 4 (2013): 531.

107 "Agranat Commission," Knesset, http://www.knesset.gov.il/lexicon/eng/agranat_eng.htm.

108 Lahav, *Judgement in Jerusalem*, 232–42.

109 Eriksson, "Israel and the October War," 45; Rabinovich, *The Yom Kippur War*, 502.

110 Ben Hartman, "Golda Meir's Fears and Uncertainty at Outbreak of Yom Kippur War Revealed in Declassified Documents," *Jerusalem Post*, 12 September 2013.

111 Abba Solomon Eban and Avi Shlaim, "Interview with Abba Eban, 11 March 1976," *Israel Studies* 8, no. 1 (2003): 9.

112 Meir Amit, "Relationship between the Decision Makers and the Head of Intelligence," in *Israel's Silent Defender*, ed. Gilboa and Lapid, 304.

113 Kissinger, *Crisis*, 12.
114 Bar-Joseph, "Lessons Not Learned," 80.
115 Shlaim, "Failures in National Intelligence Estimates," 356; See also Uri Bar-Joseph, "Strategic Surprise or Fundamental Flaws? The Sources of Israel's Military Defeat at the Beginning of the 1973 War," *Journal of Military History* 72, no. 2 (2008): 509–30.
116 Amnon Lord, "Intelligence Failure or Paralysis?," *Jewish Political Studies Review*, 2012, 52.
117 Bar-Joseph, *The Watchman Fell Asleep*, 125.
118 Blum, *The Eve of Destruction*, 327.
119 Bar-Joseph and Levy, "Conscious Action and Intelligence Failure," 485.
120 Blum, *The Eve of Destruction*, 326–7.
121 This is disputed. See Kipnis, *1973: The Road to War*, 257.
122 Shalev, *Israel's Intelligence Assessment before the Yom Kippur War*, xi.
123 Eli Zeira, The October 73 War – Myth against Reality (Tel Aviv: Yediot Ahronot 1993); Shalev, *Israel's Intelligence Assessment before the Yom Kippur War*. See also Shlaim, "Failures in National Intelligence Estimates," 376; "Why Did Israel Fail to Anticipate the Yom Kippur War?" *Wilson Quarterly*, 2014, 1–5.
124 Shalev, *Israel's Intelligence Assessment before the Yom Kippur War*, xii.
125 Zeev Maoz, *Defending the Holy Land* (Ann Arbor: University of Michigan Press 2006), 509.
126 Shalev, *Israel's Intelligence Assessment before the Yom Kippur War*, 83.
127 Gili Cohen, "Abba Eban: Israeli Leaders Wouldn't Start a War It Was Liable to Lose," *Haaretz*, 20 September 2012.
128 Cohen, "I Couldn't Face up to Army Chiefs, Golda Told Inquiry Panel."
129 Shalev, *Israel's Intelligence Assessment before the Yom Kippur War*, 214.
130 Shmuel Even, "The Revision Process in Intelligence," in *Israel's Silent Defender*, ed. Gilboa and Lapid, 311.
131 Yosef Kuperwaser, "Lessons from Israel's Intelligence Reforms," 30 October 2007, http://www.brookings.edu/research/lessons-from-israels-intelligence-reforms/.
132 Even, "The Revision Process in Intelligence," 309–15.
133 Walter Laqueur, *The Uses and Limits of Intelligence* (Pitscataway, NJ: Transaction Publishers 1993), 222.
134 Uri Bar-Joseph, "The Professional Ethics of Intelligence Analysis," *International Journal of Intelligence and CounterIntelligence* 24, no. 1 (2010): 36.
135 Amos Harel, "40 Years on, the IDF Finally Emerges from the Bunker," *Haaretz*, 13 September 2013.
136 Shalev, *Israel's Intelligence Assessment before the Yom Kippur War*, 215.
137 Shlaim, "Failures in National Intelligence Estimates," 350.
138 Bregman, "Ashraf Marwan and Israel's Intelligence Failure," 200.
139 Gili Cohen, "After 40 Years, Yom Kippur War Facts Still Disputed," *Haaretz*, 7 October 2013.
140 Nahum Goldmann, *The Jewish Paradox* (New York: Grosset and Dunlap 1978), 98.
141 Bar-Joseph, *The Watchman Fell Asleep*, 154.

142 Bar-Joseph, "Strategic Surprise or Fundamental Flaws?" 521.

143 Uri Bar-Joseph, "The Wealth of Information and the Poverty of Comprehension: Israel's Intelligence Failure of 1973 Revisited," *Intelligence and National Security* 10, no. 4 (1995): 229–40.

144 Barbara W. Tuchman, *The March of Folly: From Troy to Vietnam* (New York: Alfred A. Knopf 1984), 8.

145 Yoel Ben-Porat, "The Yom Kippur War: A Mistake in May Leads to a Surprise in October," *IDF Journal* 3 (1986): 61.

146 Amos Gilboa, "A Comparison of the Intelligence between Two Wars: The Six-Day War (1967) and the Yom Kippur War (1973)," in *Israel's Silent Defender*, ed. Gilboa and Lapid, 74.

147 Saul David, *Operation Thunderbolt* (Boston: Little, Brown and Company 2015), 115.

148 Ephraim Kahana, "Analyzing Israel's Intelligence Failures," *International Journal of Intelligence and CounterIntelligence* 18, no. 2 (2005): 273.

CHAPTER TWO

1 Roberta Wohlstetter, *Pearl Harbor: Warning and Decision* (Stanford, CA: Stanford University Press 1962); Barton S. Whaley, *Codeword Barbarossa* (Boston: MIT Press 1974).

2 Shlaim, "Failures in National Intelligence Estimates," 371–5.

3 Philip Tetlock and Dan Gardner, *Superforecasting: The Art and Science of Prediction* (New York: Random House 2016), 55.

4 Arthur M. Schlesinger, *Journals: 1952–2000* (New York: Penguin Books 2007), 109.

5 Ibid., 111.

6 Nate Jones, "Document Friday: Che Guevara Thanks the United States for the Bay of Pigs Invasion," *Unredacted*, 2012, http://nsarchive.wordpress.com /2012/02/03/document-friday-che-guevara-thanks-the-united-states-for-the-bay-of-pigs-invasion/.

7 Arthur Meier Schlesinger, *A Thousand Days: John F. Kennedy in the White House* (Boston: Houghton Mifflin Harcourt 1965), 258.

8 James Surowiecki, *The Wisdom of Crowds* (New York: Anchor 2005), 37.

9 Schlesinger, *A Thousand Days*, 259.

10 Robert Dallek, *An Unfinished Life: John F. Kennedy, 1917–1963* (Boston: Little, Brown and Company 2003), 384.

11 Robert F. Kennedy, *Thirteen Days: A Memoir of the Cuban Missile Crisis* (New York: W.W. Norton and Company 1971), 86.

12 Schlesinger, *A Thousand Days*, 797.

13 Graham Allison and Philip Zelikow, *Essence of Decision: Explaining the Cuban Missile Crisis* (New York: Longman 1999), 81.

14 Michael Dobbs, *One Minute to Midnight: Kennedy, Khruschev, and Casto on the Brink of Nuclear War* (New York: Random House 2008), 352.

15 Arthur M. Schlesinger, "Foreword," in *Thirteen Days: A Memoir of the Cuban Missile Crisis* (New York: W.W. Norton and Company 1971), 11.

16 Schlesinger, *A Thousand Days*, 802–3.

17 Kennedy, *Thirteen Days*, 36.

18 See generally Allison and Zelikow, "Essence of Decision."

19   Ibid., 346.
20   Dobbs, *One Minute to Midnight*, 353.
21   Tetlock and Gardner, *Superforecasting*, 195.
22   "President Discusses Beginning of Operation Iraqi Freedom" (White House
     Archives – George W. Bush, 22 March 2003), http://georgewbush-white
     house.archives.gov/news/releases/2003/03/20030322.html
23   Robert Booth, "'With You, Whatever': Tony Blair's Letters to George W.
     Bush," *Guardian*, 6 July 2016.
24   "Iraq Dossier 'Solid' – Downing Street," *BBC News*, 7 February 2003,
     http://news.bbc.co.uk/2/hi/uk_news/politics/2735031.stm.
25   Robert Jervis, "Reports, Politics, and Intelligence Failures: The Case of
     Iraq," *Journal of Strategic Studies* 29, no. 1 (2006): 29.
26   "The Secret Downing Street Memo," National Security Archive, George
     Washington University, http://nsarchive.gwu.edu/NSAEBB/NSAEBB328/
     II-Doc14.pdf.
27   Charles Lewis and Mark Reading-Smith, "Iraq: The War Card," Center for
     Public Integrity, 23 January 2008, http://www.publicintegrity.org/2008/01/
     23/5641/false-pretenses.
28   "Statement by Sir John Chilcot," 6 July 2016, http://www.iraqinquiry.org.uk/
     media/247010/2016-09-06-sir-john-chilcots-public-statement.pdf#search=
     rigour.
29   Irving L. Janis and Leon Mann, *Decision Making: A Psychological Analysis
     of Conflict, Choice, and Commitment* (New York: Free Press 1977), xv.
30   Irving L. Janis, *Victims of Groupthink*, 2nd ed. (Boston: Houghton Mifflin
     1972), 19.
31   Ibid., 35–6.
32   Paul 't Hart, "Preventing Groupthink Revisited: Evaluating and Reforming
     Groups in Government," *Organizational Behavior and Human Decision
     Processes* 73, nos. 2–3 (1998): 316.
33   Cass R. Sunstein, "The Law of Group Polarization," *Journal of Political
     Philosophy* 10, no. 2 (2002): 175–95.
34   Ibid., 178.
35   Ibid., 193.
36   Leo Tolstoy, *The Kingdom of God Is within You* (London: Walter Scott 1894).
37   Sandro Galea, "On Courage," Boston University, 17 July 2016, http://www.
     bu.edu/sph/2016/07/17/on-courage/.
38   Maria Konnikova, *Mastermind: How to Think Like Sherlock Holmes* (New
     York: Penguin Books 2013), 38.
39   Joseph Heath, *Enlightenment 2.0: Restoring Sanity to Our Politics, Our
     Economy, and Our Lives* (Toronto: HarperCollins 2014), 295.
40   Robin V. Spivey, "The Devil Is in the Details: The Legal Profession as a
     Model for Authentic Dissent," *International Journal of Intelligence and
     CounterIntelligence* 22, no. 4 (2009): 632–51.
41   Ibid., 640.
42   Micah Zenko, *Red Team: How to Succeed by Thinking Like the Enemy*
     (New York: Basic Books 2015), 219.
43   Cass R. Sunstein and Reid Hastie, *Wiser: Getting beyond Groupthink to
     Make Groups Smarter* (Boston: Harvard Business Press 2015), 117.

44 "News Transcript of DoD News Briefing – Secretary Rumsfeld and Gen. Myers" (US Department of Defense, 12 February 2002), http://archive. defense.gov/Transcripts/Transcript.aspx?TranscriptID=2636.

45 University of Foreign Military and Cultural Studies (UFMCS), *The Applied Critical Thinking Handbook (Formerly the Red Team Handbook)*, 7.0, 2015, 55.

46 Ken Auletta, "A Woman's Place: Can Sheryl Sandberg Upend Silicon Valley's Male-Dominated Culture?" *New Yorker*, 11 and 18 July 2011.

47 Deborah L. Rhode and Amanda K. Packel, "Diversity on Corporate Boards: How Much Difference Does Difference Make," Harvard Law School Forum on Corporate Governance and Financial Regulation, 5 January 2015, 393, 2014, DJCL, 39, no. 2, 377–426.

48 Donald C. Clarke, "Three Concepts of the Independent Director," *Delaware Journal of Corporate Law* 32, no. 1 (2007): 75.

49 Katrin Bennhold, "Where Would We Be if Women Ran Wall Street?," *New York Times*, 1 February 2009.

50 Kevin Sullivan and Mary Jordan, "In Financial Crisis, Some Britons Note, It's the Men Who Made a Right Mess of It," *Washington Post*, 11 February 2009.

51 John Carlin, "A Nordic Revolution: The Heroines of Reykjavik," *Independent*, 20 April 2012. See also "Legislative Board Diversity," *Catalyst*, http://www.catalyst.org/legislative-board-diversity.

52 Alexandra Bosanac, "Gender-Equity 'Comply or Explain' Rules for Boards Are Working—Sort of," *Canadian Business*, 18 June 2015, http://www. canadianbusiness.com/innovation/osc-comply-and-explain-boards-torys-study/.

53 Sophia Grene and Chris Newlands, "Boards without Women Breed Scandal," *Financial Times*, 8 March 2015.

54 Rhode and Packel, "Diversity on Corporate Boards," 393–4.

55 United States Senate Permanent Subcommittee on Investigations of the Committee on Governmental Affairs, "The Role of the Board of Directors in Enron's Collapse," 8 July 2002, http://www.gpo.gov/fdsys/pkg/CPRT-107 SPRT80393/pdf/CPRT-107SPRT80393.pdf.

56 Rhode and Packel, "Diversity on Corporate Boards," 397–9.

57 Alison Cook and Christy Glass, "Do Minority Leaders Affect Corporate Practice? Analyzing the Effect of Leadership Composition on Governance and Product Development," *Strategic Organization* 13, no. 2 (2015): 117–40.

58 See generally William Langewiesche, "Columbia's Last Flight," *Atlantic Monthly* 292, no. 4 (2003): 73.

59 Roger M. Boisjoly, "Ethical Decisions – Morton Thiokol and the Space Shuttle Challenger Disaster," Online Ethics Centre, 15 May 2016, http:// www.onlineethics.org/CMS/profpractice/ppessays/thiokolshuttle.aspx.

60 Diane Vaughan, *The Challenger Launch Decision: Risky Technology, Culture, and Deviance at NASA* (Chicago: University of Chicago Press 1997), 11.

61 Malcolm Gladwell, "Blowup," Gladwell.com, 22 January 1996, http://glad well.com/blowup/.

62 Michael Cabbage and William Harwood, *Comm Check ... The Final Flight of Shuttle Columbia* (New York: Free Press 2004), 94.
63 Ibid., 91.
64 John Schwartz and Matthew L. Wald, "The Nation: NASA's Curse? 'Groupthink' Is 30 Years Old, and Still Going Strong," *New York Times*, 9 March 2003.
65 Cabbage and Harwood, "Comm Check," 106.
66 Ibid., 111.
67 *Columbia Accident Investigation Board Report*, vol. 1, 2003, 204, http://www.nasa.gov/columbia/home/CAIB_Vol1.html.
68 Cabbage and Harwood, "Comm Check," 121.
69 Ibid., 131.
70 Ibid., 134.
71 Ibid., 212.
72 Langewiesche, "Columbia's Last Flight."
73 Cabbage and Harwood, "Comm Check," 202.
74 Jim Lovell and Jeffrey Kluger, *Apollo 13* (Boston: Houghton Mifflin Harcourt 2006), 159.
75 Gene Kranz, *Failure Is Not an Option: Mission Control from Mercury to Apollo 13 and beyond* (New York: Simon and Schuster 2001), 321.
76 Lee Hutchinson, "The Audacious Rescue Plan That Might Have Saved Space Shuttle Columbia," *Ars Technica*, 1 February 2016, http://arstechnica.com/science/2016/02/the-audacious-rescue-plan-that-might-have-saved-space-shuttle-columbia/.
77 "Columbia Accident Investigation Board Report," vol. 1, 195.
78 Ibid.
79 Charlan Nemeth, Keith Brown, and John Rogers, "Devil's Advocate versus Authentic Dissent: Stimulating Quantity and Quality," *European Journal of Social Psychology* 31, no. 6 (2001): 709.
80 Vaughan, *The Challenger Launch Decision*, 417.
81 Nemeth, Brown, and Rogers, "Devil's Advocate versus Authentic Dissent," 709.
82 Ibid., 708.
83 Spivey, "The Devil Is in the Details, 633.
84 Jonah Lehrer, "Groupthink: The Brainstorming Myth," *New Yorker*, 30 January 2012.
85 Nemeth, Brown, and Rogers, "Devil's Advocate versus Authentic Dissent," 709.
86 John Stuart Mill, *The Basic Writings of John Stuart Mill: On Liberty, The Subjection of Women and Utilitarianism* (New York: Random House 2002).

CHAPTER THREE

1 Linda Bren, "Frances Oldham Kelsey: FDA Medical Reviewer Leaves Her Mark on History," *FDA Consumer* 35, no. 2 (2001): 27.
2 Frances Oldham Kelsey, "Autobiographical Reflections," 2014, 8, http://www.fda.gov/downloads/AboutFDA/WhatWeDo/History/OralHistories/SelectedOralHistoryTranscripts/UCM406132.pdf.

3 Philip J. Hilts, *Protecting America's Health: The FDA, Business, and One Hundred Years of Regulation* (New York: Alfred A. Knopf 2003), 90.

4 Kelsey, "Autobiographical Reflections," 22; Carol Ballentine, "Taste of Raspberries, Taste of Death: The 1937 Elixir Sulfanilamide Incident," *FDA Consumer Magazine*, June 1981, http://www.fda.gov/aboutfda/whatwedo/history/productregulation/sulfanilamidedisaster/default.htm.

5 Bren, "Frances Oldham Kelsey," 28.

6 Bernard Dixon, "Thalidomide," *New Scientist*, 5 October 1972.

7 Roger Williams, "The Nazis and Thalidomide: The Worst Drug Scandal of All Time," *Newsweek*, 10 September 2012. Another convicted Nazi war criminal, German chemist Otto Ambros, served as chair of the company's supervisory board in the 1970s.

8 Hilts, *Protecting America's Health*, 144.

9 Ellen Rice, "Dr. Frances Kelsey: Turning the Thalidomide Tragedy into Food and Drug Administration Reform," 2, http://www.section216.com/history/Kelsey.pdf.

10 Trent Stephens and Rock Brynner, *Dark Remedy: The Impact of Thalidomide and Its Revival as a Vital Medicine* (New York: Basic Books 2001), 14–15.

11 Kelsey, "Autobiographical Reflections," 52. See Adam Bernstein and Patricia Sullivan, "Frances Oldham Kelsey, FDA Scientist Who Kept Thalidomide off U.S. Market, Dies at 101," *Washington Post*, 7 August 2015.

12 Kelsey, "Autobiographical Reflections," 53. See also Bren, "Frances Oldham Kelsey," 1–6.

13 Stephens and Brynner, *Dark Remedy*, 49; Richard E. McFadyen, "Thalidomide in America: A Brush with Tragedy," *Clio Medica* 11, no. 2 (1976): 80.

14 Daniel Carpenter, *Reputation and Power: Organizational Image and Pharmaceutical Regulation at the FDA* (Princeton, NJ: Princeton University Press 2010), 221.

15 Ibid., 215.

16 Ibid., 267.

17 John Mulliken, "A Woman Doctor Who Would Not Be Hurried," *Life Magazine*, August 1962, 28.

18 Margaret Truman, *Women of Courage* (New York: William Morrow and Company 1976), 227.

19 McFadyen, "Thalidomide in America," 80.

20 Carpenter, *Reputation and Power*, 216.

21 Kelsey, "Autobiographical Reflections," 55.

22 Insight Team of the Sunday Times, *Suffer the Children: The Story of Thalidomide* (London: Andre Deutsch 1979), 75.

23 Robert D. McFadden, "Frances Oldham Kelsey, Who Saved U.S. Babies From Thalidomide, Dies at 101," *New York Times*, 7 August 2015.

24 Stephens and Brynner, *Dark Remedy*, 20.

25 Michael Magazanik, *Silent Shock* (Melbourne, Australia: Text Publishing 2015), 71.

26 Stephens and Brynner, *Dark Remedy*, 23.

27 Magazanik, *Silent Shock*, 89.
28 Hilts, *Protecting America's Health*, 149.
29 Katherine Dedyna, "Frances Kelsey: From Cobble Hill Tomboy to Thalidomide Hero," *Times Colonist*, 17 December 2014. See also "Frances Kelsey, Scientist – Obituary," *Telegraph*, 10 August 2015; McFadyen, "Thalidomide in America," 82; Truman, *Women of Courage*, 232.
30 Kelsey, "Autobiographical Reflections," 61–2.
31 Magazanik, *Silent Shock*, 220–1.
32 Insight Team of the Sunday Times, *Suffer the Children*, 77.
33 Kelsey, "Autobiographical Reflections," 73.
34 Ibid., 62.
35 Rice, "Dr. Frances Kelsey," 3.
36 Insight Team of the Sunday Times, *Suffer the Children*, 2.
37 Kelsey, "Autobiographical Reflections," 65. Another German doctor, Kosenowand Pfeiffer, presented a paper at a pediatric meeting in Kassel in October 1960 describing two cases of children born with gross limb malformations.
38 Magazanik, *Silent Shock*, 169.
39 Morton Mintz, "'Heroine' of FDA Keeps Bad Drug Off of Market," *Washington Post*, 15 July 1962.
40 Andrew Jack, "Pharmaceutical Groups Sued over Thalidomide," *Financial Times*, 30 October 2011. See also Magazanik, *Silent Shock*, 142.
41 Kelsey, "Autobiographical Reflections," 72.
42 Jack, "Pharmaceutical Groups Sued over Thalidomide"; Magazanik, *Silent Shock*, 142.
43 Stephens and Brynner, *Dark Remedy*, 40.
44 Mulliken, "A Woman Doctor Who Would Not Be Hurried," 29.
45 McFadyen, "Thalidomide in America," 88.
46 J.F. Kennedy, "Remarks upon Presenting the President's Awards for Distinguished Federal Civilian Service" (John F. Kennedy Presidential Library and Museum, 7 August 1962), http://www.jfklibrary.org/Asset-Viewer/Archives/JFKWHA-117-004.aspx; British Pathé, "President Kennedy Calls for Stronger Drug Laws (1962)," *YouTube*, 2014, http://www.youtube.com/watch?v=2fp5sGvCdVE.
47 Kelsey, "Autobiographical Reflections," 78.
48 Gardiner Harris, "The Public's Quiet Savior from Harmful Medicines," *New York Times*, 3 September 2010.
49 Stephens and Brynner, *Dark Remedy*, 55.
50 Lyndsey Layton, "Physician to Be Honored for Historic Decision on Thalidomide," *Washington Post*, 13 September 2010.
51 Stephens and Brynner, *Dark Remedy*, 65.
52 Ibid., 68.
53 Ingrid Peritz, "Compensation Cheques Give Thalidomide Victims a New Lease on Life," *Globe and Mail*, 16 June 2016, A12.
54 David Willman, "How a New Policy Led to Seven Deadly Drugs," *LA Times*, 20 December 2000.
55 Ibid.
56 Ibid.

57 Stephens and Brynner, *Dark Remedy*, 150.
58 Harald F. Stock, "Speech to Mark the Unveiling of Thalidomide Memorial" (Stolberg/Rhineland, Germany: Grünenthal, 31 August 2012), http://www. contergan.grunenthal.info/grt-ctg/GRT-CTG/Informacion_util_en_Espana_/ Rede_anlaesslich_Einweihung_des_Contergan-Denkmals/en_EN/224600963. jsp;jsessionid=C33AC6281732F97F050878F892FA7790.drp1.
59 "Thalidomide Maker Apologizes 50 Years after Drug Pulled," *CBC News*, 1 September 2012, http://www.cbc.ca/news/world/thalidomide-maker-apologizes-50-years-after-drug-pulled-1.1264168.
60 Magazanik, *Silent Shock*, 2.
61 "Thalidomide Apology 'Insincere,' Says Mother of Australian Victim Lynette Rowe," *Telegraph*, 1 September 2012.
62 John F. Burns, "Grünenthal Group Apologizes to Thalidomide Victims," *New York Times*, 1 September 2012.
63 Insight Team of the Sunday Times, *Suffer the Children*, 81.
64 Carpenter, *Reputation and Power*, 125–34.
65 Ibid., 249.
66 Kelsey, "Autobiographical Reflections," 99.

CHAPTER FOUR

1 *Time*, 29 March 1999. See also "Rachel Carson," PBS, 21 September 2007, http://www.pbs.org/moyers/journal/09212007/profile.html.
2 "Rachel Carson Excerpts Continued," *U.S. Fish and Wildlife Service*, http:// www.fws.gov/refuge/Rachel_Carson/about/rachelcarsonexcerpts2.html.
3 I am indebted to Linda Lear for much of the biographical information that appears in this chapter. See Linda Lear, *Rachel Carson: Witness for Nature* (Boston: Mariner Books 2009).
4 Rachel Carson, *Under the Sea Wind* (New York: Penguin Books 2007), 3.
5 Lear, *Rachel Carson*, 105.
6 Rachel Carson, *The Sea around Us* (New York: Mentor Book 1954), 45.
7 Ibid., 77.
8 Ibid., 80.
9 *EPA Journal*, November/December 1978.
10 Rachel Carson and Sue Hubbell, *The Edge of the Sea* (Boston: Houghton Mifflin Harcourt 1998), 189.
11 Karen F. Stein, *Rachel Carson: Challenging Authors* (Rotterdam: Sense Publishers 2012), 50.
12 US Environmental Protection Agency, "DDT – A Brief History and Status," http://www.epa.gov/ingredients-used-pesticide-products/ddt-brief-history-and-status.
13 "Rachel Carson Dies of Cancer; 'Silent Spring' Author Was 56," *New York Times*, 15.
14 "Rachel Carson Excerpts Continued."
15 Douglas Brinkley, "Rachel Carson and JFK, an Environmental Tag Team," *Audubon Magazine*, June 2012.
16 Nancy F. Koehn, "From Calm Leadership, Lasting Change," *New York Times*, 27 October 2012.

17 G. Fischer, "Award Ceremony Speech for Paul Müller, the Nobel Prize in Physiology or Medicine 1948," *Nobel Lectures, Physiology or Medicine 1942–1962* (Amsterdam: Elsevier Publishing Company 1964), http://www.nobelprize.org/nobel_prizes/medicine/laureates/1948/press.html.

18 Rachel Carson, *Silent Spring* (Boston: Houghton Mifflin 1994), 1–3.

19 Christopher Bosso, *Pesticides and Politics: The Life Cycle of a Public Issue* (Pittsburgh: University of Pittsburgh Press 1987), 46.

20 James Stevens Simmons, "How Magic Is DDT?" in *DDT, Silent Spring, and the Rise of Environmentalism*, ed. Thomas R. Dunlap (Seattle: University of Washington Press 2008), 38.

21 Carson, *Silent Spring*, 23.

22 Stein, *Rachel Carson*, 71.

23 For a review of the pre-*Silent Spring* literature, see Pierre Desrochers and Hiroko Shimizu, "The Intellectual Groundwaters of Silent Spring: Rethinking Rachel Carson's Place in the History of American Environmental Thought," in *Silent Spring at 50: The False Crises of Rachel Carson*, ed. Roger Meiners, Pierre Desrochers, and Andrew Morriss (Washington, D.C.: Cato Institute 2012), 37–60.

24 John F. Henahan, "Whatever Happened to the Cranberry Crisis?" *Atlantic*, March 1977.

25 David Bruser and Jayme Poisson, "A Poisoned People," *Toronto Star*, 24 July 2016.

26 John Paull, "The Rachel Carson Letters and the Making of Silent Spring," *Sage Open*, 2013, 1–12, doi:10.1177/2158244013494861.

27 Stein, *Rachel Carson*, 89.

28 *Murphy v. Butler*, 362 US 929 (1960).

29 Carson, *Silent Spring*, 6–8.

30 William Souder, *On a Farther Shore: The Life and Legacy of Rachel Carson* (New York: Crown Publishing 2012), 302.

31 Carson, *Silent Spring*, 131.

32 Larry Katzenstein, "The Precautionary Principle: Silent Spring's Toxic Legacy," in *Silent Spring at 50*, ed. Meiners, Desrochers, and Morriss, 267–8.

33 Carson, *Silent Spring*, 48.

34 Ibid., 127.

35 Ibid., 225.

36 Ibid., 237.

37 Richard Conniff, "Rachel Carson's Critics Keep on, but She Told Truth about DDT," *Yale Environment 360*, 10 September 2015, http://e360.yale.edu/feature/rachel_carsons_critics_keep_on_but_she_told_truth_about_ddt/2908/.

38 Robert Caro, "Pesticides: The Hidden Poisons, Are Spray Killers Menace to Man?" *Newsweek*, 20 August 1962.

39 Carson, *Silent Spring*, 12–13.

40 Michael Jay Friedman, "A Book That Changed a Nation," *IIP Digital*, 26 May 2008, http://iipdigital.usembassy.gov/st/english/publication/2008/06/20080602124122eaifaso.7619854.html#axzz4QTnqGLR9.

41 Brinkley, "Rachel Carson and JFK, an Environmental Tag Team."
42 Ibid.
43 Mark Hamilton Lytle, *The Gentle Subversive: Rachel Carson, Silent Spring, and the Rise of the Environmental Movement* (Oxford: Oxford University Press 2007), 164.
44 Friedman, "A Book That Changed a Nation."
45 Brinkley, "Rachel Carson and JFK, an Environmental Tag Team."
46 John M. Lee, "Silent Spring Is Now Noisy Summer," *New York Times*, 22 July 1962.
47 Lorus Milne and Margery Milne, "There's Poison All around Us Now," *New York Times*, 23 September 1962.
48 Thomas R. Dunlap, *DDT: Scientists, Citizens, and Public Policy* (Princeton, NJ: Princeton University Press 1981), 161.
49 Stein, *Rachel Carson*, 93.
50 I.L. Baldwin, "Review: Chemicals and Pests," *Science* 137, no. 3535 (1962): 1042–3.
51 See, for example, Eli Lehrer, "The Church of Rachel Carson," *Competitive Enterprise Institute*, 11 June 2007, http://cei.org/op-eds-and-articles/church-rachel-carson. See also Joni Seager, *Carson's Silent Spring: A Reader's Guide* (London: Bloomsbury Publishing 2014), 164.
52 Lear, *Rachel Carson*, 462.
53 "Bill Moyers Journal" (PBS, 21 September 2007), http://www.pbs.org/moyers/journal/09212007/transcript1.html.
54 Lytle, *The Gentle Subversive*, 134.
55 Souder, *On a Farther Shore*, 15.
56 Ibid., 347.
57 Seager, *Carson's Silent Spring*.
58 Arlene Rodda Quaratiello, *Rachel Carson: A Biography* (Amherst, NY: Prometheus Books 2010), 86.
59 See generally Michael Smith, "'Silence Miss Carson!': Science, Gender, and the Reception of Silent Spring," in *Rachel Carson*, ed. Sideris and Moore, 168–87.
60 Priscilla Coit Murphy, *What a Book Can Do: The Publication and Reception of Silent Spring* (Amherst, MA: University of Massachusetts Press 2005), 106.
61 Souder, *On a Farther Shore*, 378.
62 Murray Bookchin, *Our Synthetic Environment* (New York: Harper and Row 1974).
63 Lytle, *The Gentle Subversive*, 161.
64 Carson, *Silent Spring*, 272–3.
65 President's Science Advisory Committee, Washington, D.C., Government Printing Office 1963. See also Frank Graham, Jr, *Since Silent Spring* (Boston: Houghton Mifflin Company 1970), 77–9.
66 Lear, *Rachel Carson*, 464.
67 LaMont C. Cole, "Rachel Carson's Indictment of the Wide Use of Pesticides," *Scientific American* 207, no. 12 (1962): 172–80.
68 "Rachel Carson," *Wikiquote*, http://en.wikiquote.org/wiki/Rachel_Carson.
69 Friedman, "A Book That Changed a Nation."

70   Margaret Atwood, "Rachel Carson's Silent Spring, 50 Years on," *Guardian*, 7 December 2012.
71   See Dunlap, *DDT*.
72   Bosso, *Pesticides and Politics: The Life Cycle of a Public Issue*, 141.
73   Richard Morrison, "Rachel Carson Lied, Millions Died," *Competitive Enterprise Institute*, 22 September 2006, http://cei.org/blog/rachel-carson-lied-millions-died.
74   J. Gordon Edwards, "The Lies of Rachel Carson," *21st Century Science and Technology Magazine*, http://www.21stcenturysciencetech.com/articles/summ02/Carson.html.
75   Keith Lockitch, "Rachel Carson's Genocide," Ayn Rand Institute, 23 May 2007, http://ari.aynrand.org/issues/science-and-industrialization/environmental-issues/Rachel-Carsons-Genocide.
76   Henry Miller and Gregory Conko, "Rachel Carson's Deadly Fantasies," *Forbes Magazine*, 5 September 2012.
77   Eliza Griswold, "How 'Silent Spring' Ignited the Environmental Movement," *New York Times Magazine*, 21 September 2012.
78   Thomas Sowell, "Intended Consequences," *Townhall*, 7 June 2001, http://townhall.com/columnists/thomassowell/2001/06/07/intended_consequences
79   Lisa Makson, "Rachel Carson's Ecological Genocide – Hitler, Stalin, Pol Pot … Rachel Carson," *Free Republic*, 31 July 2003, http://www.freerepublic.com/focus/f-news/955667/posts.
80   Tina Rosenberg, "What the World Needs Now Is DDT," *New York Times Magazine*, 11 April 2004.
81   "DDT Should Be Phased out of Use and Ultimately Banned," *WWF*, http://wwf.panda.org/about_our_earth/teacher_resources/webfieldtrips/toxics/our_chemical_world/ddt/.
82   Richard Tren, "How Environmentalists Opened the Door for Zika," *The Federalist*, 24 May 2016, http://thefederalist.com/2016/05/24/how-environmentalists-opened-the-door-for-zika/.
83   World Health Organization, "The Use of DDT in Malaria Vector Control: WHO Position Statement" (Global Malaria Programme, 2011), http://www.who.int/malaria/publications/atoz/who_htm_gmp_2011/en/
84   Rosenberg, "What the World Needs Now Is DDT."
85   Charles F. Wurster, *DDT Wars: Rescuing Our National Bird, Preventing Cancer, and Creating the Environmental Defense Fund* (New York: Oxford University Press 2015), 162.
86   May Berenbaum, "If Malaria's the Problem, DDT's Not the Only Answer," *Washington Post*, 5 June 2005.
87   *Rachel Carson*, ed. Sideris and Moore, 143.
88   "Rachel Carson Excerpts Continued."
89   Gerald Sirkin and Natalie Sirkin, " DDT, Fraud, and Tragedy," *American Spectator*, 25 February 2005, http://spectator.org/48925_ddt-fraud-and-tragedy/.
90   Roddy Scheer and Doug Moss, "How Important Was Rachel Carson's Silent Spring in the Recovery of Bald Eagles and Other Bird Species?" *EarthTalk, Scientific American*.
91   A.G. Smith, "How Toxic Is DDT?" *The Lancet* 356, no. 9226 (2000): 268.

92 World Health Organization, "The Use of DDT in Malaria Vector Control."

93 "A Useful Poison," *Economist*, 14 December 2000.

94 Keith Lockitch, "Reject Environmentalism, Not DDT" (Ayn Rand Institute, 19 September 2006), http://ari.aynrand.org/issues/science-and-industrialization/environmental-issues/Reject-Environmentalism-Not-DDT

95 US Environmental Protection Agency, "DDT."

96 Lindsey Konkel, "DDT Linked to Fourfold Increase in Breast Cancer Risk," *National Geographic*, 16 June 2015.

97 Jacob Koffler, "DDT, Lindane Can Cause Cancer, WHO Says," *Time*, 23 June 2015.

98 Stein, *Rachel Carson*, 87.

99 President's Cancer Panel, "Reducing Environmental Cancer Risk: What We Can Do Now," April 2010, http://deainfo.nci.nih.gov/advisory/pcp/annual Reports/pcp08-09rpt/PCP_Report_08-09_508.pdf

100 Murphy, *What a Book Can Do*, 98.

101 Quaratiello, *Rachel Carson*, 141.

102 Tim Radford, "Do Trees Pollute the Atmosphere?" *Guardian*, 13 May 2004.

103 Carson, *Silent Spring*, xxi.

104 "Hiss of Doom?" *Newsweek*, 6 August 1962.

105 Carson, *Silent Spring*, 8.

106 William P. Kabasenche and Michael K. Skinner, "DDT, Epigenetic Harm, and Transgenerational Environmental Justice," *Environmental Health* 13, no. 64 (2014).

107 Carson, *Silent Spring*, 13.

108 Ibid., 127.

109 Stein, *Rachel Carson*, 103.

110 Murphy, *What a Book Can Do*, 14.

111 Ibid., 87.

CHAPTER FIVE

1 Albert W. Alschuler and Andrew G. Deiss, "A Brief History of the Criminal Jury in the United States," *University of Chicago Law Review* 61, no. 3 (1994): 867–928.

2 Harry Kalven and Hans Zeisel, *The American Jury* (Boston: Little, Brown and Company 1966), 287.

3 *R. v. Latimer*, 134 Sask. R. 1 (1995), 31.

4 Nicole L. Waters and Valerie P. Hans, "A Jury of One: Opinion Formation, Conformity, and Dissent on Juries," *Journal of Empirical Legal Studies* 6, no. 3 (2009): 537.

5 Ibid., 539.

6 Ibid., 516.

7 Kalven and Zeisel, *The American Jury*, 453.

8 Ibid., 434–5. On the historical background, see Thomas Andrew Green, *Verdict according to Conscience: Perspectives on the English Criminal Trial Jury, 1200–1800* (Chicago: University of Chicago Press 1985).

9 *R. v. Krieger*, 2 SCR 501 (2006), para. 27.

10 Ronald H. Spector, "Vietnam War," *Encyclopaedia Britannica*, http://www.britannica.com/event/Vietnam-War.

11 Michael Singer, *Jury Duty: Reclaiming Your Political Power and Taking Responsibility* (Santa Barbara, CA: Praeger 2012), 80.

12 Magazanik, *Silent Shock*, 192.

13 Mark Fuhrman, *Murder in Brentwood* (Washington, DC: Regnery Publishing 1997), 253.

14 Ibid., xiv; Jeffrey Toobin, *The Run of His Life: The People v. O.J. Simpson* (New York: Random House Trade Paperbacks 2015), 421.

15 Paul Burstein, "Jury Nullification in Canadian Political Protest Trials: Turning Loose the '12 Angry Men,'" in *Putting the State on Trial*, ed. Margaret E. Beare, Nathalie Des Rosiers, and Abigail C. Deshman (Vancouver: UBC Press 2015), 241–63.

16 Douglas L. Keene and Rita R. Handrich, "The Dark Side of the Internet: In the Jury Room" (Boston, 9 October 2009), http://www.keenetrial.com/articles_15_2510325171.pdf.

17 *A.G. of Canada v. Lavell*, SCR 1349 (1974), 1386.

18 Ibid.

19 See Pernille Jakobsen, "Murdoch v. Murdoch: Feminism, Property and the Prairie Farm in the 1970s," in *Place and Replace: Essays on Western Canada*, ed. Esyllt Wynne Jones, Adele Perry, and Leah Morton (Winnipeg: University of Manitoba Press 2013), 40–58.

20 *Murdoch v. Murdoch*, 1 SCR 423 (1975), 439.

21 Philip Girard, *Bora Laskin: Bringing Law to Life* (Toronto: University of Toronto Press 2005), 400.

22 *Eves v. Eves*, 1 WLR 1338 (1975).

23 Susan Machum, "A Rural Woman's Impact on Canadian Feminist Practice and Theory," in *Feminisms and Ruralities*, ed. Barbara Pini, Berit Brandth, and Jo Little (Lanham, MD: Lexington Books 2015), 37.

24 J. Louis Campbell, "The Spirit of Dissent," *Judicature* 66, no. 7 (1983): 310.

25 Suzanne Zwarun, "Farm Wives 10 Years after Irene Murdoch," *Chatelaine* 59 (1983): 176–82.

26 Melvin I. Urofsky, *Dissent and the Supreme Court: Its Role in the Court's History and the Nation's Constitutional Dialogue* (New York: Pantheon Books 2015), 118.

27 Mark V. Tushnet, ed., *I Dissent: Great Opposing Opinions in Landmark Supreme Court Cases* (Boston: Beacon Press 2008), 69–80.

28 For a discussion on this case, see Urofsky, *Dissent and the Supreme Court*, 117–26.

29 Ibid., 4.

30 Ibid., 105.

31 Ibid., 122.

32 Ibid., 126.

33 Earl Warren, *The Memoirs of Earl Warren* (Garden City, NY: Doubleday 1977), 291.

34 *Brown v. Board of Education*, 347 US 483 (1954), 494.

35 Antonin Scalia, "The Dissenting Opinion," *Journal of Supreme Court History* 19, no. 1 (1994): 35.

36 Warren, *The Memoirs of Earl Warren*, 289.

37 Hughes, *The Supreme Court of the United States*, 67–8.

38 Urofsky, *Dissent and the Supreme Court*, 12.

39 William J. Brennan, Jr., "In Defense of Dissents," *Hastings Law Journal* 37 (1985): 429.

40 Joan Didion, "Why I Write," *The New York Times Magazine*, 5 December 1976; George Orwell, "Why I Write," *Gangrel*, June 1946.

41 *Burnet v. Coronado Oil & Gas Co.*, 285 US 393 (1932), 405–10.

42 Alan Barth, *Prophets with Honor: Great Dissents and Great Dissenters in the Supreme Court* (New York: Alfred A. Knopf 1974), 15.

43 Ruth Bader Ginsburg, "The Role of Dissenting Opinions," *Minnesota Law Review* 95 (2010): 3.

44 Urofsky, *Dissent and the Supreme Court*, 407–8.

45 *Edwards v. the Attorney General of Canada*, AC 124 (1930), 9.

46 *Minersville School Dist. v. Gobitis*, 310 US 586 (1940), 607.

47 *West Virginia Bd. of Ed. v. Barnette*, 319 US 624 (1943), 638.

48 This section is derived from William Kaplan, *State and Salvation: The Jehovah's Witnesses and Their Fight for Civil Rights* (Toronto: University of Toronto Press 1989), 146–58.

49 Urofsky, *Dissent and the Supreme Court*, 231.

50 Ibid., 246.

51 Campbell, "The Spirit of Dissent," 311.

52 Ibid.

53 Donald R. Songer, John Szmer, and Susan W. Johnson, "Explaining Dissent on the Supreme Court of Canada," *Canadian Journal of Political Science* 44, no. 2 (2011): 409.

54 Claire L'Heureux-Dubé, "The Dissenting Opinion: Voice of the Future," *Osgoode Hall Law Journal* 38 (2000): 512.

55 Rebecca Johnson and Marie-Claire Belleau, "Judicial Dissent at the Supreme Court of Canada: Integrating Qualitative and Quantitative Empirical Approaches," in *1st Annual Conference on Empirical Legal Studies*, 2006, http://papers.ssrn.com/sol3/papers.cfm?abstract_id=913373.

56 L'Heureux-Dubé, "The Dissenting Opinion: Voice of the Future," 498.

57 Diane P. Wood, "When to Hold, When to Fold, and When to Reshuffle: The Art of Decisionmaking on a Multi-Member Court," *California Law Review* 100, no. 6 (2012): 1453.

58 Brennan, "In Defense of Dissents," 437.

59 Ibid., 435.

60 Ibid.

61 Scalia, "The Dissenting Opinion," 35.

62 Tony Mauro, "Scalia's Law Clerks Find New Homes With Alito, Thomas," *National Law Journal*, 5 April 2016, http://www.nationallawjournal.com/id=1202754108060/Scalias-Law-Clerks-Find-New-Homes-With-Alito-Thomas.

63 Adam Liptak, "In Dissents, Sonia Sotomayor Takes on the Criminal Justice System," *New York Times*, 4 July 2016.

64 Irin Carmon and Shana Knizhnik, *Notorious RBG: The Life and Times of Ruth Bader Ginsburg* (New York: HarperCollins 2015), 3.

65 Linda Hirshman, *Sisters in Law: How Sandra Day O'Connor and Ruth Bader Ginsburg Went to the Supreme Court and Changed the World* (New York: HarperCollins 2015), 288.

CHAPTER SIX

1 Thank you to Julian Sher and his excellent book *Until You Are Dead* (Toronto: Vintage 2002), the source from which, along with the Ontario Court of Appeal's Truscott reference, much of the following section is drawn.

2 Ibid., 13.

3 Ibid., 64.

4 Ibid., 60.

5 Ibid., 75.

6 Ibid., 82.

7 Ibid., 145.

8 Ibid., 141.

9 See generally Isabel LeBourdais, *The Trial of Steven Truscott* (New York: Popular Library 1966), 74.

10 Sher, *Until You Are Dead*, 211.

11 *Truscott (Re)*, ONCA 575 (2007), para. 693.

12 Ibid., para. 715.

13 *Reference Re: Steven Murray Truscott*, SCR 309 (1967), 388.

14 Sher, *Until You Are Dead*, 245.

15 *Reference Re: Steven Murray Truscott*, SCR 309 (1967), 392.

16 LeBourdais, *The Trial of Steven Truscott*, 192.

17 *Reference Re: Steven Murray Truscott*, SCR 309 (1967), 403.

18 Ibid., 406–7.

19 Sher, *Until You Are Dead*, 256.

20 LeBourdais, *The Trial of Steven Truscott*, 206.

21 Barry Ruhl, *A Viable Suspect* (Victoria: FriesenPress 2014), 34.

22 Sher, *Until You Are Dead*, 214.

23 LeBourdais, *The Trial of Steven Truscott*, 205.

24 Ibid., 46.

25 Ibid., 221.

26 Bill Trent, *The Steven Truscott Story* (Markham, ON: Paperjacks 1971), 31.

27 Sher, *Until You Are Dead*, 270.

28 Ibid., 97.

29 Ruhl, *A Viable Suspect*, 117.

30 For the case against Talbot, see Ruhl, *A Viable Suspect*.

31 Sher, *Until You Are Dead*, 304.

32 Garrett Wilson and Kevin Charles Wilson, *Diefenbaker for the Defence* (Toronto: James Lorimer and Company 1988).

33 Barbara Meadowcroft, *Gwethalyn Graham (1913–65): A Liberated Woman in a Conventional Age* (Toronto: Canadian Scholars Press 2008), 181.

34 Julien LeBourdais, interview with author, 11 December 2016.

35 James King, *Jack: A Life with Writers: The Story of Jack McClelland* (Toronto: Alfred A. Knopf Canada 1999), 181.

36 Ibid., 182.

37 Sher, *Until You Are Dead*, 363.

38 Ibid., 364.

39 Ibid., 366.

40 Martin Friedland, "Searching for Truth in the Criminal Justice System," *Criminal Law Quarterly* 60 (2014): 519.

41 Trent, *The Steven Truscott Story*, 126.

42 Sher, *Until You Are Dead*, 397.

43 The relevant portions of the transcript of the cross-examination are in Fred Kaufman, *Searching for Justice: An Autobiography* (Toronto: Osgoode Society for Canadian Legal History/University of Toronto Press 2005), 310–12.

44 See "Steven Truscott – His Word Against History" (CBC, *the fifth estate*, 29 March 2000), http://www.cbc.ca/fifth/episodes/40-years-of-the-fifth-estate/steven-truscott-his-word-against-history.

45 *Reference Re: Steven Murray Truscott*, SCR 309 (1967), 321.

46 Ibid., 367.

47 Ibid., 327.

48 Frederick Vaughan, "Emmett M. Hall: A Profile of the Judicial Temperament," *Osgoode Hall Law Journal* 15 (1977): 308–10.

49 Ibid., 315.

50 See generally Frederick Vaughan, "Emmett Matthew Hall: The Activist as Justice," *Osgoode Hall Law Journal* 10 (1972): 411.

51 *Reference Re: Steven Murray Truscott*, SCR 309 (1967), 383.

52 Ibid., 389.

53 Ibid., 364.

54 Ibid., 390.

55 Ibid., 400.

56 Ibid., 384.

57 Ibid., 400.

58 Ibid., 404.

59 Ibid., 406.

60 Ibid., 412.

61 Kaufman, *Searching for Justice*, 312.

62 E-mail from John Wedge to Martin Friedland, shared with permission with the author, 27 July 2016.

63 Vaughan, "Emmett Matthew Hall," 422.

64 Dennis Gruending, *Emmett Hall: Establishment Radical* (Toronto: Macmillan of Canada 1985), 148.

65 Sher, *Until You Are Dead*, 447.

66 See Ed Ratushny, *The Conduct of Public Inquiries* (Toronto: Irwin Law 2009), 67–85.

67 Sher, *Until You Are Dead*, 501.

68 The Karen Daum statement was disclosed to Truscott's lawyers in advance of the Supreme Court of Canada reference, and she was not called to testify. There is reason to believe that Martin interviewed her. She was not called, possibly because she had changed her story from her first statement, as she did when called to testify at the Truscott Reference. The Ontario Court of Appeal, however, rejected her new version of events as defying "common sense" (*Truscott [Re]*, ONCA 575 [2007], para. 718). It relied instead on her original statement.

69 Sher, *Until You Are Dead*, 540. See also Kaufman, *Searching for Justice*, 307–18.

70 *Boucher v. the Queen*, SCR 16 (1955), 23–4.

71 See generally Ed Ratushny, "Is There a Right against Self-Incrimination in Canada," *McGill Law Journal* 19 (1973).
72 Kaufman, *Searching for Justice*, 307.
73 Frederick Vaughan, *Aggressive in Pursuit: The Life of Justice Emmett Hall* (Toronto: Osgoode Society for Canadian Legal History/University of Toronto Press 2004), 210.
74 *Truscott (Re)*, ONCA 575 (2007), para. 3.
75 Ibid., para. 21.
76 Roy McMurtry, *Memoirs and Reflections* (Toronto: University of Toronto Press 2013), 475.
77 Jason Michael Chin, "What Irreproducible Results Mean for the Law of Scientific Evidence," *Advocates' Journal*, 35, no. 1 (2016): 17–20.
78 Ratushny, *The Conduct of Public Inquiries*, 81.
79 *Truscott (Re)*, ONCA 575 (2007), para. 287.
80 *R. v. Stinchcombe*, 3 SCR 326 (1991).
81 Ibid.
82 Bill Swan, *Real Justice: Fourteen and Sentenced to Death: The Story of Steven Truscott* (Toronto: James Lorimer and Company 2012), 7–8.

CHAPTER SEVEN

1 Amy Goodman, *Democracy Now!* (New York: Simon and Schuster 2016), 172.
2 L.A. Kauffman, "The Theology of Consensus," in *Occupy! Scenes from Occupied America*, ed. Astra Taylor (New York: Verso Books 2011), 46.
3 Ellen Freudenheim, "Spain's 15 Mayo Protests: What Will It Mean for U.S. Youth Election Year Activism?" *Huffington Post*, 10 August 2011.
4 Raphael Minder, "Spanish Upstart Party Said It Could, and Did. Now the Hard Part Begins," *New York Times*, 29 May 2014.
5 Appropriated, of course, from Paris 1968. See Kalle Lasn, *Culture Jam* (New York: HarperCollins 2000), 121.
6 "AdBusters: The Inside Story," *Realfuture.org*, n.d., http://www.realfuture.org/wordpress/?p=372.
7 Lasn, *Culture Jam*, 24.
8 Mattathias Schwartz, "Pre-Occupied: The Origins and Future of Occupy Wall Street," *New Yorker*, 26 November 2011.
9 Micah White, *The End of Protest* (New York: Alfred A. Knopf Canada 2016), 13.
10 Ibid.
11 "#OCCUPYWALLSTREET," Adbusters Culturejammer Headquarters, 13 July 2011, http://web.archive.org/web/20110717094726/http://www.adbusters.org/blogs/adbusters-blog/occupywallstreet.html.
12 White, *The End of Protest*, 15.
13 See generally Chrystia Freeland, *Plutocrats: The New Golden Age* (Toronto: Doubleday Canada 2012), 34. Also see Matthew Desmond, *Evicted* (New York: Crown, 2016).
14 Goodman, *Democracy Now!*, 168.
15 These are the numbers for Canada for 2011. See "Individuals by Total Income Level, by Province and Territory," Statistics Canada, 2015, http://

www.statcan.gc.ca/tables-tableaux/sum-som/l01/cst01/famil105a-eng.htm;
"Who Are Canada's Top 1%?," CBC News, 13 September 2013, http://www.
cbc.ca/news/canada/who-are-canada-s-top-1-1.1703321.

16 Freeland, *Plutocrats*, xiii.

17 Timothy Noah, *The Great Divergence: America's Growing Inequality Crisis
and What We Can Do about It* (London: Bloomsbury Publishing 2012), 4.

18 Joseph E. Stiglitz, "Of the 1%, by the 1%, for the 1%," *Vanity Fair*, March
2011.

19 David Graeber, "On Playing by the Rules – The Strange Success of #Occupy
WallStreet," *Naked Capitalism*, 19 October 2011, http://www.naked
capitalism.com/2011/10/david-graeber-on-playing-by-the-rules—-the-strange-
success-of-occupy-wall-street.html.

20 Andy Kroll, "How Occupy Wall Street Really Got Started," *Mother Jones*,
17 October 2011.

21 Nathan Schneider, "Occupy Wall Street: FAQ," *The Nation*, 29 September
2011.

22 AnonOps, "Occupy Wall Street – Sept. 17," *YouTube*, 30 August 2011,
http://www.youtube.com/watch?v=zSpM2kieMu8.

23 White, *The End of Protest*, 19.

24 Jonathan Massey and Brett Snyder, "Occupying Wall Street: Spaces of
Political Action," *Places Journal*, September 2012, http://placesjournal.
org/article/occupying-wall-street-places-and-spaces-of-political-action/.

25 White, *The End of Protest*, 29.

26 Colin Moynihan, "Officials Cast Wide Net in Monitoring Occupy Protests,"
New York Times, 22 May 2014. See also Naomi Wolf, "Revealed: How
the FBI Coordinated the Crackdown on Occupy," *Guardian*, 29 December
2012.

27 USLAWdotcom, "NYPD Police Pepper Spray Occupy Wall Street Protesters
(Anthony Balogna)," *YouTube*, 24 September 2011, http://www.youtube.
com/watch?v=TZo5rWx1pig.

28 Todd Gitlin, *Occupy Nation: The Roots, the Spirit, and the Promise of
Occupy Wall Street* (New York: Harper Collins 2012), 23.

29 Chris Moody, "How Republicans Are Being Taught to Talk about Occupy
Wall Street," *Yahoo! News*, 1 December 2011, http://www.yahoo.com/
news/blogs/ticket/republicans-being-taught-talk-occupy-wall-street-133707
949.html.

30 Freeland, *Plutocrats*, 250.

31 Brian Stelter, "Protest Puts Coverage in Spotlight," *New York Times*, 20
November 2011.

32 Ibid.

33 David Brooks, "The Milquetoast Radicals," *New York Times*, 10 October
2011.

34 Bernie Farber and Len Rudner, "Selling Anti-Semitism in the Book Stores,"
National Post, 22 October 2010.

35 Jeff Sommer, "The War against Too Much of Everything," *New York Times*,
22 December 2012.

36 "Samuel Gompers," *Wikiquote*, http://en.wikiquote.org/wiki/Samuel_
Gompers.

37 Erik Eckholm and Timothy Williams, "Anti-Wall Street Protests Spreading to Cities Large and Small," *New York Times*, 3 October 2011.
38 "Adbusters Founders Cheer Their Occupy Idea," CBC News, 14 October 2011, http://www.cbc.ca/news/canada/adbusters-founders-cheer-their-occupy-idea-1.1063405.
39 Graeber, "On Playing by the Rules."
40 George Packer, "All the Angry People," *New Yorker*, 5 December 2011.
41 Taylor, ed., *Occupy!* 25, quoting from Marco Roth, "Letters of Resignation from the American Dream."
42 Paul Krugman, "Oligarchy, American Style," *New York Times*, 3 November 2011.
43 Ibid.
44 Massey and Snyder, "Occupying Wall Street."
45 Victoria Carty, *Social Movements and New Technology* (Boulder, CO: Westview Press 2015), 141–2.
46 P.J. O'Rourke, "Are the Peasants Revolting?" *World Affairs* 174, no. 5 (2012): 6.
47 Winnie Ng and Salmaan Khan, "The Year of the Occupy Movement: Imperfect Yet Powerful Acts of Love," *Canadian Social Work Review* 29, no. 2 (2012): 269.
48 Ibid., 268–9.
49 Mark Engler and Paul Engler, *This Is an Uprising* (New York: Nation Books 2016), 144.
50 "News Conference by the President" (White House Archives, Barack Obama, 6 October 2011), http://www.whitehouse.gov/the-press-office/2011/10/06/news-conference-president.
51 "Remarks by the President on the Economy in Osawatomie, Kansas" (White House Archives, Barack Obama, 6 December 2011), http://www.whitehouse.gov/the-press-office/2011/12/06/remarks-president-economy-osawatomie-kansas.
52 "Remarks by the President in State of the Union Address" (White House Archives, Barack Obama, 24 January 2012), http://www.whitehouse.gov/the-press-office/2012/01/24/remarks-president-state-union-address.
53 NYC General Assembly, "Declaration of the Occupation of New York City," *Yes Magazine*, 4 October 2011, http://www.yesmagazine.org/people-power/declaration-of-the-occupation-of-new-york-city.
54 Nathan Schneider, *Thank You, Anarchy* (Berkeley and Los Angeles: University of California Press 2013), 80.
55 Massey and Snyder, "Occupying Wall Street."
56 Keith Gessen, "Laundry Day," in *Occupy!* ed. Taylor, 198–200.
57 Mark Greif, "Drumming in Circles," in *Occupy!* ed. Taylor, 57. See also Gessen, "Laundry Day," 205–6.
58 Keith Gessen, Astra Taylor, and Sarah Resnick, "Scenes from an Occupation," in *Occupy!* ed. Taylor, 53.
59 David Greenberg, "Why Liberals Need Occupy Wall Street, and Vice-Versa," *New Republic*, 19 October 2011.
60 Ibid.

61 Meredith Hoffman, "Protesters Debate What Demands, If Any, to Make," *New York Times*, 16 October 2011.

62 Ibid.

63 Sira Lazar, "Occupy Wall Street: Interview with Micah White from Adbusters," *Huffington Post*, 7 October 2011.

64 Laura Beeston, "The Ballerina and the Bull," *The Link*, 11 October 2011.

65 Justin Elliott, "The Origins of Occupy Wall Street Explained," *Salon*, 4 October 2011.

66 Michael Greenberg, "In Zuccotti Park," *New York Review of Books*, 10 November 2011.

67 Cara Buckley, "200 Are Arrested as Protesters Clash with the Police," *New York Times*, 17 November 2011.

68 Gitlin, *Occupy Nation*, 89.

69 Astra Taylor and Sarah Resnick, "Rumors," in *Occupy!* ed. Taylor, 190.

70 Engler and Engler, *This Is an Uprising*, 147.

71 Grant Munroe, "Review: Micah White's *The End of Protest* Is Brimming with Messianic Confidence, yet Fails to Deliver," *Globe and Mail*, 25 March 2016.

72 "Statement of Mayor Michael R. Bloomberg on Clearing and Re-Opening of Zuccotti Park," Nyc.gov, 15 November 2011, http://www1.nyc.gov/office-of-the-mayor/news/410-11/statement-mayor-michael-bloomberg-clearing-re-opening-zuccotti-park.

73 James Barron and Colin Moynihan, "City Reopens Park after Protesters Are Evicted," *New York Times*, 15 November 2011.

74 Schneider, *Thank You, Anarchy*, 102.

75 Schwartz, "Pre-Occupied," 2–13.

76 Chris Hedges, "The Cancer in Occupy," *Truth Dig*, 6 February 2012, http://www.truthdig.com/report/item/the_cancer_of_occupy_20120206.

77 O'Rourke, "Are the Peasants Revolting?" 7.

78 Schwartz, "Pre-Occupied."

79 Joseph Goldstein, "Sharp Response Meets Return of Protesters," *New York Times*, 19 March 2012.

80 Ibid.

81 Schneider, *Thank You, Anarchy*, 169.

82 Micah White, "Letter to The People: Two Principles of Our War," Occupy Wall Street, http://occupywallstreet.net/story/letter-people-two-principles-our-war.

83 Ibid.

84 White, *The End of Protest*, 2.

85 Ibid.

86 Ibid., 38–9.

87 Schneider, *Thank You, Anarchy*, 163.

88 "Adbusters Founders Cheer Their Occupy Idea."

89 Ibid.

90 Andrew Ross Sorkin, "Occupy Wall Street: A Frenzy That Fizzled," *New York Times*, 17 September 2012.

91 Malcolm Gladwell, "Small Change," *New Yorker*, 4 October 2010.

92 Ibid.
93 Heath, *Enlightenment 2.0*, 17.
94 Saul Alinsky, *Rules for Radicals* (New York: Random Books 1989), 3.
95 Judith Butler, "Bodies in Public," in *Occupy!* ed. Taylor, 193.
96 Noah, *The Great Divergence*, 165.
97 Carty, *Social Movements and New Technology*, 150.
98 "The Mayor Confronts the Protesters," *New York Times*, 15 November 2011.
99 Joseph Stiglitz et al., "Rewriting the Rules of the American Economy," Roosevelt Institute, 12 May 2015, http://rooseveltinstitute.org/rewriting-rules-report/.
100 Schneider, *Thank You, Anarchy*, 16.
101 Wendi Pickerel, Helena Jorgensen, and Lance Bennett, "Culture Jams and Meme Warfare: Kalle Lasn, Adbusters, and Media Activism," Center for Communication and Civic Engagement, 2002, http://ccce.com.washington.edu/projects/cultureJamming.html.
102 Conrad Black, "The Genius of Donald Trump," *National Post*, 22 July 2016.
103 Freeland, *Plutocrats*, 251–2.
104 Stiglitz, "Of the 1%, by the 1%, for the 1%."

CHAPTER EIGHT

1 John Ivison, "How Stephen Harper Learned to Love the Omnibus Bill," *National Post*, 3 May 2012.
2 Lawrence Martin, *Harperland: The Politics of Control* (Toronto: Penguin Canada 2010), 210.
3 Campbell Clark, "Stockwell Day Cites 'Alarming' Rise in Unreported Crime to Justify New Prisons," *Globe and Mail*, 3 August 2010.
4 Donald Gutstein, *Harperism: How Stephen Harper and His Think Tank Colleagues Have Transformed Canada* (Toronto: James Lorimer and Company 2014), 174.
5 Aaron Wherry, "The Complicated Nature of Statistics," *Maclean's*, 29 June 2012.
6 Sean Fine, "Jody Wilson-Raybould Holds Private Meeting on Legal-System Reform," *Globe and Mail*, 31 July 2016.
7 See, for example, Benjamin Perrin, "Dissent from within at the Supreme Court of Canada: 2015 Year in Review," Macdonald-Laurier Institute, 2016, http://www.macdonaldlaurier.ca/dissent-from-within-at-the-supreme-court-of-canada-2015-year-in-review-by-benjamin-perrin/.
8 Joan Bryden, "Justice Department Chops Research Budget by $1.2M, Tightens Control over Subject Matter," *Ipolitics*, 11 May 2014, http://ipolitics.ca/2014/05/11/justice-department-chops-research-budget-by-1-2m-tightens-control-over-subject-matter/.
9 Anthony N. Doob and Cheryl Marie Webster, "Sentence Severity and Crime: Accepting the Null Hypothesis," *Crime and Justice* 30 (2003): 143–95.
10 Anthony N. Doob and Cheryl Marie Webster, "Weathering the Storm? Testing Long-Standing Canadian Sentencing Policy in the Twenty-First Century," *Crime and Justice* 45, no. 1 (2016): 400–1.
11 Mark Bourrie, *Kill the Messengers* (Toronto: HarperCollins 2015), 139.
12 Ibid., 141.
13 Ibid., 123.

14 Chris Turner, *The War on Science* (Vancouver: Greystone Books 2013), 21.

15 Gloria Galloway, "Clement Says He Won't Criticize Liberal Move to Reinstate Long-Form Census," *Globe and Mail*, 5 November 2015.

16 "The Census: Little Knowledge Is a Dangerous Thing," *Globe and Mail*, 3 February 2015.

17 Kathleen Harris, "Mandatory Long-Form Census Restored by New Liberal Government," CBC News, 5 November 2015, http://www.cbc.ca/news/politics/canada-liberal-census-data-1.3305271.

18 "Decision to Scrap Long-Form Census Ignites Controversy," CTV News, 19 July 2010, http://www.ctvnews.ca/decision-to-scrap-long-form-census-ignites-controversy-1.533879.

19 John Ibbitson, *Stephen Harper* (Toronto: McClelland and Stewart 2015), 300.

20 Ibid., 302.

21 See Christian Nadeau, *Rogue in Power: Why Stephen Harper Is Remaking Canada by Stealth* (Toronto: James Lorimer and Company 2011), 48–53.

22 "When Building Gazebos Violates the Public Trust," *Globe and Mail*, 9 June 2011.

23 "Death of Evidence: Changes to Canadian Science Raise Questions That the Government Must Answer," *Nature* 487, no. 7407 (2012): 271–3.

24 Maude Barlow, "Water, Water, Clean Water – but Not Everywhere," in *Canada after Harper*, ed. Ed Finn (Toronto: James Lorimer and Company 2015), 54–5.

25 David Naylor, personal communication with author, 16 August 2016.

26 James L. Turk, "Science under Siege," in *Canada after Harper*, ed. Finn, 343.

27 "National Research Council to 'Refocus' to Serve Business," CBC News, 6 March 2012, http://www.cbc.ca/news/technology/national-research-council-to-refocus-to-serve-business-1.1216848.

28 Mia Rabson, "NRC Staff Enraged by Gift Cards," *Winnipeg Free Press*, 5 July 2012.

29 Tom Spears, "NRC's Five-Year Brain Drain Dealt 'a Serious Whack' to Research," *Ottawa Citizen*, 21 September 2016.

30 "Silence of the Labs" (CBC, *the fifth estate*, 10 January 2014), http://www.cbc.ca/fifth/episodes/2013-2014/the-silence-of-the-labs.

31 Turner, *The War on Science*, 22.

32 Martin, *Harperland*, 131.

33 Bourrie, *Kill the Messengers*, 190.

34 Gutstein, *Harperism*, 171.

35 Michael Harris, *Party of One: Stephen Harper and Canada's Radical Makeover* (Toronto: Penguin Canada 2014), 150.

36 Gutstein, *Harperism*, 169.

37 Melissa Mancini, "Science Cuts: Ottawa Views Pure Science As 'Cash Cow,' Critics Say," *Huffington Post Canada*, 7 May 2013.

38 Turk, "Science under Siege," 322–46.

39 Ibid., 329.

40 Wayne Kondro, "Harper's Own Health Panel Tells Him to End Intransigence," *Ipolitics*, 17 July 2015, http://ipolitics.ca/2015/07/17/harpers-own-health-panel-tells-him-to-end-intransigence/.

41 Wayne Kondro, "Canada Launches Review of Its Research Enterprise," *Science*, 13 June 2016, doi:10.1126/science.aaf5780.

42 Ibid.
43 "Death of Evidence."
44 Turner, *The War on Science*, 32.
45 Mark Hume, "Four Former Ministers Protest 'Taking the Guts Out' of Fisheries Act," *Globe and Mail*, 28 May 2012.
46 Turner, *The War on Science*, 108.
47 "The Behavioural Insights Team," n.d., http://www.behaviouralinsights. co.uk.
48 "The Age of Willful Blindness,"comes, with thanks, from Turner, *The War on Science*. See also John Dupuis, "The Canadian War on Science: A Long, Unexaggerated, Devastating Chronological Indictment," *ScienceBlogs*, 20 May 2013, http://scienceblogs.com/confessions/2013/05/20/the-canadian-war-on-science-a-long-unexaggerated-devastating-chronological-indictment/ for a comprehensive list of cuts to science funding.

CHAPTER NINE

1 Exodus, 3:17, 32:29.
2 Dan Senor and Saul Singer, *Start-up Nation: The Story of Israel's Economic Miracle* (Toronto: McClelland and Stewart 2009).
3 Jeffrey Goldberg, "The Origins of Israel's Tech Miracle," *Atlantic*, November 2009.
4 Zionism is the movement founded in 1896 by Theodor Herzl with the goal of returning Jews to Israel.
5 On the work of UNSCOP, see William Kaplan, *Canadian Maverick: The Life and Times of Ivan C. Rand* (Toronto: University of Toronto Press 2009), 221–51.
6 Ilan Pappé, *The Ethnic Cleansing of Palestine* (Oxford: Oneworld Publications 2010), 49.
7 Benny Morris, *The Birth of the Palestinian Refugee Problem, 1947–1949* (Cambridge: Cambridge University Press 1987), 24.
8 Ibid., 63.
9 Avi Shlaim, *The Iron Wall: Israel and the Arab World*, expanded ed. (New York: W.W. Norton and Company 2014), 19.
10 John J. Mearsheimer and Stephen M. Walt, *The Israel Lobby and US Foreign Policy* (New York: Viking 2007), 96; Goldmann, *The Jewish Paradox*, 99.
11 Mearsheimer and Walt, *The Israel Lobby and US Foreign Policy*, 93.
12 Pappé, *The Ethnic Cleansing of Palestine*, xii.
13 Morris, *The Birth of the Palestinian Refugee Problem*, 113.
14 Ilan Pappé, "The State of Denial: The Nakba in the Israel Zionist Landscape," in *After Zionism: One State for Israel and Palestine*, ed. Antony Loewenstein and Ahmed Moor (London: Saqi Books 2012), 23.
15 See generally Rosemarie M. Esber, *Under the Cover of War: The Zionist Expulsion of the Palestinians* (Alexandria, VA: Arabicus Books and Media 2008).
16 Tom Segev, *1949: The First Israelis* (London: Macmillan 1998), 26. But see 72 as well: "I can forgive rape," Minister Aharon Cizling said.
17 Ibid., vii.

18 See Esber, *Under the Cover of War*.

19 It is admittedly a bit hard to follow, but see Allen Z. Hertz, "Aboriginal Rights of the Jewish People," *Times of Israel*, 18 February 2014.

20 Gershom Gorenberg, "The Mystery of 1948," *Slate*, 7 November 2011.

21 Gershom Gorenberg, *The Unmaking of Israel* (New York: Harper Collins 2011), 48.

22 Morris, *The Birth of the Palestinian Refugee Problem*, 66.

23 See Morris, *The Birth of the Palestinian Refugee Problem, 1947–1949*.

24 Ibid., 131.

25 Ibid., 292–3.

26 Noam Chomsky, "Ceasefires in Which Violations Never Cease," in Chomsky and Ilan Pappé, *On Palestine* (Chicago: Haymarket Books 2015), 191.

27 Morris, *The Birth of the Palestinian Refugee Problem*, 195.

28 Heidi Grunebaum, "Reflections in a Mirror: From South Africa to Palestine/Israel and Back Again," in *Apartheid Israel: The Politics of an Analogy*, ed. Sean Jacobs and Jon Soske (Chicago: Haymarket Books 2015), 163–4. See also Morris, *The Birth of the Palestinian Refugee Problem*, 155. Morris says thirty-five villages were depopulated. On May and the Green Party, see Marie-Danielle Smith, "Official Support for Israel Boycott Policy Causes Some Greens to Fear for Party's Future," *National Post*, 7 August 2016; and David Kattenburg, "Canadian Greens Back BDS," *Mondoweiss*, 8 August 2016.

29 Also Morris, *The Birth of the Palestinian Refugee Problem*, 170.

30 Segev, *1949*, 31.

31 Shlaim, *The Iron Wall*, 55.

32 Segev, *1949*, 30.

33 Ibid., 37.

34 Ibid., 37–8.

35 "Security Council Resolution 497 of 17 December 1981," United Nations, http://unispal.un.org/DPA/DPR/unispal.nsf/8f4ec1ce53ed321c852574740014cfd72016)./73d6b4c70d1a92b7852560df0064f101?OpenDocument.

36 Sara M. Roy, *The Gaza Strip: The Political Economy of De-Development* (Washington, DC: Institute for Palestine Studies 1995).

37 Nicholas Watt and Harriet Sherwood, "David Cameron: Israeli Blockade Has Turned Gaza Strip into a 'Prison Camp,'" *Guardian*, 27 July 2010.

38 Mearsheimer and Walt, *The Israel Lobby and US Foreign Policy*, 91.

39 "Resolution 446 of 22 March 1979," United Nations, http://unispal.un.org/DPA/DPR/unispal.nsf/8f4ec1ce53ed321c852574740014cfd7/ba123cded3ea84a5852560e50077c2dc?OpenDocument.

40 Jimmy Carter, *Palestine Peace Not Apartheid* (New York: Simon and Schuster 2006), 192.

41 Gorenberg, *The Unmaking of Israel*, 2.

42 Eyal Weizman, *Hollow Land: The Architecture of Israeli Occupation*, 2nd ed. (London: Verso 2012).

43 Shlaim, *The Iron Wall*, 754.

44 Michael Ben-Yair, "The War's Seventh Day," *Haaretz*, 3 March 2002.

45 Ibid.

46 "They Say/We Say: 'There Are Two Sets of Laws in the West Bank – One for Settlers and One for Palestinians,'" Americans for Peace Now, http://peacenow.org/page.php?name=there-are-two-sets-of-laws.

47 "Israel Demolished More Palestinian Homes in West Bank in First Half of 2016 than in All of 2015," *B'Tselem*, 27 July 2016.

48 See, for example, UNICEF, "Children in Israeli Military Detention: Observations and Recommendations," 2 February 2015, http://www.unicef. org/oPt/Children_in_Israeli_Military_Detention_-_Observations_and_ Recommendations_-_Bulletin_No._2_-_February_2015.pdf.

49 Yonah Jeremy Bob, "Livni Halts Practice of Placing Detained Palestinian Children in Outdoor Cages," *Jerusalem Post*, 31 December 2013.

50 Padraig O'Malley, *The Two-State Delusion: Israel and Palestine – A Tale of Two Narratives* (New York: Viking 2015), 215.

51 "Accountability," *B'Tselem*; Ben Ehrenreich, *The Way to the Spring: Life and Death in Palestine* (Penguin, 2016), 201–2.

52 Ibid., 44–6.

53 Jodi Rudoren and Jeremy Ashkenas, "Netanyahu and the Settlements," *New York Times*, 12 March 2015.

54 Jane Adas, "Is This 'Palestine's South Africa Moment'?" *Washington Report on Middle East Affairs* (Washington, DC: American Educational Trust 2015), 44–5.

55 "FAQ: What Happens to Those Who Torture? Are Those Who Torture Punished?" *Stop Torture*, http://stoptorture.org.il/frequently-asked-questions/ frequently-asked-questions/?lang=en.

56 "Netanyahu's Apartheid Vision for Israel's Future," *Haaretz*, 29 October 2015.

57 Segev, *1949*, 47.

58 Raphael Cohen-Almagor, "Israeli Democracy and the Rights of Its Palestinian Citizens," *Ragion Pratica*, 2 (2015): 352.

59 Mearsheimer and Walt, *The Israel Lobby and US Foreign Policy*, 88.

60 Peter Beinart, *The Crisis of Zionism* (New York: Picador 2012), 15.

61 David Remnick, "Israel's One-State Reality," *New Yorker*, 17 November 2014.

62 Jonathan Cook, "Israel's Liberal Myths," in *After Zionism*, ed. Loewenstein and Moor, 167.

63 "Israel and Occupied Palestinian Territories," Amnesty International, http://www.amnesty.org/en/countries/middle-east-and-north-africa/israel- and-occupied-palestinian-territories/.

64 Cohen-Almagor, "Israeli Democracy and the Rights of Its Palestinian Citizens," 360.

65 Shlomo Shamir, "Bush Calls on Israel to Impose Settlement Freeze," *Haaretz*, 21 September 2004.

66 Ronnie Kasrils, "Birds of a Feather: Israel and Apartheid South Africa – Colonialism of a Special Type," in *Israel and South Africa: The Many Faces of Apartheid*, ed. Ilan Pappé (London: Zed Books 2015), 34.

67 Andrew Sullivan, "Israel's Veto," *The Dish*, 29 September 2009, http://dish. andrewsullivan.com/2009/09/29/israels-veto/.

68 Ali Abunimah, *One Country* (New York: Henry Holt and Company 2006), 146.

69 Weizman, *Hollow Land*, 3.

70 Mearsheimer and Walt, *The Israel Lobby and US Foreign Policy*, 91.

71 "BDS Movement," http://bdsmovement.net/.

72 Edward Wadie Said, *From Oslo to Iraq and the Road Map: Essays* (New York: Random House Digital 2005).

73 "Letter from a Birmingham Jail [King, Jr]," *African Studies Center*, University of Pennsylvania, http://www.africa.upenn.edu/Articles_Gen/Letter _Birmingham.html.

74 See generally Omar Barghouti, *BDS: Boycott, Divestment, Sanctions: The Global Struggle for Palestinian Rights* (Chicago: Haymarket Books 2011).

75 Avi Weinryb, "At Issue: The University of Toronto – The Institution Where Israel Apartheid Week Was Born," *Jewish Political Studies Review*, 2008, 109.

76 Barbara Amiel, "School Heads Are 'Enablers' of Anti-Semitism," *Maclean's*, 30 April 2009.

77 David Naylor, personal communication with author, 18 August 2016.

78 "Naylor Responds to Claims of pro-Israel Bias," *The Varsity*, 2 March 2009, http://thevarsity.ca/2009/03/02/naylor-responds-to-claims-of-pro-israel-bias/.

79 Renee Lewis, "Hundreds of Black Activists Endorse BDS Movement," *Al Jazeera America*, 19 August 2015.

80 Jennifer Medina and Tamar Lewin, "Campus Debates on Israel Drive a Wedge between Jews and Minorities," *New York Times*, 10 May 2015.

81 Eric Alterman, "The B.D.S. Movement and Anti-Semitism on Campus," *New York Times*, 29 March 2016.

82 On the "case" for an academic boycott, see generally Bill Mullen and Ashley Dawson, eds., *Against Apartheid: The Case for Boycotting Israeli Universities* (Chicago: Haymarket Books 2015).

83 Chomsky and Pappé, *On Palestine*, 92.

84 Laurie Goodstein, "Presbyterians Vote to Divest Holdings to Pressure Israel," *New York Times*, 20 June 2014.

85 John H. Thomas, "BDS as the Third Way," *Huffington Post*, 3 September 2016.

86 John Reed, "Israel: A Bitter Harvest," *Financial Times*, 21 July 2013.

87 David Horovitz, "For SodaStream Chief, Frustration with Netanyahu's 'Politics of Hate' Bubbles over," *Times of Israel*, 3 August 2016.

88 "They Say, We Say: 'A Boycott of Settlements Is Not Only Politically Misguided but Also Pointless,'" Americans for Peace Now, http://peacenow.org/page.php?id=3270.

89 Jodi Rudoren, "French Executive Apologizes to Netanyahu after His Remarks Prompt an Uproar," *New York Times*, 12 June 2015.

90 "A Campaign That Is Gathering Weight," *Economist*, 8 February 2014, 46–7.

91 Moti Bassok, "Lapid: If Talks with Palestinians Collapse, Economy Will Be Battered," *Haaretz*, 30 January 2014.

92 Ibid.

93 Reed, "Israel: A Bitter Harvest."
94 Steven Erlanger, "With Gaza War, Movement to Boycott Israel Gains Momentum in Europe," *New York Times*, 28 August 2014.
95 "Us and Them," *Economist*, 2 August 2014.
96 C. Ross Anthony et al., "The Costs of the Israeli-Palestinian Conflict" (RAND Corporation 2015), xlii; John Reed, "Israel: A New Kind of War," *Financial Times*, 12 June 2015.
97 Patrick Martin, "Parliament Votes to Reject Israel Boycott Campaign," *Globe and Mail*, 23 February 2016.
98 But see Ethan Bronner, "Just How Far Did They Go, Those Words against Israel?" *New York Times*, 11 June 2006.
99 Tia Goldenberg, "Growing BDS Movement Raises Alarm among Israeli Leaders," *Haaretz*, 7 July 2015.
100 Rudoren and Ashkenas, "Netanyahu and the Settlements."
101 Shlaim, *The Iron Wall*, 587.
102 Ibid., 628.
103 Ibid., 627.
104 William Parry, "The Score: BDS 1, Israel 0," *The Washington Report on Middle East Affairs* (Washington, DC: American Educational Trust 2011).
105 Moshe Cohen, "Liberman: Disloyal Arab-Israelis 'Should Be Beheaded,'" *Israel National News*, 8 March 2015.
106 Thomas L. Friedman, "Netanyahu, Prime Minister of the State of Israel-Palestine," *New York Times*, 25 May 2016.
107 Yossi Melman, "Liberman Unveils New 'Carrot and Stick' Policy for West Bank Palestinians," *Jerusalem Post*, 17 August 2016.
108 Nathan Hersh, "Killing by Soldier Reveals Israel's New, Nastier Side," *Toronto Star*, 20 August 2016.
109 Asher Schechter, "If BDS Isn't a Real Threat, Why Does Netanyahu Make It out to Be Such a Big Deal?" *Haaretz*, 2 June 2015.
110 Chemi Shalev, "Netanyahu's Declaration of War on BDS Is Its First Major Victory," *Haaretz*, 2 June 2015.
111 "Poll: How Worried Should Israel Be about BDS?," *Israel National News*, 8 June 2015.
112 "Organization," *Breaking the Silence*, http://www.breakingthesilence.org.il/about/organization.
113 Anthony et al., "The Costs of the Israeli-Palestinian Conflict," 89.
114 Haviv Rettig Gur, "When It Comes to Tackling BDS, Israel Is All Talk, No Action," *Times of Israel*, 5 June 2015.
115 Ibid.
116 Peter Beinart, "When the Fight over BDS Is a Jewish Civil War," *Haaretz*, 8 March 2016.
117 Sivan Klingbail and Shanee Shiloh, "Bye, the Beloved Country – Why Almost 40 Percent of Israelis Are Thinking of Emigrating," *Haaretz*, 15 December 2012.
118 Peter Beinart, "The Failure of the American Jewish Establishment," *New York Review of Books*, 10 June 2010.
119 Beinart, "When the Fight over BDS Is a Jewish Civil War."

120 Dov Waxman, *Trouble in the Tribe: The American Jewish Conflict over Israel* (Princeton, NJ: Princeton University Press 2016), 3.

121 "Mission and Vision," Open Hillel, http://www.openhillel.org/about/.

122 Waxman, *Trouble in the Tribe*, 3, 50, 214.

123 "Canadians Split on Support for Israel, Palestine," *Forum Poll*, 30 May 2014, http://poll.forumresearch.com/post/52/fed-canadadians-split-on-israel-palestine-053014/.

124 Abunimah, *One Country*, 100.

125 John Lanchester, "Brexit Blues," *London Review of Books* 38, no. 15 (2016): 3.

126 Kasrils, "Birds of a Feather," 36.

127 Mearsheimer and Walt, *The Israel Lobby and US Foreign Policy*, 100.

128 Waxman, *Trouble in the Tribe*, 42.

129 Goldenberg, "Growing BDS Movement Raises Alarm among Israeli Leaders."

130 Goodstein, "Presbyterians Vote to Divest Holdings to Pressure Israel."

131 Beinart, *The Crisis of Zionism*, 32.

132 Alterman, "The B.D.S. Movement and Anti-Semitism on Campus."

133 Abunimah, *One Country*, 49.

134 "IDF Plans Harsher Methods with West Bank Demonstrations," WikiLeaks, Public Library of US Diplomacy, 16 February 2010, http://wikileaks.org/plusd/cables/10TELAVIV344_a.html.

135 Ibid.

136 Ori Nir, "Demographics Drive Likud's Shifting Agenda," *Forward*, 26 December 2003, http://forward.com/news/7386/demographics-drive-likud-s-shifting-agenda/.

137 Thomas Friedman, "One Wall, One Man, One Vote," *New York Times*, 14 September 2003.

138 See, for example, "Gaza: Palestinians Tortured, Summarily Killed by Hamas Forces during 2014 Conflict," Amnesty International, 27 May 2015, http://www.amnesty.org/en/latest/news/2015/05/gaza-palestinians-tortured-summarily-killed-by-hamas-forces-during-2014-conflict/.

139 "BBC Poll: Israel among World's Least Popular Nations," *Haaretz*, 25 May 2013.

140 Rudoren, "French Executive Apologizes to Netanyahu after His Remarks Prompt an Uproar."

141 "About," Canary Mission, http://canarymission.org/about/.

142 Reed, "Israel: A New Kind of War."

143 Peter Beaumont, "Israel Brands Palestinian-Led Boycott Movement a 'Strategic Threat,'" *Guardian*, 3 June 2015.

144 Jordan Cantwell, "Moderator: Upholding Democratic Rights," United Church of Canada, 27 June 2016, http://www.united-church.ca/news/moderator-upholding-democratic-rights.

145 Rob Ferguson, "Private Member's Bill over Boycott of Israel Defeated by MPPS," *Toronto Star*, 19 May 2016.

146 "S.C. Code Ann. 11-35-5300 (2015)," *Harvard Law Review* 129, no. 2029 (2016).

147 "Corrie et al. v. Caterpillar," Center for Constitutional Rights, http://ccr justice.org/home/what-we-do/our-cases/corrie-et-al-v-caterpillar#.
148 "BDS Activists Plaster Anti-Israel Labels on Israeli Products," *Canadian Jewish News*, 15 March 2016, http://www.cjnews.com/news/canada/bds-activists-plaster-anti-israel-stickers-on-israeli-products-in-calgary-vancouver.
149 Omar Barghouti, "Why Israel Fears the Boycott," *New York Times*, 31 January 2014.
150 Judy Maltz, "To Combat BDS, 'Solve the Palestinian Issue,' Say Top U.S. and EU Diplomats," *Haaretz*, 28 March 2016.
151 Ibid.
152 Gideon Levy, "Netanyahu Will Be Remembered for Speaking Israel's Truth," *Haaretz*, 22 March 2015.
153 Martin Raffel, "BDS: How Big a Threat?," *Jewish Week*, 16 June 2015, http://www.thejewishweek.com/editorial-opinion/opinion/bds-how-big-threat.
154 Avraham Burg, "When the Walls Come Tumbling down," *Haaretz*, 1 April 2011.
155 Avraham Burg, "The End of Zionism: Israel Must Shed Its Illusions and Choose between Racist Oppression and Democracy," *Guardian*, 15 September 2003.
156 Gil Hoffman, "Barak: Netanyahu in a Panic, Knows the End of His Reign Is Near," *Jerusalem Post*, 17 June 2016.
157 Amir Tibon, "Netanyahu vs. the Generals," *Politico Magazine*, 3 July 2016.
158 Beinart, "The Failure of the American Jewish Establishment."
159 "Could Two Become One?" *Economist*, 16 March 2013.
160 Scott Horton, "This Is Starting to Get Dangerous," *Harper's Magazine*, 15 March 2010.
161 Jeffrey Goldberg, "Robert Gates Says Israel Is an Ungrateful Ally," *Bloomberg View*, 5 September 2011.
162 Avi Shlaim, "Israel Needs to Learn Some Manners," *New York Times*, 30 January 2014.
163 Ibid.
164 Barak Ravid, "Netanyahu: I Don't Want a Binational State, but We Need to Control All of the Territory for the Foreseeable Future," *Haaretz*, 26 October 2015.
165 Charles W. Freeman, *America's Continuing Misadventures in the Middle East* (Charlottesville, VA: Just World Books 2016), 21–2.
166 Thomas L. Friedman, "Newt, Mitt, Bibi and Vladimir," *New York Times*, 13 December 2011.
167 Tony Judt, "Israel: The Alternative," *New York Review of Books*, 23 October 2003.
168 Merav Michaeli, "Tony Judt's Final Word on Israel," *Atlantic*, 14 September 2011.
169 Stuart Winer, "A Third of Americans Say It's Legitimate to Boycott Israel," *Times of Israel*, 30 May 2016.
170 Carter, *Palestine Peace Not Apartheid*, 215.
171 Ibid., 216.
172 Alan Dershowitz, "The World According to Jimmy Carter," *Huffington Post*, 22 November 2006.

173 Desmond Tutu, "Apartheid in the Holy Land," *Guardian*, 29 April 2002.
174 Linda K. Wertheimer, "Students and the Middle East Conflict," *New York Times*, 3 August 2016.
175 Jeffrey Goldberg, "Peter Beinart Is Right – or, a One-State Solution Is Inevitable if Settlements Continue," *Atlantic*, 8 December 2011.
176 Amos Oz, "Amos Oz Has a Recipe for Saving Israel," *Haaretz*, 13 March 2015.
177 Beinart, *The Crisis of Zionism*, 190.
178 Zeev Sternhell, "The Leadership Must Stop Pandering: Israel as a Free Nation Won't Survive the Occupation," *Haaretz*, 17 June 2016.
179 Ibid.
180 Chomsky and Pappé, *On Palestine*, 76.
181 Shlaim, *The Iron Wall: Israel and the Arab World*, 107.
182 Ibid.
183 Jeffrey Goldberg, "The Unbearable Smallness of Benjamin Netanyahu," *Atlantic*, 29 September 2016.
184 Ibid.
185 Abunimah, *One Country*, 134.
186 Ibid., 135.
187 See generally Benjamin Gidron, Stanley N. Katz, and Yeheskel Hasenfeld, *Mobilizing for Peace: Conflict Resolution in Northern Ireland, Israel/Palestine, and South Africa* (Oxford: Oxford University Press 2002).
188 "Truth or Reconciliation Mechanism: Interim Constitution Accord," Peace Accords Matrix, University of Notre Dame, http://peaceaccords.nd.edu/provision/truth-or-reconciliation-mechanism-interim-constitution-accord.
189 Tutu, "Apartheid in the Holy Land."
190 Pappé, *The Ethnic Cleansing of Palestine*, 246.
191 Raphael Cohen-Almagor, "Parameters for Two State Solution," *Palestine-Israel Journal* 21, no. 2 (2015): 117.
192 Shlaim, *The Iron Wall*, xxi–xxiii.
193 Ibid., xx.
194 William Booth and Ruth Eglash, "Israel Calls Palestinian Knife Attacks 'a New Kind of Terrorism,'" *Independent*, 26 December 2015.
195 Gidron, Katz, and Hasenfeld, *Mobilizing for Peace*, 5.
196 Burg, "The End of Zionism."
197 Al Jazeera, "Palestine Papers," 23 January 2011.
198 Itamar Eichner, "Major Poll: About Half of Israeli Jews Want to Expel Arabs," *Ynet News*, 9 March 2016, http://www.ynetnews.com/articles/0,7340,L-4775861,00.html.
199 Shibley Telhami, "How Israel's Jewishness Is Overtaking Its Democracy," Brookings Institution, 11 March 2016, http://www.brookings.edu/blog/markaz/2016/03/11/how-israels-jewishness-is-overtaking-its-democracy/.
200 Anthony et al., "The Costs of the Israeli-Palestinian Conflict," 176–7.
201 See generally Gorenberg, *The Unmaking of Israel*.
202 Nadav Shragai, "Peace Now: 32% of Land Held for Settlements Is Private Palestinian Property," *Haaretz*, 14 March 2007.
203 Virginia Tilley, "The One-State Solution: The Future of Israel and Palestine," *London Review of Books* 25, no. 21 (2003): 13–16.

204 Ian Black, "Israel and Palestine: Reappraisals, Revisions, Refutations by Avi Shlaim," *Guardian*, 24 October 2009.
205 Isabel Kershner, "Israel Quietly Legalizes Pirate Outposts in the West Bank," *New York Times*, 30 August 2016.
206 "Ministers Approve Millions in Aid for West Bank Settlement," *Times of Israel*, 10 July 2016.
207 Ibid.
208 "At the Boiling Point with Israel," *New York Times*, 6 October 2016.
209 US Department of State, "Approval of New West Bank Settlement," 5 October 2016, http://www.state.gov/r/pa/prs/ps/2016/10/262795.htm.

CONCLUSION

  1 Kennedy, *Thirteen Days: A Memoir of the Cuban Missile Crisis*, 85–6.
  2 Ibid., 95.
  3 Ibid., 98.
  4 "Ron Ridenhour Letter That Began My Lai Investigation," 29 March 1969, http://law2.umkc.edu/faculty/projects/ftrials/mylai/ridenhour_ltr.html.
  5 Christopher Hitchens, *Letters to a Young Contrarian* (New York: Basic Books 2001), 10.
  6 "Remarks by the President at Howard University Commencement Ceremony" (White House Archives, Barack Obama, 7 May 2016), http://www.white house.gov/the-press-office/2016/05/07/remarks-president-howard-university-commencement-ceremony.
  7 *Younger v. Harris*, 401 US 37 (1971), dissent of Justice Douglas, 65.

Index